Outback guide MIKE STEEL has wandered beneath the sun and stars for ten years. His red Land-Rovers roam the arid inland far beyond the normal tourist tracks, taking passengers to enchanting areas that few have been fortunate enough to see, or guiding geologists across trackless wastes in their search for mineral deposits.

He is happy to be anywhere in Australia's vast outback but there is one area that he loves more than any other. At every opportunity he returns to the Strzelecki track that winds away from the Northern Flinders Ranges over sand and stony deserts to the stream that Captain Charles Sturt named Cooper's Creek, in the beautiful land of the Yantruwantas.

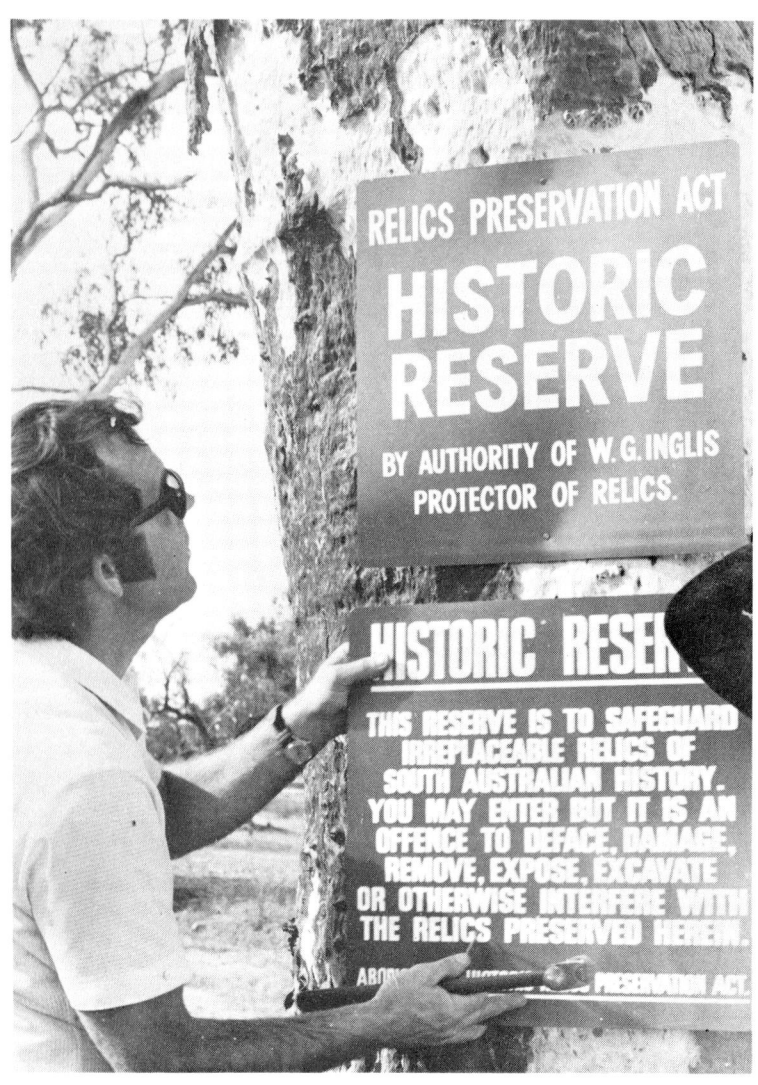

Mike Steel, a warden under the Aboriginal and Historic Areas Preservation Act erects signs in the Innamincka area.

MURTEE JOHNNY is the only surviving full-blood of the Yantruwanta tribe. He may be the oldest man in Australia. Murtee's brother, who died in 1944, always claimed he could remember the Burke and Wills expedition that camped in the land of the Yantruwantas in 1860/61.

Murtee Johnny worked for many decades as a stockman on stations along the Strzelecki Track until a bad fall from a horse forced his premature retirement when he was in his nineties. He retired to Windy Hill, a slightly raised knob of ground near the little settlement of Lyndhurst, "the gateway to the Strzelecki Track", three hundred and sixty road miles North of Adelaide, fifty-two South of Marree.

In recent years his figure has been a familiar sight along the short track that leads from Lyndhurst's balcony suburb to the store and the pub, which has a long bench seat on its verandah. Resting on that bench Murtee Johnny has watched the great Diesels pulling out to the North-East, heading for the mushrooming gas and oil fields at Moomba and Gidgealpa.

His thoughts, however, have not been of modern fuels and technology. For Murtee Johnny the dusty Strzelecki Track leads to stony wastes and sand-ridged desert, sparkling waterholes and teeming wildlife, beyond Murnpeowie, Blanchewater and Mount Hopeless, over the Cobbler, beside the vivid red stripe of the Darlingie sandhills and on to Yidninckanie, the ancestral home of the Yantruwantas, the loveliest, most awe-inspiring, stark and historic area of all Australia's great outback.

The author and publishers are grateful to the Stock Journal Publishers Pty. Ltd., Adelaide, for permission to reproduce photographs previously published in the Stock Journal.

IPPS Book Production Services
GPO Box 1892, Adelaide, South Australia 5001

Red Rover
First published 1973
Copyright (c) 1973 Mike Steel
National Library of Australia card
number and ISBN 0 85864 019 8

Registered at the GPO Adelaide for
transmission by post as a book.

Printed by Lutheran Publishing House, Adelaide.

RED ROVER

MIKE STEEL

Best wishes
Mike Steel
9-11-73.

IPPS

BOOK PRODUCTION SERVICES

Murtee Johnny

The Cobbler

The Cooper

LYNDHURST

When Murtee Johnny retired to Windy Hill he was neither homeless nor alone. He moved into a rough building
erected by "Dollar Mick" Smith, former head stockman at
Mount Lyndhurst and Murnpeowie stations. He shared the
humble shelter with Florrie, the only survivor of the Dieri
tribe from the Birdsville Track area. Murtee and Florrie
never married. By the time they teamed up there seemed
little point in going through the ceremony.

Florrie had outlived three husbands. She was brought
up at the Lutheran Mission at Kalalpaninna and was fluent
in German, while Murtee's long career as a stockman had
given him a good command of the English language. They
may each remember their tribal tongues, although there is
now nobody with whom either of them could share their dia-
lects, but they have never had difficulty in communicating.

Lyndhurst's publican Allan Dunn says the town's population is twenty-six and quite stable, because whenever there
is a birth somebody leaves town. His estimate probably included both the suburbs — Windy Hill is not the only satellite settlement of Lyndhurst. From the hotel verandah the
view is usually obscured by a giant vehicle or two or three,
resting while the drivers refuel their trucks and themselves
before tackling the long haul to the gas and oil fields. The
trucks are usually parked on the track, spurning the sign-
posted clients' car park, a flat and barren area that stretches endlessly away towards Birdsville, three hundred miles
to the North.

A little to the right, and a mile or so from Lyndhurst
town centre, is the industrial suburb of Talctown where a
few haphazard homes have sprung up beside the railway line.
Talctown is home to the carriers who cart talc from the
Mount Fitton mine to be railed South on the first stage of a
long and distinguished career. Although the white lumps ex-
tracted from the mine look very rough piled by the railway
siding, the talc is top quality and after processing the fine

Above: Dollar Mick Smith and Florrie
Below: The Lyndhurst pub

Lyndhurst publican Allan Dunn with
Mike Steel and Andrew Gassner.

A load of Menthoids on the way to Birdsville?

powder caresses many an Australian baby's bottom.

There have been rumours of impending industrial trouble at the Mount Fitton mine. It was feared some time ago that the Aborigines who worked at the mine would go on strike for dirt money because they objected to arriving home half white!

Lyndhurst is much the same as any town of similar size, or lack of it. To the city visitor it may look like the end of the earth. To people who have become acquainted with it the town had an atmosphere that is priceless and irreplaceable. At least it is virile and progressive. Both the town's businessmen, storekeeper Peter Brazel and publican Allan Dunn, are in their early twenties and carrying contractor Trevor Calliss has his own full-colour calendars printed for distribution to his clients. Allan Dunn also has some unusual calendars.

The pub is the social centre, of course, where the local population is inevitably swelled by passing truckies, doggers, rabbitters, stockmen and other characters heading North, South, East or West, or merely pausing to ponder their next move. It may take them some days to decide. The beer is cold and the showers are hot, the food is wholesome and the bar is intimate, which is what city architects say instead of small. Still, in the Lyndhurst pub the atmosphere, too, is intimate and the bar is seldom overcrowded, at least on the customers' side.

Behind the bar an endless assortment of bottles competes for space with special delicacies such as metwurst, and an ancient clock which no longer manages to move its hands from one year to the next. Not that it is useless. A notice plastered across its dial proclaims that the management, like the clock, offers "no tick".

SHAMUS O'BRIEN was a local identity of the Lyndhurst area. He once saved himself from perishing in the outback by scooping a hole in the bottom of a dam that was virtually dry and burying himself to the neck in the mud. There he survived until he was found and Dr. Gregory, the Flying Doctor, was called.

Shamus was killed near Mount Lyndhurst station in 1965 when he fell from a truck and was crushed beneath the wheels. It was ironical that a truck should cause his death, because trucks were Shamus's life. He once recited a poem in the Lyndhurst pub and I copied it down. As far as I know a fellow nicknamed "Splinter", who worked at the talc mine, is the only other person who has a copy of the poem.

TRUCKIE'S LAMENT

Swing to the cabin and press the switch
And give the diesel the gun
It's three hundred miles up the Birdsville Track
And we've got to be there with the sun.

Whether they wait for bottles or bricks
Spuds or steel or lime
Never doubt that a truckie's skill
Will get it there on time.

We cop the blame for the broken roads
We're shadowed and chased by cops
But we ride again through the quiet towns
Where we gulp down pies and chops.

We're taxed for this, and taxed for that
And cursed as a highway blight
But a thousand tons of goods will roll
Three hundred miles tonight.

Somewhere tonight in the lonely dark
A truckie is bathed in sweat
Changing a wheel or an axle stub
Or swapping a dustchoked jet.

We've wives and kids of our own it's true
Though sailors see more of theirs
We live in a cab 'neath a shuddering roof
On a floor full of pedals and gears.

Dust in our mouths, oil in our veins
And grease in our wretched souls
We roll to the west, north, east and south
Glued to a diesel's controls.

Cars for Sydney, beer for Bourke
And washing machines for Nhill
Cement for Gympie and Charters Towers
And boots for Broken Hill.

Whyalla is stuck for a load of tiles
Port Pirie is out of nails
There's a red dust cloud o'er the Condoo trail
Where a truckie goes with rails.

Two hours till dawn on a mountain road
With a roar that wakes the night
An eighteen-wheeler thunders on
Its load lashed trim and tight.

With twenty tons of water pipe
On an eight by forty deck
The man at the wheel of this great rig
Is risking his flamin' neck.

For if the booster should fail on the winding slope
Or the offside wheel should blow
She would swipe the cabin and overturn
Into the valley below.

But maybe with skill and good luck she won't
So give the diesel the gun
It's three hundred miles up the Birdsville Track
And my word we'll be there with the sun.

TO THE COBBLER DESERT

The track that winds away North-East from Lyndhurst past Avondale, Mt. Lyndhurst, Murnpeowie, Blanchewater and Mount Hopeless to the Cobbler Desert is usually dry and dusty but occasionally the creeks that carry stormwater away from the Northern Flinders Ranges put on a spectacular performance. When the occasional watercourses flow they do it wholeheartedly, carrying swift streams of water through the snaking lines of eucalypts that mark their courses towards Lakes Eyre, Blanche and Callabonna.

The explorer Edward John Eyre named Mount Hopeless in 1840 when he looked out from a small mound of earth - a poor excuse for a mountain - and found his progress to the North barred by a great inland sea. He had to turn back and report that further progress by land in that direction was impossible, in fact, hopeless. Most people seeing the area for the first time think it is well named but for the wrong reason. Except in rare good seasons it looks hopeless, arid, stony waste that is as inhospitable as it is desolate.

Eyre's report fostered two quick reactions. Another expedition was sent North under Babbage to explore the great inland sea. They lugged a large boat all the way, only to find a few drying mud flats were the only remaining evidence of the barrier that had stopped Eyre. Graziers also responded to the news and it was not long before the outlying South Australian cattle stations had reached the Mount Hopeless area.

In 1861, when Burke, Wills and King were struggling for survival along the Cooper, Burke over-ruled the others' opinions and decided to head for Mount Hopeless, a futile and strength-sapping sortie from which they had to return in far worse condition than they left. The long journey down the Strzelecki Creek and across the Cobbler is seldom possible without good transport and supplies. The explorers had neither.

Mount Hopeless has long ceased to be a station in its own right and is now a far-flung outstation of Murnpeowie, owned by the Beltana Pastoral Company. Mount Hopeless, however, retains one claim to fame. When a hole was needed for one of those typical toilets that operate on the drop system an abandoned mine shaft was brought back into service. The toilet was built at the top of the shaft and the result is the longest drop in the North, perhaps in the world. It will be a long time before they need a new hole at Mount Hopeless!

Blanchewater, too, is now part of Murnpeowie but before the turn of the century it was famous throughout Australia and overseas for the magnificent horses bred there. Blanchewater horses were in great demand for many purposes - drawing the Cobb & Co. coaches that threaded their way along outback mail and passenger routes, as stock horses, city hacks and carriage horses, remounts for the Indian army - in fact any horse from Blanchewater bearing the famous 'E brand of Thomas Elder was acknowledged everywhere as a superior steed.

In 1891, when the Beltana Pastoral Co. decided to use the station for sheep rather than horses, the clearing sale catalogue listed more than three thousand three hundred horses, about a thousand of them brood mares. Blanchewater was also an important stopover point on the inland coach routes and it was not unusual for several people, in addition to the residents, to be staying overnight.

Those infamous horse thieves, the Neaylon brothers, could not resist an attempt to spirit some of the well-bred colts and fillies away before they were old enough to be rounded up and branded during the annual muster. They were well aware that security at Blanchewater was as tight as possible on so large a holding. There was no chance of approaching within miles of the homestead without being spotted but around the fringes of the great horse station it was impossible for the employees to patrol all the boundaries all the time. The boundaries covered many hundreds of miles and it was easy for the thieves to watch from a secluded vantage point and await their opportunity. They rounded up a batch of foals - nobody knows how many - and drove them away to the North, to the uninhabited areas where they had built horse yards far from inquisitive eyes. There they put a brand on the fillies and colts and were then ready to sell

19

Remnants of Blanchewater —
Above: The crumbling walls of the homestead.
Below: Relics of the horse yards.

them in populated areas as superior horses, "as good as those from Blanchewater". The horses looked as good as the way they were described and there was no trouble finding buyers at good prices. The holding yards the Neaylon brothers used were far away from anywhere. They may have remained undiscovered until they had rotted away into oblivion if it had not been for the modern demand for fuel and the search for oil and natural gas in South Australia's Far North. It is possible now to sit on a rotting remnant of those secret horse yards and gaze across the arid plain to the giant towers at Moomba, to watch the perpetual flame fluctuating on the skyline while pondering the enormous hardships the horse thieves must have endured in harsh country in order to make a success of their illicit business.

The remains of the buildings at Blanchewater look much the same as many other ruins in the outback. There is little in the crumbling walls to suggest the rich and colourful history of the previous century. To the discerning visitor, however, there are a few clues that suggest there was something of class about Blanchewater. The remains of the walls have been ripped and torn by floodwaters from the MacDonnell, now shown on some maps as Blanchewater Creek, but they retain a faint air of distinction. There is a sense of superiority in the stonework and a hint of class in the layout. Nearby there are a few giant posts still standing like silent sentinels saluting the glories of Blanchewater's past. The oblong holes in them still testify to the skill of the craftsman who adzed away the slots to hold the rails and their height and solidity proclaim that they were not constructed for a mere sheep or cattle station.

Nobody who knows Murnpeowie uses its full name. It is always shortened and mispronounced "Mumpy". By the mid-1890s there were more than a hundred thousand sheep on the run and the wool clip weighed nearly three hundred and fifty tons. Transfer that to modern metrics and prices and even at $2 a kilo it would be worth about $700,000! The Murnpeowie woolshed, built in 1890, is a most attractive building of stone with a rounded roof structure that reflects the lack of local timber suitable for rafters. An eye-catching exhibit near the homestead is an old steam traction engine, one of

21

Above: The Neaylon brothers' yards and Moomba towers.
Below: Mount Hopeless outstation.

several massive power units installed in the pastoral country by Peter Waite who later donated the land near Adelaide on which Urrbrae Agricultural High School and the Waite Agricultural Research Institute have developed. These great engines generated power to operate shearing machinery, saw wood, pump water and a dozen other tasks.

Although the great horse-breeding enterprise was abandoned, horses have continued to play a part in Murnpeowie's development and progress but not without opposition. Mules, donkeys and camels have each been used extensively. Early in this century, during a run of poor seasons when the rainfall fell well short of the yearly average of nearly five inches, Don Ricardo and Don Pablo were two of the most important animals on "Mumpy". Both were donkeys. Don Ricardo produced many fine foals from a mob of twenty-five female donkeys while Don Pedro's progeny were mules, their dams being superior mares descended from the Blanchewater horses. The donkeys and mules were used for every station chore from pack animals to buggy hauling and proved invaluable through the tough times, surviving and thriving where horses would have faltered. The donkeys now belong to the past, except for those that went wild and are a recurring nuisance, while horses remain to serve where vehicles cannot be used and the station's vast plains and ridges are grazed by cattle.

Over the years economic circumstances have caused many changes in types of animals on Murnpeowie but people are not so easily replaced. The present manager, Ron Napier, carries a name that has become as much a part of the pastoral country as camels, horses, mules and donkeys once were. Four-wheeled vehicles may replace four-footed animals but there is no mechanical gadget to compete with the people born and raised in the outback, who know and understand the harsh country's moods and needs, respect it and use it sparingly to preserve its future.

Aboriginal rainmakers had a difficult job in the country North of the Flinders Ranges. They could sit on hilltops for weeks, perhaps years, chanting incantations to cloudless skies which replied only with blazing sunlight to dim their sight and wind-whipped sand to stifle their monotonous calls to "send 'er down, Hughie", or whatever it was they pleaded.

Walter and Wilpi were the last remaining rainmakers in the Innamincka area and poor Wilpi could never do anything right - according to Walter. When rain was needed Walter would perch on a sandhill and chant away while Wilpi did the same thing from another dune. On the rare occasions when it did rain Walter claimed all the credit, scoffing at any suggestion that Wilpi could have exerted any influence. Walter did, however, admit that Wilpi had certain powers. Whenever his incantations failed to produce a deluge his excuse was the same.

"I bin singum up rain all right but that fella Wilpi bin singum back again."

The ritual of chanting from a hilltop may have been developed because the high ground was closest to the source of rain, or the hilltop site may have come with experience, because on the odd occasions when it does rain wholeheartedly in the outback the lower ground is quickly inundated. In January, 1972 I was lucky enough to be stranded on the track through Murnpeowie, following torrential rain which fell over a vast area of the inland.

Some people wonder if I am crazy when I say I was lucky to be stranded; others are sure I am crazy to be travelling the Strzelecki Track in January, but they are all wrong. It was quite a mild summer, really, and the hottest we experienced on that trip was a mere 126°F. on the Cordillo Downs airstrip, which might sound uncomfortable but is no harder to take than 100°F. in the humid cities. In any case, it makes little difference when you travel in an air-conditioned Land-Rover. As for being stranded by floodwaters and mud, it was an experience I will always remember without regret.

It had been a successful and exciting trip. We had set out to search for the remains of the last stage coach to run in the area and we found it. Unfortunately it lay on its side in the bed of the Strzelecki Creek, almost covered with sand and far beyond restoration. Then we went North to Innamincka and again we were fortunate in re-locating the spot where the explorer Wills died. We went on to Cordillo Downs before starting the long return trip to Lyndhurst and on to Adelaide.

Cordillo Downs manager Roger Beckwith mentioned that he could use some rain because the waterholes were getting low. There was nothing unusual in that but he asked for it

Murnpeowie
Manager —
Ron Napier.

Below: Blanchewater Creek in flow, with water backing
up along the approach track.

and he got it! So did everybody else, except us.

We travelled about three hundred miles down the track in leisurely fashion and experienced only one light shower. The track, however, was very wet in places and every time we stopped and put the transceiver aerial up the speaker crackled with voices talking about falls of rain that would have washed Walter and Wilpi off their hilltops. From behind us Roger Beckwith reported receiving six months' rain ration since breakfast, Betty Hearne from Innamincka said the great Cullyamurra Waterhole had risen four feet in a hurry, from ahead Mike Searle at Moolawatana said the whole countryside was saturated and creeks were running in all directions. From every direction excited voices talked of rain, rain and more rain. One character said he had recorded more than five inches "and it looks like setting in". We travelled on down the slippery track, watching great storm clouds pass constantly overhead without spilling enough of their cargo to wash the dust from the Land-Rover. From all around us the reports of it raining rabbits and dingoes (the local equivalent of cats and dogs) kept flowing through the transceiver. We knew the creeks would be running like startled brumbies but we were dumbfounded when we drove over a crest and saw the scene ahead. I had just made one of those classic predictions that go in the file marked "famous last words".

Petermorra Creek, a few miles behind us, was quite dry and I was sure Blanchewater would be the same.

"There are sure to be some creeks flowing and the Frome will probably be a problem but there are no worries about this one. I've never seen water in it yet."

Blanchewater Creek was flowing like the Murray in full flood, swirling great trees and branches along in its turbulent stream that was still rising and increasing its pace and ferocity. We drove down to the water's edge but soon had to back off - and again. With nothing to do but wait we drove the few miles back to Petermorra and found a raging torrent of water tearing the causeway to pieces - only an hour or so before we had driven across it. The noise was terrific. Bob, the boundary rider from Mount Hopeless, stood with his horse on the other side but there was no way to communicate across that roaring stream.

The causeway crossing of Petermorra Creek — an hour earlier the creekbed was dry.

Back at Blanchewater we settled down to wait for the creek to subside. We listened to the " galah sessions" on the transceiver network and everybody was talking about the same subject. As night approached the creek was obviously dropping and we felt confident of having breakfast on the other side. Some old coolabahs made a friendly fire and we sat around yarning to pass the early hours of darkness.

It was a unique situation. We were effectively marooned between two streams only a few miles apart, sitting beside a track but with no chance of anyone approaching from either direction, rather like being on an uninhabited and unapproachable island. Apart from one heavy, warm shower the rain stayed away from us. We had plenty of supplies and a transceiver to fall back on if any emergency arose, so there was nothing to worry about. We were discussing the strange and wonderful experience of being completely isolated from the rest of the world when we had our second big shock for the day.

Twin lights suddenly appeared over the rise half a mile away and a vehicle came down the track towards us. It was Don McGowan from the Highways Department camp near Mount Hopeless, with his wife. Petermorra had fallen as quickly as it had risen and although the causeway was no longer there Don had managed to cross and come on down the track to survey the scene ahead. Blanchewater was obviously the end of the trail for the moment so Don returned to pass the news to others who had arrived at Petermorra. It was not long before another set of lights appeared and a giant International, with Chris Cullin at the wheel, joined the Land-Rover at Blanchewater.

During the night the creek rose again but by morning the flash flood had subsided and before the day was very old we were on the other side. Not that we progressed very far. At Koortanyaninna Creek we joined a Highways Department crew, a party from the Mines Department, a French exploration crew and others waiting at the crossing, while more vehicles trickled in from the North to join the queue. Soon there were a dozen vehicles and about twenty men waiting to cross and it looked as though it might take a long time.

Koortanyaninna had settled down to a steady stream about two feet deep but there was a much bigger barrier to be

Above: Stranded at Koortanyaninna Creek.
Below: The suction of the silt bar defied the hydraulic
strength of the loader and grab.

Above: The aircraft from Moomba dropping supplies.
Below: The assault on the silt bar.

Red Rover, all over! The men gather to man-handle
the next vehicle across the barrier.

crossed. The flood had left a great silt bar, thirty feet across and four feet deep. Among Highways equipment at the spot was a back hoe loader and grab but it could make no impression on the silt. It seemed we might be there for days until heavy equipment could be brought into the area to clear the crossing. As some of the crews were short of supplies a radio message was sent to Moomba to arrange an air-drop of food.

The aircraft duly arrived, skimmed in over the transceiver aerials and released a bundle which thudded to the ground, took one enormous bounce and landed right in the middle of the stream. All hands plunged in to retrieve the groceries while the aircraft made a second drop, this time leaving the supplies on the bank.

By that time, however, the situation had already changed. My Land-Rover was already across Koortanyaninna.

Two vehicles had appeared on the other side - a four-wheel-drive Bedford truck and a Toyota driven by Ron Napier from Murnpeowie who had driven out to see if anyone needed help. We decided to tackle the silt bar, using the Bedford and Toyota to pull from the other side while a dozen fellows man-handled the Rover forward inch by inch. I doubt if anyone really thought it would work but there was not much else to do so there was nothing to lose - except my Land-Rover if another flash flood came down the creek!

Slowly the straining cable, strong shoulders and swift shovelwork edged the Land-Rover through the oozing silt and when it finally stood on the other bank a few inches had been sheared off the barrier. A Holden utility was then hauled and half-carried over, then Chris Cullin put the big International through and the silt bar was flattened into submission. There were other problems ahead but we enjoyed the hospitality at the Lyndhurst pub that night.

The Cobbler Desert — a 40-mile stretch of white sand that
was a great natural barrier to transport in the earlier days.

Above: The soakage well in the bed of the Strzelecki Creek
        at Accalana.
Below: The remains of the old stage coach, lying on its side
        and almost buried in sand.

Monticollina bore, originally established as a watering point
for stock crossing the Cobbler, is no longer serviced but the
hot artesian water still gushes out to maintain an oasis in the
desert. A Highways Department crew working on the Strzelecki track bulldozed a deep hole to form a swimming pool,
now seldom used but deeply appreciated by the few who have
enjoyed the sensation of swimming in the middle of a desert.

The Cooper, viewed from the causeway at
Innamincka.

A white-faced heron.

Brolgas near the spot where explorer W.J. Wills died in the bed of the Cooper.

Above: Corellas resting beside the Cooper.
Below: Pelicans fishing in a shrinking waterhole.

They may look cute but they will grow up to be troublesome dingoes.

Famous drover Bill Gwyder on the track.

Towing a Holden utility through the flooded Frome Creek.

Outback cattle sometimes live in a land of plenty — but sometimes food or water runs out.

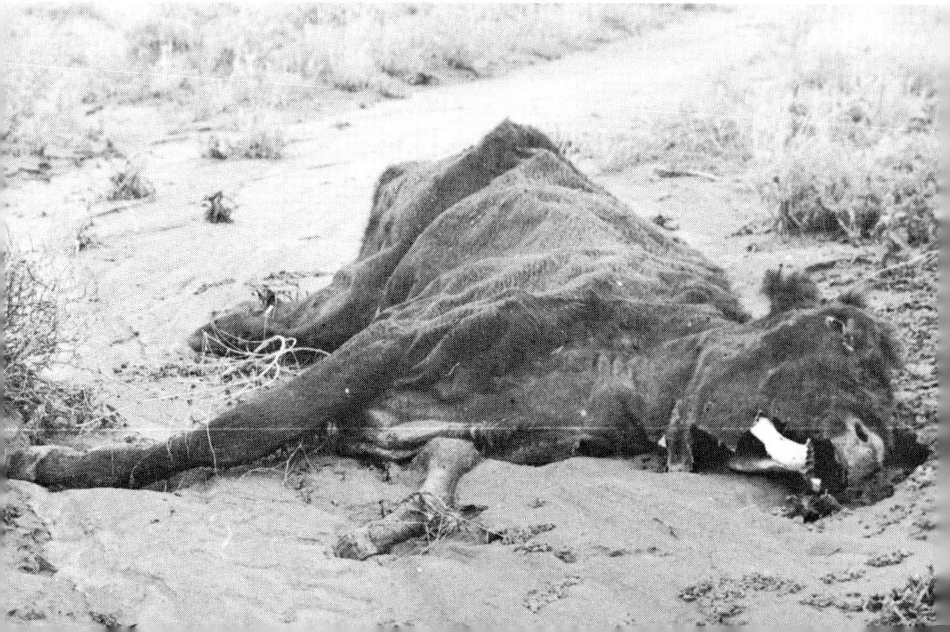

Storm clouds gather in the morning — and disperse in the
evening.

Every rain fosters vibrant life.
Every drought causes lonely death.

Sacred To The Memory
of
LITTLE JACK.
HENRY WALTER SMITH
BORN NOV. 2ND 1867.
PERISHED FEBY 24TH 1889.
—
R.I.P.

Above: Grave of a Yantruwanta tribesman.
Below: Grave of a shearer who perished while
walking from Innamincka to Cordillo Downs.

Above: The administration building at Innamincka airport.
Below: Moomba installations, with an important strip of
concrete in the foreground.

Sandhills come in various colours and sizes.

COBBLER DESERT AND
STRZELECKI TRACK

The word " cobbler" is a shearing term, a name for the last sheep to feel the shears harvesting its wool. Usually it would be the biggest, strongest and toughest of the mob because none of the shearers would be anxious to get it. After all, they are paid by the number of sheep they shear, so it's only natural they avoid those that will require more muscle and time, hoping somebody else will grab them.

Cordillo Downs, in the North-East corner of South Australia, used to be a sheep station. The wool had to be sent down to the railhead at Farina, now a ghost town between Lyndhurst and Marree. Bales of wool were carried on camels for hundreds of miles and barely an inch of the way was easy going, although it was a relatively simple journey over the final stretch from the Mount Hopeless area to Farina. The long arduous haul down the Strzelecki Track was always a trial and the final obstacle was a forty-mile stretch of white sand dunes, so it is not surprising that they were also called " cobbler".

The Cobbler Desert is actually one massive sand hill, sprawled over the land as a shallow plateau, its surface undulating with thousands of small ridges. When the seasons have been harsh there is little but rippled white sand, magnificent in its stark barrenness and isolation, compelling to some people, frightening to others. After rain the sandhills — like all areas of the outback — may be carpeted with a great flush of wild flowers and stock food. Anyone coming across the Cobbler in a good season could be excused for thinking it was good cattle or sheep country, as happened in so many places before the vagaries of our outback climate were learned through bitter experience.

Although the Cobbler soon disillusioned early squatters about its potential carrying capacity, it was necessary for stock to cross it periodically as the white sand stood between the stations further North and the markets to the South. Water was essential for stock crossing the dunes. Soakage wells proved unreliable and finally, early in this century, a bore was put down in the Cobbler. As with many similar bores over a vast area of the outback, Monticollina never needed a pump to bring the water to the surface. The artesian water is under pressure and once it is provided with an escape channel to the surface it flows freely without assistance. Monticollina bore is no longer services because modern stock transports have almost made droving obsolete, but the water still flows from a rusted pipe to splash down into a large, deep hole in the sand. A Highways Department crew, camped in the Cobbler while forming a track for the transports, gouged out the hole to form a swimming pool where they could cool off at the end of their days in the desert. The crew has long moved on but their pool is still used — many of my passengers have enjoyed an unexpected dip in the middle of the great stretch of sand dunes. The water is hot when it comes from the earth but gradually cools as it flows towards the other end of the pool, so swimmers can even choose the temperature of their plunge.

From the swimming hole the water seeps away, gradually shrinking back into the earth, but not before it has left a few shallow "lakes" covering perhaps half an acre in all. There are always a few ducks on Monticollina, resting during long flights between more imposing waterholes, and plovers, corellas, zebra finches, hawks, kites, crows, dotterels, wrens and a dozen other species. Some, like the wrens, probably arrived there in a good season when there was plenty of surface water for them to follow and have been marooned there for generations. People who have seen wrens make a big drama out of a fifty-yard flight find it incredible that they flit and twitter happily around the stunted bushes at Monticollina but they seem to survive very well in their tiny oasis.

Beyond the Cobbler is the Strzelecki Track. When I was eleven years old I saw the film "Back of Beyond" and was enthralled by the adventures of the mail contractor as he battled his way up the Birdsville Track. I rushed home and pored over my school atlas until I found the dotted line through the wilderness where the film had been made and I vowed that someday I would see that country. My attention, however, was drawn away from the Birdsville Track to another series of dots on the map — an outback route even more

Above: Shallow lakes formed by the overflow from
      Monticollina bore.
Below: Strange sand formations near the bore.

vague, mysterious and intriguing because it was marked "closed since 1935". The Strzelecki Track also went on my list for "someday".

I was always a wanderer. My mother had to chase me around the block when I was just old enough to walk. As soon as I was old enough to ride a bicycle I went further afield, pushing out as far as possible and always regretting turning back. A motor cycle later extended my range but it was never enough — there was always another sandhill, another range, another horizon ahead to be explored and savoured. As soon as I completed my apprenticeship as a mechanic I found an old short-wheel-base Land-Rover and headed inland. The vehicle had only the bare essentials but the country had everything I had ever dreamed of. The vehicle situation has changed dramatically. I still use Land-Rovers because I have always had a great run from them, but they are big station wagons with special water and fuel tanks, V-eight motors, two-way radio, air conditioners to take the sting out of summer tours and refrigerators to put a little of it back again. The country, however, has changed very little — it is still the most wonderful country in the world, unchanging but ever-changing, simultaneously stark and beautiful, desolate but stirring with vibrant life — and every time I return to the city I am impatient to be on the way North again. I have travelled the Birdsville Track and the Strzelecki Track scores of times and roamed the trackless country between them but whenever I see a map of the area I still gaze at it with the same eager anticipation I felt staring at my old school atlas.

North of the Cobbler Desert the Strzelecki Track never strays far from the Strzelecki Creek. There is seldom water in the creek. The twisted trunks and branches of the coolabahs that mark its course show that they have led a stop-and-start existence, growing new wood when there has been an occasional flood or heavy rain, struggling for survival through long periods of drought. In tough times they may even "grow backwards", shedding leaves and branches so there is less to support and the tree will have more chance of survival. Life was never easy for them, nor for the people who settled the area many decades ago.

The ruins of Tinga Tingana give little impression of life

there sixty years ago. It was a busy place then, with people, cattle, sheep, horses, goats, camels, chickens and dogs all contributing sound, colour and movement to the scene. Stage coaches came and went, carrying passengers and mail South to Blanchewater or North to Innamincka. A soakage well in the creek bed supplied water for a flourishing vegetable garden near the homestead. They even grew peanuts! Now there are only a few rotting remains of the station buildings and the well to show that people once lived there, and a grave to show that at least one person died there.

Wrought iron railings formed in the station blacksmith shop in 1917 surround a concrete headstone that marks the last resting place of Archie Patterson, who died at Tinga Tingana at the age of ninety-four. His grandson, Arch Burnett, was there when the old man died, and helped his uncle Jack Patterson make the headstone and railings. Arch Burnett now lives in retirement in Adelaide and recently published a book "Wilful Murder in the Outback" in which he recalls early days at Tinga Tingana.

Further North at Nappacoongie there is another grave surrounded by iron railings, perhaps the deepest grave in the outback. A fellow called Harry Bird and his partner contracted to re-timber the Nappacoongie well. Harry was lowered to the bottom and was doing some preliminary work when the well caved in, burying him beneath tons of earth as his partner above wound the handle off the winch in his frantic efforts to drag the poor fellow to safety. As nothing else could be done the rest of the well was filled in and the railings and plaque were placed on top.

A few miles from the remnants of old Toolachie outstation is the grave of "Little Jack" Smith, who perished during a cattle round-up. He had ridden out from the camp to examine a waterhole and found it dry. On the way back his horse had knocked up and he started to walk back to camp, apparently quite confident he would make it with strength to spare because he actually carried his saddle several miles from the spot where the horse died. It was a strange and fatal mistake for an experienced stockman to make.

The graves suggest the Strzelecki Track is a deadly place and it is certainly an area where inexperienced travellers should take no chances, but many people lived and

Above: The grave at Tinga Tingana.
Below: The grave at Nappacoongie.

Above: Rotting remains of the outstation at Toolachie.
Below: The grave near Toolachie.

Sacred To The Memory
of
LITTLE JACK.
HENRY WALTER SMITH
BORN NOV. 2ᴰ 1867.
PERISHED FEBʸ 24ᵀᴴ 1889.
R.I.P.

worked there in the early days and it was inevitable some should die there. Without vehicles, aircraft, radio and other modern innovations outback stations had to be entirely self-sufficient, with people skilled in many trades to supply the needs of a self-contained community.

A few years ago workers began building a road which ran West from the Strzelecki Track, then turned North towards nothing. Local people soon began referring to it as "the No road" and the name has stuck, although the reason for the strange construction became apparent a few months after it was laid down. Now the lofty towers and sprawling buildings of Moomba stand at the end of "the No road".

When "the No road" was first built it was easy to follow it to its end but at that time there was little to see there. Now there is plenty to see but it is almost impossible for a stranger to the area to follow any track to Moomba and Gidgealpa. Drilling rigs are moved around the country from time to time, fulfilling their roles in the comprehensive program of exploration that has already proved successful and promises much more for the future. Every time a rig is moved to a new site a fresh track is formed so vehicles can travel between the exploration point and supply routes with a minimum of delay. There are tracks running all over the countryside, some leading to rigs, some to deserted rig sites, but there are no signposts to help strangers find the right track to follow. I have come across battered vehicles that have limped back to the Strzelecki Track after spending a few days "somewhere out near Moomba", without their hopeful drivers and passengers seeing even a sign of the great oil and gas development program. It is no place for inquisitive strangers. Nor are they likely to be made welcome if they are lucky enough to arrive at an active site.

In 1642 Abel Tasman set out from Batavia in search of the "Great South Land". He sailed South through the Indian Ocean, then East to Tasmania and New Zealand and returned via the North coast of New Guinea. He sailed all the way around Australia without sighting the mainland — it was perhaps the biggest miss in history until people started heading for the outback to have a look at Moomba. At least Tasman was able to find his own way home!

The men who work on oil, gas and mineral exploration

The devil's golfcourse — formed by drying
slurry pumped out from an oil rig.

in the outback are Australia's modern pioneers but the hardships they face are nothing compared with those endured by the old-time pastoralists and prospectors. The mining crews may put up with extreme heat, flies and other discomforts but they have many services on call. If someone is injured a call on a transceiver will have a doctor there quickly, usually in less time than it takes for city dwellers to get medical aid — and cheaper.

At Moomba itself the men live in comfortable air-conditioned quarters with lounge-reading rooms and other facilities adjoining their bedrooms. An ultra-modern kitchen complex which an hotel would be proud to own adjoins a spacious dining room, recreation area with indoor swimming pool, theatre, billiard tables and bar — a big improvement on the "after five" life of the original pioneers. Out on the rig sites there are fewer luxuries but most of the men like the life, the money and the short holiday down South every month.

There are many impressive and exciting scenes around the oil and gas fields — giant rigs thrusting deep into the earth, massive engines and equipment worth millions of dollars, everything on a gigantic scale of effort and expenditure — but the most awe-inspiring sights are the burn-offs to test oil or gas flows. When an oil burn-off is in progress the black cloud may be visible from fifty miles or more. At close range the great writhing cloud that leaps from earth to sky is more colourful, with fierce tongues of red flame twisting and swirling through the dense black smoke. Gas, on the other hand, burns cleanly. There is no smoke-cloud and the burn-off is only visible at close range, although it might well be heard much further away than it can be seen. Squeezing out of a narrow outlet under tremendous pressure, the gas screeches like a thousand demented cockatoos and anyone who approaches within a quarter of a mile is likely to be rubbing his ears for a few hours afterwards.

Wallace Johnston, a Canadian bore contractor who worked in the North-East corner of South Australia about sixty years ago, put down quite a few successful holes and also had some failures. One of the failures was at Patchawarra, between Innamincka and Cordillo Downs. No artesian water came gushing to the surface and the drillers turned away in

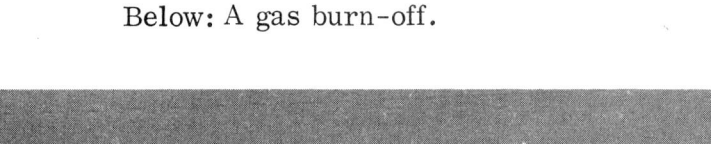

Above: A hole sealed off for future tapping.
Below: A gas burn-off.

An oil burn-off — Note the tiny vehicles in the background.

Inside scenes at Moomba.

disappointment but not before they noticed a strange thing about the dry hole. Gas bubbles seeped out of the bore and when lit they burned for some time. The drillers, interested only in water, had no idea they were seeing a preview of an enormous project that was to develop two generations later. The old Patchawarra bore, a long way North from the centre of the Moomba-Gidgealpa complex, still produces its burning bubbles.

On Murtee Murtee station there is a fascinating old "water-wheel", a relic of the days when power had to be supplied by muscle and sweat rather than electricity or fuel engines. An iron wheel, obviously designed and hand forged in the station blacksmith shop, is mounted horizontally on solid timber supports and is about ten feet from ground level. The wheel is about eighteen feet in diameter and around its perimeter are many hitching bars, to which camels or other animals were harnessed. The animals walked in a circle and kept the big wheel turning, drawing water from a well to nearby troughs where stock could drink.

Although the "water-wheel" is a relic of another era, Murtee Murtee station itself is very much alive. I lost one of my regular passengers there. A group of teachers from Victoria have an annual booking for a tour during the September holidays and after several trips their enthusiasm is greater than ever. One, however, was not satisfied with a mere two weeks a year in the outback. Marlene is now married to Lew Tomsil, who works for Ted Rieck at Murtee Murtee.

The country through which the Strzelecki Track runs is mostly off-white with soft yellows and browns but the Darlingie sandhills provide a vivid contrast of colour. Like a ragged red stripe painted across the landscape the fiery dunes parallel the track for eighty miles, showing the way to Innamincka, the white man's corruption of the Yantruwanta name, Yidniminckanie.

Above: The "water-wheel" at Murtee Murtee.
Below: A King-sized windmill.

Above: Water from artesian bores leaves the pipes at
near boiling point.
Below: A King-sized pipe on the way to Moomba.

In Loving Memory
of
PETER PARKER
HEAD STOCKMAN DURHAM DOWNS
ACCIDENTLY KILLED
RACE MEETING
NOV 25TH 1943
ERECTED BY HIS FRIENDS

Graves in the Innamincka cemetery.
While most of the graves are parallel, a few are laid
out at an angle of about 30° from the general direction.
They mark the last resting places of Afghan camel
drivers and their families, whose religion decreed they
be buried pointing to Mecca.

The causeway crossing at Innamincka.
Above: Under 10 feet of floodwater.
Below: In more normal times.

A memorial cairn to explorers who first saw the Innamincka area stands near the ruins of the mission hospital. One plaque is a tribute to Sturt, who named Cooper's Creek in 1845. The other is for Burke and Wills, who came 15 years later.

A choice of tracks!

Above: Two ways to spell Innamincka.
Below: Youngsters get acquainted.

Above: An assortment of ducks on a shallow lake.
Below: A white-breasted wood swallow.

A coolabah that refused to die.

At Gidgealpa station, fuel drums have been converted for a useful purpose. The rotating arm at right is the "occupied" signal.

Above: The home of a marsupial rat.
Below: An outback pilot rescues tourists that blundered into
the outback with insufficient petrol, spare parts,
water, food, knowledge and common sense.

Above: Drovers rest their cattle beside the Strzelecki track.
Below: Emu in the scrub.

Most exploration companies clean up their old camps but occasionally litter despoils the countryside.

A portable transceiver maintains contact with the rest of
the world.

Above: The Strzelecki Creek runs only when the Cooper overflows.
Below: Everybody waves in the outback — it keeps the flies on the move.

When vehicles break down —
it may be a long time before help arrives.

THE COOPER COUNTRY

"I would not trust the largest of them further than the range of vision. They are deceptive, all of them, the off-spring of heavy rains, and dependent entirely on local circumstances." Those words were written by Captain Charles Sturt. He was referring to Australia's inland rivers and waterholes, thinking particularly of the stream he named Cooper's Creek. Perhaps there is a hint of bitterness in the words, a suggestion that there was something unfair about the fickle nature of water supplies in the vast outback. If there were any such thoughts in Sturt's mind, history has proved them to be entirely justified.

Sturt set out to reach the centre of Australia and passed the area where Broken Hill now stands in January, 1845. He had a theory that the arid inland could be conquered by following the course set by flights of birds that swept overhead during long journeys from waterhole to waterhole. Sturt was convinced the birds knew the way and by following them he would conquer the stony and sandy deserts that stretched out between the occasional sources of water. The great explorer followed his theory — and failed! He was bitterly disappointed but his theory was not wrong. Neither he, nor anybody else, will ever know how many birds also failed to reach their intended destinations in that unusually harsh year.

Eyre was turned back from Mount Hopeless by water in country that seldom saw water. Sturt was repelled from "The Centre" by lack of water where water was usually available. Still, his remarks about the streams and water-holes are valid — they are unreliable and unpredictable, as many outback travellers have found to their final sorrow.

In a good season, even a moderate one, Sturt would have named the stream a river rather than a creek. Queensland-ers sometimes claim that South Australia deserves to be the driest state in the driest continent because it squanders most of the water Queensland gives away. In Queensland the Bar-coo River, the Thompson River, the Wilson River and sev-

81

eral other water-courses join together to form one great stream which flows across the state border near Nappamerrie Station homestead. This is the watercourse that Sturt discovered inside the present South Australian border and named Cooper's Creek. South Australians scoff at Queenslanders and claim it takes several of their rivers to make a creek in South Australia but it is true that the water that flows across the border is spread indiscriminately over the countryside and finishes up either deep under the ground or evaporates into the outback air.

Periodically people propose schemes for damming the Cooper to conserve and ration out the water that otherwise runs "to waste" in an endless system of shallow lakes and sandy flats where it seeps away underground or is absorbed into the hot, dry air. That water is not wasted. When the vast areas of lakes and swamps dry out after a Cooper flood has filled them the water no longer lies on the surface of the earth but that does not mean it has been wasted. In one of three ways it has served a vital purpose.

If it has evaporated the old saying "what goes up must come down" applies. Perhaps it will fall in Arabia. It is equally likely that water evaporating from the South Atlantic ocean will fall in the catchment areas of the Barcoo, Thompson and Wilson rivers. The world is round and everything goes around with it.

If it has seeped away deep into the earth it will help replenish the great artesian water basins on which hundreds of cattle and sheep stations and outback towns depend for their existence. Underground water supplies have already failed in more closely settled areas because man has tapped the supply and used it faster than nature can replace it. Man cannot have it both ways.

The third cycle in which the Cooper floodwaters are involved is in vegetation. When the flooded lakes and swamps dry out there is a great flush of growth on the flats. Native grasses and clovers form lush carpets of greenery that provide feed for fattening cattle to supply a hungry world.

None of the water that flows down the Cooper is wasted. It merely goes into one of those three cycles that nature devised. The whole ecology of the outback has evolved over thousands of years. Man can no more tame the outback than he can regiment the tides or the sun. The plants that grow when there is water to nourish the soil have adapted to the situation. They survive and flourish under occasional and irregular floodings and corresponding terms of drought. Any attempt to regiment or regulate water supplies would be an ecological disaster, a thousand times more obvious and regrettable than the results of man's attempts to tame and harness the River Murray.

Anyone who still wants to dam the Cooper has one more problem to face. There is only one place where a dam would be a practical possibility — a short way downstream from Cullyamurra Waterhole near Innamincka. A massive dam wall there would certainly imprison an enormous volume of water and flood a vast area of country. That area has been declared an Aboriginal and Historic Relics Reserve. Anyone who proposed burying that area under water would be about as popular as a skunk in a submarine.

With all due respect to Captain Sturt, nobody in the outback ever mentions "Cooper's Creek". The watercourse is always referred to as "the Cooper", perhaps because the people who have seen its various moods know it is seldom a creek but sometimes a raging river and sometimes a dry ditch. In full flow it is a magnificent and noble river. When there has been no rain in the Queensland catchment areas the Cooper basin is sand and dust and rock — nothing more, except for the permanent waterholes. There are several waterholes near Innamincka which survive the fiercest droughts and the largest — indeed the greatest waterhole in Australia — is Cullyamurra.

Alfred Howitt, the explorer who led the relief party which found the bodies of Burke and Wills and rescued King from his struggle to survive with friendly natives, described Cullyamurra as four hundred yards wide, several miles long and very deep. It is in fact about six miles from the ancient rock carvings at the head of the great waterhole to the crossing at its lower end and pastoral inspector Jim Vickery once sounded its depth at nearly a hundred feet. As for the width, most people think Howitt may have over-estimated, until they try swimming across and find it is a lot further than it looks.

Cullyamurra, like the other permanent waterholes in

Above: Looking across Cullyamurra to the site
of Howitt's camp.
Below: A construction camp beside Cullyamurra.

the area, is simply a very deep stretch of the Cooper. When the river is flowing freely it is merely a part of the river but when the river dries up the great waterholes remain as beautiful oases in a harsh and arid land.

When a severe drought has devastated the country for hundreds of miles in all directions, reducing it to a desolate and deadly region where few forms of life can survive, the permanent waterholes are even more busy and beautiful than usual. Most of the long-flying birds wing their way South to the Murray, the Coorong and other retreats but some of the ducks, swans and pelicans remain to feast in and around the waterholes. Other birds, their wings not strong enough to carry them across the surrounding deserts, congregate at the waterholes until the Cooper flows again.

From the great river red gums and coolabahs on the banks of Cullyamurra the ringing calls of thrushes and honeyeaters fill the air with music, rainbow birds on their annual pilgrimage from New Guinea flash their colours in the sunlight, kingfishers ply their trade from low branches overhanging the water, corellas and galahs create a crashing crescendo of sound as they fly around in thousands, kites and crows, plovers and dotterels, herons and egrets, chats and budgerigars, parrots and finches all add their colour and sound and movement to a scene of vibrant life.

Beneath the surface it is much the same, although the water is seldom clear enough to give more than a hint of the activity that goes on in its depths. Cullyamurra is crowded with bream, callop and catfish, tortoises and water rats. The same applies to the other permanent waterholes.

Corellas are noisy birds and I doubt if anyone or anything except a corella finds its squawk particularly pleasing. We camped beside Cullyamurra one night when a flock of about twenty thousand came in at sunset and decided to settle in the red gums around us. It was a magnificent sight as they came in, blotting out the rosy sunset with a dense wall of white feathers. We had finished eating and were settling down around the campfire to yarn the evening away, but when the corellas arrived we found we could not hear each other shout. There was nothing to do but wait until they settled down for the night.

Unfortunately, corellas have no idea of the number of

85

birds that will fit on a branch. They perch shoulder to shoulder, filling every inch from the trunk to the end of the branch, then a latecomer tries to squeeze in the middle. The inevitable result is a couple of irate corellas are tipped off the end of the branch and they let everyone know about it. These displaced corellas obviously have friends who take off in sympathy with them and do two or three circuits of the red gum, squawking as raucously as possible. They then return to the tree and try to push in the middle of a branch, which tips a couple of corellas off the end. As this sort of thing happens simultaneously on about twenty different branches about half the flock is kept on the move — and on the squawk — until they gradually get organised.

For about three hours we sat drinking coffee and tea and shrugging our shoulders at each other, until finally the great flock lapsed into silence and slumber, except for one bird still flapping around and uttering muffled protests. Luckily he blundered onto an uninhabited twig and stayed there. I picked up a torch to get my bedroll organised, tripped on a camp stool and dropped the torch which flashed its beam through the trees and startled about ten thousand corellas into violent protest. The corellas left at dawn but we slept late that morning.

At the upstream end of Cullyamurra there is a great expanse of large black boulders, many with their flat faces scored by ancient carvings. Some of the rock carvings are many thousands of years old, others are of more recent origin. Of the oldest carvings, the Yantruwanta tribesmen knew only that they were done in the Dreamtime. They are different in form and style from the more modern carvings, more reminiscent of Egypt than Australia, mysterious messages left by people no longer known or remembered.

When the Cooper is in full flood its water rushes and pounds its way over some of those rocks. When the stream is quiet the rock faces are blistering hot under the outback sun. When strong winds blow the rocks are scoured by sand whipped away from drifting dunes. That the carvings have survived such treatment for so long illustrates the hardness of the rock. How, then, were the carvings made? What implement known to primitive man would score deeply into rock so hard it would resist the wearing effects of sun, sand and flood for thousands of years?

Perhaps it is fortunate that the rock carvings are not accessible to casual visitors. They can only be reached after a long, rough walk over boulder-strewn slopes but recently somebody has been in there and scratched over some of the ancient impressions to make them more obvious. Perhaps he is under the deluded impression that he is "restoring" the age-old symbols but in his ignorance he has utterly destroyed priceless relics.

The fringes of Cullyamurra are littered with artifacts and other remnants of the days when the Yantruwantas frequented the great waterhole. Along each bank there are dozens of "workshops" where the natives sat patiently chipping away at the rocks to form Pirri (spear) points, knives, grinders and other implements. The framework of wurlies, native graves covered with branches and decorated with sacred "stones", and extensive heaps of broken mussel shells have survived although it is more than fifty years since an epidemic of influenza decimated the tribe, leaving only a few survivors. Cullyamurra is far from unique in providing a pageant of the past — there are many waterholes and lakes in the Cooper country that show similar signs of the primitive civilisation that survived so many obstacles, only to falter and flounder when afflicted by a disease to which the Yantruwantas had no resistance.

Upstream from Cullyamurra, just over the border, is the "Dig Tree", where Brahe and his party waited more than four months while Burke, Wills, Gray and King made a dash to the Gulf of Carpentaria. On April 21, 1861, Brahe left the depot and started the long journey back to civilisation. He had waited more than a month longer than Burke told him to and his own men were suffering severely from scurvy and other ailments. Brahe buried food at the depot so the natives would not find it and calved the word DIG and directions on a tree.

Just seven hours after Brahe and his party left Burke, Wills and King staggered into the deserted depot. Gray was already dead, buried on the fringes of Lake Massacre.

There have been many stories about Gray's death and just as many about his body but I do not intend to compete with the multitude of theories and evidence advanced by historians. One persistent claim, however, deserves to be squashed and forgotten. The story is that Gray's skull was used as a doorstop at Coongie for some years. It makes a good yarn but it is not very logical. Any piece of rock would make a more efficient doorstop than a skull which is too light and rounded to offer much resistance. Artie Rowlands, a great old cattleman who knows more about the early days of the Innamincka and Coongie areas than any other ten men, described the story as "rubbish".

The weary explorers dug up the food and Wills and King wanted to follow Brahe, knowing he was only a few miles away. Burke decided they would head for Mount Hopeless. He left a note in case Brahe returned, but buried the message in the same hole and covered it carefully. Brahe did return but found no sign that the others had been there, so he hurried back to Melbourne to organise search parties.

Two amateur wood carvers who worked for a time on Innamincka station about fifty years after Brahe blazed his message on a tree, added their own memorial to the explorers — they carved their impression of the face of Robert O'Hara Burke on a coolabah trunk. Recently the carving has shown signs of decay so, with the approval of the appropriate authorities, I give the "face" a coat of preservative whenever I visit the site of the "Dig Tree".

There is a cairn at the site, with a plaque repeating the message carved by Brahe, but somewhere along the line the message became garbled. Brahe buried the provisions three feet West of the tree, the plaque records it as forty feet West.

Not far from the "Dig Tree" are the ruins of Oontoo, which was a customs station on the Queensland/South Australia border before Australia became a Commonwealth and trade between the States became free. Only a few decaying posts and a scattered bottle heap remain to show where the old customs station stood.

Innamincka township is about eight miles downstream from Cullyamurra but in between is another picturesque waterhole, Yidniminckanie. The name of the town is a corruption of the name of the waterhole. About fifty yards from the steep, sandy bank of Yidniminckanie a memorial cairn marks the second last resting place of Robert O'Hara Burke.

Applying preservative to the carving.

Above: The plaque on the cairn near the "Dig Tree".
Below: The scattered bottle heap at Oontoo.

Howitt buried the bodies of Burke and Wills where he found them but when he reported back to Melbourne he was sent back to the Cooper country to exhume the bodies and return them to Melbourne where they now lie.

After returning from their attempt to reach Mount Hopeless Burke, Wills and King struggled for survival along the Cooper, wandering upstream and downstream from one waterhole to another, hoping desperately for the arrival of a relief party.

The friendly Yantruwantas gave them fish and they learned to collect nardoo seeds and grind them to a coarse flour to make a type of cake. The nardoo cakes were filling but there was little nourishment in them. Burke foolishly drove the natives away.

When Wills lost the strength to walk Burke and King left him as much food as they could and travelled upstream again but Burke died beside Yidniminckanie with his pistol in his hand — a typically flamboyant gesture. King returned thirteen miles downstream to find Wills also dead. Then King did what he and Wills had wanted to do all along — he went to the Yantruwantas and lived with them for two and a half months until he was rescued by Howitt.

It is difficult, standing by a sparkling waterhole teeming with fish and with plenty of edible birds within easy range, to understand why the explorers wasted away and died in the midst of apparent plenty. Wills' journal provides the explanation. He wrote that Burke shot at a bird and missed, but could not be bothered trying again. Obviously the terrible hardships of their journey had sapped not only their physical strength, but also their will power and judgement. They were ravaged by scurvy and had little protection from the penetrating cold of the winter nights.

Innamincka township never progressed beyond a hospital, police station, pub and a couple of houses. In the early days there were plans to establish a flourishing country centre there, to be called Hopetoun. The town was surveyed and the possibility of building a railway from Farina to the Cooper was seriously considered but both the railway and Hopetoun were first deferred and finally forgotten.

About twenty years ago Innamincka was deserted. Little trace remains of the police station and the hotel. Even the world-famous Innamincka bottle heap, an enormous stack of "dead marines" many times larger than the pub itself, has gone. A super flood from the Cooper swept the bottles and most of the buildings away, leaving only the walls of the former mission hospital as a substantial reminder of the old town. Nearby is a large cairn with two memorial plaques — one for Sturt, the other for Burke and Wills.

Beside those tattered remnants of old Innamincka there are now new buildings. A store and fuel supply has operated for some time and the new hotel recently opened.

A few hundred yards away on a stone-strewn slope is the cemetery, some of the graves adorned with headstones that tell their own stories of old-time tragedies, others merely unmarked mounds of earth and rock. Most of the graves are laid down in orderly parallel rows but a few slant away at an angle — even at Innamincka the Afghan camel drivers and their descendents knew the direction of their Mecca.

Nearby is an airstrip, used by light aircraft but not by the Twin Otters that fly regular services for freight and passengers to the Channel Country. They use the strip at Innamincka station, a few miles away on the other side of the Cooper. Innamincka is a Kidman property and in its heyday there were few holdings in the world which could even compare with it for size. Some of its outlying areas have since been taken over by other stations, but it is still big enough to give Texans an inferiority complex.

When the Cooper is in flood and the concrete causeway near Innamincka is under water, normal traffic between the station and the town is impossible. The only power boat in the area belongs to Artie Hearne, who runs an outback contracting business and has his headquarters at a camp near Cullyamurra.

When someone from the station wants to cross the Cooper they drive down to the edge of Cullyamurra, fire a rifle to attract attention in the camp, then somebody takes the speedboat across to get them. After a trip to the store in another vehicle they return the same way — a very simple and effective way around a problem and also an example of the difference modern transportation has made to life in the outback.

Above: The Cooper near Innamincka township.
Below: A tourist tries a transceiver.

Before aircraft, vehicles, transceivers and power boats, stations could be completely isolated by floods from supplies and medical services. Generations ago a row boat was kept at Cullyamurra in case it was necessary to cross the Cooper when the normal crossing points were flooded. Anyone who has seen the Cooper in full flow will turn a shade paler at the thought of tackling it in a rowing boat!

Artie Hearne's daughter Tracy has a horse called Princess Sheena, which periodically creates chaos in the camp. Sheena is a half-brumby with extraordinary habits and tastes. She eats clothes, meat, cigarettes, bread and soap packets with obvious relish but has little time for such mundane foods as hay or lucerne. It is useless tying up the Princess — she merely eats the rope and trots off to the clothesline for a three-course meal of a juicy jumper, tasty trousers and a delicate dress for desert.

A barbed-wire enclosure keeps Sheena out of mischief most of the time but she breaks out occasionally. Once she wandered into the recreation caravan, flipped up the lid of the deep freeze unit, ate five loaves of bread and then ambled around the room chewing the ends off all the curtains. A few days later she sneaked into another caravan and ate the ski-boat ropes.

There are two other crazy horses at the camp, young colts brought in by brumby shooter Ray Haylock. Like Sheena, they spurn normal nourishing horse feed and wander away into the sandhills to gather their tucker. The brumby colts spend the rest of their time lounging around by the camp lighting plant. They may be "hooked" on carbon monoxide or perhaps they are smart enough to realise the gas and noise keep the flies in check. Whatever the reason, the young colts obviously find something soothing in the machine's noisy vibrations.

We always take special precautions when we camp beside Cullyamurra, where we often stay for two or three nights while making day trips around the Cooper country. Any clothes or towels left around will soon disappear if Princess Sheena is on the loose and all supplies have to be safeguarded from Heckle and Jeckyl, two half-tame marauding crows that can make an incredible mess of a campsite in a few minutes.

Above: Princess Sheena finds some of her favourite
food inside caravans.
Below: The brumby colts in their favourite spot.

The speedboat on Cullyamurra.

The "Dig Tree", scene of one of the many mistakes
that brought disaster to the Burke and Wills expedition.

Floodwaters sprawl over sand and gibber plains.

Ancient rock carvings near Cullyamurra waterhole.

Cullyamurra, the magnificent permanent waterhole near Innamincka.

Cullyamurra waterhole

HOWITT'S DEPOT
HERE IN SEPTEMBER 1861
ALFRED HOWITT CAMPED
WHILE SEARCHING FOR THE EXPLORERS
BURKE & WILLS
THIS CAIRN WAS ERECTED BY TED CONRICK AT
THE EXPENSE OF DONALD MACKAY
1st JANUARY 1941

Near Cullyamurra waterhole — Howitt's camp and
the framework of a native mia-mia.

Along the track to Cordillo Downs.

King's Lookout, an enormous sandhill that dwarfs the tiny Land-Rover on the plain below.

At Cordillo Downs - the historic woolshed and
the meathouse.

Contrasts in transportation.

The sprawling Coongie Lakes cover hundreds of square miles and support a great variety of wild life.

Sunset over Coongie.

Above: The channel where the north-west distributary of the
Cooper flows into the Coongie lakes.
Below: Terns, 400 miles from the sea, rest on a sandbar.

Narrow strips of higher ground divide
the shallow water into scores of lakes.

Water ski-ing on Cooper floodwaters.

REBIRTH OF A RIVER

Immediately after passing Innamincka township the Cooper loses some of its water to the Strzelecki Creek, although it is only during a very big flood that there is a substantial flow in the distributary that meanders away to the South. The crossing of the Strzelecki near the town is often cut during minor floods, preventing conventional vehicles from using the Strzelecki Track, but with four-wheel-drive it is often possible to drive across country for a short way downstream, cross the dry creek bed and come back on the other side.

The reason is that the water going out of the Cooper into Strzelecki Creek has to flow up hill, which means it will not go very far unless it is pushed forward by a great volume of floodwaters. There is a gradual incline over the first few miles of the creek and unless the flood is big enough to cover the crossing with about six feet of water there will be no flow beyond the bar five miles downstream.

The main volume of water flows West for about twenty miles before the Cooper again distributes its strength into side channels, first to the South-West, then to the North-West Branch which carries a tremendous volume of water to the great network of lakes that stretch away beyond Coongie. Before those distributions are made the Cooper passes the spot where Wills died.

There is general agreement among historians that the choice of Robert O'Hara Burke to lead the expedition to cross Australia from South to North was a poor one. Burke was a dashing policeman in Melbourne but he had no experience in the bush and little tolerance with other people's opinions. The expedition cost the people of Melbourne £50,000 — an enormous fortune for the times — and was equipped with every possible aid to success. The farewell cheers of the crowd had scarcely subsided before there was a preview of disaster. The camel expert, Landells, who began the trip as Burke's second-in-command, returned to Melbourne following a violent disagreement with his leader. The carefully

113

planned expedition had quickly lost one of its key men and Burke continued to sap the strength of the party by dividing and redividing his men and equipment.

Wills, chosen as astronomer and surveyor, became Burke's new lieutenant. All accounts of the tragic expedition show Wills as an able young man who might well have been a success as leader but was dominated by the aggressive and impatient Irish policeman.

A memorial cairn was erected on the spot where Burke died many years ago. I always felt that the young English scientist deserved at least as much recognition as his Irish leader. Other people had the same thoughts years ago.

Joe Mack, a keen student of history who lives in the River Murray town of Waikerie, tried to raise enthusiasm and support for a project to build a cairn in 1961, the centenary of the explorer's death. The response was disappointing. Ten years later I had the same experience — people generally were interested and offered encouragement but not practical assistance.

Some financial aid would have been most welcome. After all, it costs money to run Land-Rovers on a round trip of nearly two thousand miles in the outback, plus supplies and materials for the cairn. It seemed reasonable to hope that the Government might at least supply the bronze plaque to be attached to the cairn. But which Government?

The explorers set out from Victoria, traversed long stretches of New South Wales and Queensland and died in South Australia. The South Australian Government said it was a Victorian expedition, the Victorians already had memorials to Burke and Wills in Melbourne and the Federal Government said it was obviously a State matter.

By this time I had met Joe Mack and we were both determined to go ahead with the project. We had to be quite sure the cairn was built in the right place.

A Queenslander, Alex Towner, spent a lot of time in the area in 1948, tracing the tracks of the explorers and reestablishing points of interest. Towner carefully studied the journals kept by Wills, Howitt and McKinlay, the leader of another relief expedition who arrived shortly after Howitt and made detailed maps and descriptions of the country, including the grave sites.

I had previously located the markers left by Towner to record the spots where Wills died and where King was found living with the Yantruwantas. Howitt found Wills' body in the broad channel of the Cooper which was dry at the time, but naturally buried him on the bank so the grave would not be washed away when the stream flowed again. Towner placed a pipe in the ground near the grave and found a fine tree growing in the channel where the body had been recovered. He blazed the tree and carved "Wills 1861" on the trunk. In the intervening twenty-five years the bark has grown back over the edges of the carving.

With a few willing helpers and a television crew from ADS7, Joe Mack and I headed off from Adelaide in March, 1973 to build the cairn. Where Governments had failed, private enterprise had joined in with a practical contribution. Adelaide photo engravers, Porter and Barnett, had supplied a fine magnesium plaque.

We stopped overnight at Lyndhurst and the next day reached the Cooper which was flowing freely and rising rapidly. We set up camp beside Cullyamurra and prepared to begin the cairn the next morning. We had discussed camping near the work site which would give us more hours of daylight for the job but three factors finally influenced the choice of Cullyamurra, twenty miles away. We had to call there to pick up cement which I had arranged to be delivered to Artie Hearne's camp. There were no suitable rocks near the grave site but on the track from Cullyamurra to Innamincka township there were a couple of rock-strewn hills where we could pick up ideal material to cart to the grave. And as some members of the party had not been to the area before I wanted them to have the pleasure of camping beside Australia's greatest waterhole.

Next morning we loaded the Land-Rovers with cement and as much rock as we could carry and drove to Wills' grave. From my own investigations I was satisfied Towner had done his work well and pin-pointed the spot accurately. Joe, who had not seen the site, was cautious until he had surveyed the scene himself, but he certainly knew what was in the explorers' journals. As we approached the site he began to get excited as he recognised landmarks.

"There's the big nardoo flat. There's the big sandridge

Eric Loffler at work on the cairn

The completed memorial cairn

WILLIAM JOHN WILLS
second-in-command of the
Burke & Wills expedition
born
Totnes, Devon, England, 1834
died
near here about June 29, 186
Erected by the passengers of a Rover Charter To
March, 1973.

Above: The plaque
Below: The builders.

that runs down to the channel. And there's the sandbar between the two waterholes."

We expected to take two days, perhaps three, to complete the cairn but we reckoned without Eric Loffler, one of Joe's friends from Waikerie. Eric is a fruitgrower but he likes building things and he knows how to go about it. He is also a tough foreman!

Within minutes of our arrival he had everybody on the move, digging out foundations, carting sand from a nearby deposit and water up the steep bank of the Cooper, mixing cement, fixing wires and bolts to the plaque so it would be firmly fixed to the cairn, boiling the billy to keep up the tea supply, facing rocks and driving back to the stony hills for more materials.

The sun climbed high and so did the temperature but Eric kept building away and yelling for more sand, more cement, more rock and more tea. Before the day was over he had given the cairn a last careful stroke with the trowel. Wills' memorial was complete, and a very fine cairn it is.

As it was still warm in the late afternoon some of us celebrated with a plunge into the Cooper while the others settled for yet another billy of tea. With the current flowing strongly we were unable to get to the tree that Towner blazed, nor see the actual spot where Wills died because it was under feet of water. Still, looking out across the cairn to that tree in the stream brought a deep feeling of satisfaction.

The next day we erected signs so tourists would be able to find both Burke's and Wills' grave, then decided to head downstream to see how far the rising flood in the Cooper had progressed. It takes months for floodwaters to get from Innamincka to the Cooper's final destination at Lake Eyre — if they get there at all. Countless lakes and side channels have to be filled along the way and progress along the main channel is slow. Although the causeway crossing at Innamincka was under ten feet of rushing water I felt we would not have to travel too many miles downstream to reach the head of the flood.

I have seen the Cooper country die week by week and month by month when there have been prolonged droughts over both the local area and the Cooper's catchment areas in Queensland. With no rain and no flow in the streams for many months, perhaps years, the vegetation withers and blows away with the drifting sand. The coolabahs and gidgie trees stand like silent sentinels mourning the death of the land that produced them, clinging desperately to life through the long wait for rejuvenating water.

Birds and mammals disappear from thousands of square miles of desolate country, leaving only those equipped by evolution to survive. Some that leave reach greener pastures, many do not.

Cattle leave the watercourses and congregate around the artesian bores that provide a permanent supply of water. They eat the flimsy feed remaining around the water point, then they have to walk out further for feed and further back to water, every day a longer journey until they can no longer walk from one essential to the other.

Modern transports carry thousands of bullocks and steers away from drought areas to other districts, a big improvement on the early pastoral days when the stock could only be moved on their own legs, but still many cattle die when severe droughts hit the Cooper country.

The water life, too, must have an enormous casualty list. I have been water-skiing on a spillage lake from the Cooper when there were hundreds of tiny black heads protruding from the water. There must have been thousands of tortoises in that shallow lake, completely cut off from the rest of the world once the inlet channel dried up. Yet I have landed an aircraft and driven a Land-Rover on the same spot when seepage and evaporation have exhausted the water and the sun has baked the surface to a hard claypan.

The thought of all those tortoises losing their water will upset a lot of people but it is all part of a cycle. The same process has been repeated on that same lake hundreds of times over the ages. When the water supply dies, so do many creatures that depend on it. When the lakes and channels are refilled the water is suddenly, miraculously, teeming with wildlife.

I have seen the incredible transformation that occurs in drought-stricken areas of the outback when rain finally falls. It is astonishing how quickly the yellow-brown country is tinged with green shoots that flourish into lush carpets of native grasses, shrubs and wild flowers, the coolabahs and

The crossing below Embarka Waterhole,
with the first floodwater flowing.

gidgeas lift their heads and sprout new leaves, the birds and mammals appear in thousands to add their sound and colour to a panorama of vibrant life.

But that day when we drove down the Cooper to see how far the floodwaters had progressed we witnessed another intimate chapter in the rebirth of a river. On Gidgealpa station we came to a crossing a few miles below Embarka Waterhole. The water was just a few inches deep in the channel but it was rising rapidly. Quickly we drove the vehicles across, knowing they would be the last to make that crossing for months.

It was not the main channel of the Cooper, merely one of the distributories that break away to the South. Still, it turned on a memorable performance.

We left the vehicles and ran downstream, soon outstripping the infiltrating water. The surface of the channel was dry and bare, laced with a network of cracks that had swallowed a few decaying leaves and twigs discarded by the thirsty coolabahs on the bank. Underfoot the soil crumbled, sending dust and pellets cascading down into the yawning cracks.

The water approached in spasmodic spurts, splashing forward a few feet as it reached a forward slope, pausing to consolidate and broaden its hold on level stretches. The leading edge of the stream was a tumbling mass of foam, twigs and leaves.

Hundreds of miniature waterfalls formed as the water reached the gaping cracks and poured down to fill the crevices. Some filled in an instant, others ran deeper and connected with other cracks, for in places the water went down one fissure and up another, bubbling to the surface a few inches ahead of the swelling stream.

From other cracks ahead of the water startled geckos scrambled to the surface, running frantically to the sides of the channel and pausing to glance back at the strange fluid that was engulfing their retreats. And from the deepest cracks in the lowest part of the channel little bream and catfish jerked their way to the surface, flipped their tails and launched themselves into the air. Some fell straight into the fringe of the advancing water, others bounced two or three times on the dusty surface before the spreading stream rea-

The sun-baked channel ahead of the floodwater.

The first water flows in.

Floodwaters sprawl far beyond the channel.

ched and engulfed them.

Cameraman Jan deWit had placed his TV camera on the surface a short distance ahead of the encroaching water to get a low level shot of the advance. Some of the little fish emerged right in front of the lens and showed up clearly on the film, so thousands of television viewers were fortunate enough to see the phenomenon.

Some of the bream and catfish were three inches long, some smaller. How they came to be wriggling out of cracks ahead of the advancing water I do not know — I will leave it for the experts to argue about that.

Three weeks later when I took another party out the same way we all commented on a shimmering mirage that distorted the big plain ahead — only it was not a mirage, it was the real thing. Floodwaters sprawled for miles and I wondered how many little bream and catfish were swimming contentedly in that vast expanse of water.

While watching the floodwaters restore life in the dry channel was a unique experience I did not find it altogether surprising. I have spent too much time in the Cooper country to be surprised at anything that happens there. Looking back over scores of trips I cannot remember one when nothing unexpected occurred.

When passengers ask what they will see on the road ahead I have learned to be cautious. Even if I have been over the same track a fortnight or so earlier and found it devoid of vegetation, and also know there has been no rain reported from stations in the area, it is still possible to drive around the next sandhill and be confronted with a few square miles of flourishing greenery. A local thunderstorm, too far away from any homestead to be noticed, can transform a small area in a few days. When that sort of thing happens the passengers tend to sit up straighter, glance at me suspiciously and ask if there is a road map handy.

Most people expect to see large numbers of kangaroos and emus when they go outback but we seldom see more than a few stragglers except around the Northern fringes of the Flinders Ranges. They have never been common in the Cooper country.

On the other hand those who are apprehensive about snakes would be safer in the outback than in the outer suburbs of most cities. There is always a chance of coming across a womma, a green monster that is quite harmless, but venomous snakes are very rare. The heat of the inland summer is more than they can stand. Lizards, however, seem more at home and quite a few species may be encountered.

Echidnas survive around the permanent waterholes and dingoes roam far and wide. Occasionally wild camels, donkeys and goats appear and brumbies are quite common away from the regular tracks.

Marsupial rats and mice are very numerous in places but they are seldom seen. They are nocturnal and keep out of sight during the day, leaving only tiny tracks criss-crossing sandhills to show that they have been out for their usual midnight supper.

Another animal which few people have seen but demands respect from everyone is the murramurra, the legendary monster that lives in the great waterholes. Anyone wanting to swim the waterhole must first bow to the murramurra if he wants to reach the other side.

The variety and number of birds is a surprise to most travellers, particularly water birds but also some that are familiar to city dwellers. People tend to stare in disbelief when they see a familiar willy wagtail performing aerobatics in pursuit of a bush fly, or the same honey-eaters that sip nectar from their garden fuchsias fossicking around the leaves of a coolabah.

Brolgas seem to cause more excitement than anything else. While driving quietly along one day in the lakes country a stentorian voice from the back seat yelled "Stop!" Before I could bring the Land-Rover to a standstill the door flew open and Jack Kaines leapt out onto the sand. As Jack was seventy-six years old I thought a womma must have appeared from under the seat but he had merely spotted some brolgas across the lake. They are now very rare and seldom gather in large numbers but we usually come across one or two small parties during a tour.

Budgerigars in the wild are quite different from budgies in cages. For one thing all wild ones are green, the coloured varieties having been bred in captivity. Their flight is swift and beautiful, like a volley of arrows crossing the sky and when they wheel in unison and the sunlight catches a thousand wings at once there is a brilliant flash of emerald in the sky. When hundreds of them settle on a dead tree it is a great spectacle, as if the tree has sprouted fresh new leaves over every inch of its surface.

Gulls and terns, supposedly sea birds, often appear in large numbers when the Cooper has filled some of its spillage areas. Like the ducks that head for the inland as soon as the rains fall there, the gulls and terns somehow know when there is an inland sea waiting to offer them an alternative home for a while.

Cormorants, too, desert the coastal fringes when the lakes are full, to gorge themselves on fish that have little chance to escape in the shallow water. I have camped beside a sprawling lake which was apparently the cormorants' chosen meeting place for the night, quietly watching in wonder as squadron after squadron flew overhead in their echelon formations to sideslip down and land on or beside the water. We could not keep an accurate count but we all agreed that there were at least twenty-five thousand water birds sharing our secluded spot that night.

Pelicans also gather in great numbers when the fishing is good. When they are resting between meals they sometimes squat close together in a great white mass that looks like chalk cliffs across the lake.

Above: A deserted home.
Below: A deserted vehicle.

Above: When a load of horse meat capsizes —
Below: The salvage operation requires special equipment.

The camp of a seismic crew near a station bore.

Above: Sacred grave-stones of the Yantruwantas.
Below: Chipped stones in a Yantruwanta "workshop".

In bad seasons outback tracks are hidden by drifting sand, in good seasons by vegetation.

Above: A veteran — at 76, Jack Kaines is still an
enthusiastic outback traveller.
Below: A beginner — an emu chick.

Above: The days can be hot —
Below: The nights can be frosty.

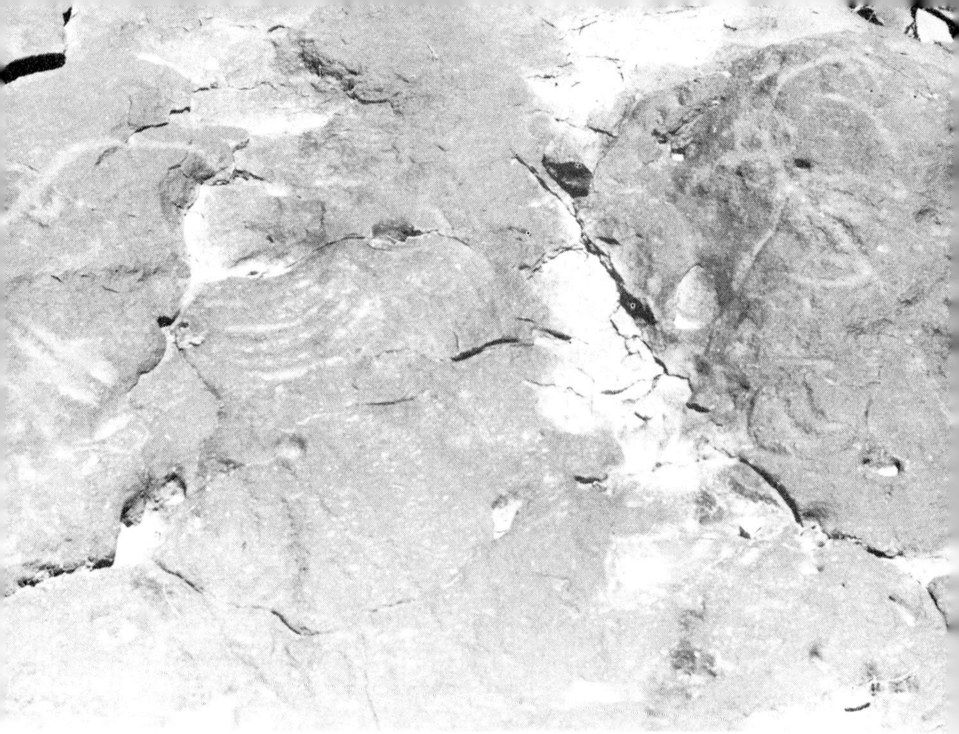

Ancient rock carvings near Cullyamurra.

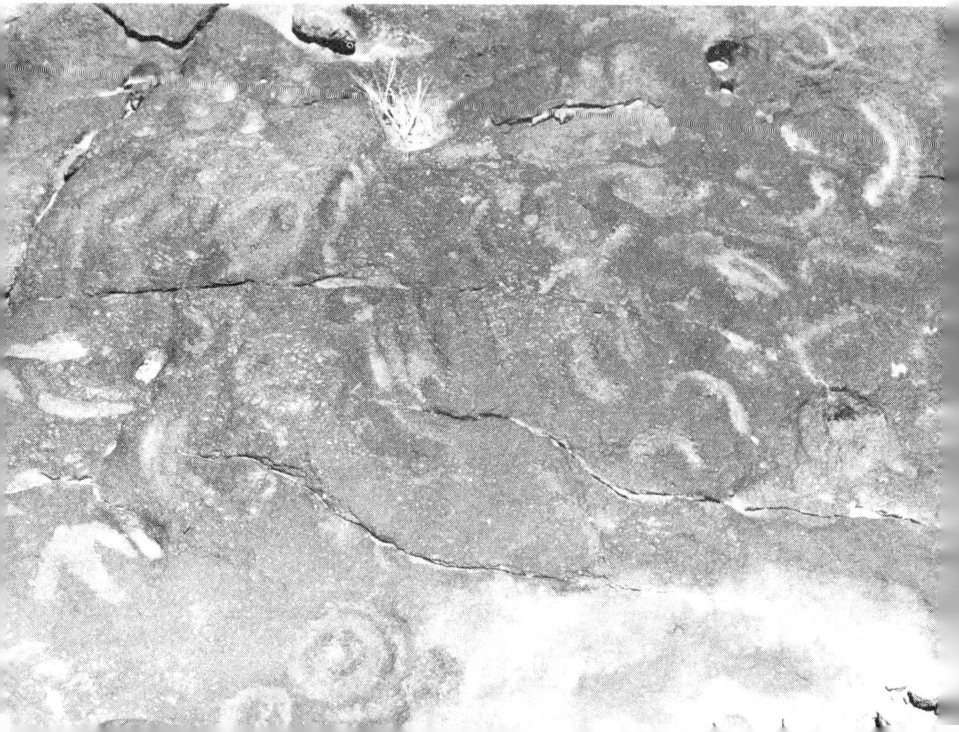

In the lakes country near Coongie.

Above: Lake Massacre, scene of Gray's grave.
Below: Bulloobulloo, scene of the "Dig Tree".

Burke's face, carved on a tree beside Bulloobulloo.

Above: Yidniminckanie, scene of Burke's death.
Below: The dry bed of the Cooper where Wills died.

The tree blazed by Alex Towner at the scene of
Wills' death.

The blazed tree, second from left, engulfed in
Cooper floodwaters.

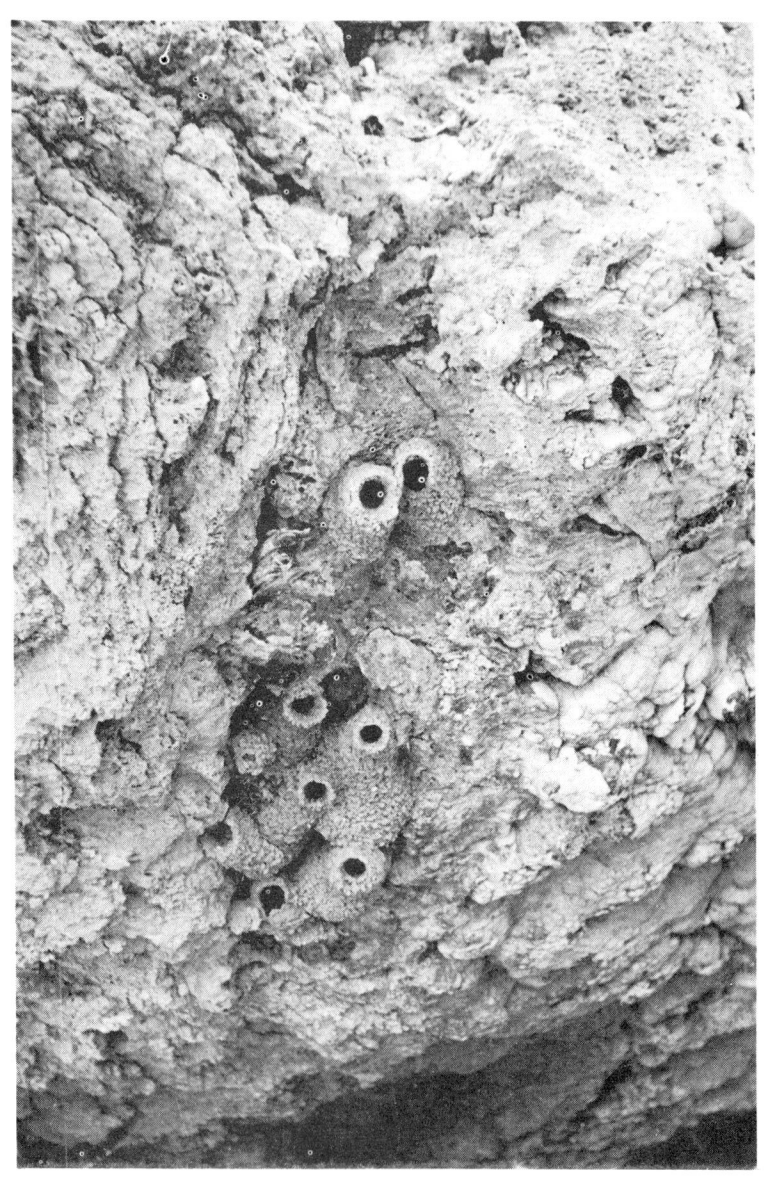

Nests of a colony of fairy martins beneath an overhanging rock ledge.

Stock feed flourishes following a flood
in an outback watercourse.

Above: Two trains in an outback siding.
Below: A camel boot used in stony country.

Above: Cattle on the move.
Below: Brumbies on the plains.

COONGIE LAKES AND CORDILLO DOWNS

The North-West Branch of the Cooper channels water to a vast network of lakes and streams that sprawl out over an enormous area of country. Near the unfrequented Coongie outstation, about sixty miles by track from Innamincka, the lakes are divided only by narrow strips of land that support fine stands of trees. Further West the lakes are more scattered with ranges of sandhills and extensive plains between them.

Whenever the Cooper flows the lakes receive a liberal share of the water, so it is only in periods of prolonged drought that they dry out completely. Usually at least some of the shallow depressions are inundated.

The variety of bird life around Coongie is quite fantastic. Ibis, herons and egrets swarm around the shores while pelicans, swans, ducks, cormorants, coots and other waterfowl float in great congregations further out from the trees and shrubs that fringe the water. Dozens of species of small land birds flock around the lignum bushes that grow luxuriantly beneath the eucalypts. Parrots and cockatoos fill the air with flashes of colour and raucous screeching.

When approaching Coongie I often ask my passengers which way they would go if they were suddenly left alone without water. At about that point there is a lofty sandhill to the right of the track but a mile or so to the left there is a line of coolabahs that mark a wandering watercourse. Having by this time spent a few days in the outback, most of them spot the straggling trees and suggest there would be a chance of finding water there. My only reply is to turn the Land-Rover to the right and churn up to the top of the dune. From there the view is breath-taking.

The lakes stretch away to the horizon and beyond, reflecting the blue sky, the vivid green of the trees and shrubs and the rusty red of the sandhills that tower in the distance. There is usually a minute or two of silence as incredulous eyes sweep across the expanse of beauty, then a frantic rush to get the doors open and the cameras into action.

It is rarely possible to travel West from Coongie to the more scattered lakes that sprawl out over lonely country towards the Birdsville Track. And on the odd occasions when it would be possible there would be little point in doing it, for if the lakes at Coongie were dry, those further West would also be dry, dusty flats.

In all but the worst seasons there is plenty to see in the country West of Coongie and it is an area that very few people have seen. It is uninhabited and inaccessible, isolated, untamed and trackless. One could wander there for months without ever seeing a sign of another human being.

Not that the area is entirely and permanently deserted. Stockmen from Clifton Hills occasionally penetrate deep into the lakes country following cattle that have wandered out to the boundaries of the big station. Doggers and brumby shooters also venture far from the recognised tracks and there is plenty of prey for them in that area.

Brumbies are never approachable. They run for their lives at the first sign of an intruder entering their domain and it is seldom possible to get close to them. Even in the distance, however, it is exciting to see a mob of the wild horses galloping away across the plain, leaving a great pall of dust as they head for the shelter of the nearest dunes.

Dingoes are sometimes quite unafraid and inquisitive, especially in areas like the lakes country where they have little contact with people. Some appear to have no previous experience with human beings or their vehicles and I have had dingoes trotting along behind the Land-Rovers for miles, standing back to stare curiously when we stopped and emerged, falling in behind again when we climbed aboard and continued on our way.

After many attempts and failures I finally succeeded in finding a practical route from the Birdsville Track through the beautiful lakes country to Innamincka. It is rough and rugged but can be accomplished in all but the wettest seasons. Only a few people have been through there but they have all rated the experience as one of the highlights of their holiday in the Cooper country.

A lot of tall stories have been told about Cordillo Downs. Old bushmen claim that at shearing time there were so many blokes on the station that the cook used an outboard motor to

149

THE BURKE & WILLS EXPEDITION
1860—1861

CHARLIE GRAY DIED NEAR THIS SPOT
ON THE SIXTEENTH OF APRIL 1861. HE WAS ONE OF FOUR
MEN FIRST TO CROSS THE CONTINENT FROM SOUTH TO NORTH.
HE & KING ACCOMPANIED BURKE & WILLS. BURKE & WILLS
DIED ON COOPERS CREEK. KING BEING RESCUED BY
ALFRED HOWITT ON THE FIFTEENTH OF SEPTEMBER 1861.
HE HAD BEEN LIVING WITH THE NATIVES FOR THREE MONTHS,
THEY HAVING BEFRIENDED HIM.

Above: Notice erected by Towner near Lake Massacre.
Below: An inquisitive dingo.

stir the porridge and his off-sider cruised through the stew in a midget submarine to see if the spuds were cooked. It took two men to see across the cookhouse to the clock on the opposite wall.

The soil would grow anything on the odd occasions when it rained. Whenever there was a good fall the head gardener would saddle his fastest horse and circle the homestead at full gallop, throwing pumpkin seeds into the soft ground. He had to keep moving fast, otherwise the horse's legs would become tangled in the sprouting vines. Despite the gardener's efforts the pumpkins were never any good. The vines grew so fast they wore the pumpkins out dragging them along the ground!

Two shearers heading for Cordillo camped out one night near an old water tank. They were attacked by ferocious mosquitoes and in desperation they pulled the tank over themselves to keep the giant insects at bay. The mosquitoes changed their tactics and attacked the tank, plunging their great barbs through the galvanised iron in the hope of spearing the men cowering inside. One of the shearers grabbed a big rock and began bending the barbs as they came through the tank, so the mosquitoes could not withdraw them. When he had bent four barbs the mosquitoes flew away with the tank!

Some of the yarns may seem to be exaggerated but it is almost as difficult to believe the true story of Cordillo Downs. The homestead and station buildings are on a slight rise which gives a view in almost every direction. There is little variation in the scene — stony plains stretching away to distant red and yellow sandhills, blurred and distorted by the inevitable mirages that are as much a part of that country as the sand and rock.

When rabbits sprawled in plague proportions over vast areas of the inland many sheep and cattle stations were ruined as the invaders ate all the grass and shrubs, even the bark from the struggling trees. Fortunes were spent on building and maintaining rabbit-proof fences to contain the infiltrating pests.

One of the major barriers built to stop the progress of rabbits was along the Queensland/South Australia border. The rabbits were working their way North and the Queensland authorities approached their South Australian counterparts, suggesting a jointly-financed rabbit-proof fence along the border. The South Australians said "bunnies to you", or words to that effect, because nothing would have pleased them more than to see all the rabbits hopping across the border.

Not surprisingly the Queenslanders accepted the verdict philosophically and financed the whole project themselves. Men were employed to patrol the fences and keep them in effective order, a constant job because drifting sand kept changing the height of the land and the level of the fence had to be adjusted accordingly. The system worked well until shortly after World War I when an inspection by a Union official revealed that the boundary riders were working under primitive conditions. When minimum standards of housing and other amenities were demanded the employers decided it would be cheaper to accept the rabbits, so the whole scheme was abandoned.

Cordillo Downs had its own barrier that the rabbits could not overcome — the country itself. The fierce heat of the summer sun on the stony deserts where there was not room for even a rabbit's foot to fit between the gibbers was too much. The rabbits, like Sturt, were forced to retreat from the forbidden landscape.

Yet Cordillo Downs, hundreds of miles beyond the dog-proof fences that separate sheep country from cattle country, survived as a sheep station for nearly seventy years despite the rabbit-repelling conditions and the ravages of dingoes. Only in 1941 were the Merinos replaced by Shorthorn cattle.

There are few buildings in Australia to compare with the famous station woolshed. Although used now only for storage it remains a solid structure stretching away over hundreds of feet. Like most buildings at Cordillo, it has the distinctive rounded roof used where there was no timber for rafters.

The woolclip had to be carted three hundred and seventy seven miles to the railhead at Farina, a big job for the camel trains, especially as the wool was heavy with dust, sand and grease. It cost a lot of money to have all that extra weight carried to Farina, so in 1885 a complete wool scouring plant was installed at Cordillo. The remains of the plant can still be seen near the station waterhole but it gives little

Typical buildings on Cordillo Downs.

Roger Beckwith, manager of Cordillo Downs.

Above: A derelict rabbit-proof fence.
Below: A typical Cordillo Downs mirage.

impression of the size of the operation or the number of sheep carried on the desolate land.

In 1891 more than fourteen hundred bales of scoured wool were carried by camels to Farina!

By that time there were so many people permanently on the station that a fellow called William Sturdy was appointed as schoolmaster. When the shearers arrived the cook must have wished for that outboard motor to stir the porridge.

Many of the shearers walked the eighty-odd miles up the short track from Innamincka, some all the way from Farina. They had bicycles but they were used only as two-wheeled carts to carry their swags and meagre possessions. Not all of them reached Cordillo Downs. There are graves along the short track.

This track has long been replaced by another further East and it is impossible for anyone who does not know the area well to follow it. Only in odd places is the route visible and there are long stretches where memory is the only guide and one false turn can have the vehicle floundering in soft sand. Although about thirty miles longer the new track is hours faster but I like to follow the route the shearers trudged.

There is some magnificent scenery along the way. Stony areas are interspersed with picturesque sandhills and patches of vegetation where watercourses occasionally run. Some of the rarest and shyest of our wildlife can be seen there, particularly the wild turkeys that have retreated from frequented tracks seeking secluded survival.

The dunes vary from white to yellow to red. King's Lookout is an enormous red sandhill which towers over the surrounding ridges, making the long climb to the top well worth the effort. The spectacular views span hundreds of square miles of uninhabited wilderness, a vast panorama of colour and isolated splendour that is simultaneously exciting and sobering.

Many years ago Cordillo Downs was involved in experiments which brought great benefits to people in the outback. Messages were transmitted from Beltana on Alf Traeger's "pedal wireless" and successfully picked up at Cordillo. From that humble beginning the complex and efficient Royal Flying Doctor Service radio networks have developed.

156

Footprints in the sand.

Heading for home —

FRONTISPIECE
Her Majesty The Queen, Patron of the Royal United Services Institute, at the Trooping of the Colour ceremony, 1981.

RUSI

and

BRASSEY'S

Defence
Yearbook
1982

Edited by
The Royal United Services Institute for Defence Studies
London

92nd Year of Publication

BRASSEY'S PUBLISHERS LTD
a member of the Pergamon Group
OXFORD · NEW YORK · TORONTO · SYDNEY · PARIS · FRANKFURT

U.K.	BRASSEY'S PUBLISHERS LIMITED, a member of the Pergamon Group, Headington Hill Hall, Oxford OX3 0BW, England
U.S.A.	Pergamon Press Inc., Maxwell House, Fairview Park, Elmsford, New York 10523, U.S.A.
CANADA	Pergamon Press Canada Ltd., Suite 104, 150 Consumers Rd., Willowdale, Ontario M2J 1P9, Canada
AUSTRALIA	Pergamon Press (Aust.) Pty. Ltd., P.O. Box 544, Potts Point, N.S.W. 2011, Australia
FRANCE	Pergamon Press SARL, 24 rue des Ecoles, 75240 Paris, Cedex 05, France
FEDERAL REPUBLIC OF GERMANY	Pergamon Press GmbH, 6242 Kronberg-Taunus, Hammerweg 6, Federal Republic of Germany

British Library Cataloguing in Publication Data

RUSI and Brassey's defence yearbook.
1982
1. Armed Forces - Periodicals
I. Royal United Services Institute for
Defence Studies
355'.005   UI
ISBN 0-08-027039-5 (Hard cover)
ISBN 0-08-027040-9 (Flexi cover)

Library of Congress Catalog Card No. 75-641843

Frontispiece photograph of Her Majesty the Queen reproduced by kind permission of the Public Relations Office, London District.

Printed in Great Britain by A. Wheaton & Co. Ltd., Exeter

Contents

PREFACE   v

EDITOR'S COMMENTARY   vii

Part I—Strategic Review

AIR POWER AND THE ROYAL AIR FORCE   2
Air Chief Marshal Sir Michael Beetham

TRIDENT—A CANDIDATE FOR CANCELLATION?   15
Professor Ian Bellany

THE ARMED FORCES OF GREECE   28
Professor James Brown

THE JAPANESE ARMS INDUSTRY, 1981: AN ASSESSMENT   50
I P S G Cosby

MERCHANT SHIPPING AND THE MARITIME THREAT   66
H G Davy

COMPUTERS AND COMMANDERS IN THE SOVIET MILITARY SYSTEM: A GENERAL SURVEY   79
Professor John Erickson

DEFENCE IN THE 1980s   96
Dr Gwyn Harries-Jenkins

AN ANATOMY OF DEFENCE POLICY   109
Admiral of the Fleet the Lord Hill-Norton

THE ARMS TRADE AND ARMS CONTROL   124
Dan Smith

OUR COMMON DEFENCE FOR THE EIGHTIES   139
Senator John G Tower

iv

Part II—Weapon Developments

SUBMERSIBLES   152
Captain Francis Bruen

STRATEGIC WEAPONS   163
Dr Lawrence Freedman

WEAPON DEVELOPMENT IN THE 1980's
— SEA   180
Captain Roger Villar

FUTURE TRENDS IN MARITIME WARFARE
— NATO AND THE WARSAW PACT   196
Captain Roger Villar

WEAPON DEVELOPMENT IN THE 1980's
— LAND   217
Ian V Hogg

TRENDS IN LAND WARFARE: INFANTRY
SUPPORT VEHICLES   233
Ian V Hogg

WEAPON DEVELOPMENT IN THE 1980's: AIR   261
Air Commodore F W Thompson

FUTURE TRENDS IN AIRBORNE WEAPONS SYSTEMS   284
Air Commodore F W Thompson

THE FAR EAST NOTES ON MARITIME AND AIR FORCES   297

Part III

DEFENCE LITERATURE OF THE YEAR   326
Robin Stephenson

CHRONOLOGY OF MAIN EVENTS OF DEFENCE INTEREST
APRIL 1980 — MARCH 1981   339
Joanna Chapman

THE CHESNEY GOLD MEDAL   377

INDEX TO ADVERTISERS   379

Preface

FOR 150 years the Royal United Services Institute has played an important part in the advancement of the literature and science of the Armed Forces and in keeping the public informed on defence matters. For the past 92 years one of the most authoritative sources has been the Yearbook which bears the name of its originator Lord Brassey. As the *RUSI/Brassey's Defence Yearbook* it carries on the tradition of high standards in the breadth and quality of its contents. Such is the reputation which the Yearbook has earned that the Editors can enlist the support of contributors of the highest prestige and qualifications as the contents lists so clearly indicate.

We are honoured that By Gracious Permission, the 92nd edition of *RUSI/Brassey's Defence Yearbook* carries as its frontispiece a photograph of Her Majesty the Queen, Patron of the Royal United Services Institute for Defence Studies.

Editors' Commentary

WE ARE honoured that by Gracious Permission this 92nd edition of the *Defence Yearbook* is introduced by a portrait of Her Majesty the Queen, Patron of the Royal United Services Institute, which celebrates its 150th anniversary this year. The Institute, formerly (or originally) the Royal United Service Institution, has a proud record of continuous activity, not only as the repository of the records of British military history but also as a centre dedicated to the advancement of the literature and science of the Armed Services of the Crown. Its membership embraces representatives of other Commonwealth countries across the world, of the allied countries, and of men and women of many vocations and professions in all the continents. The Institute is located literally at the centre of a great capital and prides itself on being at the hub of affairs. Indeed, it can justly claim that by its independent status and international reputation it has promoted the public exchange of thoughts and ideas in advance of the general run of strategic, tactical, and logistic appreciation. A list of those who have been awarded the Chesney Gold Medal of the Institute is included as an appendix to emphasize this point.

A NEW DECADE

The hopes and fears which accompany the birth of a new decade are soon proved to be illusory. The calendar exerts an influence upon political change, which is at best ephemeral. The 1970s opened amid optimism over the future of arms control, following a series of agreements during the 1960s and the start of the Strategic Arms Limitation Talks (SALT). They ended, however, with the arms marathon still an awesome spectacle, while *détente,* the springboard for so many aspirations 10 years earlier, was sagging in the middle.

The Vietnam War had ended. But South-east Asia remained dangerously unsettled and the new Vietnam, united by bloodshed, looked like a country drugged on violence. The ambitions of post-Mao China to achieve First World status by the end of the century seemed almost certain to fail. The new Age of

Multipolarity which strategic thinkers had predicted during the early 1970s — an age in which world power would be shared by five central sources, the United States, the Soviet Union, China, Japan, and Western Europe — had simply not happened. The European Community in many ways appeared less united than it had 10 years before. We were still living in the Age of the Superpowers, for better or worse — and it looked like being for the worse. The start of the 1970s had been characterised by a spirit of hope. The start of the 1980s was surrounded by fear and uncertainty.

The high hopes of the Carter Administration in the United States, in particular, continued to be set down, whether over the release of hostages held in Iran or the response to the proposed boycott of the Moscow Olympic Games. The realities of superpower diplomacy were emphasised by the agreement of the Soviet leaders that talks on Theatre Arms Limitations could be pursued. This change at last came about when it was evident that NATO's plans for Theatre Nuclear Force (TNF) modernisation would go ahead, as a response to the continuing deployment of SS-20 missiles by the USSR, unless mutually satisfactory agreements were reached. If President Carter left office with ambitions unfulfilled, the Soviet leaders who rebuffed his idealistic efforts had little cause for joy. The aftermath of the Afghanistan invasion hangs round the Kremlin with stark evidence of ground lost to the Soviets among the nonaligned countries. The economic state of the Soviet empire is demonstrated in extreme form in Poland, and the politico-industrial consequences have caused grave concern to Communist Party leaders inside and outside Poland. The disillusionment of the people in other parts of the Soviet empire, even within the Soviet Union itself, is a crucial factor which must affect Soviet policy. Poor economic performance, dependence on imperialist/capitalist grain supplies, tribal, nationalist and religious aspirations, and indiscipline in satellite countries add up to a gloomy scene for ageing Soviet leaders to contemplate. The experience of international outrage over Afghanistan seems to have encouraged restraint in the handling of the temerity of Polish trade unionists. The coincidence of the election of President Reagan was probably beneficial in the sense that the response of the United States can in future be expected to be robust and, more importantly, consistent. Inconsistency — the swings from open-armed pursuit of arms control to tight-lipped embargo and boycott — can be misunderstood east of the Iron Curtain, and lead to unnecessary tensions.

At the same time the new US Administration is more likely to create positive policies and a healthy climate for the maintenance of freedom if offered wise counsel by its European allies, not least in the United Kingdom. Such counsel will not carry weight if Britain and its Allies do not maintain a proper military posture and give support for actions taken for the common good. It will be hardly reasonable to complain of isolationism in the United States if the European Community is beguiled by insularity and its members by self-interest. It is by unity of purpose, freely achieved, that fear will be dispelled, and by the determination to resolve problems that uncertainty can be removed.

This uncertainty was nowhere better exemplified than in the Middle East and its surrounding territories. The Camp David settlements between Egypt and Israel, the overthrow of the Shah in Iran, and the Soviet invasion of Afghanistan, together upturned the complicated jigsaw of people and places which has represented the Middle East to a generation. While the big powers were scrabbling around trying to pick up the interlocking pieces, they were shaken by a fourth crisis when Iraqi forces marched into Iran in September 1980. Would they have to begin all over again?

THE GULF WAR

The origins of the Gulf War lay partly in Iraqi discontent with the terms and consequences of the Treaty of Algiers 5 years before and partly in the Iraqi perception, not unfounded, that the new rulers in Tehran were trying to export their revolution to Baghdad, with its large Shi-ite Moslem population. But they were also rooted in historic mistrust between the two countries, sharpened by disputes over control of the Shatt al-Arab. The personal ambitions of Saddam Husain, Iraq's formidable president, added a fourth dimension.

Prophecies of a quick and easy victory by Iraq over Iran's depleted and demoralised forces were soon confounded. Iraqi troops seized territories ceded but never actually relinquished by Iran under the Algiers Treaty. They thereby established some sort of control over the east bank of the Shatt. But by early 1981 they had failed to capture Abadan or any other of the important border towns except Khorramshahr, whose fall might have persuaded Ayatollah Khomeini to enter into peace negotiations. Not that the capture of Ahwaz, Abadan, and Dezful would necessarily have achieved the desired result. Khomeini remained largely an irrational fanatic, bloody but not easily bowed.

Nor were there any clear indications of how long he would be allowed to stay in power. Clashes which developed between his own supporters in the revolutionary guard and those of the more pragmatic and now deposed President Bani Sadr encouraged hope of Iranian discontent after a chilly winter with fuel in short supply. Other revolutionary movements like the Fedayeen, the Mujaheddin, and the Tudeh (Iran's Communist party), remained dormant, the last of these acting no doubt on promptings from Moscow. It was arguable anyway how far anyone outside Moscow — even Iraq — would welcome the consequences of another period of anarchy in Iran. The Army meanwhile had failed to recapture the public imagination by its performance during the fighting - much of any glory there was to be had, had gone to the stubborn if amateur revolutionary guard - and looked some way off establishing itself as a stabilising political force.

INTER-ARAB RELATIONS

The outcome of the internal conflict in Iran and of the war with Iraq were hard to predict, beyond, that is, a period of armed attrition between the two countries. Its effect upon inter-Arab relations, however, was more clearly discernible.

'The Arab World' is a convenient short form for a number of countries united by a common religion and language. The same countries are divided, however, as is the Christian community, by religious schism and political interest. The 1980s opened amid a series of continuing disputes — not all of them very lively — between Morocco and Algeria over the Western Sahara; between Libya and Tunisia; Libya and Egypt; Saudi Arabia and the United Arab Emirates, Saudi Arabia and South Yemen; and between South Yemen and Oman.

To these long-standing quarrels, three more have now been added. First, Egypt was ostracised as a result of her peace agreement with Israel. Secondly — though not chronologically so — Syria and Jordan squared up to each other, ostensibly because President Assad accused King Husain of giving sanctuary to the Moslem Brotherhood, a militant organisation opposed to his own ruling Alawite clique in Damascus.

The widest fissure opened, however, at the Arab summit in Amman in November 1980, when five states — Algeria, Libya, Syria, Lebanon, and South Yemen — absented themselves. Their official complaint was that by launching his country on the campaign against Iran, Saddam Husain, with Jordanian support (though not military aid) had diverted attention from the anti-Zionist crusade—the single cause which had previously united the Arab world.

A more convincing reason, however, was resentment against Saddam's obvious claim to be the leader of the Arab states, particularly after the so-called defection of Sadat. Economically and geographically, Iraq is well placed to lead the Arab states. Saddam is also a strong—if ruthless—personality. But the resentment of the radical powers led by Libya and Syria was to some extent justified by his miscalculation over the war. As oil and blood drained together into the sand, one wondered if Saddam's ambition to emerge as an undisputed force in the Middle East had also disappeared.

The result has been to leave the Arabs in a state of some confusion, divided between the radicals, on the one hand, and the conservatives, on the other. Iraq, whose Baathist ruling régime had shown a new spirit of pragmatism in recent years, might have bestrode the two worlds. Now the Arabs had to search for a new Colossus.

ARABS AND ISRAELIS

The *jihad* against Israel remains the one secure force in the Arab world. In January 1981 the call to unite behind the Palestinian cause was repeated by Prince Fahd of Saudi Arabia, and was endorsed by not just the Arab nations but by 42 assorted heads of state at the Islamic summit in Taif. There would be no lasting peace in the Middle East until the Palestinian right to found an independent state under the leadership of the PLO had been accepted.

Fahd was probably right. Among those who enthusiastically supported him was King Husain himself who, not for the first time, made it clear that the PLO, not Jordan, should represent Palestinian aspirations in the struggle. Neither Fahd, nor Husain, nor anyone else, could explain, however, how the aim would be achieved. Meanwhile Israeli settlements mushroomed on the West Bank to make the task of the Arabs/Islamics seem more difficult than ever.

The world thus advanced into the 1980s with the Palestinian problem still resembling the 'intellectual and diplomatic quagmire' which was how Mr Edward Heath described it in an article in *The Times*. Would President Reagan be able to make headway on the road already explored by his predecessor in the Oval Office?

AFGHANISTAN

The Islamic powers found it equally easy to call upon the Russians to leave Afghanistan and equally difficult to decide how to make them do so. In early 1981 the Soviets still had about 80,000 troops in the country, and Mr Brezhnev, in a display of generosity which was quite unnecessary under the circumstances, had promised to leave them there for as long as was required.

No doubt many Russians themselves would also like to return—and a number of senior people in Moscow must think the same way. Even the Soviet Union does not permit itself to call up reservists for more than 3 months in any one year except in times of national emergency. The constant rotation of the troops which this means hardly damages the country's overall security, but it is an irritant which the Army would prefer to do without. Though Western reports of heavy Russian casualties at the hands of the Afghan tribesmen have been exaggerated, there have certainly been a number of dead and injured.

As far as world pressure for a Soviet withdrawal goes, the Russians might feel justified in shrugging their shoulders and forgetting it. Trade agreements with Moscow, cancelled at the time, are now being signed again, and the leaders of Islam themselves are calling not for a *jihad* against Moscow, but a political settlement to achieve their goal.

If, as some commentators originally predicted, the Afghan adventure was the first stage in a new Soviet push towards the Indian Ocean and the old Tsarist dream of a warm-water port—a *very* warm water port indeed—the Moscow government would be reluctant to pull out. Similarly, they might want to cling on to the bases there as outposts of the Russian security system. But it seems more likely that their aim is to see Karmal established before withdrawing in any strength.

OIL

Gulf oil remains the reason why so many countries take so much interest in the Middle East and the surrounding region. It is not the only reason but it is the most common one. This being the case, outside interest in the area is likely to grow rather than diminish.

CIA estimates suggest that oil production in the world has reached its peak and is likely to decline from now on. The prospects vary from one part of the world to another, and in the Gulf itself production will probably remain about the same throughout the 1980s, although there will presumably be a local increase when the Gulf war is finally resolved and the installations are repaired. The general conclusion though is that world reserves are going down, and new wells were being discovered during the 1970s at only half the rate at which old stocks were declining.

The Soviet Union is not immune to this. Its production of 11.5 million barrels a day has been 2 million more even than the Saudi output and has made it the biggest producing country in the world. Now the CIA has calculated that the Russians themselves are likely to become major oil importers by the end of the 1980s. This view is not universally accepted. But most commentators agree that Eastern European powers at least will have to fall back upon the Gulf to make up supplies which were once provided by the Soviet Union.

Until now the Russians have been able to take a dilettantish interest in the Gulf's internal affairs. The inference to be drawn from the world's oil situation is that they will probably feel a need to become more closely involved. It could mean a period of more positive Soviet policy in the region. On the other hand, it could give the Russians a vested interest in the Gulf's political stability.

Mr Brezhnev has already snatched the odd opportunity to call for a security conference on the Gulf and to urge the creation of a zone of peace in the Indian Ocean. It was pointed out with some acidity that he might begin himself by withdrawing his forces from Afghanistan — and he must have made his proposal with the hope of propping up Russia's sagging reputation in the Third World — rather than with any real expectation that the West would give a positive response.

RESPONSES

The Middle East in general and the Gulf in particular remain politically unstable and economically important to the rest of the world. Can the rest of the world do anything to make it more stable — and should it even try to? Those who deplore the power vacuum left in the Gulf by the withdrawal of British forces may or may not be right in their judgements. The withdrawal itself inevitably disturbed the pattern of Gulf politics and security, and the continuance of the small unobtrusive presence would probably have done more good than harm. New Western military deployments into the Gulf states are quite another matter.

There is no longer any serious suggestion that NATO's boundaries might be extended to encompass the Gulf or anywhere else. It is generally accepted in the West that the United States alone is equipped to be the custodian of the collective interests of the Free World in the region. The two carrier task groups steaming in the Indian Ocean and the planned Rapid Deployment Force of 200,000 men signify American preparedness to take on the role. Nonetheless it seems imperative that other countries of the Free World should be seen to be giving the United States support. This could be either by direct representation in military deployments when this is appropriate or by relieving the United States of other burdens, e.g. replacing forces detached from NATO commitments. There has already been pressure from the United States for increased military effort by Japan in defence of her own interests—if not those of friends and neighbours.

The important point is for the United States to take counsel with her Allies and their friends so that the influence exerted on the situation is a stabilising one. Ideally the Gulf countries would like to sort out their own security, and the Saudis have now brought Oman, the UAE, Qatar, Kuwait, and Bahrain together in a local block to tackle security problems on a joint basis.

It is after all internal security which is the most potent threat to the sheikhdoms. The Saudis have been jittery since the attack on the Grand Mosque in Mecca and have taken steps to ensure that the royal princes are well represented in the country's armed forces. They are also well aware that the overt support of big powers like the United States encourages rather than deters unrest at home.

There is another reason why Western powers should be wary of identifying too closely with the sheikhs. Violent political change can arrive quite suddenly in the Middle East—rather like nightfall. Iran was the outstanding example of a country where the West was outpaced by events. In the Gulf, therefore, the policy of countries like the United States or the United Kingdom should be one of support, not involvement. That is a lesson which the Russians, too, have yet to learn.

It is evident that the chief danger spot in international relationships remains the Arab-Israeli problem. The primary force which may generate a solution is the influence of the United States. It is therefore doubly unfortunate that the development of US foreign policy under the new administration has been impeded by the incapacitation of President Reagan after the attempt upon his life. However one may applaud the resilience he has displayed, it has to be recognised that no man past his seventieth birthday can resume his grip on the reins of a superpower immediately after absorbing an assassin's bullets. The murderous attack on His Holiness the Pope, following so soon after the shooting of the President of the United States, may mark a watershed in the attitudes to terrorism and violence used in pursuit of political aims. The attitude of Israel's Prime Minister, Mr Menachim Begin, may be conditioned by the approach of an election but with his personal record of service in a terrorist group it is surprising that he has sought to revive old memories. His personal attacks on the German Chancellor may win him votes at home but are unlikely to attract many supporters elsewhere for a policy which seems to contain more unseeing obstinacy than realism. It will be interesting to see whether the EEC is able to establish a position of influence on this and other major international problems. The relationships between the Federal Republic of Germany and the United Kingdom appear to have improved after discussions between the Chancellor and Mrs Thatcher. French policies are likely to be substantially changed in style and content with the arrival of M Mitterand in the Elysée Palace and a newly elected National Assembly. West European countries have a key role whatever the interplay between individual members of NATO and the EEC in the development of international relationships in the world at large. Deterrence and arms control provide one aspect of the problems to be faced and politico-economic matters the other. The change in economic climate from dark recession to renewed activity and growth must encourage development of long-term policies. Unless the industrial countries are able to devise and implement Marshall-type plans for the developing and underdeveloped countries, the future will be bleak, not rosy. It is time to act on the appreciation that sound and unselfish energy policies must be worked out and that the centre piece of all Free World policies must be a workable system for the production and distribution of food. It has become evident to the peoples of the Soviet colonies in Europe that Soviet Communism has nothing to offer for the improvement of their lot. It would be deplorable if West Europe and the United States were found to be equally bankrupt in their moral attitudes and material generosity to less-fortunate countries in the world.

WE, THE LIMBLESS, LOOK TO YOU FOR HELP

We come from both world wars. We come from Korea, Kenya, Malaya, Aden, Cyprus . . . and from Ulster.

Now, disabled, we must look to you for help. Please help by helping our Association.

BLESMA looks after the limbless from all the Services. It helps to overcome the shock of losing arms, or legs or an eye. And, for the severely handicapped, it provides Residential Homes where they can live in peace and dignity.

Donations and information:
Major The Earl of Ancaster, KCVO, TD
Midland Bank Ltd., 60 West Smithfield,
London EC1A 9DX

Help the disabled by helping BLESMA. We promise you that not one penny of your donation will be wasted.

Give to those who gave — please.

BLESMA

BRITISH LIMBLESS
EX-SERVICE MEN'S ASSOCIATION

International Year of
Disabled People

Right on target –
Arab Defence Journal

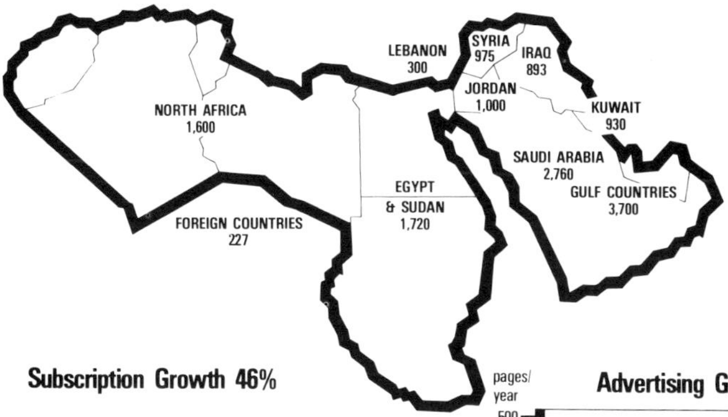

LEBANON 300
SYRIA 975
IRAQ 893
JORDAN 1,000
KUWAIT 930
NORTH AFRICA 1,600
SAUDI ARABIA 2,760
GULF COUNTRIES 3,700
EGYPT & SUDAN 1,720
FOREIGN COUNTRIES 227

Subscription Growth 46%

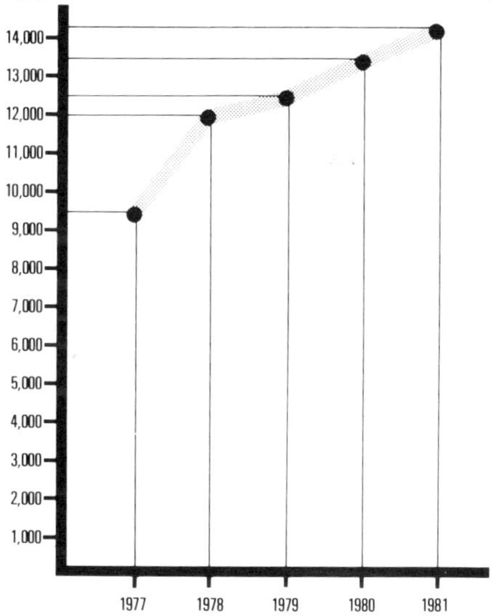

copies/month

14,000 · 13,000 · 12,000 · 11,000 · 10,000 · 9,000 · 8,000 · 7,000 · 6,000 · 5,000 · 4,000 · 3,000 · 2,000 · 1,000

1977   1978   1979   1980   1981

Advertising Growth 388%

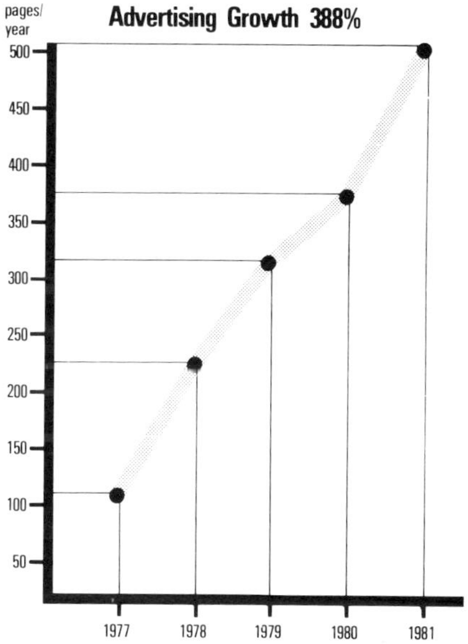

pages/year

500 · 450 · 400 · 350 · 300 · 250 · 200 · 150 · 100 · 50

1977   1978   1979   1980   1981

The readership of Arab Defence Journals is restricted to military officers, government defence organisations and military attaches in the 18 Arabic speaking countries. You will reach the news-stand in vain for Arab Defence Journal as it is sold at a cost which keeps the enthusiasts away (US$ 80 for 12 issues). Monthly, 14,105 subscription copies are eagerly awaited by Arab ministries of defence and military academies.

On the marketing front Arab Defence Journal got the confidence of over 120 major companies dealing with exportation of military products. These companies are mainly American, British, Italian, French, German, Swiss, Danish, Brazilian and from Singapore.

Arab Defence Journal: Exclusively the leading defence magazine of the Arab World.

DAR ASSAYAD S.A.L.

5 Moore Street, London SW3.
Telephone (01) 589 6743
Telex 918046 Assayad G.

c/o Al Tayar (France)
65 Avenue d'Iena, Paris 16eme
Tel 5015050

Membership of the RUSI

The Royal United Services Institute for Defence Studies exists to promote independent study and discussion of all matters relating to national security. Membership applications can be made not only by serving and retired members of Commonwealth Armed and Civil Services and NATO Services, but also by those who may benefit from membership and through it make a positive contribution to the activities of the Institute. The existing membership includes men and women from many walks of life including Parliament, the Universities, the Legal and Medical professions, Industry and Commerce, the Church, the Police and all branches of Journalism.

The interests of the Institute embrace the strategic, tactical, logistic and technological aspects of defence in the modern world and the study of the human problems to which they relate. History, economics, moral ethics, disarmament, and the behavioural sciences are included in the Institute's study programme of lectures, seminars, discussions and conferences.

The RUSI *Journal*, published quarterly, reflects the wide-ranging interests of the Institute and its readership extends across the world from Korea to Argentina and from Australia to Finland.

Further information about the RUSI can be obtained from the Secretary, Royal United Services Institute for Defence Studies, Whitehall, London SW1A 2ET

"Our customers reflect our shipbuilding knowledge."

Our customers expect a lot. So did Nelson. Whether they want an ocean-going frigate for the South Atlantic, or a fast patrol boat for the Persian Gulf, our customers demand the best – and expect a little more. Any group which builds ships for the Royal Navy is used to meeting the most demanding standards.

British Shipbuilders has brought together a group of companies such as Vickers, Vosper Thornycroft, Yarrow (Shipbuilders), Brooke Marine, Hall Russell, Swan Hunter, Cammell Laird and Scott Lithgow, all well known to the navies of the world and providing them with the finest capabilities in design and workmanship.

Submarines, surface ships as big as HMS Invincible with Sea Harriers and helicopters, frigates, fast offshore patrol boats, new GRP countermeasure vessels, survey and support vessels, are in the range of the types constructed by these companies.

This is all backed up by the most advanced equipment – machinery, weaponry, and electronics – together with repair services and training and support services second to none.

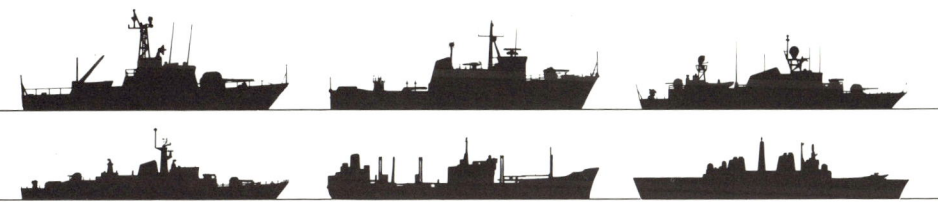

New Books in the field of
INTERNATIONAL AFFAIRS

PLANNING US SECURITY †
Defense Policy in the Eighties
A Study Developed at the National Defense University

Edited by **P S Kronenburg**, *Virginia Polytechnic Institute and State University, USA*

In this critique of the national security planning process, experts assess the government's ability to make effective policy choices for national security and identify major structural weaknesses impeding the development of rational long term policies.

180pp approx   107 lit refs   September 1981
0 08 028082 X Hardcover £11.20 $22.50 approx
0 08 028081 1 Flexicover £ 3.50 $ 7.95 approx

INTERNATIONAL ARMS †
PROCUREMENT
New Directions

Edited by **M Edmonds**, *University of Lancaster, England*

At a time when modern weapon systems are becoming increasingly costly and complex, **International Arms Procurement** examines the possibilities for international cooperation, collaboration and exchange.

"Excellent case studies illuminate some of the darkest corners . . . a book of real gravity which will be valued by those in government as well as in the academic world and in industry. I commend it."
General Sir Hugh Beach, KCB, OBE, MC,
from the Foreword

200pp approx   1981
0 08 027558 3 Hardcover £12.00 $24.00

LESSONS FROM AN
UNCONVENTIONAL WAR
Reassessing US Strategies for Future Conflicts

Edited by **R A Hunt**, *Department of the Army* and **R H Schultz, Jr**, *Catholic University, USA*

Using for the first time recently declassified data files, key military experts examine the complex strategy issues raised by American involvement in Vietnam. The authors discuss ways to increase US effectiveness in future low-intensity conflicts.

Contents: Province advisers in Vietnam, 1962–1965, **J W Dunn**. Strategies at war: pacification and attrition in Vietnam, **R A Hunt**. The Vietnamization-pacification strategy of 1969–1972: a quantitative reassessment, **R H Shultz,**

Jr. Requirements of strategy in Vietnam, **L E Grinter**. The sources of US frustration in Vietnam, **D S Blaufarb**. American culture and American arms: the case of Vietnam, **D Vought**. Policy and strategy for the 1980s, **R H Shultz, Jr** and **A N Sabrosky**. Abbreviations. About the contributors. Map of South Vietnam.

250pp approx   October 1981
0 08 027186 3 Hardcover £12.50 $25.00 approx

NATO'S STRATEGIC OPTIONS †
Arms Control and Defense

Edited by **D S Yost**, *Naval Postgraduate School, USA*

"An unusually rich and healthily controversial collection of essays . . . . These essays serve usefully to remind us that military problems exist on a truly major scale and that we ignore them at our peril. . . . This is a superior work."
C S Gray, Hudson Institute

"A very timely and useful collection of essays by an impressive group of authors. It will benefit policymakers, academicians and students equally."
Professor W R Van Cleave, Director
Defense and Strategic Studies Program,
University of Southern California

288pp   July 1981
0 08 027184 7 Hardcover   £14.50 $29.00

STRATEGIC MILITARY DECEPTION †

Edited by **D C Daniel** and **K Herbig**, *Naval Postgraduate School, USA*

Based on new data from recently declassified World War II documents, this book presents a clear and systematic approach to the nature, variants, processes and factors influencing strategic deception. All aspects of military deception, from communications and organizational factors to psychology and the counterdeception problem, are considered.

300pp approx   1982
0 08 027219 3 Hardcover £16.20 $32.50 approx

Sterling prices applicable to UK and Eire customers only. Prices subject to change without notice.

† Pergamon Policy Studies on Security Affairs

PERGAMON PRESS
Headington Hill Hall, Oxford, UK
Fairview Park, Elmsford, New York 10523, USA

What's the vital difference that makes Ferranti simulation so realistic?

Operational experience.

One of the chief reasons for the strong leadership of Ferranti in trainer and simulator systems is our deep involvement in operational systems for the armed forces, particularly the Royal Navy. It is well known that virtually every Royal Navy warship now in service or on order carries a Ferranti computer system for Action Information and/or Weapon Control.

It means that when we simulate, we know exactly what we are simulating.

In close co-operation with your Operational and Training Staffs we design and manufacture trainers and simulators for training at all levels— for individual operators, for teams of operators, for crews and for command teams.

Trainees working with them get the feel of the real thing. This is what simulation is all about.

Choose the simulators with the operational background. Ferranti.

Ferranti Computer Systems Limited, Bracknell Division, Bracknell, Berkshire, RG12 1RA Tel: 0344 3232 Telex: 848117

FERRANTI
Computer Systems

Part I — Strategic Review

Air Power and the Royal Air Force

MICHAEL BEETHAM

Air Chief Marshal Sir Michael Beetham, GCB, CBE, DFC, AFC, is Chief of the Air Staff

MANY influences account for the place of air power in our defence planning over the past three decades or so, among them simple geography, national and Alliance security commitments and the imperative to extract an optimum leverage from comparatively modest economic and other resources. Beyond those general considerations, however, there are two others of particular importance. The first is that in a strategy that is wholly defensive, air power has a unique offensive capability and the ability to carry hostilities to an aggressor. The second is that air power is a dynamic concept, not only in the literal sense that it deals with movement and with force in action, but also in the sense that it has a wide potential to adapt to the shifting challenges of contemporary warfare.

To put that potential and those challenges into perspective, something should first be said about the place of air power in contemporary strategic thought and about the intrinsic attributes that air power can bring to war. They are attributes that have changed very little, but our perceptions of them certainly have altered a great deal, and it is interesting, for example, to compare air power thinking in, say, the late 1940s, with that of today. In the early years after World War II, strategy was still largely about total victory, about unconditional surrender, and, as far as air power was concerned, it was about strategic bombardment on a massive scale. In an age of approximate nuclear balance, however, it is precisely those absolutes that strategy seeks to avoid, and the result is a concern with restraint and therefore with the more precise applications of military force. In an interesting parallel with aeronautical science, which over the same period explored the limits of performance in, for example, speed and altitude, the emphasis now is on the ways in which available attributes can best be employed, rather than on any further pursuit of extremes.

THE ATTRIBUTES OF AIR POWER

The attributes of air power start with the capabilities that are offered by a freedom to operate in the third dimension and from the ability to use this freedom to project or to transmit military force. It is high mobility that makes it possible, for example, for aircraft to reach out to very distant targets and to attack them with great selectivity and precision in the bomber role, or to remain on station at long range and there to carry out surveillance or control functions, as they do in the anti-submarine warfare (ASW) role over the Atlantic or in airborne early warning (AEW) and control work. Air mobility makes it possible to transport men and supplies over great distances, and aircraft can deploy with great speed the fighting units of other arms.

One role in which high mobility plays a particularly important part is that of interception. In the case of the United Kingdom, this calls for air defence aircraft to move out to long ranges at very high speed and to engage attacking enemy aircraft before they can launch stand-off missiles at targets on our home territory or on the ocean surrounding us. In many circumstances, the interceptor role makes use of air-to-air refuelling tankers which then offer the option of intercepting incoming attacks at greater ranges or maintaining patrol for a longer period of time but closer to the targets being defended.

In a more direct form of mobility, tactical aircraft from widely scattered operating bases can concentrate their efforts in key operational areas, deliver intense firepower against targets on the ground or at sea and disperse to prepare for further attacks before a coherent enemy defence can be mounted. The choice of timings, tactics and target options make this kind of tactical concentration extremely difficult to counter without a massive enemy investment in defensive capability, and for the enemy to produce that level of defence at all his key points would almost certainly mean a militarily ruinous diversion from his primary objectives.

Mobility is thus an obvious aspect of the application of air power, but the impact of that quality is greatly enhanced by two other attributes: versatility and adaptability. Versatility is best seen as the capacity of a weapons system to react to operational surprise, to meet the changing priorities of combat and where necessary to accept local improvisation. This quality is often a question of the design features of weapons systems, but it is also an area in which imagination and the ability to seize opportunities, not only at the combat level, but also in the command echelons, can play a key part in air operations. Versatility can thus be defined here as a measure of the extent to which the full potential of a weapons system can be exploited by combat formations.

Adaptability, on the other hand, should be seen as a measure of the facility with which a weapon system can absorb new or improved capabilities to match emerging combat challenges, and the extent to which it can accept structural modification or even undergo a complete change of role. It is therefore the ability of a system to accommodate more permanent shifts in its operating environment. It is the combination of these three main attributes — mobility, versatility and adaptability — that give air power its most valuable single quality, that of flexibility, the ability to carry out a varied range of changing military functions over widely scattered geographical areas.

To carry the analysis to a stage where it moves from the abstract to the practical, flexibility in air power can be seen to have an application at three overlapping but distinct levels: one tactical, one operational and one strategic. The tactical level of flexibility is essentially about the ability to switch effort between targets or between destinations within a particular limited operational area. Given an aircraft with basic characteristics appropriate to the mission, it is therefore about tactics, about weapons and perhaps above all it is about crew skills and training. To a greater or lesser degree, this kind of flexibility is seen in most weapon systems — land, sea or air; but the essential feature of tactical flexibility in air power is the rapidity with which aircraft can re-direct their efforts, and, for example, the ability of combat aircraft to deal with rapidly varying operating conditions and targeting problems.

Perhaps more complex than that tactical level of flexibility, and certainly unique in its degree of effectiveness, is the whole field of operational flexibility: the ability of air power to shift its impact from one target system to another within an overall theatre of operations, or to transfer its whole potential from one theatre to another. No other arm can change its point of application or its weight of effort with the responsiveness and with the reach that is available to air forces, and it is at this level in particular that air power can make its most significant contribution to high defence preparedness as well as to the actual conduct of warlike operations.

Finally, there is flexibility at the strategic level in which air power has the potential to change the whole thrust of its efforts in order to match the changing demands of longer-term strategic trends. The development of strategic bombing to its devastating climax at the end of World War II is one clear example of this kind of change; the shift to an emphasis on theatre operations once nuclear-armed ICBMs had first absorbed most of the strategic bombardment role, and then relegated it almost entirely to a deterrent function, is another. Other changes in strategic emphasis may lie ahead, and it will be suggested later that the first indications of a shift may be with us now. Those are the abstracts of air power, and they say something about the broad framework within which air capabilities are designed and operated. Not all the attributes are relevant in all roles, but experience shows that where they have been relevant and have been ignored, air power has been less than fully effective.

To translate the abstracts into the tangibles of an air force is, however, not always a straightforward process. There is, for example, the difficulty of reconciling conflicting operational demands within one design, and it has been found that those demands and the problems of reconciliation tend to proliferate at a faster rate than can be met or solved by the aeronautical sciences. Specialisation is thus inevitable and it acts as a constraint on total flexibility. A further difficulty is the inescapable dilemma of defining military needs in terms of contemporary circumstances, but in the knowledge not only that aircraft lead times between conception and front line service are usually in the order of 10 to 15 years, but also that once an aircraft does enter service it may well remain in the inventory for perhaps another 20 years. On the whole, however, aircraft design has historically been remarkably successful in meeting the demands on adaptability that are implied by such lengthy periods of service, and in more recent years an emphasis on our weapons as well as on platforms has had the effect of extending the general flexibility that has so far been available.

Beyond those general considerations that affect all air forces there are the constraints and pressures of purely national factors, and in the post-war era the Royal Air Force has been profoundly affected by a number of influences. Three are worth particular mention since they help explain not only the size and shape of the Service today, but also why the emphasis in the procurement programme lies where it does.

THE BRITISH EXPERIENCE

The first influence was the process of British withdrawal between about 1947 and 1969 from its many overseas commitments, followed by a more explicit commitment to the defence of the Central Region of the Alliance. This process not only led to the loss of overseas bases, but the air units that had been based abroad were disbanded rather than brought to Europe, and most of the air transport forces that had served the overseas garrisons were also dismantled. The result was an overall loss of numbers, a consequent loss of overall flexibility and a narrowing focus in the kind of role for which the Royal Air Force was equipped.

The second factor has been the almost unbroken pressure on defence resources, mainly caused by the disappointing performance of the national economy. Twice this pressure has led to far-reaching Defence Reviews, one in 1957 and the other in 1966. In 1957, defence was absorbing 10 per cent of our GNP, and about 7 per cent of the working population was either in the Services or supporting them. Drastic cuts were made to reduce both burdens. One result was the abolition of conscription, a decision that returned British defence to the traditional pattern of small but high-quality regular forces. A second result was a massive reduction in the forces themselves, including for example, a cut of half in the strength of the Royal Air Force based in Germany.

A third consequence of the 1957 decisions was in the long term even more serious for the Service. The decision to make savings on the scale that was planned coincided with the conviction that since there was no defence against a nuclear attack on the United Kingdom, the emphasis should be placed on our own force of bombers in the deterrent role. Since that was so, the only air defences necessary were thought to be the very much reduced ones essential for the protection of the bomber bases, and the rest were cut. And since it was believed that the bombers themselves would soon be replaced by long-range ballistic missiles, development both for bombers and fighters was cancelled.

Many of the consequences of these decisions are with us still, and if the 1957 decisions proved anything it was that to reconstruct defences is infinitely more difficult than to dismantle them.

In the 9 years after 1957, some progress was made in restoring the front line of the Royal Air Force, but other blows fell in 1966, when, in order to make further economies in defence spending, several important projects, including the advanced TSR-2 tactical strike aircraft, were cut, and although a series of efforts was later made to restore the front line by various measures such as off-the-shelf procurements, these were less than wholly successful.

Finally, there has been our national defence policy within the

NATO Alliance, and in particular the shift in 1967 from a strategy of massive retaliation to one of flexible response, a change that led to an even stronger emphasis on the continuing efforts to restore a full range of capabilities for conventional war in our front line.

Taken together, all these influences have helped to mould the Service into what it is today; a relatively small but very high quality air force, heavily oriented towards three tasks: the air defence of the United Kingdom, overland operations in Europe — particularly in the Central Region of NATO, and maritime operations in the Eastern Atlantic. These responsibilities and the measures that are being taken to improve the capabilities of the Service to discharge them, lie at the centre of almost all Royal Air Force activities today.

THE ROYAL AIR FORCE TODAY

The air defence of the British Isles, of the surrounding seas and of the friendly navies using those seas, is a particularly important function. Without the secure base offered by these islands, the defence of Europe would be deprived of a vital element of depth, many key ports of Europe would be exposed to naval and air threats from the Western Approaches and Alliance naval forces would be deprived of their support in the eastern half of the Atlantic.

The huge area covered by our air defences forms one part of a very extensive Alliance air defence system that includes a chain of radar sites the whole length of Europe, and an interlinked network of air defence sectors in which interceptor aircraft as well as ship- and ground-based surface-to-air missiles of all nations work in the closest cooperation.

The UK radar cover is now being modernised by the purchase of advanced transportable equipments with a high resistance to hostile electronic warfare counter-measures (ECM), and these shore-based units will in the next few years be complemented by a new squadron of Nimrod AEW aircraft. All this will be backed by a new ground communication system to replace the existing land-lines, ground-to-air communications will be given a data-link facility and a new command and a control system will be introduced that provides a comprehensive picture of the whole air defence battle area derived from a wide variety of static and mobile sources. Even in peacetime the UK air defence cover detects and intercepts intruders such as Soviet Tupolev Tu20 Bear aircraft, which make regular surveillance flights over the Norwegian Sea and often penetrate the UK Air Defence Region, which surrounds our territorial airspace.

In war our air defence radar cover would be used to detect the approach of attacking aircraft, and to direct interceptor aircraft onto them several hundred miles from the coasts of these islands. The interception task is one that has for many years been undertaken by Lightning and Phantom aircraft, but it will increasingly pass to the air defence variant of the Tornado. With its advanced radar system, its endurance on station and its capacity for multitarget engagement with Skyflash missiles, the Tornado F2 will be one of the most advanced interceptors in the world. The first of these aircraft will join the front line in the middle of this decade.

That first line of air defence will shortly be backed by Hawk aircraft equipped with air-to-air missiles for the local protection of our airfields, more Rapier missiles are being deployed for point defence and our aircraft and control centres on key airfields are being protected under hardened and secure shelters. When complete, this extensive programme of improvements across a wide spectrum of passive and active measures will give a qualitative effectiveness to our air defences that has not been available for more than a quarter of a century. Numbers of fighters will then be the limiting factor on the overall effectiveness of the system, but this claim on our resources has to be balanced against other demands on a finite budget.

Below that air defence cover, maritime surveillance and shore-based ASW tasks in the Atlantic are carried out by Nimrod aircraft of No 18 Group, an aircraft which, particularly in the Mark II version now entering service, is one of the most effective anti-submarine platforms in the world today. This remarkable aircraft has a wide range of equipment that enables it, on the one hand, to locate and destroy hostile submarines, and, on the other, to maintain a plot of maritime disposition over a very wide area so as to provide targeting information to surface and air forces. It is fitted with a computer controlled radar, an advanced acoustic processor, a much improved tactical computer and it will later be given a greatly enhanced ECM fit. Depending on the range and the operational profile, the Nimrod can remain on station for around 10 hours, and its excellent performance at altitude enables it to reach distant operating areas at high speed.

Strike and attack missions against surface targets are fulfilled by the Buccaneer, armed with both the television-guided and anti-radar versions of the Martel stand-off missile; in due course the Buccaneer will be succeeded in this role by Tornado GR1s.

Equally important in the developing front line of the Royal Air Force are two other operational formations based in the United Kingdom, No 1 and No 38 Groups. No 1 Group, the successor to Bomber Command, operates in the nuclear-strike, conventional attack, reconnaissance and air-to-air refuelling roles. Its squadrons include the last of the Vulcans, still making a valuable contribution in the strike and maritime reconnaissance roles, as well as Victor tankers, to which will shortly be added a squadron of specially modified VC10s. These aircraft will be invaluable in extending the range, endurance and general flexibility of several front-line capabilities, and they give the Royal Air Force an enhanced capacity to deal with the unexpected. No 1 Group controls the unique tri-national British/German/Italian Tornado Training Establishment which began training crews for the air forces of all three nations at the beginning of 1981. The Group will receive the first of its operational Tornado Squadrons in 1982 — Tornado GR1s, a version of the aircraft that has been specifically designed to fill the interdiction strike, attack and reconnaissance roles, and thus to meet the vital operational requirements of overland operations. These aircraft, with their very advanced navigation and attack system, will give the front line of the Royal Air Force the ability to operate at high speed at very low level and in all weathers to an extent that has never before been available.

Although the Royal Air Force now devotes almost all its efforts to the North Atlantic and European area, the need for air transport capacity and air mobility generally have proved to be as great as ever, both within the Alliance area and for occasional deployments outside it. The transport force forms part of No 38 Group, and consists of one squadron of VC10s and four of C130 Hercules, which in peacetime make trooping flights and offer support for the many exercises that are necessary if the three Services are to maintain a high level of operational preparedness. They have also taken part in many emergency relief operations in various parts of the world, and in a time of crisis or war they would provide an invaluable capability for tactical lift, e.g. to move reinforcements from one part of Europe to another. In a recent move to increase the capacity of the air transport force at minimum cost, work is under way to lengthen the fuselages of the Hercules force. This will have the effect of adding the equivalent of several aircraft to the present fleet but without the penalties of further crews or ground support.

High mobility is also a characteristic of the four Harrier and Jaguar squadrons of No 38 Group, units which in a crisis could expect to deploy rapidly to, say, Denmark, Norway, Italy or the Central Front to augment the forces already based there. This Group also holds a small force of helicopters which provide essential flexibility at the tactical level to certain Army units in the field. A programme of improvements to the helicopter force is now under way, and two squadrons of Chinooks will enter service in the next few years.

The forces of the Alliance in Europe include the 12 squadrons of Royal Air Force Germany, which make an essential contribution to the air power shield in one of the most critical areas of the Alliance.

In peacetime, the interceptor squadrons of Royal Air Force Germany, at present equipped with Phantom air defence aircraft, are responsible for the integrity of the airspace of the northern part of Germany. In war they would form part of the air defence of the same area. Other squadrons of the same Command are assigned in the strike/attack and reconnaissance roles, all of which imply all-weather and low-level penetration of enemy airspace and thus call for the high quality of navigation and target-acquisition equipment which the Tornado IDS aircraft will bring to these missions as it joins the front line. For shorter range attack and reconnaissance missions, particularly those in more direct support of the Alliance ground forces, there is a wing of Harriers in the Command. This wing holds itself ready to deploy in the field at very short notice, and from there provides a very high level of response in delivering fire-power to meet the changing priorities of the battle area.

THE POTENTIAL ADVERSARY

The place of air power in the Central Region is crucial to the successful defence of Alliance territory, and a mention of the particular challenges in Europe may be useful here. The function of air power in the Central Region is essentially to offset the potential of the Warsaw Pact to impose an overwhelming numerical imbalance of force in the air and on the ground. The high mobility of the air weapon gives it the ability not only to deal with land and air target arrays beyond the reach of other weapons systems, but also to lay down intense concentrations of fire-power in critical areas of combat laterally along the whole of the Central front. Air power can uniquely bring effort to bear rapidly where it is most needed and transfer that effort as the situation changes.

In recent years, however, the Warsaw Pact itself has recognised the contribution that air power can make in a theatre conflict, and great efforts have been made to catch up and, if possible, to overtake the Alliance in its air power expertise. One result is that they now have a new generation of combat aircraft in service, with ranges and payloads so improved that they are able for the first time to reach out over virtually the whole of Western Europe, and to do so from bases further back in Warsaw Pact territory and thus behind deeper defences.

Some of these modern types are multirole aircraft, giving the Warsaw Pact a level of flexibility that was once almost exclusively the preserve of the Alliance, and the importance of numbers has not been neglected. In fixed-wing aircraft alone, the Warsaw Pact outnumbers the Alliance in the Central Region by between 2 and 3 to 1. Not only that, but very large numbers of attack helicopters have been deployed which release even more fixed-wing aircraft for missions beyond the immediate battle area. These developments put a new emphasis on the importance of our own air defences, but above all they make it vitally necessary for Alliance air power to attack and destroy enemy air forces where they are most vulnerable—on their airfields. Offensive counter-air operations would thus be an early charge on the air power resources of the Alliance so that the levels of freedom of the air that will be essential to the success of all other operations of war can be gained.

Those important changes in the air capability of the Warsaw Pact have not, however, been the only changes in the overall balance. The ground forces in Eastern Europe contrive to show an alarming increase in numerical strength, and, for example, the number of Soviet main battle tanks has increased by 35 per cent over the past decade, while their force of artillery has grown by 38 per cent and their number of APCs by no less than 83 per cent. In the Central Region alone, the ground forces of the Warsaw Pact now outnumber those of the Alliance by 1.2 : 1 in troops, almost 3:1 in tanks and nearly 3:1 in artillery pieces. The potential imbalance of force that can be imposed on our defence has thus become more serious, and the imperative on Alliance air power to redress it has become even more pressing. That quantitative feature of the threat is paralleled by a qualitative change in which Warsaw Pact ground force echelons are held in a high state of forward readiness to enable them to launch powerful attacks towards key Alliance targets from their normal peacetime positions. This has put new demands on the ability of Alliance air to respond in the first critical hours of any conflict with a decisive weight of fire-power wherever it might be needed along the whole front of the Central Region. An ability to intervene with concentrated, flexible and decisive fire-power in key sectors is therefore a critical role for air power in the Central Region.

Finally, there is evidence that the Warsaw Pact ground formations are now so organised, equipped and deployed that rear echelons can move up with great rapidity to maintain the momentum of an attack once it has been launched. It would be a vital part of our defence plan to disrupt or destroy these advancing echelons before they could play a part in the main battle, a task that air power is uniquely suited to undertake. Successful interdiction will neutralise an aggressor's potential to impose critical imbalances of force, thus not only inhibiting his advance, but freeing our own land forces to take the initiative. Interdiction is likely to be a decisive role in any conflict in the Central Region.

MEETING THE CHALLENGE

It is a characteristic of modern war that no firm priorities can be allocated beforehand between the three roles of offensive counter-air, battlefield intervention and interdiction, and it is the key feature of flexibility both at the tactical and at the operational level that enables air power to meet the changing demands as they arise. Those flexibilities are well founded in the design of Tornado GR1, which will undertake all three roles, but it will be further consolidated in three principal ways. First, by the introduction of more advanced weapons such as the airfield denial weapon at present under development. Second, it will be consolidated by the ability of commanders to assess the operational situation with speed and accuracy, and then to put into effect their decisions on force allocation. In this whole crucial areas of command, control, communications and intelligence, greater use is now being made throughout the Alliance of satellite communications and automated data processing, while a number of national measures are in train to improve our capabilities in all aspects of electronic warfare and in communications at all levels.

The third element of consolidation lies in tactics and in the training of our personnel, particularly the aircrew. As to tactics, our continuing emphasis on operations at low level gives two advantages to our offensive units. Low-level tactics enable our air-craft to slip beneath the cover of most enemy air defence radars, thus making it difficult to detect, and then to plot our attacks, and they give enemy guns and missiles so little warning of the ap-proach of our aircraft that their opportunity to engage is cut to a minimum. These tactics call for a complex technique of flying that demands extremes of skill, concentration and constant prac-tice over terrain as varied as can be made available. It is for this reason that the Royal Air Force carries out a continuing pro-gramme of training at low level over Western Europe, in North America and over the greater part of the United Kingdom.

This broad review of present deployments and future plans gives the outline of a Royal Air Force that has been shaped to meet the contemporary demands of strategy and suggests some of the areas in which the attributes of air power are being exercised to produce high operational value from very finite resources.

Flexibility in particular has been stressed, because not only is it essential to meet a wide range of future possibilities within the Alliance area, but it is also the quality that offers at least some resilience in the force of the unforeseen. We cannot say what the future may bring, but there does now seem to be growing evidence that the Soviet Union may be prepared to exert pressure on the West in other and more ambiguous parts of the world. A convergence of three factors supports this view.

First, it seems to be generally agreed among Western defence analysts that the 1980s will be a period during which the Soviet Union is likely to hold a margin of strategic advantage over the United States, and if there is to be a favourable opportunity to ex-ert military pressure, then it will be during the present decade. Second, the West is increasingly dependent on overseas resources, particularly on oil and other raw materials. And third, in Afghanistan the Soviet Union has resorted for the first time to the use of direct military intervention outside its immediate sphere of influence, thus breaking the past pattern of indirect support and the use of proxy forces.

New levels of Western vulnerability may thus come to be mat-ched by a new Soviet preparedness to exploit them, and the future seems likely to add long-term and subtle threats to the short-term and direct threats that we have faced for three decades in Europe. That kind of possibility has led to the start of con-tingency planning for Western intervention forces, and there is no doubt that the range and the speed of response of air power make it particularly appropriate for that type of operation. This is not to advocate any substantial or permanent redeployment of forces, since it is clear that the transfer of anything more than a token force would be likely to incur risks in Europe that would outweigh any possible advantages further afield. Token forces may, however, be all that is needed. It seems unlikely that European nations would launch an out-of-area initiative on their own, yet it might become essential to indicate a European concern, and it could become necessary to signal a European readiness to turn a developing local crisis into a wider one. In any such contingency the ability of air power to make rapid deployments to distant theatres without any permanent loss of effectiveness in the primary area of concern, Europe, could be a vital factor.

If that kind of future demand does come to be made on European air power resources, it will be a factor that has played little if any part in the planning process for the European air forces of today. Defence resources are allocated to meet perceived threats, and those threats presently lie in the Alliance area of interest. But the comprehensive improvements now underway in the Royal Air Force to enable it to meet its very varied responsibilities within the Alliance area will produce new flexibilities as well as improved capabilities at all levels, and thus put the Service on a sound footing not only to meet the challenges that have so far been assessed but to react to that most telling feature in all politico-military affairs — the unforeseen.

Trident—A Candidate for Cancellation?

IAN BELLANY

Professor Bellany is Head of the Centre for the Study of Arms Control and International Security, University of Lancaster

THE DECISION to replace the Polaris flotilla with a new flotilla of similar size based upon the Trident C4 missile will almost certainly have to face reconsideration sometime in the next few years on grounds of economy. The reason is that British defence expenditure chronically outstrips British resources, and British resources are shrinking, relatively, and even (at the latest count) absolutely.

The diagram in the Appendix shows that the British share of (or contribution to) Western European defence expenditure far exceeds the British share of the Western European GNP. Put another way, and slightly more tendentiously perhaps, the British contribution to the defence of Europe substantially exceeds its share of that which is to be defended.

It is not within the scope of this article to account for the 'excessive' British contribution to Western European defence, but the fact of its existence is strong circumstantial evidence that the protection afforded to defence expenditure in the early period of the Thatcher government will not be indefinitely extended.

Once the search for cuts in defence expenditure is begun, a prime target will be the Polaris replacement programme. Not because it is particularly expensive compared to other, conventional, defence programmes and activities, but because it will be at the dangerous stage of sucking in large amounts of money while still some years away from entering service. And, unlike the run of defence programmes, which can always rely upon fierce protective lobbying from their parent branch of the Armed Services, the strategic nuclear force is a comparative orphan—not without supporters, certainly, but they are widely dispersed. Nor, as we shall see, can the Polaris replacement programme, by its nature, equip itself with the various anti-cancellation protective devices that military aerospace projects, for instance, have evolved in recent years.

15

A clearer picture of what is being said here may be obtained by use of an analogy. Suppose that instead of defence policy we were dealing with energy policy. Suppose the replacement issue in question concerned the new generation of nuclear power stations. Argument would then rage over whether new power stations were needed at all; what the balance should be as between nuclear and conventionally fired stations; and if there were to be any nuclear, what type they should be.

How would the choice of new power station be settled? It would be settled in two parts. The first part would be 'rational'. Careful assessment would be made of the costs and benefits of the various choices available and the decision made according to what maximised the latter and minimised the former. But implementing the rational choice always takes time, and the rational choice then has to enter the political arena and survive changes of government, unexpected shifts in the external environment which seem to call into question the correctness of the original choice (shifts the relative prices of fuel, in this example), and technical and managerial failures in the construction phase, all of which give new heart to the supporters of the alternative possibilities that have been discarded at the rational stage.

The survival rate of the rational choice amongst British publicly funded capital projects is not markedly good, whether we are speaking of power-station choices or new sites for the third London airport. Those that do survive are those that by luck or design have about them qualities that make the choice politically robust in the buffeting phase between the end of the rational choice-making process and the coming into operation of the project in question.

THE RATIONAL CHOICE

There is little doubt that the decision to replace Polaris is 'rational' enough.

The British defence budget pays for a deterrent, defensive strategy of bare but calculated sufficiency. In theory, NATO declares that it pursues what the United States has for a long time wished it would pursue in practice, namely a flexible response strategy which is supposed to be about being able to deter Soviet aggression by offering resistance in depth to Soviet force at whatever level of violence it is pitched at. In fact NATO's conventional forces are too small and its reinforcement capabilities too arthritic to stop a full-scale push by Soviet conventional forces, and the balance is maintained by leaving the Soviets in doubt as to the exact point at which their conventional successes (or semi-conventional, if battlefield nuclear or chemical weapons had already been used) would force the West to escalate the war to the highest possible level of attacking Soviet cities with strategic nuclear weapons.

The exact size of the conventional armies NATO needs in order for this strategy to work cannot be calculated very precisely. Very large armies would probably be read abroad as a signal that the introduction of strategic nuclear weapons would be long delayed, perhaps indefinitely so; by contrast very small armies might be read as signifying that defence was simply not being taken seriously and that an application of Soviet pressure would actually meet with no resistance. But between these extremes a wide range of conventional or semi-conventional capabilities, provided this was coupled with an unquestioned ability to take the war to the extreme pitch of violence, will do.

This method of keeping the peace was conceived in the days of Western nuclear superiority and it was officially disbanded for flexible response when this superiority began to dissolve as the Soviet Union equipped itself with a full range of nuclear and thermonuclear weapons and delivery systems to match. In practice it has remained undisbanded since the original expectation that the strategy would become untenable because the Soviets would not be daunted by what amounted to a Western threat to commit suicide, i.e. to trigger a nuclear exchange at the highest pitch of violence, has been modified. A threat to commit suicide gains in credibility (as aircraft hijackers remind us almost daily) the more desperate the threatener's position seems to be. And desperation will be the last thing the West will be short of when its comparatively feeble armies are on the point of being crushed by a Soviet offensive.

NATO practice is British practice writ large. If NATO were to disappear tomorrow, the balance between Britain's conventional and strategic nuclear capabilities would not need to be altered at all. Moreover, Britain's strategic nuclear capacity helps to maintain in working order the mechanism that connects NATO reverses in the field to the introduction of US strategic nuclear weapons. The Soviets could scarcely offer to leave US territory out of the war once its own chief cities had been razed by a British strike. Or to put it another way, provided the British strategic nuclear force can hit the most cherished Soviet targets, Britain has a veto upon any wartime arrangement being reached between the superpowers, tacitly or otherwise, to limit the European war to levels of violence acceptable to them.

If savings are to be forced on British defence expenditure, what the defence budget buys will be least affected if the savings were made on the conventional side, since British defence policy is in fact, whatever may be declared to be the case, relatively insensitive to the size of its conventional component. And, of course, there is far more scope for cuts in the conventional side since it nowadays amounts to 95 per cent of the budget.[1] The main danger of making large conventional cuts is not that they would shorten an already fairly short fuse between the outbreak of war and the point where strategic nuclear weapons were used, but the psychological one that the Soviets might read into such cuts that the will in Britain (and, by implication, in NATO) to resist Soviet pressure was evaporating. To avoid that risk the best point at which to cut conventional capabilities is at the same time as improvements are being made to the nuclear force.

The rational choice may of course be disputed as not so much incorrect as fundamentally misconceived. Just as a rational national energy policy choice may dictate that a certain proportion of nuclear-fired stations should be built, and this may be objected to on the principle that nuclear stations are (allegedly) peculiarly unsafe and not to be built at any cost, so obviously can there be root-and-branch objections to a defence policy with such a prominent nuclear element. The defence policy being pursued certainly does not include much of a margin of safety in the event that deterrence fails. It may also very well be judged morally inferior to possible alternatives, since it rests upon a willingness not only to use nuclear weapons but also to use them first and, moreover, to use them deliberately to kill civilians in their many hundreds of thousands. But any orthodox strategy which placed more weight on conventional forces would be extremely expensive. To push nuclear weapons firmly into the defence background, to become solely a means of deterring nuclear attack, NATO would need a conventional capability in

---

[1] Ninety-five per cent may overstate things slightly, 5 per cent of the defence budget goes on pensions, for instance. The round 5 per cent that the strategic nuclear force accounts for is a figure which also includes an allowance for the replacement of the Polaris flotilla by another of similar size, in four new submarines, based on the Trident C4 missile. Historically the strategic nuclear force has not always been so cheap. Before the Polaris purchase in 1962, when the nuclear force was based on bombers, it accounted for nearer 15 per cent of defence expenditure. It could be said that, therefore, the 'productivity' record of the strategic nuclear force has been very good in that it still accomplishes all it ever did whilst taking up a much smaller share of the defence budget.

Europe at about twice the current level, with the British contribution up in proportion.[2] Since this article is not unreasonably predicted upon economic stringency portending cuts in British defence expenditure, of as much as 20 per cent (see Appendix), an orthodox conventional strategy calling for a substantial increase in defence expenditure is out of the question.

It may be retorted that this is no answer to radical objections and is merely a defence of the rational choice. Defending a large nuclear energy programme by showing that relying solely on conventionally fired stations would work out very expensive, says almost nothing about the viability of a programme based upon a mass of windmills and solar panels. Equally it is true that this procedure for making a rational defence policy choice is not capable of considering the merits of a British or West European defence policy modelled, say, upon the Swiss, revolving around light armaments and a citizen army.

THE ROBUSTNESS OF THE RATIONAL CHOICE

The rational choice made, in this instance to replace Polaris and to replace it by Trident C4[3], we can now turn to assessing its chances of surviving cancellation and reaching the point of coming into service some 10 or 15 years hence.

The sign of a public capital expenditure project in distress is either cost over-run or failure to keep to schedule or both, and a prime cause of both is the unexpected technological hitch. In the case of Trident, technological problems have been guarded against virtually entirely by the purchase of as tried and tested a system as is feasible — short of buying something already on the verge of obsolescence. And buying off the shelf obviously also helps. Trying to develop a similar missile within Britain or even a

---

[2] This is based upon what would be needed to match, on paper, unit for unit, the Warsaw Pact offensive capacity in Central Europe. This probably overstates somewhat the extra expenditure that would be required, but it takes no account of the cost of meeting subsequent Warsaw Pact force increases stimulated by the NATO move.

[3] With the rational decision to replace Polaris taken, it is not altogether accurate to assume that the specific replacement choice, Trident C4, emerged purely on the basis of cost/benefit calculations. It was no doubt preferred over its nearest rivals — sea-based or air-based cruise missile systems — partly for reasons of this kind, but it was also preferred (in the same way the pressurised water reactor is now being preferred over the steam-generating heavy-water reactor) because it is more of a known quantity, not certain to be free of problems in the development and construction phases but more likely to escape the sort of embarrassingly large problem a relatively untried system might encounter. Students of game theory will recognise they are in the presence of a 'maxi-min' decision — aiming not at obtaining the best possible outcome but at avoiding the worst possible.

greater part of the missile than simply the warheads, as is the plan, would have been exceptionally risky. And this is known, as near as can be, for certain, because the evidence of the until recently secret, homemade, Chevaline project—to make the British Polaris A3 missiles better at penetrating Soviet anti-missile defences—is before our eyes.

The Chevaline development phase alone took about 8 years (1972 - 80) and cost at least £1000 million (1980 prices). The object seems to have been to retro-fit into the Polaris A3 missile a British-made front end to produce a hybrid system with most of the features of the American Poseidon missile, except that no front-end can be used to hit more than one area target.[4] In other words, Chevaline is a two-dimensional MIRV capable of subjecting Moscow (or any other Soviet city) to a spatially well-separated multiple warhead attack, with some warheads plunging in almost vertically and with others arriving at a flatter angle.

But Chevaline cannot be deemed a success. It appears to work, but it is coming into service very late, much nearer the end of the useful life of the Polaris system than can originally have been planned. Moreover, its cost does seem astounding, especially when set against the £5000 to £6000 million that will apparently buy the entire new Trident system, submarines included. And, besides, Chevaline was begun after the 1972 Moscow Agreements, which strictly limited the number of Soviet anti-missile interceptors and which inaugurated an era of low Soviet interest in this area of military activity: in other words, Chevaline, even had it come in at a much lower cost, and more quickly, was probably unnecessary anyway.

It might be wondered why Chevaline survived cancellation when doubts are in order about the robustness of the Trident project. The answer is that Chevaline was smuggled through behind the Official Secrets Act and was thus never exposed to the buffeting open projects have to endure. If it had been conducted openly it might have been cancelled in mid-stream; alternatively, openness might have imposed better discipline on the project managers and got the thing completed sooner and more cheaply.

The Trident project cannot be conducted wholly secretly; it is too prominent politically, looms too large in the defence budget to be overlooked, and, anyway, nothing can be kept secret which

---

[4] The name 'Chevaline', assuming that the Ministry of Defence is only human, is itself a slight give-away. Chevaline means 'horsy' or perhaps 'horse-like'. Poseidon, as well as being god of the sea, was also the god of horses.

involves £1500 - £2000 million worth of key components being bought from the United States.

Two other classic project defence mechanisms are also out of reach. Military (and civilian) aerospace projects find a safeguard against cancellation in international collaboration. Involving other governments as joint participants in major aerospace projects may or may not reduce unit costs below what could have been achieved nationally; equally it may or may not improve equipment standardisation amongst allies; but it does give a kind of guarantee against cancellation. If it had been possible to build the Polaris replacement in collaboration with a foreign partner (and France would have been the only feasible contender), some new freedom from cancellation would have been won. But to set against this there would have been greater technological risk, problems about how far Britain could be open with France with respect to American technical information Britain already had, and possibly too a sense that the collaboration would have been unequal since such an arrangement would have given France a theoretical veto on the future of the British strategic nuclear force without giving Britain a reciprocal veto (since France apparently has a national capability, with or without foreign assistance, to stay in the nuclear weapons business indefinitely).

The other defence mechanism denied the Polaris replacement project is the export market: it is not inconceivable, on the other hand, that should the Trident C4 have encountered development problems in the United States, one or two voices might have been heard saying that pressing on would permit some to be sold to the British.

Of course no project can be made cancellation proof, because while it is well enough understood that in the United Kingdom almost every medium or high technology capital project with a unit cost of about £300 million upwards has a tendency to outwit its managers and to cost much more and take far longer to build than had been planned, no-one quite understands why. Ordinary inflation may play a part and so may also the absence of economies of scale: possibly if Britain required fifty nuclear power stations, or SSBNs, rather than (typically) five, the average unit cost and completion time would be acceptable.

What the Trident planners seem to have done to protect the project is to choose a route, which will be as free as possible of technical and managerial surprises, by 'cloning' the earlier Polaris project, which was even for those less inflationary days a triumphant exception to the rule of budget overshooting and production delays. It is not exactly clear why the original Polaris project behaved as well as it did, but it is probably connected with the fact that its managers resisted the temptation to tamper with the original American designs.

But there is one important obstacle to a successful cloning. The marriage of the Trident C4 missile to a purpose-built sixteen-tube SSBN, which is apparently what is being proposed, has never actually been made before, even in the United States. There, the sixteen-tube Trident C4 boats now in existence were originally built for the Poseidon missile but with Trident in mind in that the boats were deliberately built over-size so that when the time came they would be roomy enough to take Trident C4 (just as the later Polaris A3 boats were built a little over-size so that they could subsequently be fitted out with Poseidon). Thus there is no complete sixteen-boat American blueprint for the British to follow. There are complete blueprints for a twenty-four-tube boat (the *Ohio* class), purpose-built to carry Trident C4, and built over-size so that it can later also take the successor missile Trident D5. But such boats will be more costly than the sixteen-tube models, and, moreover, themselves a managerial risk in that British yards have no experience of building submarines of this size.[5] The smallest managerial risk would seem to be associated with a sixteen-tube Poseidon-style boat with tubes reamed out to their full diameter to take Trident C4 from the beginning. The flaw in this choice would be a vulnerability to a shift in the external environment. The Trident C4 will be rather old by the time it enters service with the Royal Navy: older than the SSBNs carrying it. Soviet anti-submarine warfare techniques may have improved so much and Soviet anti-missile defences been strengthened so far that the greater range and payload of a retro-fitted D5 might be seen as necessary to maintain the British capability to wage war at the furthest extremity of violence.

The other change since the days of the original British Polaris project is that the depressing knowledge that the British capacity to manage large-scale projects is very limited, has sunk in everywhere. The responsible planner, then, will be torn between doing what he can to protect the project from cancellation—and if this means getting on with the job cheaply and quickly so much the better—and taking out some insurance against cancellation being a complete disaster, by arranging from the beginning for

---

[5] The lack of American experience at building boats of this size has been reflected in cost over-runs and completion delays: and it is too early to be certain that the *Ohio* class will not in fact itself be cancelled.

the project to be capable, if necessary, of taking on a cheaper and more acceptable form as an alternative to outright cancellation. The responsible planner in this case might want to be able to offer as an alternative the conversion of the SSBN boats to SSN boats (by removing, or not building, the middle, missile tube, section) and the sale back to the United States of the missiles. The responsible planner will also know that planner's logic is not always political logic; for projects have sometimes been carried through to completion because there was no escape and for no better reason. A politically more astute form of insurance might simply be an eventual unspoken willingness to see the four-boat flotilla cut down to three.

SUMMARY

What makes the Polaris replacement project special is not its cost (conventional weapons programmes are at least as expensive as nuclear these days) but its cancellability. Unlike Chevaline it cannot be smuggled through in secret, and unlike, say, the Stingray torpedo project, it has high political visibility and cannot expect simply to be overlooked; unlike the MRCA-Tornado aircraft there is no foreign partner, for fear of offending which cancellation becomes unthinkable; and, unlike the through-deck cruiser, export markets do not even exist in theory. The rationality of the original decision is no safeguard; the long-term cost advantages of a defence policy with a prominent strategic nuclear component will mean very little to a government anxious for immediate savings.

In the absence of a miraculous transformation of the national economy, pressure for a substantial reduction in defence expenditure cannot be long delayed. What is cancellable will be cancelled. If the Polaris replacement project is perfectly managed, perhaps a 2 in 3 chance of escaping the axe would be about right. But if, as seems more likely, the project will encounter turbulence over the choice of the appropriate size of the SSBN and its manufacture, since there is not today as there was in 1962, an obvious and proven American design to be replicated, a 1 in 2 chance may be more accurate.

Appendix

COMPARATIVE DEFENCE EXPENDITURE

The main shifts in British defence policy since the war have usually been justified by reference to economic difficulties of one kind and another. The figure below suggests that at least since 1968, when defence spending outside Europe was finally cut back to insignificant levels, pressure to cut back on defence was only to be expected, for there is a reasonably objective sense in which British defence expenditure does chronically exceed resources.

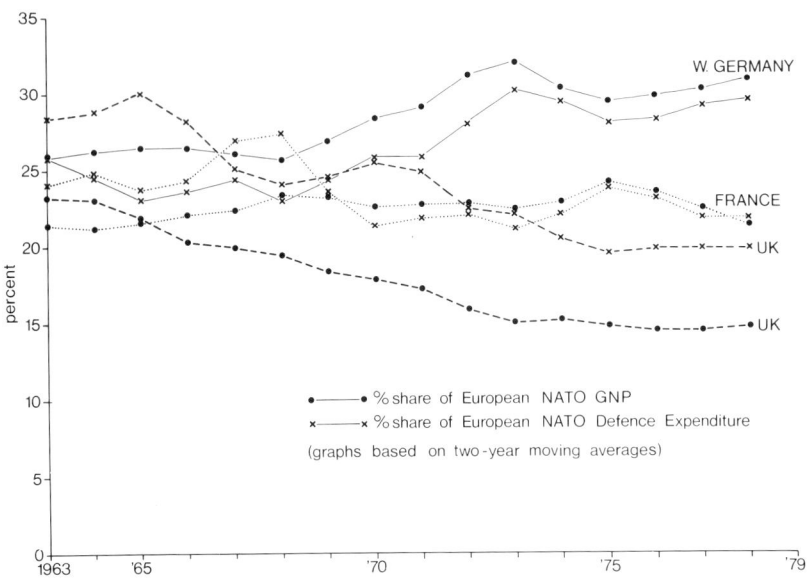

The data behind the figure, of course, are not exact. It is based upon annual estimates published by the International Institute for Strategic Studies[6] and these in turn are based upon figures provided by governments, and it is highly probable that French defence expenditure, for instance, is somewhat understated. Equally, some distortion will also have been introduced by exchange rate movements. But the general picture is clear enough,

[6] In the successive annual editions of the *Military Balance,* IISS, London

and if the British defence sector were at all like the farming sector, the excess of contributions to what is in effect the common defence over the British share by value in what is to be defended, would have been part of national folk-lore by now.

The explanation of excessive British defence expenditure is not obvious. Theories of Alliance burden sharing all point in the opposite direction, saying that where allies are unequally rich, the burden of common defence falls most heavily on the richest members of the Alliance. Presumably a range of special factors is at work in this case. But the close match between the German GNP share and its defence expenditure share is not surprising, given the restricted range of German defence policy. And for France, total defence expenditure may be kept in proportion as a result of heavy nuclear costs being used to justify a tight rein on conventional defence expenditure.

In theory Britain's share of defence expenditure could be brought into line by its two main partners increasing their defence budgets: but that in turn would push their defence share out of line with their GNP share. The more obvious and neater solution would be for Britain to reduce its defence budget. At 1980 prices the reduction required to match the British defence share with its defence share would be about £2000 million.

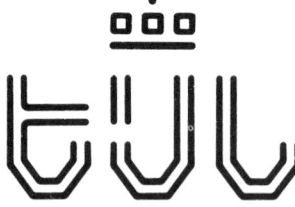

**Magazine
for technical training,
further education
and information in the Army.**

**Issued
in co-operation
with the Federal Ministry
of Defence.**

▶ SOLDAT und TECHNIK is published in co-operation with the Federal Ministry of Defence, and has been issued each month since 1958 primarily for members of the armed services of all types and ranks and for those members of the public displaying interest, at home and abroad.

▶ SOLDAT und TECHNIK brings factual reports which are nevertheless generally understandable, with plenty of illustrations, drawings and graphs devoted to:

— activities of the Ferderal Republic of Germany and allies within NATO for the defence of Europe,

— up-to-date aspects of the use of modern weapons systems in the armed forces of Germany and other world forces, particularly those of the Warsaw Pact,

— technical and economic results of research, development, tests and production of armaments in East and West.

The Armed Forces of Greece

JAMES BROWN

*James Brown is Professor of Political Science at the Southern Methodist University,
Dallas, Texas*

HISTORICALLY, but especially in this century, the Greek Armed
Forces have assumed an internal political function. The assumption of this role came with the encouragement, and at times the
cooperation, of the civilian sector to such an extent that a sym-
biotic relationship often existed between officers and various
political interests. As a result, intervention of the Greek Armed
Forces in the domestic political arena has become institutionalis-
ed with roots deeply embedded in the socio-culture of the country.[1]

Greek civil-military relations can be divided into six major
phases: the Westernisation phase (1828 - 90), the nationalistic
phase (1897 - 1922), the interventionist phase (1922 - 35), the
anti-communist phase (1936 - 48), the Americanisation phase
(1949 - 74) and the differentiated phase (1974 - present).[2]

Greek society in the 19th century contained a distinct but small
civilian élite whose power lay in its wealth, education, mobility
and foreign alignments.

> A predominantly rural society, one fragmented into kinship groups, integrated only
> through competitive institutions, and linked with other social groups by patronage,
> hampered attempts at modernization and affected the formation of a regular army
> profoundly.[3]

Political and military leadership tended to coincide with very

---

[1] Seven *coups d'état* have taken place in this century: coups led by Col N Zorbas in
1909, Col George Plastiras in 1922, Gen John Metaxas in 1933 and 1936, Gen George
Kondyles in 1926 and 1935 and Gen Theodore Pangalos in 1925. Other attempted coups
either failed or never got 'off the ground' (May 1951, March and early April 1967,
February 1975 and February and June 1981). Most of these interventions have been implemented by the Army, which today comprises two-thirds of the Greek Armed Forces.

[2] The basic typology of civil-military relations was developed by George Kourvetaris in
'Greek Service Academies: Patterns of Recruitment and Organizational Change', in Gwyn
Harries-Jenkins and J van Doorn (eds), *The Military and the Problem of Legitimacy*. Sage
Studies in International Sociology, (Sage Publications Inc, Cal, USA, 1976), pp 118 - 27.

[3] Thanos Veremis, 'Some Observations on the Greek Military in the Inter-War Period,
1918 - 1935, *Armed Forces and Society*. 4(3) (1978) p 527.

little differentiation between military and civilian élites. Until 1897, officers tended to act in unison with politicians to enforce constitutional reform or even to produce changes in government.[4] The penetration of the Armed Forces into the political arena was ingrained in the officer corps and set the tone for the 20th century.

The Military League's *pronunciamento* of 1909 was the first instance of independent military action against the political establishment. The architects of this movement, primarily junior officers, were initially motivated by professional grievances. But their grievances were soon aligned with more fundamental criticisms and even contempt for many aspects of civilian society and for the political élites who exercised control.[5] In spite of its ultimate subordination to Eleftherios Venizelos, a civilian politician, the *pronunciamento*[6] of 1909 later became a stereotyped justification for military intervention against civilian corruption, as in the *coup d'état* of 21 April 1967. Venizelos acceded to the Military League's demand for drastic military reform, and, as a result, the military budget reached an all-time high. British and French military missions were instrumental in training, educating, reorganising and strengthening both the Army and the Navy. Thus, when the Balkan Wars (1912 - 13) broke out, Greek victories demonstrated that the period from 1910 had been used for a profitable revitalisation of the Armed Forces.

By 1914 the Greek officer corps had achieved excellent morale, its reputation was intact, and it was quite popular in civilian society. During this time the social structure of the officer corps had also changed. The élitism of the late 19th and early 20th centuries came to an end when members of the less-privileged classes were admitted to the military academies. In addition, large numbers of reserve officers admitted into the Army with regular commissions perpetuated the system of patronage and further

---

[4] Both instances of major intervention in the 19th century (the absolutist reign of King Othon ended on 15 September 1843; he remained on the throne, but his powers were greatly curtailed: the *coup d'état* of October 1862 forced the abdication of Othon and brought to the fore King George I from the House of Glucksburg) were planned by civilians. The ability of the officers in active service to hold ministerial positions provided an outlet for their political aspirations. For a detailed discussion, see Keith Legg, *Politics in Modern Greece* (Stanford University Press, Stanford; 1969)

[5] For a detailed discussion of these events, see S Victor Papacosma, *The 1909 Coup d'état* (Kent State University Press, Kent, Ohio, 1977). Also Spiros Melas, *H Epanastasi tou 1909* [The Revolution of 1909] (Piris Press, Athens, 1957)

[6] Military intervention was justified because order was restored and 'responsible' politics reinstituted. Parallels with the 1909 *coup d'état* begin and end with the rhetoric of the coup makers.

politicised the officer corps. Military conspiracies were the rule among the reserve officers. This may be attributed to their insecurity. Whenever promotion lists became too crowded, the reserve officers were the first to be dismissed. Dependence upon military and political patrons became a condition for survival. Individual self-interests increased the disposition of the military toward intervention.[7] Whatever professionalism the officer corps attained up to 1915 as a result of the training by the foreign military missions was disrupted by the schism over World War I.

The schism resulted from differences over the position to be taken by Greece in World War I — support of the policy advocated by the anglophile Venizelos or support of the policy of neutrality advocated by germanophile King Constantine.[8] This schism set the tone of Greek politics during the interventionist period, to 1936, and to some extent Greece today continues to feel the repercussions of this crisis.[9] The implications of 13 years (1922 - 35) of military conspiracies and the Asia Minor débâcle were far reaching in both the military and civilian sectors. Venizelos came to symbolise the liberal elements in Greek society. The conservative elements tended to support the royal family. Each group had its personal followings in the Armed Forces and maintained traditional clientage structures within the military. The implications in the 20 years (1916 - 36) of military intervention in Greek politics were far reaching. Contrary to the intentions of the Venizelist officers who fomented most of them, these interventions ultimately resulted in the return of the monarchy. The entire period was marked by continuing purges of the officer corps. Fanatical anti-Venizelists became a dominant force in the officer corps after the return of the monarchy in 1935. This began the anti-communist phase. Metaxas' rule confirmed civilian supremacy over the military and the authority of the monarch over the Armed Forces.

The schism that began in 1915 manifested itself again during World War II. Republican officers served primarily in two

---

[7] Thanos Veremis, *The Greek Army in Politics* (PhD. diss, Trinity College, Oxford University, England, 1974).

[8] The terms *Venizelist, Republican, liberal, anti-Venizelist, royalist,* and *conservative* defy precise definition. They designate individual elements comprising various political groupings.

[9] The reign of Constantine I came to an end in March 1924 as a result of the débâcle in Asia Minor. A republic was established, but it was short-lived and came to an end in November 1935. King George II assumed the throne. Shortly thereafter, in 1936, General John Metaxas assumed power and created a dictatorial régime.

resistance forces, the National Republican Greek League (EDES) and the Social Liberation Movement (EKKA). Both organisations had regional power, but neither was successful in establishing a broad national base. Ultimately, the resistance movement was dominated by the National Liberation Force (EAM), a popular front coalition headed by communists. The EAM and its military arm, the People's Army of Liberation (ELAS), challenged the Greek government at the end of World War II.

These forces were opposed by several organisations. Regular Greek military units of approximately 10,000 men escaped Nazi occupation in the Middle East and formed the nucleus of Greek forces in exile. In Greece, the government created paramilitary units, such as the National Security Battalions (TEA), to combat the EAM/ELAS forces, particularly after the Germans left Greece. Regular officers in the Middle East formed an anti-communist organisation, which became known as IDEA (Sacred Union of Greek Officers) in 1944 when the Middle Eastern units returned to Greece.[10] Elements of this organisation were instrumental in the *coup d'état* of 21 April 1967.

Shortly after the liberation of Greece from German control in December 1944, bitter fighting erupted in Athens between Greek communist elements and Greek national forces backed by the British Army. This costly civil war ended in 1949, but, in the interim, King George returned to the throne; the communists lost the struggle; and, after proclamation of the Truman Doctrine (March 1947), the United States became actively involved in Greece. From 1947 forward, the United States provided Greece with most of its military equipment and professional training from the commissioned and non-commissioned officer corps.[11]

The defeat of the communists, coupled with the military assistance received from the United States, marked the beginning of the Americanisation phase and was a new era for the Greek military, which emerged as a major domestic political bloc independent of traditional parliamentary factions and leaders.

As symbols of national unity, the Armed Forces, especially the Army, felt that their main purpose was to protect the nation from

[10] More precisely, a splinter group of IDEA known by the acronym EENA (Ethniki Enosis Neon Aksiomatikon—National Union of Young Officers) was the group that actually implemented the *coup d'état* of April 1967. For a concise discussion of secret organisational activities of the Greek officer corps, see N Stavrou, *Pressure Groups in the Greek Political Setting.* (unpublished dissertation, Ann Arbor, University Microfilms, 1979), pp. 212 - 93.

[11] In 1951 Greece joined the North Atlantic Treaty Organisation, and billions of dollars of US military aid secured this nation for the West.

communism, both from within and from without. The military possessed a combination of pragmatic and ideological commitment based on common experiences and a heightened sense of self-esteem. From all outward appearances, the Greek Armed Forces appeared united and apolitical. But, in reality, the officer corps retained the belief that it should act if it perceived a potential or actual threat to Greek national security. Thus, the inability of the politicians and the monarchy to solve Greece's post-war political crises, particularly during the period of 1965 - 67, predisposed some elements of the officer corps to institute the *coup d'état* of 21 April 1967.[12]

Five factors appeared to predispose the officer corps towards military intervention: the communist threat, political incompetence of parliamentarians, decline of the growth rate of the economy, social and moral decay of Greek society, and Greece's geopolitical and strategic role in the Western Alliance. The 1967 *coup d'état* was easier to implement because most of the Greek population perceived the factors that led to the action. The longest period of military rule in Greece (1967 -74) produced extensive factionalism in the military junta. This culminated in 1973 with the overthrow of George Papadopoulos by Brigadier General Dimitrios Loannides, head of the military police. Ultimately, the junta's inability to cope with a worsening economic situation and student unrest at the universities (especially at the Athens Polytechnic) led to its own demise. In 1974 it launched an ill-fated *coup d'état* against Archbishop Makarios' Cypriot government in the hope of uniting Cyprus with Greece.

Turkish leaders asserted their rights as guarantor under the 1959 Zürich - London agreement and landed forces on the island in the early hours of 20 July. The military junta responded with a call for general mobilisation, but mobilisation fell into complete disarray, primarily because of failure to follow a phased plan. The junta had gambled that Turkey would not respond or that

---

[12]Two events set the stage for the April *coup d'état*: first, the discovery in May 1965 of a left-wing secret organisation known as ASPIDA (Shield) and connected to Andreas Papandreou; second, the elections scheduled for May 1967, which George Papandreou's Centre Union and the Left were certain to win. The latter event precipitated discussions within the General Staff (including King Constantine) for a possible *coup d'état*. Serious discussions began as early as February 1967. Several members of the General Staff were against a *coup d'état*, thus no decision appeared forthcoming. Col George Papadopoulous and his cohorts were aware of these discussions, and when no decision by the General Staff was eminent they instituted their own *coup d'état*. The actual coup plan, given the name IERAX (The Hawk), was a General Staff contingency plan to implement a NATO plan known as Prometheus II.

the United States would again intercede (as in 1963 and 1967) to prevent Turkish intervention, and it lost the gamble.

Discredited and diplomatically isolated, the junta exited on 23 July 1974 under heavy pressure from the officer corps. Konstantine Karamanlis created a new civilian government. One of the first goals of this government was to re-establish civilian control over the military. It accomplished this by appointing as minister of defence the Conservative politician E. Averoff-Tossizza, a respected political ally of the military establishment. In fact, it might be the case that the leaders of the Armed Forces, seeing that the junta's position was untenable, swallowed their pride and turned to Karamanlis in order to preserve, intact, the power position of the Armed Forces.[13]

The legacy of the junta and the 1974 Cyprus humiliation still dominates Greek foreign and national security policy. Since that date the country has been engaged in a crash rearmament programme to counter the perceived Turkish threat. Greek bitterness at the unwillingness of their NATO allies to take their side against Turkey in 1974 led to the immediate withdrawal of the Greek Armed Forces from the Alliance's military command. After 6 years' absence, Greece returned in October 1980 to NATO's military wing.

The original issue that led to Greece's withdrawal from NATO, and the Aegean Sea problems[14] that emerged shortly thereafter, have not as yet been resolved. An impartial analysis of what facts are available indicate that Greece, as well as Turkey, made concessions in order for Greece to return to the Alliance. This has provided fuel to the liberal elements of Greek politics led by Andreas Papandreou and the PASOK Party.[15] These elements ad-

[13] The issue of the monarchy was swiftly closed by a referendum confirming the Republic, and in January 1975 a new constitution was adopted. The leading junta members and the more notorious torturers were tried and imprisoned, and the Army purged of the more prominent adherents of the previous régime.

[14] In addition to the Cyprus question, two other issues further complicate Greece's relations with Turkey, NATO and the United States. The first issue concerns the right to explore for minerals, primarily oil, beneath the Aegean Sea. The second issue concerns the right to control the airspace over this body of water. This latter issue was partially resolved by creating two NATO commands—the Seventh Tactical Air Force (Larissa, Greece) under a Greek commander. This command has its Turkish equivalent in the Sixth Tactical Air Force (Izmir, Turkey), which is commanded by a Turkish general. Specific air and sea operations in this area are governed by NATO headquarters in Naples (CINCSOUTH).

[15] The November 1977 elections showed that the conservatism of the Greek electorate, in the midst of an acute crisis, was more apparent than real. Mr Karamanlis's party was re-elected with a severely reduced popular vote of less than 42 per cent. This was at the expense of Andreas Papandreou's PASOK party and the combined Communist Parties' votes.

vocate Greek withdrawal from NATO, the closing of American bases and a policy of non-alignment. The first signs of renewed polarisation in Greek politics may now be discerned. There are, as yet, no viable solutions to these problems that contain a substantial military dimension. The Greek Armed Forces, however, are back in their barracks, and likely to remain there, at least for some time.

STRENGTH, EQUIPMENT, BUDGET and ARMS INDUSTRY

Strength

The total regular strength of the Greek Armed Forces is about 182,000.[16] Of these, 132,000 are conscripts serving for an average of about 26 months. The ratio of military personnel to the civilian population is 1.9 per cent, a ratio surpassed in the entire world only by Israel, Jordan, Syria, Taiwan and the Democratic People's Republic of Korea. More specifically, the strengths of the three Services are as follows:

ARMY: The largest of the Services consisting of about 75 per cent of all men under arms. Army strength is 140,000 (110,000 conscripts) with about 290,000 reservists. The officer strength is approximately 20,000.

Organisationally it consists of 1 armoured division, 2 armoured brigades and 11 infantry divisions, and 15 artillery, surface-to-surface (SSM-Honest John) and surface-to-air (SAM-Hawk) missile battalions with nuclear capabilities.

The tank division consists of 6 tank battalions of 55 tanks each, 4 motorised infantry battalions (800 men and 50 armoured personnel carriers (APCs)) and 2 reconnaissance battalions and 4 self-propelled (SP) artillery battalions (105-, 155- and 203-mm howitzers), plus several logistical support units. Total strength is about 13,000 men and 360 tanks. The independent armoured brigades consist of 2 tank battalions, 1 SP artillery battalion and other support units bringing the total to about 3650 men and 120 tanks.

The Greek Army, being primarily an infantry force, resembles the motorised infantry formations of other NATO countries. The strength of a Greek infantry division is approximately 14,000 men

---

[16] Much of the following information is from *The Military Balance, 1980 - 81* (International Institute for Strategic Studies, London).

with 60 tanks, 80 APCs, 1800 vehicles, 76 howitzers (203-, 155-and 105-mm), 114 mortars, 50 (106-mm) recoilless launchers and 450 anti-tank guided weapons (Cobra, TOW and Milan). More than half of the infantry divisions are manned at the 60 - 70 per cent level. They are all trained for combat in both nuclear and non-nuclear conditions. Greek military doctrine and combat training is, for the most part, American in origin.

NAVY: A total of 17,000 personnel (11,000 conscripts) and approximately 1700 officers. There are also an additional 20,000 reservists.

The main strength of the Navy lies in 11 submarines, 12 destroyers, 4 destroyer escorts, 11 Combattante fast patrol guided-missile boats (8 with Exocet SSM systems, 1 with Penguin SSMs and 2 with SS-12 SSM), and 14 fast attack torpedo boats. In addition, the Navy has 2 coastal minelayers, 14 coastal minesweepers and 83 landing ships of various sizes.

AIR FORCE: Consists of 24,500 members (15,000 conscripts) and some 2300 officers. In addition, there are some 20,000 reservists.

The Air Force is organised into 8 fighter, 5 intercept, 1 reconnaissance, 3 transport and 3 helicopter squadrons, consisting of about 247 combat aircraft. Three of the fighter squadrons are equipped with 57 A-7H Corsair IIs, 3 others with 50 RF-4E Phantoms, and 2 with 33 F/TF-104 Gs. The 5 interceptor squadrons are comprised of 3 with 43 F-5As, and 2 with 38 Mirage F-ICG. These squadrons are all armed with Sparrow, Sidewinder, Falcon and R-550 Magic air-to-air missiles. In addition, there is 1 reconnaissance squadron with RF-5 AS and RF-4Fs and 1 maritime squadron with Albatross (8 HU-16Bs) and Alouette III helicopters.

The Air Force also has 3 transport squadrons equipped with 12 C-130H Hercules, 20 C-47s, 30 Noratlas, 1 Gulfstream and 7 CL-215 amphibians. The 3 helicopter squadrons have 12 AB-205s, 2 AB-206A, 10 Bell 47 Gs, 8 UH-19Ds and 35 UH-IDS. There is 1 surface-to-air missile (SAM) battalion equipped with Nike Hercules missiles.

Furthermore, Greece presently claims paramilitary forces consisting of 26,000 Gendarmerie, 100,000 National Guard and an unspecified number of National Defence Battalions (TEA).

Equipment
Since 1975, when it faced possible confrontation with Turkey,

the Government has undertaken an ambitious programme to purchase and upgrade the equipment of the Greek Armed Forces.

Major arms agreements have been consummated with the United States for the purchase of 7 destroyers, 300 air-to-air (AAM) Sidewinder missiles, 16 CH-47C helicopters, 18 Phantom F-4E fighters, 32 Harpoon surface-to-surface missiles (SSM), 37 Chaparral SAMS and an undisclosed number of TOW anti-tank guided weapons (ATGW), 155- and 105-mm self-propelled guns. Also, France will supply Greece with Exocet SSM systems, 115 AMX Medium tanks and AMX-10P mechanised infantry combat vehicles. The Federal Republic of Germany intends to manufacture 4 submarines and supply Milan ATGW to the Armed Forces. In addition, negotiations are now taking place with the United Kingdom, the Federal Republic of Germany and Italy for the purchase of tanks, heavy guns and naval support helicopters.

In 1977 Greece initialled an agreement with the United States that provides for $US 700 million in military aid over 4 years. This agreement was never ratified. Recently an attempt was made to re-negotiate the 1977 protocol to no avail. Negotiations will resume after the parliamentary elections in late 1981. In return the United States will continue to operate four military bases in Greece, but under the command of Greek officers. These are Suda Bay and Heraklion, Crete, Ellinikon Air Base, which is part of Athens International Airport, Tanagra Air Base (outside Athens) and a communications station at Nea Makri (north of Athens). All of these bases serve as major telecommunications and surveillance stations to monitor Soviet activities in the Mediterranean. In addition, Suda Bay also serves as a naval support base of the US Sixth Fleet. The importance of these installations has been greatly heightened by the Afghanistan and Iranian crises.

Budget

The defence budget has remained relatively stable since the demise of the Junta. Total governmental spending is about 5.6 per cent of the GNP. For 1980 the total defence expenditures will be approximately 75 billion Drachmas ($US 2 billion) or 21 per cent of the total budget.

Arms industry

Greece's domestic arms industry is a fledgling, but a parliamentary bill introduced in 1977 provided assistance to state-owned and private factories manufacturing armaments in order to attract advanced foreign technology. The first results were a cooperative venture between Greece and the firm of Heckler and Koch of the Federal Republic of Germany to build a light weapons plant at Aigion. This plant is producing the G-3 automatic rifle and also barrels for anti-aircraft guns. In addition, a tank plant is located in Velestion (Thessaly) which will rebuild and modernise Greece's ageing M-47/48 tanks. This plant has the capacity to assemble approximately 100 tanks per year. Tendered offers from France (AMX-30s), the FR of Germany (Leopard I and Marder), Italy (Lion I) and Great Britain (Chieftain) have been received for assembling this armour. As yet a decision has not been reached by the Ministry of Defence. Recently, Greece also purchased a controlling interest (60 per cent) in the Austrian Steyr army truck plant in Thessaloniki.

The Hellenic Shipyard at Skaramangas is now constructing three Combattante fast patrol guided missile boats under French supervision.

Lastly, three US companies[17] are cooperating with the Hellenic Aerospace Industry for the establishment of an aircraft industry at Tanagra. Its primary purpose will be the maintenance, repair and modification of Phantom jets and other aircraft. The Hellenic Aerospace Industry and Air Italia have also signed an agreement to assemble several sections of a twin-engine military transport at this installation.

As a result of the above activities a new advisory group was created within the Ministry of Defence to oversee matters that relate to the production and control of these arms industries.

CONSTITUTIONAL STATUS

Historically, several régimes have pressed for institutional changes in the role of the military. However, the military régime during the 1967 - 74 period undertook the most extensive change in its Constitution of 1968 (and revised in 1973). The role assigned to the Armed Forces under that document did not provide for a complete withdrawal from political responsibilities. This constitution differed from all its predecessors in that it included a separate section of two articles which dealt exclusively with the military.[18] In effect these articles legalised the historic extra-parliamentary function of the Armed Forces.

[17] These companies are Lockheed, General Electric and Westinghouse. A total investment of $130 million is anticipated.

[18] See Articles 129 and 130 of the 1968 Constitution.

The present constitution firmly places the Armed Forces under civilian control.[19] The present Defence Minister has spoken out on numerous occasions on the reliability of the Greek Armed Forces and their subservience to civilian rule. In fact, several hundred officers (primarily colonels and general officers) were cashiered or chose forced retirement after civilian rule was restored because of their juntist activities and mentality.[20] However, very little purging of the officer corps took place at the junior ranks (captain and below). This could possibly portend problems for future Greek governments. It is these junior officers who were graduates of the military academies at the time of military rule and were inculcated with values that were anti-parliamentarian, values that exalted the role of the Greek Armed Forces as protectors of the state.

As we have said, the norm of civilian supremacy is not firmly rooted in the ethic of the officer corps. Conspiratorial organisations and activities have been an indigenous part of the Greek officer corps. In fact, the 21 April *coup d'état* was spawned from such activities. These organisations are not limited to any one part of the political spectrum; at times they have even included in their membership foreign elements.[21]

The behaviour of the Greek officer corps has been influenced by its perceived role of defender of the national interest. This does not necessarily coincide with that of civilian authorities. In fact, it indicates a lack of faith on the part of the military regarding the ability of civilian authorities to hold or achieve the same objectives.

Motivated by their perceived interests, the officers corps has often sought to influence those in power and, at last resort and if unsuccessful, replace civilian rule with military rule.

ROLE COMMITMENT: EXTERNAL and INTERNAL SECURITY

Greece occupies a critical position, both geographically and strategically, in the eastern Mediterranean. This position has affected Greek politics. Nations historically have sought to control or influence Greece's decision-making process and in so doing

---

[19] The present constitution of Greece was ratified on 7 June 1975. See Article 45.

[20] On 25 February 1975 a plot was uncovered to overthrow the Karamanlis government. Thirty-seven officers, including six generals, were involved.

[21] For an excellent treatment of this topic, see Nikolaos Stavrou, *Pressure Groups in the Greek Political Setting* (unpublished dissertation, Hunter College, 1970). See, in particular, pp 245 - 55.

gain dominance in that part of the world. Since World War II, this control and influence has been further exaggerated because of the influence of the Soviet Union in the countries that border Greece; countries that have long been in conflict with Greece. Furthermore, Greece fought a civil war, 1946 - 49, the bloodiest fratricide in the history of modern Greece. It was from these nations—Yugoslavia and to a lesser extent Bulgaria—that the Greek communists received aid and comfort. Naturally enough, this has heightened Greece's suspicions about these nations.

Today there is no perceived military threat from non-aligned Yugoslavia, with whom relations have been cordial in the last two decades. Diplomatic relations with Albania were only established in 1971, and there is little warmth in them due to the ideological difference between the two countries. On the other hand, the Bulgarian threat is taken very seriously. There are no Soviet troops stationed permanently in Bulgaria, but the Bulgarian forces of 149,000 men possess almost twice as many tanks as Greece. The geography of north-eastern Greece (Thrace), moreover, makes it very difficult to defend: a strip of land several hundred miles long between Bulgaria and the Aegean Sea, averaging only 30 - 50 miles in width. Although it is likely that in any general European war the bulk of the Bulgarian forces would be directed eastward towards the strategically vital objectives of Istanbul and the Dardanelles, few Greeks doubt that a substantial proportion would be reserved for an attack on western Thrace.

Greece's perpetual foe, Turkey, even in periods of normal relations, poses a perennial problem for Greek politics. The Cyprus crisis of 1974 caused a complete deterioration of relations with Turkey. In the end it affected Greece's membership in NATO and her relations with the United States, causing Greece to withdraw her forces from NATO in protest against the ineffectiveness of the Alliance, but without denouncing NATO itself or evicting all American installations. The developments in the Middle East and the strengthening of the Russian fleet in the Mediterranean are further arguments used by the Greek officer corps to indicate the importance of Greece and her Armed Forces for the defence of the West.

All of these factors create a mood of uneasiness in the officer corps and colours their perceptions, which, in the end, dictates how they view their role and define for themselves what constitutes the maintenance of the internal and external security of Greece. More specifically, the officer corps does not sharply differentiate between an internal and external communist threat.

They perceive them as one and the same, emanating from the Soviet Union. Therefore, how to defend the country from a communist threat, real or imagined, is the dilemma the Greek officer corps is continually faced with, which ultimately sets the tone of their relations with civilian governments and further dictates their military preparedness and strategy.

At present, their views regarding the Left and its incursions into the political arena and their perception of civilian governments, in general, are quite muted. In part, this is attributable to the posture the Minister of Defence, Evangelos Averoff-Tossizza, has taken regarding the officer corps' non-involvement in politics.

They do, however, make a sharp distinction between the state (with themselves cast in the role of protector) and the government in power. The norm of civilian supremacy, as inherent in the United States and Western European officer corps, is not implicit in the Greek officer corps.

Greece's return to the NATO Alliance still leaves several problems unsolved which ultimately impinge upon her national security. The Cyprus question still eludes solution, with Turkey and its Armed Forces still occupying approximately 39 per cent of the island. This relationship is further complicated by the Aegean Sea conflict. Turkey seeks to change the *status quo* and exert more economic and military influence in the region, which Greece firmly resists. Three specific issues are involved here; first, the right to explore for minerals, primarily oil, beneath the Aegean Sea. According to international practice, nations have the right to explore for mineral wealth on their continental shelf, but the Greek islands and the Turkish mainland share the same shelf. Second is the clash that concerns the right to control the airspace over the Aegean, which to this day has not been resolved. The third dispute centres on the military balance of power. By international treaty, Greece is obliged to demilitarise the coastal areas that abut upon Turkey. She has strengthened the High Military Command for Interior and Islands (ASDEN) and also created 'D' Corps with headquarters in Xanthi (60 miles from the Turkish border) to offset the mobilisation and deployment of Turkish troops on the Maritsa River.[22]

These problems will continue to affect the NATO Alliance and its viability in the Eastern Mediterranean in spite of Greece's re-

---

[22] Turkey has also created an army of the Aegean headquartered in Izmir. Its purpose is to counteract Greece's mobilisation in the Aegean Islands.

cent reconciliation. Aggravating this problem are the bi-lateral relations that the United States has with both Greece and Turkey. Negotiations are presently taking place between Greece and the United States on a new base agreement. The United States still maintains the 7 to 10 ratio in its military assistance agreements with Greece and Turkey.

Greece's relations with the United States, Turkey and NATO became clouded with the November 1977 election victory of Andreas Papandreou's PASOK Party. Although K Karamanlis's New Democracy Party still retained a majority in parliament, its majority eroded. Papandreou's challenge to the government is to-day quite vigorous.[23] In fact, Papandreou is against giving quarter on any of the above issues. New parliamentary elections are planned for late 1981, and speculation exists that A Papandreou will emerge with a parliamentary majority.

Primary responsibility for internal security in Greece rests with the Gendarmerie and City Police Departments. But these elements are backed up by National Guard units and the National Defence Battalions (TEA), which were created during the late 1940s and were instrumental in the success of the Armed Forces to hold liberated territories during the Civil War. These battalions, found primarily in the rural areas, are headed by regular military officers and usually train on Sunday mornings in small unit tactics.

ORGANISATION

The organisational structure of the Armed Forces was recently changed under the Armed Forces Act of 1977. This new plan supersedes the Hellenic Armed Forces Act of 1968, which was enacted under the military junta. The Supreme Hellenic Armed Forces Command (AED), which had direct command and control of all three Services, was established under this plan. The Commander of Hellenic Forces had full authority to manage all facets of military activity including promotions, personnel, logistics and organisational matters. Minimal civilian control was exercised internally over the Armed Forces. In reality, however, the Armed Forces were continually interfered with by the then military government. In fact the Military Police (ESA) became an

---

[23] On 6 May 1980 Konstantine Karamanlis and his government resigned. Karamanlis then took the post of President of the Republic. A bitter fight ensued within the New Democracy Party with George Rallis emerging as victor. He formed a new government and now serves as Prime Minister.

authority unto itself and reported to junta leaders rather than to the Supreme Hellenic Armed Forces Command. An additional by-product that had been anticipated by the 1968 Act was the prevention of internecine rivalry among the Services. This was not fully realised. Lastly, AED deferred most decisions to each of the Services and did not exercise control over them.

Under the provisions of the 1977 Act the Ministry of Defence reasserts its full control over the Armed Forces. The Supreme Armed Forces Command has been abolished and is replaced by the National Defence General Staff (GEETHA)[24] and the three Services — Army (GES), Navy (GEN) and Air Force (GEA) — are now independent of each other with coordination by the Chief of the General Staff. In times of war he assumes command of all Services. Naturally this plan and its predecessor give the lion's share of power to the Army. Although it is anticipated that the Minister of Defence will be the ultimate authority, it is conceivable that compartmentalisation of the Services will reassert internecine rivalries, but more importantly may lead to conspiratorial politics within and among the Armed Services.

Specifically the three Services are organised as follows:

ARMY: It is headed by the Chief of the Army General Staff. Under him is the General of the First Hellenic Army, which command is subdivided into 4 Corps. Of these Corps, D Corps is the élite of the Hellenic Army. The commander of D Corps is crucial to any kind of planning and is usually elevated to head of the Hellenic Army and then is 'tapped' to become the Chief of the National Defence General Staff. This Corps is the best trained and equipped and has the most outstanding officers. Below this are found 14 divisions plus special commands for the Interior and Islands and for Central Greece, and below these levels it follows organisationally along traditional lines.

AIR FORCE: The Chief of the Air Force Staff heads this Service. Below this level is the Tactical Air Command consisting of 13 combat wings and an early warning wing plus a Nike Hercules Battalion.

The commanding general of the Tactical Air Command usually succeeds to the position of Chief of the Air Force. It further consists of an Air Material Command and an Air Training Command, plus other specialised units.

NAVY: The Chief of the Naval Staff heads 8 squadrons, a

---

[24] The Chief of the General Staff is always an Army officer. He is assisted by two deputies from each of the other Services.

logistical command, a navy training command and special commands for the North Aegean and Ionian Seas. The two élite elements of the Navy are the submarine force and the fast attack craft, Combattante. These elements are always manned at full complement.

Some general problems arise in the operational aspects of the Greek Armed Forces. Because Greece is a poor nation, its economic ability to maintain modern armed forces is limited. As a result, limited allocation of funds affects its military preparedness as follows. Its Armed Forces battlefield efficiency is somewhat restricted when it involves the formational training of large units (i.e. brigade strength) and combined theatre operations. Its logistical abilities are limited. Parts, supplies and munitions are not always readily available when needed, and are used sparingly during field exercises. Furthermore, long-range planning is lacking. As a result, necessary equipment and weapons systems are not purchased on a regular and planned basis. New weapons are purchased at the cost of other military needs.

The promotion system is quite archaic, and merit is not the only criterion for promotion (especially for colonels and general officers) or job assignments. As a result, there is a tendency in the Greek Armed Forces for officers to avoid responsibilities in making decisions. This requires that most decisions be made at the highest levels, which in turn makes decision making an antiquated process and lessens innovation on the part of the officer corps. This naturally impacts on their professional ethic. Corrective steps are now being taken to minimise this. Furthermore, because of its adverse promotion and assignment system, inflated staff positions exist especially at the field grade level. This creates an overabundance of lieutenant colonels and colonels which the General Staff cannot bring itself to retire early.

An officer who completes 30 years of service will most likely reach the rank of colonel. Usually he will retire with a 'hip pocket' promotion to brigadier general.

RECRUITMENT AND TRAINING

The recruitment patterns for personnel of the Greek Armed Forces vary between Services. More specifically these variances exist in the recruitment of the officer corps.

The main sources of recruitment for the officer corps are the military academies.[25] Reserve officer training programmes provide only temporary officers at the sub-lieutenant and 2nd lieutenant levels. These individuals serve from 24 to 30 months.

Career advancement is regulated by a more rigid pattern of screening and meritocracy than in the civilian sector. However, patronge is still evidenced somewhat today in the Army and Navy and to a lesser extent in the Air Force, especially in the area of assignments more so than in promotions (below the rank of colonel). This whole process was greatly distorted during the 1967 - 74 period.

The professional training of the Greek officer is similar in format to that of the American officer's training and education. However, the Greek officers differ from their American counterparts in that Greek officers are less specialised, reflective of Greece's semi-developed status as a nation.

Both the Service academies and the reserve officer's training schools (OCS) are state-supported institutions under the direction of the Ministry of Defence. Requirements and academic standards for the academies compare favourably with a university education. Upon graduation the cadet receives a diploma as a graduate of the academy but it does not compare to a university degree. Admission to one of the military academies is through competitive examination and presupposes a clean political and civil record, excellent health and a strong grounding in mathematics and natural sciences. As is true of all such institutions, the purpose of the academies ideally is to prepare the cadet for future military leadership roles in the Armed Forces and society. At times the academies have been used by various governments to inculcate in the cadets political values of the existing régime rather than a professional military ethic (i.e. the 1920s and 1967 - 74 periods).

The curriculum of the academies, military and non-military, is structured to reflect a professional socialisation process. Some specialisation occurs in the fourth year, but instruction tends to be of a generalised nature. Instruction at the academies is conducted by both military and civilian instructors. Upon graduation as a 2nd lieutenant, the new officer attends one of the specialised

---

[25] The size of each class for each of the academies varies: Sxoli ton Evelpidon (Army), pp 225 - 50; Sxoli Dokemon (Navy), pp. 50 - 60; Sxoli Ikaron (Air Force), pp 100 - 20. There is also a Services Military Academy in Thessaloniki which provides officers for the medical, financial and judge advocate corps.

courses of instruction for his basic branch.[26] Throughout an officer's career a pattern of rotation will be followed from command to professional training to staff assignments.

After being commissioned an officer usually is assigned to two or three years in a command position (i.e. platoon leader, or in the Navy to fleet assignment). After this command assignment the officer usually is sent to a special school of his branch or service to expand further the basic knowledge and tactics he acquired at the academy, a pratice that is continued at various intervals during his career. These schools may include inter-branch or inter-Service training. In addition, officers are selected or 'tapped' to attend specialised schools in the United States, the United Kingdom, France or those of NATO.[27] Those officers selected to attend such schools will usually have the inside track on promotions, and are the top 10 or 15 per cent of the officer corps.

The turning point in an officer's career takes place when he enters the War College.[28] Beginning with the rank of major and lieutenant colonel, officers must pass an examination in order to gain admittance into the War College. If an officer does not attend the War College of his respective Service, for all intents and purposes his career is at an end. The number of officers attending the Army War College in Thessaloniki is usually about 100; for the Navy and Air Force the enrolment is quite small, numbering 20 - 25 officers. The length of study at these schools is usually for one year. Training at the war colleges deals with advance problems of military strategy and tactics and prepares the officer for staff assignments and leadership roles in large size units (brigade, corps, etc.).

The pinnacle of postgraduate work for an officer is the National Defence School. Prerequisite graduation from a war college is necessary. This school not only provides training for officers of the Armed Forces but also for the gendarmerie, coast

---

[26] The combat branches in the Army are Infantry, Artillery, Armoured Cavalry, Engineer, Signal. Only the combat arms of the Army, the line officers of the Navy and the flight officers of the Air Force are eligible to be considered for promotion above the rank of brigadier general.

[27] The Schools most attended are the US Special Weapons School in the Federal Republic of Germany, the US Command and General Staff College, Army, Naval and Air Force war colleges, and the NATO Defence College. Approximately 15 - 20 officers annually attend NATO schools while some 300 officers attend schools in the United States.

[28] Each service has its own War College. The Army's is located in Thessaloniki, the Navy's in Pireaus and the Air Force's in Tatoi outside of Athens.

guard and high-ranking civil servants.[29] No entrance examination is required, and officers are selected by the Minister of Defence. The average class membership is about 30 - 40 students, and the curriculum varies from large-scale simulations of military exercises to topics on international relations, politics, economics and sociology.

The military profession, and in particular the officer corps, serves in Greece as a channel of social mobility.[30] This is especially true of the Army and Air Force. The Navy has been viewed as the more prestigious Service and historically perceived as élitist, having links with the Royal Family, with shipping magnates and with the more affluent sectors of Greek society. This situation still prevails today but to a lesser degree.

Data indicates that the Army officer has roots in the rural areas. The two major cities of Greece, Athens and Thessaloniki, do not contribute substantially to the officer corps of the Army and Air Force. Recruitment patterns of the military academies indicate that Athens supplies 37.7 per cent of the naval cadets, 11.05 per cent of the Air Force cadets and only 7.3 per cent of the Army cadets.[31] A partial explanation for the over-representation of naval cadets may be the recruitment patterns from different socio-economic strata. The Army and Air Force officer corps are derived primarily from three geographic areas — Peloponnesos, central Greece and Crete — which contribute 52.3 per cent and 59 per cent respectively to these two branches, while at the same time they represent only 22 per cent of the population. All three of these areas are relatively poor economic regions, and the mobility, security and prestige offered by the military appeals to many of the inhabitants. The regions of Thrace, Epirus and Macedonia also contribute a high proportion of the Army and Air Force officer corps.

[29] Officers at the rank of colonel and brigadier general, or comparable ranks, are eligible.

[30] For a detailed discussion, see James Brown 'The Military and Society in Greece', *European Journal of Sociology* 15 (1974) 245 - 261; Kourvetaris op cit; *Meleti Epi Tes Exelixeos Tou Monimou Axiomatikon Stratou Xeras* (A Study of the Development of the Professional Officer of the Army) (Greek General Staff, 1967); *Statistika Stexia Epi Ins Proeleusseos kai ton Senthikon Biabioseos ton Monumon Axiomatikon Stratou Xeras* (Statistical Study on the Origins and Social Characteristics of the Professional Officer of the Army) (Statistical Office of the Army, June 1969); Dimitrios Smorkovitis, *Kenoniologika Problemata Enoplon Denameon* (Sociological Problems of the Armed Forces) (unpublished dissertation, Panteos School of Political Science, Athens, Greece).

[31] *Meleti Tes Sxoles Evelpidon* (Study of the Army Military Academy), (Greek General Staff, 1974); Kourvetaris, op cit, pp 113 - 42.

Again, social mobility is a factor, but, in addition, these regions border neighbouring countries long hostile to Greece; so war, with its attendant chaos and devastation, arming and the use of weapons, may have become ways of life for the people in these regions. This, then, furnishes ample and active reason for young men to eye a military career.

Since the officer corps is recruited from the rural areas, we may also infer that they tend to come from rather humble circumstances, and, if so, a career as an officer does serve as a vehicle for social mobility otherwise unavailable to them. One's father's occupation is utilised as a criterion to measure social origin and may also be employed as an indicator for locating an officer's parents at some point on the social pyramid. Farmers and bureaucrat-tradesmen produce the largest percentage of all officers in the Greek Armed Forces, which is another indication of the aforementioned social mobility. The naval officers tend to come from the older wealthier families, the highest social base of recruitment, which coincides with our previous statement.

Another aspect of social origin is the proportion of military officers who have entered the profession through self-recruitment, i.e. who are the sons of professional officers. The percentage of self-recruitment in the Navy is 23.9 per cent, while the extent of self-recruitment for the Army is 11 per cent and 4 per cent for the Air Force. The Air Force's relatively small percentage of self-recruitment may reflect the fact that it is a fairly new service, as compared to the Army and Navy, and has not had the advantage of time to develop self-recruitment patterns.

Non-commissioned officers (NCOs) are divided into two groups—command and technical. They are recruited from the ranks of enlisted men for the Army and the Air Force. The Navy has the Poros Training School which selects youngsters (ages 10 -16) and educates them: upon graduation they receive a high school diploma and enlist in the Navy for 12 years as petty officers. Of the three Services, the Army suffers a serious shortage of NCO personnel. Part of this shortage is the unattractiveness of the Army as a career and the lack of financial rewards. Generally speaking, in the Greek Armed Forces professional expertise is not recognised in the ranks of NCOs.

Career NCOs have the opportunity of being promoted to warrant officers (WOs). These are also divided into two groups—command WOs and technical WOs. The number of command WOs that may be promoted to 2nd lieutenants in the Army cannot exceed one-fifth of the number of cadets graduating from the military academy (usually 25 - 30 annually). Technical WOs are promoted to 2nd lieutenants in the Army as vacancies occur (usually 35 - 40 annually). Compulsory military service varies among the Services: Army - 22 months; Navy - 26 months; Air Force - 24 months.[32]

Since the rapid post-1974 expansion of the Armed Forces, the number of young men entering military service has not been adequate to meet requirements, due to a birth rate that has been static for years. Accordingly, the Greek government mandated under Public Law 705 and 1977 to conscript women between the ages of 20 and 32 (prior to this time they were restricted to the Nurses Corps) into non-combatant roles of all Services. The first women completed their training in March 1979. By the end of 1980 approximately 1800 women entered service. At the moment, women cannot enter the officer corps except as nurses.

Ranks follow the British system, and uniforms have been very similar to the British in colour and design. Recently, however, an army officer's uniform, more American in style, has been introduced.

A distinctive visual element in the Greek Army is the Presidential guards or Evzones. Consisting of two companies, they wear the traditional mountain dress—tasselled cap, embroidered waistcoat and pleated skirt, known as the *foustanella*.

CONCLUSIONS

To be sure, much has changed since the April 1967 *coup d'état* some 13 years ago. The Greek military's image has been tarnished by its mismanagement of affairs during the dictatorship.

The norm of civilian supremacy is not as firmly rooted in the officer corps (trained and educated by American and NATO officers) as it is elsewhere in Western Europe, although the likelihood of renewed military intervention in politics is quite low at the moment, and the officer corps today seems thoroughly loyal to the present constitutional régime. However, it is within the realm of possibility that military intervention may rise again over the longer term. If such an event did occur, it would be due to the re-emergence of the kind of political chaos that existed in the mid-1960s. Should Greek politics again polarise and create a powerful leftist force (of which the 1977 election gave some hint), then it is conceivable that the military will again inject themselves into the political arena. Already such signs are now appearing on

---

[32] *The Government Gazette,* 12 April 1979.

the horizon. The parliamentary elections scheduled for 1981 will
be quite telling. By all present indications the popularity of Andreas Papandreou and PASOK is at an all time high. Should his
party prove successful and win a parliamentary majority (alone or
in coalition), the military's interest in politics will be greatly
heightened and hastened.

Several major issues of strategic and military importance — i.e.
Cyprus and the Aegean Sea — are still unresolved. Greece's return
to the military wing of NATO in the long run may be a hollow
victory for the Alliance. Papandreou's ideas about moving Greece
into the non-aligned sphere, removing Greece from NATO and
severing its military linkages with the United States would create
great consternation for the officer corps. Such policies are laden
with great risks for any Greek government, but most especially
one that leans toward the left of centre. If history is any indicator,
then there is no reason to believe that the cycle of intervention
and withdrawal has yet been finally and decisively broken in the
civil-military relations of Greece.

The Japanese Arms Industry, 1981: An Assessment

I P S G COSBY

Mr. Cosby is a Reserve Officer in the Royal Hong Kong Regiment (The Volunteers) and is currently lecturing at Aichi University, Japan

THE arms industry in Japan is becoming a subject of interest at a time when the Japanese are being encouraged by their allies to improve the capabilities of their armed services. By drawing attention to the peculiarities of the industry and to certain changes likely to affect its development, an attempt can be made to assess what can be expected of the industry during the next few years.

It is important to stress how most Japanese still regard with deep suspicion anything which might precipitate a return of pre-war militarism. It is this, not fear of invasion or commercial opportunism, which is the overriding concern when considering matters affecting the country's defence. By taking this order of priority as a premise, it becomes easier to understand the inherent difficulty of developing an arms industry in Japan, but, more importantly, to appreciate how much effort is being made to assume greater military responsibilities in Asia.

ORGANISATION

Hostility towards rearmament affects the arms industry in so far as the government imposes restrictions on what weapons may be manufactured and on how much money will be available for procurements. Although there is no law to prevent the sale of armaments abroad, it has also been customary to prohibit it. Ministry of International Trade and Industry (MITI) guidelines exist to define what equipment related to defence may be exported. Automobiles, for example, will be approved for export, regardless of whether they will be supplied to the armed forces of the importers' country. Items which are clearly components will be withheld, but military equipment, which is not for combat, such as a fighter simulator or an auxiliary ship, will be dealt with

50

on a case-by-case basis. In practice, if the importer can reasonably demonstrate that the equipment is for civilian purposes, an export licence will be granted in accordance with a principle of the country's foreign exchange law that with three exceptions cargo be exported freely. Whatever the restrictions it is inevitable that some products will be found as components in weapons manufactured abroad, although it is not so easy to dismiss the construction at Vladivostok of a ¥13-billion floating dock which has since been used to service the Russian aircraft carrier *Minsk*. Although the Swedish International Peace Institute has reported to the contrary, there is for all intents and purposes no exportation of armaments.

Since there is no export trade, the arms industry is confined to supplying the needs of the Japan Self-Defence Force (JSDF). As a result, weapon production runs are short and costly, with a small margin for profit. During the period of fast economic growth in the 1960s and early 1970s, therefore, industrialists showed little interest in the trade. One notable feature of the industry is the length of time it takes to develop and manufacture a weapon which may be approaching obsolescence by the time it is deployed. The reasons for this can be attributed to a shortage of funds and technology at the outset, and to priority being given to the other non-military projects. But an important contribution to delay may also be the system of piecemeal manufacture which results from farming out production to a large number of subsidiary companies.

It has been convenient to write of the Japanese arms industry as if it were a clearly defined entity consisting of manufacturers whose sole or main function is weapon production. In this sense the Japanese arms industry is almost non-existent. Except in certain marginal areas, there are no companies whose main preoccupation is arms production. Nor is there a government-managed enterprise like the Royal Ordnance Factory in the United Kingdom. On the contrary, all weapons are manufactured as a subsidiary venture by private companies, using facilities that most managers feel could be put to more profitable use. Mitsubishi Heavy Industry, for example, the largest single manufacturer of weapons in Japan, relies on weapon sales for only 8 per cent of its sales. This compares with over 60 per cent for some of the major manufacturers in the United States. The total value of contracts has also been small, amounting to Y 460 billion in 1980, and in 1978 accounted for only 0.38 per cent of total industrial output. One exception to this as a feature of the industry is that arms contracts account for about 86 per cent of the aircraft industry's turnover.

Although the arms industry is relatively small in relation to industry as a whole, a disproportionately large percentage of all contracts go to a very few companies, who admittedly then farm out the business. Nevertheless, overall control resides with the principal contractor. There are 2270 companies presently registered as arms suppliers, but 80 per cent of the business goes to less than ten companies as compared with approximately 35 per cent in the United States. The Mitsubishi Group alone handled about one-third of the business in 1978.

The types of weapon that may be manufactured have also been subject to restriction. The National Defence Programme Outline of 1976 stated that weapons that constitute an offensive threat would be prohibited, and then listed types. What is of interest here is that as the performance of a type of weapon is improved, but at a rate inconsistent with progress made in other types of weapon, what might once have been reasonably defined as offensive has now become essential for defence. The effect therefore of making the distinction is to impose on the choice of weapons for service with the JSDF a certain built-in factor of obsolescence, which helps account for this being a feature of some Japanese equipment.

Apart from the political, there are financial restrictions, which in the event are likely to prove more difficult to circumvent. A first priority for the government is to control the phenomenal growth since 1974 in government bonds which will account for 26 per cent of revenue in the 1981 budget, making bond servicing, at ¥6.6 trillion, one of the two largest items of expenditure, besides grants to local government. While this deficit will be met in part by an increase in taxation, it can be appreciated that a rise sufficient to reduce the imbalance to manageable levels will be out of the question. It can be expected, therefore, that strict limits will be applied for some time to come on what funds will be available to the Defence Agency to spend on armaments.

Between 1955 - 70 the ratio of defence spending to the total of the General Account dropped sharply from 13.6 per cent to 7.2 per cent since when it has continued to drift down to reach the present figure of 5.2 per cent, following much the same pattern as for expenditure on education and the promotion of science. This can be explained by the high priority given to building up social services and infrastructure to a level comparable to those of other developed countries. Those standards have now been reached and one would expect in future a certain readjustment of priorities. The Ministry of Finance has so far succeeded in keeping to a minimum any compromise on its draconian measures to prevent any large-scale increase in public expenditure during 1981, with the result that expenditure on weapon procurements will amount to only ¥458 billion in 1981.

Opposition to any extraordinary increase in defence expenditure is not confined to the Ministry of Finance. That faction of the Liberal Democratic Party (LDP), which used to be led by Masayoshi Ohira, is still strongly imbued with the pacifism of Shigeru Yoshida, and its members are reluctant to show undue sympathy for the Defence Agency's financial problems or for relaxation of the conventions restricting the arms trade.

UNITED STATES - JAPAN COOPERATION

A particular feature of the Japanese arms industry is the extent of its ties with its counterpart in the United States, and derives from the peculiar circumstances in which the former was revived during the Korean War. The procurements boom, which resulted from supplying and servicing USF equipment not only resuscitated the arms industry, but was instrumental in getting Japan's post-war economic recovery underway. However, the main demand for weapons came following a decision to convert the National Police Reserve into an armed National Defence Force in 1952. Two years later a Mutual Defence Assistance Agreement was signed, enabling the force now renamed the JSDF to be supplied with American equipment, much of which was surplus World War II stock and had to be modified in Japan. Another factor consolidating the close relationship has been the importance the Japanese Government attaches to smooth functioning of the US Security Treaty, which in practice means close cooperation on arms procurement. With the subsequent formation of the Security Consultative Committee and production of the 'Guidelines for Japan - US Defence Coordination' in 1978, the trend towards standardisation of equipment has intensified. A product of this trend has been the formation of a committee which meets biannually to discuss technical problems arising from weapon production. If the argument for standardisation is taken to its logical conclusion, both forces should be equipped with the same weapons. Any tendency in this direction is going to favour an American product since in terms of cost effectiveness, apart from any technological superiority, the Japanese product is usually uncompetitive.

Two phenomena during the 1970s have had a significant effect on the relationship between the two industries. During the fourth Year Plan (1972 - 76), it was usual for Japanese tenders for contracts to lose in favour of their American competitors. This may have been due to a policy, later explained in the 1976 Defence Outline, to carry out as cheaply as possible, without upsetting service morale, the minimum improvements necessary to keep abreast of technological developments elsewhere. However, the situation changed somewhat when the US Government reversed its policy of allowing force levels to decline after the Vietnam War. American industry, which had been adjusting to the run down, now found itself unable to meet the sudden change of demand, with the result that the Americans have been looking to Japanese industry to meet the shortfall for equipment of a non-combatant nature. This may in part account for a recent change in the Pentagon's procurement policy, which will in future permit Japanese companies to supply front-line forces much as manufacturers in NATO countries do.

One important feature of the Japanese arms industry, which has developed from this close association, has been the tendency to rely on importation or on manufacturing under licence, for advanced technology. Reasons for not participating whole-heartedly in the technology race have been expense, small profit margins, the difficulty of catching up with leading arms producers abroad and the ease with which American weapons and licensing arrangements have been available. But another reason has been a reluctance on the part of Japanese manufacturers, themselves aware of the widespread aversion in Japan to the manufacture of armaments, to be seen pioneering weapon technology. There has, therefore, been a relatively low priority attached to the need for self-sufficiency. As a result the industry has in some cases missed out on a complete generation of weapon production, which has meant that there is now a marked gap between the technology available and that required to produce the kind of weapons the JSDF needs. Should the country now wish to become self-sufficient, it will only be able to do so at immense cost.

An interesting characteristic of the industry is the close liaison achieved between the Defence Agency, the Services, and the manufacturers, which contrasts with the latter's lack of interest in the industry as an area for business. That there has been such a marked degree of cooperation may be attributed to Japanese ethos, and a well understood client/profession relationship. But it derives also from a tendency among serving officers to transfer on retirement to a company associated with the manufacture of weapons. As a result, there is at a personal level a clear appreciation of the requirements and limitations of the parties concerned. It is usual practice for the Defence Agency to make over *in toto* its procurement and R&D funds to private industry, and treat projects as a kind of joint venture. The Agency largely confines itself to measuring standards of performance and to making selections. The responsibility for innovating design and testing, besides actual production, usually rests with the manufacturer. Where there is controversy, it is pecuniary, and usually concerns the margin of profit allowed, which in theory is about 5 per cent.

Two bodies, in particular, help to coordinate and promote the interests of the industry. The first is the Defence Production Committee of the Federation of Economic Organisations (Keidanren), whose members are drawn from the senior ranks of industry. The aims of the committee are to achieve maximum self-sufficiency, to improve the quality of weapons and to promote interest. The other body is the Technical Research and Development Institute, which operates within the Defence Agency, to coordinate work done in R&D and equipment to be supplied to the services.

RECENT DEVELOPMENTS

Having outlined some of its main features, it will be seen from what follows that the arms industry is entering a certain transitional phase. The government, largely reacting to the growth of Russian military power in the region, seems to be changing its policy on matters affecting the industry, and in doing so is reflecting a perceptible change in popular antipathy to the manufacture of armaments in Japan. Partly because of this change of attitude, but also for purely economic reasons, industrialists are beginning to take a much more positive interest in developing the arms industry.

While it is beyond the scope of this article to analyse the extent and reasons for the change taking place in public opinion, it is important to note that change, since what is perceived to be public opinion will not only affect the attitude of industrialists but is the basis upon which political action is at least justified, if not taken.

A significant development that is likely to affect the arms industry was a decision taken in October 1980 to define again what weapons are excluded by the Constitution. Instead of making a distinction between offensive and defensive weapons, now only weapons that are capable of totally destroying another country will be excluded. Any reference to the type of weapon has been carefully avoided. Although Japan's adherence to its three non-nuclear principles has been unequivocally reaffirmed, as have its obligations as a signatory to the Nuclear Non-Proliferation Treaty, it was stated categorically in answer to a parliamentary question that possession of nuclear weapons was not unconstitutional. A distinction was then made between strategic, theatre and tactical nuclear weapons, but not as to which, if not all, would be excluded under the new definition. The inference clearly is that provision has been made to permit the use of tactical nuclear weapons in due course should the need arise.

It also seems that the principle of 'basic and balanced defence power' is at least being qualified if not abandoned. When used in the 1976 National Defence Outline Programme this principle was understood to mean the minimum defence capability practicable. In contrast the 1980 Defence White Paper has stressed that since it takes a comparatively long time to build up a capability to meet a sudden worsening of a situation, it would be prudent to take due precautionary measures. The inference here is that a capability somewhat greater than that to meet the circumstances of the moment is needed. Even the Foreign Ministry, in a Blue Paper published in August 1980, drew attention to the fact that the concept, 'minimum force required for defence,' had now become, 'an appropriate capacity for defence'.

Another significant development during the last year has been the Foreign Ministry's change of policy on defence. It had been policy to play down both the extent of the Russian threat and the need to improve Japan's defence, which would have been contrary to an overall policy of maintaining a position of equidistance between the Great Powers. But now, and it can probably be attributed mainly to the Russian invasion of Afghanistan, the Ministry's policy appears to be that independence, which was fundamental to the former policy of equidistance, is more likely to be attained if Japan is rather more independent in defence. It can be expected that this reconciliatory move on the part of the Foreign Ministry will do much to diminish the antipathy toward rearmament.

Two clear pointers exist to show that there has been a change of attitude on defence. First are the references in the 1980 Defence White Paper to the effect that Japan is required to make a contribution to the maintenance of international peace, to increasing its own defences in a manner commensurate with its actual strength and to seeing that, in its arrangements with US forces, a power vacuum is not allowed to occur. Second, is the decision to exempt the Defence Agency from the maximum limit imposed on all other government departments for increasing budgetary appropriations. Although the extent of the exemption actually allowed will be less than Japan's allies had come to expect, an important principle and precedent have been established.

As mentioned, there has recently been a change in the attitude of industrialists. But enthusiasm for developing the arms industry has not been confined to the leaders of industry; in July 1980 the Japan Junior Chamber of Commerce, which has 54,000 members under 40 years of age, adopted two resolutions advocating that the Constitution should not be allowed to impinge on the country's ability to defend itself, and that defences be increased as necessary.

There are certain commercial reasons to explain this change of attitude. In the first place many manufacturers find their facilities for producing armaments are greatly under-used, and if used to capacity could produce weapons much more economically. Being a registered arms supplier has certain advantages; it is understood that if a company produces something required for national security, the government will see that the company survives a recession. For this reason registered arms suppliers usually enjoy better credit ratings with the banks. It is also thought to enhance a company's reputation in foreign markets. Be that as it may, realistic appreciations suggest that sooner or later the arms industry must expand. There is little doubt, too, that some firms take what is known in the trade as a 'flying start', which means that a company will try to produce something potentially very useful, which the Defence Agency will be bound to commission.

As regards trading in armaments the point is made that an increase in production would reduce costs and so the burden placed on taxpayers. Athough not particularly apt, the argument is sometimes heard that arms be exported in exchange for oil, and the French arms trade is quoted to show that it need not adversely affect a country's international trade in other commodities. Certainly as manufacturers become more confident of the performance of their weapons they will not be averse to comparing their market potential with foreign products. The element of contradiction in a policy which forbids export but permits the import of weapons has not gone entirely amiss. Whether or not exports are ever allowed, as the Japanese economy begins to assume a pattern of lower growth and has to rely more on domestic demand than on export trade to stimulate growth, defence spending is likely to be seen as a useful source of demand. The arms industry is also attractive in that it is relatively unaffected by cyclical changes in the economy and world trade, being subject to its own market factors. Furthermore, as already inferred, the trade is monopolistic in character, whether it is the government as sole buyer, or the manufacturer as sole supplier of a special product. As a result the trade enjoys safe if not high profit margins, a point that was brought home to the shipping industry during the recent recession.

But the most compelling reason for the growing interest in the arms trade is that it is believed to call for a high degree of technology. As the other industrialised economies of north-east Asia, particularly those of Taiwan and South Korea, become more competitive in the 'bulk' secondary industries, which require much energy but relatively little technology, it becomes essential for the Japanese economy to be based mainly on technologically advanced manufacturing. The situation is serious because the industries most threatened—shipping, crude steel, and motor-cars—are the three mainstays of the economy. It is hoped, therefore, that 'spin-off' derived from the arms industry would be instrumental in making the necessary transition.

The Japanese arms industry, for the reasons mentioned, is not particularly noted for its technology, but there is every reason for believing that much more will be spent on developing technology than hitherto. Not only was technology relatively cheap to buy, there was a tendency for foreign companies to short-sell it. Besides being afraid of early obsolescence, or piracy of their patent, it was tempting to make a quick profit without going to the expense of marketing a product. However, because of the Japanese penchant for manufacturing a more competitive product with the technology gained, it has now become much more difficult to come by. There are several areas in the manufacture of aircraft, for example, where the American companies concerned refuse absolutely to disclose information, and where joint ventures are negotiated on a take-it-or-leave-it basis. It is no longer unusual for a foreign company to refuse to participate in a joint venture unless it is confident of being at least 5 years ahead in its technology.

Although the Japanese lag behind in some significant areas, such as in gas-turbine engines, some aspects of metallurgy and in electronic countermeasures, they have largely caught up in others, as in fire-control systems and short-range missiles. As the process of catching up continues, not only will there be less incentive to buy foreign, but also foreign manufacturers seeking a joint venture will find they have fewer bargaining counters than before. In some quarters the opinion is expressed that in the world at large progress in research and development has been stagnating to the extent that Japan can no longer rely on being able to import technology.

The situation in Japan regarding R&D is unique in that it is undertaken for the most part by private industry, which provided 71.9 per cent of the finance in 1980 for natural science research. When the government does participate in a project the aim is to help realise a programme whose costs and risks are too great for a private company to handle rather than to influence or control the project. It can be expected that much more will be spent on research than hitherto. The government has undertaken to give a lead, and in a report published by MITI in 1979 (August) proposed to raise the money spent to 3 per cent of GNP by 1990, and the government share of expenditure to 50 per cent. It is perhaps significant that the declared motives for encouraging R&D are to promote economic growth and to assist negotiations in international trade. Given that there will be greater emphasis on research, it is important to the arms industry to know how it will be spent. The government, however, has decided that priority will be given to new sources of energy, high-speed transportation and to developing electronics in the consumer and labour-intensive industries.

Conclusions that can be drawn from the foregoing are, first, that the often held opinion that Japanese are adept at improving upon known technology but are dependent on others for innovations, may prove untrue as industry starts investing in research rather more than hitherto. Secondly, although the government may spend more on research, the emphasis will be on enhancing the competitiveness of the economy, not on security. As a result the amount spent on improving armaments may be somewhat less than one would otherwise expect. Thirdly, since the emphasis will be on making progress in areas of commercial interest, it may well be a question (with certain notable exceptions, e.g. the aircraft industry) of the arms industry having to borrow 'spin-off' from civil industry, as was the case in the wiring for the 'heavy Mat' missile, and not the reverse. In any event, if the arms industry is to make any significant contribution to technological progress, rather more than the present figure of 1 per cent of the Defence

Budget (14 per cent in the United Kingdom) will have to be spent on R&D.

FUTURE POSSIBILITIES

Whatever the reasons for wanting to expand the arms industry and possibly develop a foreign trade, there are also grounds for hesitation. To begin with the mass-production argument must be qualified. It is not unusual for extensive remodelling to be done to suit the particular requirements of a customer, but also the disparity in price between the domestic and the foreign model is so great that it is questionable whether even the most optimistic degree of mass production could significantly reduce the differential. Secondly, even if the Japanese product is proved to be technically superior under test conditions, until it is exported it will continue to suffer from the disadvantage of not having been proved in active service conditions. Although it can certainly be argued that there has been a certain change in public opinion, there is still sufficient residual antipathy to the idea of trading in armaments for manufacturers to conclude that the threat of adverse public criticism would not be worth the risk. There are also doubts about how much technology would be available in practice for commercial use. Not only is much of it likely to be classified, but being designed for a specific purpose, it may have limited application elsewhere. Private industry is also likely to question the value of devoting valuable resources to improving weaponry instead of developing more profitable commercial interests. It has also been argued that more progress is made in developing technology as a result of the competitive conditions which prevail in civil industry, than is the case when serving a public body such as the Defence Agency.

In the wider context of international trade there are doubts that even if a limited trade in armaments were to develop, it would create customer commitments that would force the government to compromise its policy of pursuing as nearly as possible an impartial and non-interventionist role in foreign affairs. There is concern, too, at what adverse affect expanding the arms industry would have on the market for other products, particularly in Asia. It is feared an increase in arms production would be evidence that Japan was about to assume a more dominant military role in the region, and thereby arouse dormant but not quite forgotten fears of Japanese militarism. There is concern that Asian countries having been content to allow extensive penetration of their respective economies in the certain knowledge that Japan had no military ambitions in the area, may now reconsider the position. On this issue, the Japanese appear to be more sensitive than their neighbours. Partly because of the deep concern felt everywhere in Asia at the continuous growth in Russian military strength, and partly as a result of long exposure to Japanese commercialism, popular aversion to Japan is disappearing. Rather it is increasingly being relied upon to represent Asian interests and to service local needs. In so far as there is concern, it is that funds which would otherwise have been allocated to development aid may now be spent on rearmament. Generally there is cautious optimism that Japan is discarding its pacifist policy in favour of close cooperation with its neighbours to assume due responsibility for security in the region. If asked to comment on what is the Asian attitude to Japanese rearmament, it may not be far wide of the mark to say that if the Japanese remain pacifist in deference to Asian sensibilities about their militarism, and in the event Japan's strength is not brought to bear to contain a common danger, the Japanese will not be thanked for their pacifisms. But if their actual military forces are of sufficient strength to be seen to be effectively deterring foreign aggression, the traditional fear of Japanese militarism will be forgotten.

From the foregoing it should be possible to deduce what may be the trends in the arms industry during the next few years. It will be seen that, unlike in the past, high priority will be given to being self-sufficient, a trend that will be encouraged by a growing scarcity of foreign technology; to some extent by more being spent on R&D and by the fact that arms production will increasingly be seen as a measure of the country's state of advance and independence. Although this new stress on self-sufficiency is likely to persist, there is reason to believe it will be qualified. In the first place finance, whether in terms of funds at Defence Agency disposal or in terms of the cost of domestic weapons, will be a restraining influence. Although there is reason to believe the limit of 1 per cent GNP will soon be breached, if the order of priorities that determined allocations for the 1981 budget are any guide, it can be reasonably concluded that the Defence Agency is not going to get the funds it needs to re-equip the JSDF adequately, purchasing the most economic weapons on the market, let alone expensive Japanese ones. The probable formula for deciding on whether or not to buy a domestic weapon will be that if the domestic weapon has reached the production stage after a long and expensive period of development it will be bought even if it is not in the class of the latest weapons of its type on the market. But, if there is likely to be a long indeterminate period of research ahead, then further development will be deferred in favour of importing or assembling under licence. An important factor to be taken into account when deciding whether or not to import will be the state of the exporting country's balance of payments with Japan. Importing arms is likely to be seen as a convenient way of alleviating possible pessure on the manufacturers of civil products to reduce their exports if the balance is strongly in Japan's favour.

Two factors which will continue to make domestically produced weapons expensive will be the cost of trying to narrow the wide technological gap and not being able to defray costs over production lines longer than those needed to supply the JSDF. Despite the fairly wide interest shown in Japanese weapons, it can be assumed there will be no export trade for the time being. Even if the restrictions were removed, price, relative obsolescence and slow rates of production are likely to be disqualifying factors. The most competitive weapons are likely to be those which could be deployed in a theatre of war which did not require the latest technology so much as reliability, and where price was not an overriding consideration.

Although there may be no immediate change of policy on exporting armaments, there may well be a more liberal interpretation of what constitutes armaments. One significant development in this respect, and assisted by the recent change in the Pentagon's procurement policy, has been a noticeable growth in the trade of strategic metals and products indirectly related to the manufacture of armaments.

A major restraint on becoming self-sufficient will be the policy of coordinating ever more closely with the United States on defence, which will tend to favour outright purchase of American equipment. Even when opportunities for joint development arise, the usual experience for the Japanese manufacturer has been to come in as a junior partner, and for the 'black box' material, which primarily interests the Japanese, not to be made available. The prospects of building up a domestic industry using information gained from bilateral ventures, is, therefore, very limited. It is possible that in the present circumstances with the US government exerting what pressure it can on the Japanese to spend more on defence, it may be willing to release more classified information. However, much of this information will be withheld by the companies concerned, as they will refuse to divulge trade secrets.

Although understandable, it is a moot point whether it is in

Japan's best interests strategically to insist too strongly on self-sufficiency. The country's vulnerability is the concentration of its industries along a narrow exposed belt on the Pacific coast; quite apart from the expense of defending it adequately, the greater the degree of self-sufficiency the greater will Japan's security and supply of weapons depend on keeping the belt intact. However if the weapons used by the JSDF can be supplied also from elsewhere, not only will the advantages of diversification apply, but also, although it would increase dependence on lines of communication, access to Japan is sufficiently diverse that arguably it would be more difficult to impose a total embargo on supplies than it would be to destroy the country's essential industry.

A more immediate criticism concerns Service morale. Given that the JSDF has a not undeserved reputation for employing equipment that is frequently quite inadequate, and given the peculiar difficulty of attracting recruits in Japan, keeping morale high becomes more than ever important. The task becomes immeasurably more difficult if it is known that better equipment is available at lower cost. Whatever may be the provisioners' preference, the weapon's operator is primarily concerned with its performance, not its place of origin.

One solution to the problems of short production lines, the dearth of technology, the insufficient funding, the vulnerability of industry strategically and the desire to make a constructive contribution to maintaining international peace, would be to participate in multinational consortia for the construction of weapons. Little thought appears to have been given to the idea on the grounds that it might be unconstitutional. But it is questionable whether this would be so if at least part of the weaponry was produced specifically for the JSDF. Participation in the multinational venture would be in Japanese interests in several respects. It would improve the chances of negotiating a more equitable partnership, would give Japan greater access to a variety of sources of technology, enable the JSDF to be equipped with more advanced weaponry at a fraction of the cost of trying to do so alone and might even be seen by Japan's allies as a convenient way for Japan to make a contribution to security without compromising the Constitution. It would also help achieve the standardisation sought without surrendering wholesale to importation or to unsatisfactory licensing.

Given that participation in a multinational project is practicable, what Japan could provide of interest to the other partners would be efficient production methods, a high degree of quality control, an additional entrée into Asian markets, in some cases technology, and capital. The Japanese partner, on the other hand, will be looking for testing facilities, an equitable partnership, joint sharing and development of technology, and an advanced weapon for deployment with the JSDF.

The unknown factor besetting a multinational venture involving Japan is the likely consensus of opinion to the idea in Japan itself. As mentioned, public feeling is becoming increasingly sympathetic to the need to equip the JSDF adequately. If a project could be justified on the grounds that it would save substantial expenditure on defence, would deter the formation of a powerful armaments cartel within Japan, would alleviate what is seen for a developed country as an embarrassing dependence on importation and would show that Japan was no longer taking its 'free ride', and once it begins to dawn on people, first, that Japan's neighbours—far from being apprehensive—are now expecting Japan to increase its military strength, and, secondly, that the present urgent need to improve Japan's military strength bears no resemblance to pre-war militarism, arguably the consensus of opinion would be favourable. In the last analysis the decision will be a political one. Although the number of present cabinet members sympathetic to the problems of security, and the extent to which the opposition parties in Japan are having to re-evaluate their policy of opposition to rearmament, may be cause for optimism, it is important not to underestimate either the pacifist tendency still evident in some factions of LDP, or the importance which the present administration attaches to government by consensus, which means that there will be more concern to accommodate the opposition than its small size would appear to justify.

When deciding how to procure arms, the decisive factors must surely be the most efficient weapons at a price the economy can afford and with the best chance of being re-supplied. In conclusion suffice it to say that when commercial friction threatens to estrange Japan from its allies, experience suggests that co-operation in defence to meet a common threat promises to be one of those areas where there will be a large measure of mutual understanding.

POSTSCRIPT

Since writing the above article there have been two developments affecting the Japanese arms industry. First, it was discovered that a number of firms, but principally Hotta Hagane,

Osaka (not a member of the Japan Ordnance Association) had since 1976 been exporting semi-finished parts of weapons to South Korea and Taiwan. Major items included 800 barrels (euphemistically called 'seamless steel piping') worth Y750 million for trench mortars and howitzers, and 30 tons of SNCM steel, 6.35 mm thick, which was thought to have been intended for tank armour. Following these discoveries an appeal was made in some business and political quarters to relax the Miki rulings on arms exports as they appeared to be unduly prejudicing the export of certain general purpose items. But in the main the opinion of business leaders was that on balance it is not in Japan's interest to encourage an arms trade, and that this was an isolated case serving only to give the arms industry a bad reputation. However, there was concern that no more restrictive legislation be introduced to prevent the export of arms as enforcement would be disproportionately costly, and threatened to upset the flow of exports especially in the electronics, computer and steel industries. In the event the government resisted Opposition proposals to impose a total ban and instead tried to stop what was seen as a possible loophole in existing regulations by extending the ban to include semi-finished products designed exclusively for military use. A watch-dog committee comprising MITI and Ministry of Finance officials was set up to help detect future infringements.

The second development concerned a government decision to allow Japanese companies to build military installations overseas. This effectively projects Japanese companies at present constructing naval/air facilities at Lumut, Diego Garcia and at Subic Bay.

Merchant Shipping and the Maritime Threat

H G DAVY

Mr H G Davy, MBE, is the Director responsible for Defence affairs at the General Council of British Shipping

THE phrase 'We are an island nation' once immediately evoked patriotic outbursts about its implications, not least in defence terms. Nowadays it is treated as a statement of the obvious, of a fact of life with which we must live and to which no special considerations need apply. A few moments thought will, however, bring a somewhat changed reaction.

There is the fact that we still import some 93 per cent (by weight) of our requirements by sea, that the EEC imports about 60 per cent of its requirements by sea and that 98.2 mn tons of goods move between the United Kingdom and the Community annually by sea. There is, of course, also our trade with other NATO partners.

A conflict in Europe would necessitate massive supply and re-supply of men and military equipment from the United States and there would be the need to sustain fortress Europe under siege with the food and essentials of life for civilians as well as troops, quite apart from home production of military supplies. In world defence terms one must add the consideration that major hostilities centred elsewhere than in Europe will surely necessitate extended lines of communication in which merchant shipping will play a major part.

Then there is our experience during two world wars. Looking at the United Kingdom alone, between 1914 and 1918 we lost 7.7 mn grt. Between 1939 and 1945 we lost 11.4 mn grt (2570 ships) and over 30,000 merchant seamen. In 1942 the Allies lost over 6.0 mn grt of shipping—1160 ships all by submarine attack.

These factors surely underline the implications of the position of the United Kingdom and the dependence which it and, indeed, Europe must place on adequate maritime communications. They demonstrate also the vulnerability of these lines of communication to attack at sea, especially from submarines.

THE SIZE OF OUR MERCHANT FLEET

The United Kingdom, and for that matter most of its Allies, cannot afford to sustain a merchant fleet of a size and composition entirely suitable to military or other wartime requirements. Allied merchant fleets have to live in an increasingly competitive international environment, and thus the size of merchant fleets and their composition must reflect the basic economic considerations and ship types. We Allies are competing with each other and the United Kingdom must certainly keep in the lead in developing specialist ships necessary to achieve the maximum economic potential which, in turn, can require specialist port facilities. The growing trend towards specialist ships (e.g. containers) and specialist port facilities involves extreme vulnerability in war. So a very relevant factor is the size and composition of our merchant fleet and that of the other members of NATO.

In 1939 the United Kingdom owned 27 per cent of the world tonnage. By 1950 that figure was 21 per cent; now it is about 6 per cent. But the UK merchant fleet remains comparatively large — we are still fourth in the world league table. Much of it is normally engaged in cross-trading, which is, of course, of tremendous value to the nation in terms of invisible exports. In 1979 UK-owned merchant ships contributed £1139 mn (net) to the UK balance of payments.

It is not only the British merchant fleet which has changed in size, so too have most of our NATO partners. The tables at the end of this article indicate what has happened in general terms. The following tables summarise developments regarding some specific types of ship.

GENERAL CARGO

	1971		1975		1980		Change	
	Ships	dwt /000	Ships	dwt /000	Ships	dwt /000	Ships	dwt /000
UK	1356	8889	1086	6508	830	4374	−526	−4515
Greece	1330	7955	1514	9629	2041	15,521	+711	+7566
USA	1042	10,393	558	5850	446	5057	−596	−5336
Balance of NATO	6062	20,676	4756	16,398	4043	14,630	−2019	−6046
Total NATO	9790	47,913	7914	38,385	7360	39,582	−2430	−8331
USSR	1507	7900	1757	9494	1793	9929	+286	+2092

CELLULAR CONTAINER

	1971		1975		1980		Change	
	Ships	dwt /000	Ships	dwt /000	Ships	dwt /000	Ships	dwt /000
UK	51	647	91	1242	74	1529	+ 23	+ 882
Greece	—	—	4	44	7	43	+ 7	+ 43
USA	75	1054	103	1628	87	1572	+ 12	+ 518
Balance of NATO	60	613	78	1211	116	2757	+ 56	+ 2144
Total NATO	182	2314	276	4125	284	5901	+ 98	+ 3587
USSR	—	—	11	69	37	274	+ 37	+ 274

It is true that the Greek fleet has increased, much of the superior tonnage registered under flags of convenience is under the control of the United States or other NATO countries and could be expected to become available to NATO if required. But so far as the United Kingdom is concerned the trend in overall fleet size and certainly numbers of ships has been downward and must be kept under continual scrutiny. The size and composition of Free World merchant fleets is a matter of general concern because undesirable dependency on the fleets of others must be avoided.

THE SOVIET MERCHANT FLEET

Western shipowners have become increasingly concerned about the build-up of the Eastern Bloc, particularly the Soviet, fleet in the past few years. The Soviet fleet is now the sixth largest in the world with over 23 mn grt. It is not, however, the total size of the Soviet fleet which causes anxiety but that of the Soviet cargo liner fleet, which is now the largest in the world.

Already in the bilateral trades, Soviet shipping carries 78 per cent of imports and exports between the USSR and the United Kingdom and 75 per cent between the USSR and Western Germany and the USSR and Japan.

This is achieved by the manipulation of cargo to their own ships, by the use of cif (carriage - insurance - freight) sale/fob (free on board) purchase terms and by enforcing artificially low rates for such balance of general cargo as the ships of their trading partners and of third flags are permitted to carry.

British and other Western shipowners recognise the desire of COMECON countries to engage in international trades. On the liner side they are prepared to encourage Soviet lines to become conference members under normal conference criteria (e.g. taking account of traffic generated by the applicant's country, the number of cross-traders already in the conference, access by other members to the trade of the applicant's country, whether or not the whole conference trade is over-tonnaged and whether it is growing or diminishing). But in recent discussions with most conferences Soviet lines have made demands which are unreasonable by these criteria, having first established themselves as 'outsiders' by charging rates which are uneconomic by free market economy standards.

The Trans-Siberian Railway (TSR) is a special problem, not perhaps obvious from the viewpoint of maritime defence in a narrow sense. However, it carries as a transit operation 10 per cent of the high-quality containerised general cargo moving in both directions between Western Europe and the Far East: further TSR expansion, even up to a hypothetical 50 per cent of the traffic, is envisaged. More is said about this later.

FUNCTIONS AND ORGANISATION OF SOVIET MERCHANT SHIPPING

In the Soviet Union the division of functions between the merchant fleet and the Navy is less sharp than in the West. The Soviet commercial fleet appears to have at least five main functions and at any moment any particular ship may be serving more than one of these:

(i)   the transport of Soviet internal and external trade, the most important single function;

(ii)   the improvement of the Soviet Union's hard currency position, both by earning foreign currency in cross trades and also by reducing the need to import foreign shipping services in the Soviet Union's direct trades;

(iii) direct auxiliary support for the Soviet Navy, principally involving logistic support but also possibly involving mine laying and sabotage within enemy harbours during times of war;

(iv)   as an intelligence-gathering organisation;

(v)   the support of Soviet political objectives by facilitating trade, including the arms trade with Soviet allies.

Broadly speaking, there is a hierachy of organisation at three levels:

(i)   at the head is the Ministry of Merchant Marine in Moscow (MORFLOT);

(ii)   at the next level are the three state self-financing shipping corporations SEVZAPFLOT, YUZHFLOT and DALFLOT, which are responsible respectively for the North-west, South and Far East regions and are based at Leningrad, Odessa and Vladivostok;

(iii) the 17 individual shipping companies, divided 6, 6 and 5 to the 3 regional groupings in (ii) respectively.

However, despite these apparent differentiations and the overt delegation of responsibility, the important point about the Soviet Merchant Marine is that it is essentially a single, centralised whole. Personnel and ships are interchanged between the shipping companies and organisations. It is not fully clear where and at what level the main important decisions concerning investment in shipping and the allocation of ships to particular services are taken, but a decision at the top will always override the wishes of the lower organisms in the last resort (e.g. if an oceangoing roll-on/roll-off (ro/ro) ship has to be diverted from a hard-currency-earning cross trade to land military material at a client country's port).

USSR FLEET SIZE AND CARGO-CARRYING PATTERNS
— PRESENT AND FUTURE

Indications (admittedly in some ways ambiguous) about the Soviet next Five Year Plan suggest that its merchant fleet expansion will slow down a little in 1981 - 85. The main concern of the West, in terms purely of commercial fleet activity, will be the extent to which MORFLOT attempts to expand further its use of modern ocean-going liner-cargo tonnage in rate-undercutting competition against the established freight conferences worldwide.

For example:

1. Lloyd's Register figures in mn *grt,* for Soviet commercial plus other types, are as follows: July 1975, 19.2; July 1980, 23.4; an increase of 22 per cent. The Soviet Register's July 1980 figure of 22.1 mn grt roughly corresponds.

2. MORFLOT's own figures in mn *dwt,* for commercial tonnage only, are January 1976, 15.1, January 1981, 18.6, a rise by 23 per cent.

3. The 1976 - 80 commercial increase was 3.4 mn dwt, net of scrappings. This rise is supposedly to be 'halved' in 1981 - 85, to 1.8 mn. This would be a 10 per cent rise, roughly matching a recent Soviet declaration that fleet effort in ton/kilometre terms will increase 8 - 9 per cent in 1981 - 85.

MORFLOT tonnage increase forecasts by ship types contradict the 1.8 mn dwt increase and reach a *minimum* of 4.0 mn (tanker nil, dry-cargo multipurpose 0.6, container/ro -ro (ocean only) 0.5, dry-bulk 1.6, timber 1.0, ice class 0.3). But there could be less contradiction if any of the details by types are gross increases: Soviet statistical statements often leave one in such doubt.

4. Apart from ocean-going container/ro-ros, the fleet has shown no startling technological/vessel-size features in 1976 - 80: the present dry-bulk maximum size is 100,000 dwt, so-called Soviet 'super' tankers reach only 150,000 dwt (and there are only six of them). For 1981 - 85, there is no apparent present intention to continue with new tanker acquisitions beyond 60,000 dwt size. The general restrictions in vessel sizes would reflect general Soviet restraints, because of port draughts, on vessels operating in their national trade. It may be asked if there will be any new atomic ice-breakers beyond the present three: *Lenin* (running since 1959) could well soon need replacement. The Finns are to help, at least by building the hulls of new atomic breakers, but the first delivery date could be after 1985.

5. If planned 'doubling 1981 - 85 of the container/ro-ro fleet' is applied to ocean-going types alone, 40 ships totalling 500,000 dwt and 25,000 TEU* at end 1980 could become 60 - 65 ships, 1,000,000 dwt and 45/50,000 TEU at end 1985. It is difficult to forecast the additional tonnage/TEU rise of smaller types, e.g. for round-Europe, Soviet Far East/Japan - Hong Kong use.

6. The 22 - 23 per cent dwt fleet capacity rise in 1976 - 80 has been modest compared with a 43 per cent increase in seaborne USSR export/import trade volume (mainly bulk cargoes), from 140 mn t (1974) to 201 mn t (1979) by all flags. USSR coastal carriage is probably static around 75 - 80 mn t pa, and MORFLOT liftings in cross trade all types were up from 30 mn pa 1974 to 34 mn 1979 (latter probably 28 mn bulk, 6 mn liner). MORFLOT share of 1979 foreign trade of 120 mn - 201 mn all flags = 60 per cent. There has been at least one MORFLOT claim to have lifted 140 mn of 1979 foreign trade, not just 120 mn.

7. TSR. This railway presently carries about 100,000 loaded TEU annually between the United Kingdom/Western Europe

---

*TEU = 20-foot equivalent units, the standard indicator of container capacity.

and the Far East in both directions. This means 10 per cent of the combined total traffic—indeed the TSR carries 25 per cent of the Japan/Europe traffic. With marginal costs using an existing railway mainly serving domestic traffics, rates for transit containers are as much as 50 per cent below those of the Far Eastern Freight Conference (FEFC) lines, the traditional carriers. The declared Soviet long-term aim is to have by TSR a capacity to lift 50 per cent of the trade, especially once the new BAM railway in Eastern Siberia is completed about 1985. The problem for FEFC lines is compounded by the fact that MORFLOT is also serving their Western Europe/Far East trade by a non-conference service of modern cellular container vessels via the normal wholly seaborne route through Suez.

8. The Soviet merchant fleet's expansion will slow down a little in general terms, on overt evidence which is in some ways ambiguous. The West's main concern will be caused by the forecast doubling of big ship cellular/ro-ro tonnage. This will mean the extra capacity being necessarily aimed mainly at cross-trades because of the probable continuing dearth of high-quality liner goods in USSR export/import trade by sea. Such an increase of specialised tonnage would be far beyond any overall share of world cross-trades which conferences collectively could prudently allow MORFLOT (a) as the UN Code of Conduct for Liner Conferences takes effect and the activities of third flags generally become progressively constrained, and (b) with no reciprocal sacrifice of USSR national liner trade to established carriers.

NON-COMMERCIAL TYPES OF SOVIET 'CIVILIAN' SHIPPING

The USSR owns half the whole-world tonnage of fishing/whaling fleets (6.7 mn grt out of 12.8 mn by Lloyd's Register at 1 July 1980). This is of critical importance in its heavy depletion of world fish and whale stocks to provide protein for a USSR population ill-served by an inefficient agricultural system. Additionally, this tonnage (with 306,000 grt of research ships: half world total of 624,000 grt) spends much time 'fishing' for unsubstantial harvests whose accumulation is of real concern to the free world.

In the context of East/West political relations, it is naive and irresponsible to consider Soviet expansion as an international carrier as an ordinary commercial development of no greater consequence to Western defence or to Western political presence in the Third World.

The creation of dependency, to which reference has been made already, is as serious in terms of the means of carriage of mercantile freight as dependency on one source for a particular commodity which might be part of the freight.

NATO MERCHANT SHIPPING AND AN EMERGENCY

What would the NATO merchant fleet be called upon to do in the event of rising tension or hostilities?

It is well known that in a period of rising tension a factor of deterrence, though also of final preparation, would be the movement of men and military equipment across the Atlantic to reinforce Europe. Equipment particularly would move by sea and plans are laid for it. On the basis of military planners' requirements, sufficient allied merchant ships of various types would at present be available to carry these cargoes within the envisaged time scale and on the assumption that actual hostilities have not broken out.

The plans as to the military requirements and the availability of shipping are kept under review. But as time passes these plans need particular scrutiny to ensure that changes in the size of the allied merchant fleet, its composition, the time scale and the requirements for protection are all taken into account.

During such a period of rising tension merchant shipping would expect to be harassed in various ways. They may find strategically placed and exceptionally large exercise areas being used by unfriendly countries; their ships may be brought under close surveillance at sea — some may even be boarded under some pretext or other — they could experience problems at unfriendly ports and so on. In all such situations close liaison with governments and with NATO is vital, including, on the one hand, the availability of some form of physical protection and, on the other, complete understanding as to the commercial considerations which may face an owner in avoiding what may or may not be a hazard to his ship and cargo. This is another area where existing NATO planning must keep up to date.

If attempts to deter aggression fail, merchant shipping must expect to face merciless attack, either at long range or by close encounter, especially by submarines.

The permanent and semi-permanent installations in the North Sea would be particularly vulnerable to long-range attack and to sabotage, as would the ports generally and the highly sophisticated terminal installations (e.g. for containers) in particular. Our planning must surely rely on very restricted use of highly specialised ships requiring comparably specialised facilities, but it would not be realistic or feasible to equip the entire dry-cargo fleet with ro-ros. However, it should be noted that the handy-sized general-purpose fleet is the one which is being driven out by economic progress.

Those responsible for sustaining civilian life and production of essential goods as well as military equipment need to be clearer as to their requirements, both in commodity terms and in their transportation needs.

It may be that hostilities would not focus wholly on Europe and/or that other areas of conflict would develop. Relatively few sophisticated ports would be readily available under friendly control and, over extended lines of communication, there would probably be a great responsibility on sea transport for troop movements by comparison with air. One should reflect also on the limitations of planning between all NATO countries because of the limitations of the NATO area and the constraints on mutual assistance between such countries elsewhere. Other alliances are needed.

Our capacity to defend ourselves in the modern world, just as much as in the past, depends on economic strength as well as the amount of hardware and the number of effectives that we can put into battle. Not only military strength but political influence and intelligence, in the widest sense, are dependent on trade and shipping.

The tremendous increase in Soviet naval power in the last two decades has been matched by rapid expansion of the Soviet Merchant Navy which not only serves the requirements of Soviet foreign trade but increasingly participates in cross-trading and acts as logistic support in intervention abroad.

Operating in the Western world market economy, shipowners have sought efficiency, and in most countries they wish to remain free of government support and direction. They are now equipped with specialist ships of much greater carrying capability and lower unit cost than we were operating 10 years ago, or are operated by the Russians.

In comparison the Russians have a very large fleet of multideck conventional liners, with a growing proportion of roll-on/roll-off ships; so-called Combo ships, which carry containers and have deep capacity for break-bulk cargo with their own discharging gear aboard, and a few LASH—lighter aboard ships vessels—which are not commercially viable but are ideal for military support.

Historically, most bulk cargoes were carried by handy-sized tramp ships. Their modern equivalents are of a much larger size and more efficient economically. But their numbers are relatively fewer, certainly in the British fleet, and the rate of attrition which can be contemplated raises serious questions.

The tanker fleet has developed in much the same way but to even larger sizes. The supply of oil is obviously crucial and thus raises serious questions.

A fleet of 18 large container ships can do the work of 120 conventional ships: only 18 missiles are needed to do the work of 120 torpedoes in the last war. The implications are obvious.

SHIPPING AND NATIONAL SECURITY

Those nations which have sought to exercise imperial power without proper application of the influence of sea power have in the end been humbled by it. Sea power, commonly referred to as maritime power to embrace all forms of air-power at sea, consists not only of fighting units but also of the strength of a strong mercantile fleet developed and maintained in peacetime. This element is the safeguard against dangerous dependency on others, the means of support of national existence and the support of the armed services in time of war.

The failure of Allied governments to consider the role of merchant shipping in terms of national security may result in the Alliance finding itself without adequate tonnage under Allied control for diversion to wartime military use and maintenance of civilian supply.

To have reached such a point in a time of tension, together with the failure to provide enough fighting ships to defend the sea lanes, means that it is too late to seek a remedy.

World Merchant Fleet by Type and Flag, Selected Years 1939 - 79

Dry Cargo

Flag	3 September 1939		1 July 1950		1 July 1970		1 July 1975		1 July 1979	
	000 grt	000 dwt	000 grt	000 dwt	000 grt	000 dwt	000 grt	000 dwt	000 grt	000 dwt
United Kingdom	13,863	—	13,680	17,421	12,669	16,546	15,182	21,917	12,284	17,866
Belgium	319	—	406	516	706	988	930	1,388	1,242	1,939
Denmark	986	—	1,095	1,579	1,865	2,576	2,143	2,924	2,365	3,158
France	2,416	—	2,230	2,823	2,598	3,227	3,128	4,452	3,403	4,982
Germany, FR of	3,929	—	152	246	5,971	9,289	5,443	8,281	5,314	7,903
Ireland	—	—	—	—	—	—	190	267	171	219
Italy	2,890	—	2,293	3,099	4,424	5,591	5,649	8,101	6,152	9,260
Netherlands	2,250	—	2,499	3,314	3,014	3,946	2,704	3,594	2,367	3,322
Norway	2,573	—	2,842	4,376	9,797	14,982	11,703	18,858	8,121	12,989
Greece	1,736	—	966	1,889	5,500	10,279	14,077	22,419	25,915	41,836
United States	5,826	—	26,340	38,056	13,018	18,320	8,399	10,881	7,869	10,310
Liberia	—	—	20	34	13,703	23,288	23,662	41,936	29,431	52,889
Panama	248	—	1,379	1,934	2,164	3,057	7,595	11,388	14,792	22,439
USSR	1,024	—	868	1,121	6,165	7,491	8,524	10,677	10,258	13,164
World	49,860	—	66,674	91,370	126,576	181,119	170,891	257,726	209,080	319,873

World Merchant Fleet by Type and Flag, Selected Years 1939 - 79

Tanker

Flag	3 September 1939		1 July 1950		1 July 1970		1 July 1975		1 July 1979	
	000 grt	000 dwt	000 grt	000 dwt	000 grt	000 dwt	000 grt	000 dwt	000 grt	000 dwt
United Kingdom	3,029	—	4,165	6,329	12,227	21,515	16,969	30,780	14,621	26,430
Belgium	67	—	91	127	305	491	367	624	447	709
Denmark	107	—	169	256	1,361	2,408	2,196	4,158	3,008	5,724
France	332	—	651	1,031	3,591	6,145	7,255	13,473	8,120	15,524
Germany, FR of	256	—	26	37	1,666	2,897	2,756	5,180	2,880	5,616
Ireland	—	—	—	—	—	—	7	10	10	16
Italy	432	—	590	943	2,863	4,615	4,244	7,410	5,281	9,716
Netherlands	542	—	636	921	2,015	3,363	2,711	4,864	901	1,609
Norway	2,113	—	2,493	3,876	9,240	16,233	14,061	26,566	13,633	26,121
Greece	27	—	106	172	3,882	6,606	8,318	15,106	11,276	21,420
United States	2,896	—	5,235	8,621	4,799	8,114	5,267	9,424	8,429	15,316
Liberia	—	—	259	444	19,533	35,297	42,098	84,075	51,997	107,057
Panama	474	—	1,758	2,837	3,443	5,807	5,752	10,560	6,731	12,806
USSR	130	—	101	148	3,481	4,929	3,739	5,524	4,966	7,541
World	11,566	—	18,605	29,293	88,214	151,642	154,137	286,472	183,215	349,064

World Merchant Fleet by Type and Flag, Selected Years 1939 - 79

All Ships

Flag	3 September 1939		1 July 1950		1 July 1970		1 July 1975		1 July 1979	
	000 grt	000 dwt	000 grt	000 dwt	000 grt	000 dwt	000 grt	000 dwt	000 grt	000 dwt
United Kingdom	16,892	—	17,845	23,750	24,896	38,061	32,151	52,698	26,905	44,296
Belgium	386	—	497	643	1,011	1,479	1,297	2,012	1,689	2,648
Denmark	1,093	—	1,264	1,835	3,226	4,984	4,339	7,082	5,373	8,883
France	2,748	—	2,881	3,854	6,189	9,372	10,383	17,924	11,523	20,506
Germany, FR of	4,185	—	178	283	7,637	12,186	8,199	13,460	8,193	13,519
Ireland	—	—	—	—	—	—	197	277	181	235
Italy	3,322	—	2,883	4,042	7,287	10,206	9,893	15,510	11,433	18,977
Netherlands	2,792	—	3,135	4,235	5,029	7,309	5,416	8,458	3,268	4,931
Norway	4,686	—	5,335	8,252	19,037	31,215	25,764	45,425	21,754	39,111
Greece	1,763	—	1,072	2,061	9,382	16,885	22,395	37,525	37,191	63,256
United States	8,722	—	31,575	46,677	17,817	26,434	13,666	20,305	16,298	25,626
Liberia	—	—	279	478	33,236	58,585	65,760	126,011	81,429	159,947
Panama	722	—	3,137	4,771	5,607	8,864	13,347	21,948	21,532	35,245
USSR	1,154	—	969	1,269	9,646	12,420	12,263	16,200	15,224	20,705
World	61,426	—	85,277	120,663	214,790	382,761	325,028	544,199	392,295	668,937

Computers and Commanders in the Soviet Military System: A General Survey

JOHN ERICKSON

The author is Professor of Defence Studies at the University of Edinburgh

ALMOST 25 years ago General Sir Richard Gale in his discussion of the art of command in the nuclear age observed that 'concentration in terms of space' must henceforth give way to 'concentration in terms of time', thus requiring nothing less than a 'scientific approach to the problems of deployment and movement'.[1] Such a prescription would have received—and will still receive—enthusiastic endorsement within Soviet military circles, particularly the General's neat encapsulation of the 'art of command' with an insistence on a 'scientific approach' to military operations. Indeed, if any single term permeates Soviet military writings, it is the word *nauchnyi* (scientific), though it should be said at once that this is accompanied by the strongest emphasis on the 'creativity' of the individual commander.[2] For all the thrust of the 'scientific' approach and the increasingly complex applications of automation and mechanisation, algorithms and computers, operational research and the theory of games, there is the sternest reminder that automation is no substitute for traditional military skills: as one Soviet officer put it: 'victory cannot be computed, it must be won'.[3]

[1] See General Sir Richard Gale, 'The art of Command in the Nuclear Age', *Military Review,* July 1957, p 78.

[2] On 'scientific methods', see Marshall of the Soviet Union M V Zakharov, *O nauchnom pokhode k rukovodstvu voiskami* Moscow, Voenizdat, 1967, 80 pp (Marshal Zakharov was then Chief of the Soviet General Staff): also Major - General E F Sulimov and Rear-Admiral V V Shelyag, *Voprosy nauchnovo rukovodstva v Sovetskikh vooruzhennykh silakh,* Moscow, Voenizdat, 1973; also Army General S P Ivanov, *O nauchnykh osnovakh upravleniya voiskami,* Moscow, Voenizdat, 1975, 111 pp. On 'initiative/creativity', see V V Serebryannikov and M I Yasyukov, *Initsiativa i tvorchestvo v voennom dele,* Moscow, Voenizdat, 1976, 296 pp. Note that *initsiativa* is an imported word and by 'creativity' I understand tactical deftness and dexterity.

[3] Engineer Lieutenant-Colonel A Volkov (PhD candidate), 'Primenenie sredstv avtomatizatsii i matematicheskikh metodov v voennom dele', *Vestnik protivovozdushnoi oborony (VPVO),* No 10 (1975) 18.

At first sight it might seem that much of this could be subsumed under the rubric of 'command and control', but this takes
no account of the distinctive Soviet approach involved in
upravlenie voiskami (loosely translated as 'troop control') and
Western concepts embedded in C_3I. As for the latter, M I Thom
has recently demonstrated that C_3I is a runaway concept,
developed out of the more correct command and control information systems (CCIS). This speedily became C_3 (an advance on
C_2) and thence C_3I, even to a suggested C_4 and now C_4I, bringing
about some confusion between 'optimum management of forces
in live operational situations' and 'enhancing management' via
electronic aids.[4] Without being unduly pedantic, perhaps an attempt should be made to understand what the Soviet military
understands by *upravlenie voiskami,* and, more particularly, the
term *upravlenie.*[5] It must be said at the outset that the Soviet
literature of *upravlenie voiskami* is massive, comprising both
general commentary on automation and the man-machine mix as
well as technical military-engineering investigations of automated
systems, military cybernetics (of which a recent example is
Kibernetika v sistemakh voennovo naznacheniya, edited by V N
Zakharov and published in 1979 by *Voenizdat* in an edition of
7,500 copies). If nothing else, this paper might be construed as a
commentary on the body of Soviet military-technical writing on
'command/control systems', *upravlenie* in short.

Lieutenant-General Smirnov has recently defined *upravlenie
voiskami* as:

> the purposeful activities of the commanders, staffs and other
> agencies to maintain combat readiness, their preparation for
> combat actions and their guidance during the execution of the
> assigned tasks. The purpose of control is to assure the maxi-
> mum effectiveness of the use of available forces and means in
> the specific conditions of the situation and with the least
> losses.[6]

---

[4] M I Thom, 'The Evolution of C_3I', *International Defense Review* No 7 (1980)
1033 - 5.

[5] *The Russian - English Military and Technical Dictionary,* Moscow, Voenizdat, 1975,
p 559, under *upravlenie,* gives: 'board, administration, directorate: management: control, regulation: handling, direction'. Control, direction and management (battle
management) seem to be relevant here. For a detailed discussion of Soviet terminology,
see Colonel (now Brigadier) John Hemsley, *Soviet Command and Control (Upravlenie
voiskami): An Investigation of Theory and Practice,* Defence Fellowship Study, University
of Edinburgh, 1980.

[6] Lieutenant-General (Artillery), B Smirnov, 'Nekotorye voprosy upravleniya v
takticheskom zvene', *VPVO* No 7 (1979) 14.

If anything, *upravlenie* is programmed control (so described by Colonel-General Druzhinin, a senior officer of the Air Defence Command, *PVO Strany,* and Deputy Chief of the Soviet General Staff).[7] Even at this stage it will be readily seen that we are entering the domain of a special Soviet terminology and particular Soviet concepts which do not correspond entirely with Western notions of C_3I. Druzhinin concentrated on the meaning of *upravlenie* in the context of optimised decision-making, command organisation and operational planning, the 'control of technical means' (applicable throughout the system), 'control of material resources' (supply), 'control of combat training', 'control of combat readiness', 'control of military operations' and, not least, enemy C_3 which must take account of enemy policies, ideology, military doctrine, composition of forces, psychology, morale and capability of commanders.

Mention of the system *in toto* necessitates looking at the architecture of Soviet arrangements followed by a discussion of the technology involved and the degree of effectiveness attained (or anticipated).

ORGANISATION

Centralisation receives the most pronounced emphasis (though this is not to be confused with rigidity—on the contrary, centralisation is that arrangement which induces 'adaptive flexibility').[8] The 'top-down' structure brings all Soviet military elements under the centralised command of the General Staff, which is a unique organ in existing military structures with its 'command in being' functions: Soviet operations (land, naval and air) come under the operational control of the General Staff with its own operational directors and battle staffs.[9] Thus, there are

[7] The two principal works on *upravlenie* by Colonel-General V V Druzhinin and Colonel D S Kontorov are: *Ideya, algoritm, reshenie* Moscow, Voenizdat, 1972 (available in USAF translation) and the more advanced treatise *Voprosy voennoi sistemotekhniki,* Moscow, Voenizdat, 1976, 224 pp. *Sistemotekhnika* seems to have come into wider usage in the 1970s. For a commentary on Druzhinin, see Colonel John Hemsley, 'Command Technology: Voennaya sistemotekhnika', *RUSI Journal,* September 1980, pp 58 - 64. See also under *upravlenie voiskami* (entry by P K Altukhov) in *Sovetskaya voennaya entsiklopediya (SVE)* Moscow, Voenizdat, 1980, Vol 8, pp 203 - 04 (also bibliographical note).

[8] See Ch 6, 'Sistemnoe rukovodstvo', in V V Druzhinin *(Voennaya sistemotekhnika),* op cit, pp 191 - 94, on types of *upravlenie.*

[9] See the extensive analysis by Lieutenant-Colonel (now Colonel) Lynn M Hansen, USAF, *The Soviet Command Structure,* Appendix L to *The Soviet Military District in Peace and War: Manpower, Manning and Mobilisation,* Washington DC, 1979. Also research monograph, *The Imperial and Soviet General Staff (1860 - 1980),* Defence Studies, University of Edinburgh

two requirements, those of the 'large system' related to strategic HQs and those of specialised tactical tasks (such as air defence or naval forces), information systems and action data system, both subject to varying degrees of automation and with a subdivision into automated systems of controlling weapons (ASUO) and automated systems for controlling troops (ASUV), with the latter not amenable to total automation.[10]

To what degree can all this activity, *upravlenie voiskami,* be reduced to a general theory? A decade ago Captain (2nd Grade), V Morozov of the Soviet Navy examined this question in *Voennaya Mysl* and attempted to delineate a 'theory of troop control' particularly 'cybernetic approaches to the processes of control'.[11] Operational research (OR) as an aggregate of methods would solve only problems of 'a certain class', the theory of games seeks optimum decisions under various conditions, but both techniques simply comprise a set of methods. The 'large system' (large meaning complex) implies a 'systems approach',[12] where systems control in a 'live operational situation' is able to elaborate on reactions to varying situations and effectiveness is dependent upon the availability of information on enemy systems. Sufficient density of observation in the combat area is a prerequisite for the 'large system', as well as the formulation of 'patterns' (algorithms) for controlling the manner of the functioning of the system. Information acquisition is fundamental and control (*upravlenie*) is essentially a process of the elaboration of a plan (or an operational plan) and those measures needed to secure the implementation of the plan. Above all, this implies 'the resolution of tasks of varying scale under conditions of a shortage of both time and information',[13] but here the system operates to convert incoming data (status information) into an aggregate of orders and commands (control information).[14] Thus, control rests basically on the conversion of status information into control information. Disruption of status information will deprive the control entity of the capability of making a correct decision. The continuous acquisition of status information is crucial to the provision of control,

[10] Engineer Colonel A Volkov, 'Chelovek i EVM v avtomatizirovannykh sistemakh upravleniya voiskami', *VPVO* No 7 (1976) 12.

[11] Captain (2nd Rank) V Morozov, 'Development of a Theory of Troop Control', *Voennaya Mysl (VM)* No 9 (1971).

[12] On the systems approach and 'large systems', see the major work edited by Professor V A Baranyuk, *Osnovy sozdaniya bol'shikh ASU,* Moscow, 'Sov Radio', 1979, 360 pp.

[13] Morozov, loc cit.

[14] Ibid.

while the object is to facilitate a particular commander decision (as opposed to the general operational plan).

So much for theory, though it is difficult to disentangle certain theoretical positions from practical operational interests. An obvious instance is the Air Defence Command with its highly specialised tactical - operational requirements, where time was (and is) the critical factor and where the human operator could not exercise complete control. The human controller is perforce taken out of the loop under AUSO, while the computer is also used to relieve the commander of routine functions. The same might be said for naval action data systems and it is no accident that the Air Defence Command (*PVO Strany*) and the Soviet Navy did much to pioneer the cybernetic approach.[15] Manual and even semi-automated air defence systems can no longer cope with high density coordinated attacks designed to saturate the defence and to overwhelm both the surveillance and C_3 systems: fully automated systems are mandatory from initial target detection through fire control and interceptor vectoring, with the human operator assuming only a 'problem resolution' function and monitoring (controlling) identification and weapon assignments.

This is clearly recognised by the Soviet command, beginning with improved radar performance (beam agility, waveform control and operation in a 'radio-electronic warfare' environment),[16] surveillance coverage and track accuracy to engage high speed, manoeuvring targets at long range, coupled with higher data rates and measurement quality. Improved tracking and identification will inevitably provide the basis for improved control of

---

[15] From a very large body of publication see A N Romanov and G A Frolov, *Osnovy avtomatizatsii sistemy upravleniya*, (Ed V V Druzhinin), Moscow, Voenizdat, 1971; also *VPVO, PASSIM*. Also A L Lifshitzs, *Kibernetika v voenno-morskom flote*, Moscow, Voenizdat, 1964, 258 pp; also V D Skugarev and K O Dubravin, *Nauka upravleniya i flot*, Moscow, Voenizdat, 1972, 216 pp.

[16] On 'radio-electronic warfare' see the Soviet engineering text *Zashchita ot radiopomekh* (Ed M V Maksimov), Moscow, 'Sov Radio', 1976, 496 pp. Advances in Soviet radar include power and frequency usage, processing technology radar/optic combinations, site vulnerability, control netting, multi-mode transmission and reception: radar processing factors include monopulse, PRI jitter, frequency agility, antenna technology and sidelobe cancellation: see, for example, V G Glagolevskii and Yu A Shishov, *Antenny radiolokatsionnykh stantsii*, Moscow, Voenizdat, 1977, 111 pp; on training of radar operators A N Romanov, *Trenazhery dlya podgotovki operatorov RLS s pomoshchyu EVM*, Moscow, Voenizdat, 1980, 126 pp. Soviet use of monopulse radars involves multiple antenna beams (in place of single beam), also switching between transmission and reception: new Soviet equipment involves frequency-agile magnetions, millimetre tubes with frequency and PRI agility.

all weapons systems (in particular, SAMs),[17] with automation facilitating the solution of the multiple engagement problem by displaying information to each SAM battery of targets engaged by other batteries. The range of Soviet military-technical discussions bearing on these problems is very considerable, as might be expected, comprising mathematical - technical investigations of the time factor involved in the interception process, target distribution, detection and engagement, analytical methods for the solution of combat problems, combat simulation and the decision-making process (data analysis, determination of its significance, choice of the optimum decision) and game theory (determination of the optimum strategy under conditions of incomplete information).[18]

The transition from the primary formulation of a specific operational - tactical problem to the programming of its solution on the computer is demonstrably complex, a process which involves formulating the task (operational - tactical description) as a first stage, followed by developing the algorithm for its solution, describing the algorithm in one of the algorithmic languages (the 'input' stage for the programmer)[18a] with a final stage involving the verification of the result (comparison with control values, estimating the effectiveness of the algorithm and the optimisation process). All this, however, magnifies the contradiction between bringing the commander 'nearer the computer' and the actual limitation on his capabilities, which are further constrained by the time factor. One way out of this impasse is to assemble a library of standard computer programmes which embrace a wide range of operational - tactical problems occurring most frequently in the control process. This is to suggest special software serving specific command levels, necessitating the development of an algorithm and a programme for each of the most frequently

---

[17] See A S Mal'gin, *Upravlenie ognem zenitnykh raketnykh kompleksov*, Moscow, Voenizdat, 1976, 143 pp.

[18] From yet another very considerable body of publication, with at least 200 main references, see as sample Yu V Chuyev, *Issledovanie operatsii v voennom dele*, Moscow, Voenizdat, 1970; V R Durov, *Boevoe primenenie i boevaya effektivnost istrebitelei -perekhvatchikov*, Moscow, Voenizdat, 1972; V A Abchuk *et al*, *Vvedenie v teoriyu vyrabotki reshenii*, Moscow, Voenizdat, 1972; F A Matveichuk (Ed), *Spravochnik po issledovaniyu operatsii*, Moscow, Voenizdat, 1979.

[18a] *Algorithm*—any *rule which specifies the form of computation* to be pursued in order to arrive at the solution of a given problem, the solution to a mathematical problem in a *finite* number of steps. For an example, see an earlier publication by A L Lifshitz, *Kibernetika v voenno-morskom flote*, Moscow, Voenizdat, 1964, Ch 4, on algorithms and the automation of control processes.

recurrent control problems, plus the creation of a single data field and a single library of mathematical methods and procedures for problem solution. Such complexes would enable the commander to call up by single command the programme suited to process initial data and then formulate a programme from the algorithms of subproblems solved at an earlier stage. Systemwide software (*matematicheskoe obespechenie*) with respect to automatic control systems can be provided with up to 90 per cent of the requisite programmes from 'packaged components' drawn from the overall system programming.[19] Multiprogramming and computer time sharing also widen the utilisation of and access to the computer.

MACHINE INTELLECT

Raising the level of 'machine intellect' and improving the man - machine interaction are obvious priorities and preoccupations fully and faithfully advertised, not least in *PVO* circles, though there continues to be what might best be called a persistent campaign in favour of the 'mathematisation' and the 'algorithmisation' of *upravlenie*. It is now virtually standard practice for Soviet military writing on military affairs at large to contain a section on the automation of troop control and the relevance of mathematical methods including probability theory, the theory of games, information theory, queueing theory and some discussion of programming. None of this is designed to turn Soviet officers into computer experts; rather the object appears to be the inculcation at every level of the officer corps of some grasp of the relevance of mathematical methods and computer applications to operational situations.[20] A prime example is the section on mathematical methods in the work edited by Army General I E Shavrov and compiled by a group of specialists from the General Staff Academy, *Metodologiya voennonauchnovo poznaniya*.[21] Another is Tarakanov's treatise on mathematics and armed combat, *Matematika i vooruzhennaya bor'ba*,[22] which has a useful

[19] The figure cited in Colonel Volkov, *VPVO*, No 7 (1976) op. cit, p 16; also N G Zaitsev, *Matematicheskoe obespechenie avtomatizirovannykh sistem upravleniya*, Moscow, 1974.

[20] Typical of this programme or campaign, 'Upravlenie v boyu', *Krasnaya Zvezda*, 20 March, 1980; 'Komu podvlastna avtomatika', *Krasnaya Zvezda*, 17 June, 1980.

[21] Edited by Army General I E Shavrov and Colonel M I Galkin, published Voenizdat, 1977 (18,000 copies, which presumably means circulation in military academies/military schools as a standard text).

[22] Published in 1974 by Voenizdat. See also Colonel A Postovalov, 'Modelling the Combat Operations of the Ground Forces', *VM* No. 3 (1969).

section of the kinematics of combat operations, terrain features[23] and the utility of a kinematic model[23a] operating jointly with a damage infliction algorithm.

Before looking more closely at the technical means involved in automation and *upravlenie,* it might be useful to set out certain trends in the Soviet approach to 'man and the computer in automated systems', differentiation depending to some degree on particular Service perceptions and requirements, 'systems management' as opposed to specialised tactical commitments. One point in common, however, seems to be the insistence on the value of the human operator and the notion that automation neither bypasses nor displaces traditional military skills and competence, particularly efficient staff work. Within the Ground Forces, for example, the problem of *upravlenie* is seen largely as a matter of institutional adaptation, that is, by improving staff organisation and planning procedures via automation and mechanisation, precisely in the area of planning and decision making; without recourse to mathematical methods, the optimisation of operational decisions is well nigh impossible, nor can the commander rely on his intuition alone. Mathematical methods must be utilised to produce the requisite type and number of tactical calculations (*takticheske raschëty*). These calculations pertain to: the combat effectiveness and potential performance of friendly arms and services; the 'correlation of forces' in terms of tactical densities; combat losses for both sides; and the effects of regrouping or extensive troop movement. All have the aim of establishing 'coefficients of commensurability' (*koeffitsienty soizmerimosti*) relating to probable combat outcomes with given levels of manpower and weapon mixes.[24] The tactical calculations can be supplemented by operational typologies (*typovye raschëty*), while these calculations can be prepared either by the use of nomograms or with calculators and

[23] On 'operational calculations' and terrain passability, see Colonel V Korneichuk *et al,* 'Method for Evaluating Terrain Passability', *VM* No 4 (1967) also on terrain passability Colonel V Shchedrov and Colonel M Yeresov, *VM* No 12 (1967) (on the use of digital computers); also *Spravochnik po voennoi topografii,* Moscow, Voenizdat, 1973.

[23a] *Kinematics*—the science of motion without reference to force (viz. General Sir Richard Gale on 'deployment and movement').

[24] See D A Ivanov *et al, Osnovy upravleniya voiskami v boyu,* Moscow, Voenizdat, 1977 (2nd edn), pp, 244 ff: I regard this as an invaluable work and assume that it has been translated/disseminated in Western military circles, hence my foreshortened referencing. Equally I would draw attention to a Polish study by Z Golab and S Kolcz, *Wspólczesne dowodzenie wojskami,* Warsaw, MON, 1974 with its extensive references.

computers.[25] Tactical calculations are held in unit logs and workbooks, with as much planning material as possible held as pro-formas, *formalizatsiya* (for at least 50 per cent of a document consists of permanent 'fixed' items).

The automation and mechanisation of staff work, coupled with a shift from sequential to parallel planning, can appreciably reduce the time needed for planning and thus enlarge the time available for decision making. Here wartime experience has been rigorously analysed, pointing to the wisdom of an enlarged and efficient staff organisation which frees the commander from discharging secondary tasks, centralises 'rear services' (logistics) and creates new coordinating elements to control the interaction process (*vzaimodeistvie*)[26] for combined arms operations. While the staff exercises its traditional functions, staff work is appreciably assisted by modern 'command aids' ranging from computers to calculators, plus a wide variety of sensor information.

This institutional approach has given rise to an assorted literature on such matters as the psychology of operational thinking and the psychological element in troop control,[27] though the proponents of automation go much further, even to introducing an engineering concept into command. *Avtomatizirovannaya sistema upravleniya voiskami (ASUV)* places heavy emphasis on technical means for the collection, storing, processing and dissemination of information, which must be used for operational tactical calculations.[28] The most sophisticated modern 'weapon' is automated troop control. Algorithmisation is at a premium; many thousands of algorithms being needed (though even ardent exponents realise that it takes a team of 3 - 5 men 18 - 24 months to elaborate such algorithms, hence 'formalisation' still has its place). A complete systems approach has been outlined by none other than Colonel-General Druzhinin in his exposition of *voennaya sistemotekhnika* (systems engineering combined with com-

[25] See A Ya Vainer, *Takticheskie raschëty*, Moscow, Voenizdat, 1977, 112 pp.

[26] *Vzaimodeistvie*—interaction process, combined-arms cooperation. See Ivanov, op cit, Ch 6; also *vzaimodeistvie* discussed at length in *The Theory and Practice of Combined-Arms*, Defence Studies, University of Edinburgh, research monograph. 1979.

[27] See Lieutenant-General (Tank Troops) I Petrov, 'The Psychology of Operational Thinking', *VM* No 9 (1967) and 'Equipment and the Psychological Factor', *VM* No 9 (1971). Also A F Shramchenko, *Voprosy psikhologii v upravlenie voiskami*, Moscow, Voenizdat, 1973, 196 pp; also V D Ryadchuk and V I Kovalev, *Psikhologiya resheniya komandira*, Moscow, Voenizdat, 1976, 206 pp.

[28] See *Avtomatizatsiya upravleniya voiskami* (Collective authorship), Moscow, Voenizdat, 1977, on the *automating* of military systems.

mand/control technology).[29] The 'automation complex' does not merely imply a data retrieval system, but might be seen as the operation of the 'electronic consultant', the 'electronic assistant' (with large computers and permanent lines to communication, with lower level links equipped subsequently with systems to convert 'assistants' into 'consultants' and an entire system of interconnected command posts — and where the 'assistant' is indispensable under conditions of uncertainty, dispersal and surprise), with the electronic 'comrade in arms' (*soratnik*) servicing through computer channels lower level elements.[30]

A CAUTIONARY NOTE

A third school, however, advises caution with respect to automation. Navy Captain Makhrov reminded his readers that chance still plays a large part in war and that it might be ill advised to turn operational - tactical calculations into absolutes.[31] There is also something of the belt-and-braces approach in the event that the computers are knocked out or that none is available. There is also the prominent contradiction where the automation process is presented as one which does not make the human operator redundant (indeed, a higher performance is required from the human agent) but at the same time the automation of data processing and machine aids to decision making reduce the human role (as well as adding to support/ maintenance costs, itself no mean factor). Operational planning under conditions of severe time constraints has received much attention. Where the use of parallel planning can cut the time involved, though the information flow can be very large and the time for decision making small,[32] the use of computers at army/ divisional level (in the 'information-computer centre') and the use of 'tactical calculations' can speed up the process. But *automated* aid to decision making can only be carried through when the specific operational/tactical tasks have been translated into machine language via algorithms.

---

[29] Druzhinin, *Voprosy voennoĭ sistemotekhniki*, loc cit.

[30] For full details see id, *Ideya, algoritm, reshenie*, op. cit. Part III on technology.

[31] Captain (1st Grade) N Makhrov, 'Sluchainost v reshenii komandira', *Morskoi sbornik* (MS) No 3 (1980) 19; probability studies are related to abstract mathematical models rather than *actual situations*.

[32] See Army General I Gerasimov, 'Iz opyta podgotovki operatsii v korotkie sroki', *Voenno-istoricheskiĭ Zhurnal* No 8 (1978): for details, see 'Metody planirovaniya' in Ivanov, op cit, p 269. Also *Soviet Command Technology, 'Troop Control' and Time*, Defence Studies, University of Edinburgh, Research Paper, April 1980.

Consider the automation process and an operational assignment at, say, divisional level, with an admixture of the 'information control process' and 'parallel planning'. The divisional commander can develop his situation analysis from the data retrieval system (deployment of forces, enemy forces, Soviet forces, flank formations and units, signals and communications, the state of enemy forces) with further information on the enemy derived from documentary resources, materials which cover non-quantifiable data (such as enemy morale and the capabilities of enemy commanders). The next step is closer familiarisation with Soviet forces as well as current operational orders, logistics, contact with subordinate commanders, with data display completing this process. The area (or zone) of operations can now be displayed on stereoscreens, supplemented with digital data and documentary information. Here the computer comes into play in order to investigate possible variants of operational forms, logistics requirements and the state of operational preparation. Here we come to the search for optimum combat decisions, projections of probable outcomes and estimates of enemy intentions based on a search of probabilities. After these preliminary steps, the commander using the 'parallel-planning' method would make his inspections of subordinate units, a method designed to save up to 20 - 30 per cent of the time previously absorbed by the 'sequential' mode, followed by the initial command decision, duly matched against the computer which will furnish alternatives and variations (*varianty resheniya*).[33]

The decision is the key. Decision making may begin with a review of computer-based variations, each variant setting out positive and negative features as well as measures of effectiveness, though it is left to the commander to select that decision which eliminates weaknesses and incorporates alternatives, working down to a single alternative which can be optimised. The computer can be used for two purposes, one pertaining to information and the other to calculation and quantification. Operational - tactical information (*operativno-takticheskaya informatsiya*) (*OTI*) can be further divided into three categories: situation information (data on friendly and enemy forces, disposition, area of military operations); control information (situation information in relation to assigned missions expressed algorithmically and also relating to the experience of the commander taking the command decisions); and command information (*komandnaya informat-*

---

[33] See Druzhinin, *Ideya, algoritm, reshenie*, Part III.

siva) comprising orders, signals, the disposition of subordinate units in relation to situation information displays.[34] However, while the automation of the information process does permit the commander to develop his own optimised decisions, data on enemy forces — such as readiness, morale - psychological condition and the capabilities of individual commanders — it is not amenable to machine treatment and here it is back to the drawing-board for the staff.

The requirement centres on flexibility and rapid reaction (subsumed in the Soviet term *operativnost*) as well as uninterrupted operational control and a proper rhythm (*ritmichnost*), plus the security and continuity of communications. The relationship between information processing and decision making is obviously critical, leading to some extensive discussion of what types of data lend themselves to automation and to what degree decision making can be automated, particularly with human agents in the operating loop.

TECHNICAL MEANS

Much is made in the Soviet military press of the technical means involved in automation at large and in the 'automation and mechanisation' of staff work. As might be expected, the problems inherent in macro-systems (strategic air defence systems, strategic missile forces, satellite surveillance) have proved to be more tractable than those related to tactical handling, where systematisation and automation is more difficult and where the man - machine mix is a further complicating factor. Starting at the lowest level, at battalion, the adding machine and the calculator can be used to speed up routine work and can be employed to make rough 'tactical calculations', though higher up the scale more sophisticated calculators are in service (semi-automatic VK-2, VK-2M, BMP-2, automatic VK-3, VMM-2, *Bystritsa-2*), leading in turn to the computer.[35] The automation of 'tactical calculation' is handled by machines such as the NAIRI series,[36] though punched-card systems seem to enjoy wide use for processing information in spite of the labour involved and the

[34] See O S Razumov and V Shurakov, *Osnovnye printsipy i metody obrabotki voennoi informatsii na EVM*, Moscow, Voenizdat, 1975, 326 pp, Ch 1.

[35] See A V Prokof'ev *Sredstva mekhanizatsii i avtomatizatsii v shtabakh*, Moscow, Voenizdat (1969 and 1976 edns); also Ivanov, op cit, Chs 2 and 4.

[36] A G Geoletsyan, *EVM "Nairi-3"*. Programmirovanie i mikroprogrammirovanie, Moscow, 'Statistika', 1979, 208 pp.

cumbersome nature of the equipment. Other office aids include electric typewriters (Ukraina PEK-46), dictaphones and tape-recorders, photocopiers (ERA and ELEKTROFOT), copiers for field use (SKN-2M, SKN-22), map/chart copiers (KM-8M) and hectographs for staff use (type *Yantar*).[37]

'Tactical calculations' (*takticheskie raschëty*) which might be compared to staff tables, can be prepared by using nomograms, calculators and computers in the highest instance, all as an aid to decision making, whatever the level of command. Such calculations are direct, inverse and optimisation (with the latter presenting more complex aspects and usually requiring recourse to the computer, as opposed to the nomogram or the calculator). Such calculations include assessing relative strengths (Soviet and non-Soviet) not merely at the outset of operations but also taking account of probable losses incurred during intermediate phases of operations and executing secondary assignments, e.g. the numerical analysis of breakthrough operations conducted off the march, repelling enemy counter-attacks, assault river crossings and, under nuclear conditions, assessments of the post-strike situation.[38] 'Co-efficients of commensurability' related to probable outcomes, duly assembled, should enable commanders to modify their combat deployments and mix of weapons in order to gain maximum superiority along the line of the main attack. When the computer is involved, staffs perforce need a specially trained group of officers and NCOs (sergeants) to handle this work and the existence of such a group can demonstrably save time which might otherwise be expended by the less expert.

In a recent Soviet study the gamut of 'technical means' related to automated systems is described as follows:

(1) Information collection (sensors, satellites, radar, optical reconnaissance), (2) information recorders (punch card systems, electric typewriters, dictaphone/tape recorder, reproduction and coding), (3) information processing (computers, calculators, tabulators), (4) information coding and transfer, (5) information display, (6) search and storage of information, (7) communications/signals (telegraph, telephone, radio, radio-relay, information call-up and search).[39]

---

[37] See Ivanov, op cit, pp 95 - 109.

[38] Vainer, *op cit*. See also Engineer Colonel V M Kryat, *Metodika otsenki vodnykh preyrad*, Moscow, Voenizdat, 1978, 158 pp, also Colonel E K Malakhovskii, *Strel'ba na porazhenie opornykh punktov*, Moscow, Voenizdat, 1978, 112 pp (on artillery calculations and *norms*).

[39] See *Avtomatizatsiya upravleniya voiskami*, op cit, p 85.

The heart of the automated system is, however, the computer. Few would argue, nevertheless, that progress with Soviet computer technology has been spectacular and part of the disillusionment with 'military cybernetics' — much touted in the 1960s — lay with the fact that the requisite 'technical means' were not to hand. The discussion of military cybernetics took on a decidedly philosophical cast which contributed very little to resolving the commander's operational problems and difficulties. On the technical side the first Soviet attempt to produce an upward-compatible standardised set of computers failed and it had to wait upon the RYAD project, launched in the late 1960s, for the realisation of a major, unified computer system (involving also the COMECON nations, not least Hungary, Bulgaria and the GDR). First in the field as general purpose computers were the MINSK machines (MINSK-2, MINSK-22), with the MINSK-32 a considerable advance on the MINSK-22. In 1973 the MINSK-32 was operating with a disc unit and could support both multi-programming and limited remote processing. Until the mid-1970s and the development of the RYAD series, the MINSK machines (M-20, M-220, M-222) formed the backbone of the computer servicing of the Soviet Armed Forces as well as the space programme.

Lack of peripheral input/output and secondary storage devices hampered the development of modern software and wider computer applications. Input/output was via paper tape and typewriter console (with poor quality of card readers and printers); secondary storage used poor quality tape and drum units, since disc storage did not come into use until 1973. Programming used machine (binary) or assembly language, with high-level languages coming into use only in the 1970s. In 1971 the first of the RYAD computers (ES: unified system) made its appearance, the ES-1020 computer (comparable with the IBM 360/30) and by the mid-1970s and ES computer programme seems to have found its feet, albeit somewhat painfully, with the Czechoslovak ES-1021 and the East German ES-1040 in production. The ES-1020 is a joint Soviet-Bulgarian medium-sized computer, while the East German ROBOTRON ES-1040 — whose production started in 1973 — forms a vital and impressive element of the whole ES system.[40]

[40] See table of Soviet computer characteristics: based on *Osnovy sozdaniya bol'shikh ASU,* Moscow, 'Sov. Radio', 1979.

For a comprehensive and very expert survey of the RYAD/ES system (the reverse engineering of the IBM S/360 system), see N C Davis and S E Goodman, 'The Soviet Bloc's Unified System of Computers', *Computing Surveys* 10 (2) (1978), 93 - 122 with an excellent bibliography.

Disc-storage capacity remains a problem, though peripherals have improved, while the RYAD-2 series of computers promises considerable advances—machines with larger primary memory, semi-conductor primary memory, virtual-storage capabilities, block-multiplexor channels, relocatable control storage and improved peripherals. (A RYAD-3 computer has been mentioned in connection with the Soviet Air Defence system coupled with discrimination radars capable of handling large numbers of targets, while the computer will be capable of ABM data processing). Recent examination of a Soviet microprocessor also tends to suggest that Soviet designers and Soviet industry fully understand the specific logic functions and their interaction (the Soviet microprocessor being a copy of INTEL's microprocessor, the 8080A chip, and eight-bit processor unit).[41] Standardisation of procedure and structure for computer usage has been incorporated into the 'standard military computing centre' (*typovyi voennyi vychislitel'nyi tsentr*) (*TVVTs*), though large time-sharing centres in the Soviet Union have not generally fared too well, due largely to shortcomings in the communications system. Data transmission by telegraph line remains in wide use and the telephone system can scarcely sustain large-scale remote data-processing operations (though the Soviet military presumably uses all channels, telegraph, telephone, high-frequency telephone channels and television), though the ES computers are equipped with ES-8401 and ES-8410 multiplexors, as well as several types of *modems* (ES-8001, ES-8002, ES-8005 and ES-8006).[42]

EFFECTIVENESS

For all the improvement in 'technical means', such as computer technology, technological advance is no sure guarantee of efficiency and effectiveness in the automation of command/control processes. Criteria of effectiveness has come to occupy increasing importance in Soviet discussions of *ASUV*. Early in the 1970s Major-General Fedorenko put forward criteria of effectiveness designed to reflect the properties of the control system—the degree to which it accomplishes the operational mission, the rapidity of information exchange between the

[41] On the microprocessor test, *International Herald Tribune*, 7 November, 1980, p 9.

[42] See details in *Osnovy sozdaniya bol'shikh ASU*, op. cit, 'Svedstva obmena dannymi v bol'shikh sistemakh', p. 141.

elements of the system, the degree of resistance of enemy action
and environmental effects, adaptability to sudden change and
the cost/support factor. Selecting a single criterion of
effectiveness (domination method) is not satisfactory, though 'the
time of the control cycle' has been suggested as one measure of
operational efficiency. The measure of the 'coefficient of averted
loss' under nuclear conditions hardly makes sense to General
Fedorenko, who proposes additive weighting of particular
criteria — particular or partial criteria covering such aspects as
combat readiness, reliability, relative vulnerability, survivability,
concealment, flexibility and mobility.[43] A more recent study,
Avtomatizatsiya upravleniya voiskami, has suggested that each
system has its own specific set of indicators or operational
effectiveness, e.g. the automation of radar reconnaissance has a
different set of effectiveness indicators from those pertaining to
the efficiency of automation in logistics or in the missile and
artillery arms.[44] Though 'troop control' has now been placed
firmly on a scientific basis, the question of effectiveness and
efficiency has yet to be solved. Even as the Soviet system continues
its technological advance, there is much reliance on robustness,
redundancy and some degree of invulnerability. Perhaps the last
word should remain with V Morozov, who scouted the notion of
an 'ideal system', all-singing, all-dancing automated *upravlenie
voiskami:* 'for all practical purposes, it is sufficient if the system
ensures not optimum control but control which is at least no
worse than control effected solely by human operators.'

[43] Major-General K Fedorenko and Colonel A Lelekhov, 'On the Method of Evaluating
the Effectiveness of Troop Control Systems,' *VM,* No 12 (1973)

[44] *Avtomatizatsiya . . .,* op. cit, pp 274 - 94: for further investigation of criteria of effectiveness, see Yu V Chuyev, *Issledovanie operatsii . . .,* op. cit, pp 119 - 23.

Designation	ES-1020	ES-1030	ES-1040	ES-1050	ES-1060
Origin (country)	Bulgaria/USSR	Poland/USSR	DDR	USSR	USSR
Processor					
Operating speed (k ops/sec)	20	100	300	500	1000+
Selected performance: short operations	20-30	7-12	1.4-2.0	0.65-2.24	0.32
Floating point: add/subtract	20-30	10-16	2.5-3.6	0.8-2.24	0.32
Fixed point: multiply	300-500	36-52	6.5-13.1	1.5-2.24	1.6-2.4
Processor control	Microprog.	Microprog.	Microprog. Hardware	Hardware	Hardware
Primary memory					
Capacity (k bytes)	64-256	128-512	256-1024	256-1024	512-2048
Cycle time (μsec)	2	1.25	8	8	8
Channels					
Selector channels					
Number	2	3	6	6	6
Transmission rate	200	680	300-1200	1300	1300
Multiplexor channel transmission rate (k byte/sec)	10-16	40	20-25	110-670	110-670

Defence in the 1980s

DR GWYN HARRIES-JENKINS

Department of Adult Education, The University of Hull

AS WE move into the 1980s, a question, which has increasingly to be faced by government and governed, is whether a democratic society can 'afford' to maintain armed forces of a traditional type. It is a question which invites emotional responses. On the one hand, we meet the comment that a society has to pay for strong military forces and that a government has a duty to ensure the safety of the State at all costs. On the other hand, a totally different response rejects any preference for guns rather than butter. This often vehement criticism of military spending argues that a society should not bankrupt itself to maintain armed forces, the utility of which has declined, is declining and should decline still further. In the light of these contrasting approaches, the time is now opportune to explore those arguments which discuss at greater length the potential economic, political and social costs of contemporary and armed forces.

THE COST OF ARMED FORCES

Much contemporary discussion about the role of armed forces in the 1980s focuses on the economic costs of defence. This is very understandable. In a Western society based on a market-place economy, policy-orientated research into the problems faced by the military has, of necessity, to look critically at economic models. Moreover, it can be argued that the escalating costs of Western defence are such as to encourage a greater concern with these problems.

This concern clearly recognises the importance of expenditure trends over the past decade. Following the phasing out of conscription, the proportion of the gross national product (GNP) allocated to defence expenditure in the United Kingdom, for example, has until recently declined consistently. This reflects the specific political decision to reduce a defence commitment which in the 1950s generated an expenditure averaging 10 per cent of the GNP and which involved 7 per cent of the working population either in the armed services or in supporting functions. It has to be noted, however, that a similar move characterises the defence expenditure of most of the member countries of NATO, other than Greece, Portugal and the United States. This suggests that we are witnessing a common trend in all Western industrialised societies toward the reallocation of economic resources that were formerly assigned to defence expenditure, and that this trend is most noticeable in those countries where the GNP has increased during the decade under consideration. In Great Britain, where this growth rate has been less marked, it is, however, significant that it has hitherto been found to be impossible to bring the proportion of the GNP spent on defence into line with the Western European average of 4.4 per cent (1973). This constrasts very markedly with the allocation of resources to the maintenance of an all-volunteer armed force in the United Kingdom in the pre-conscription period, when before World War I some 3 per cent of the GNP was defence expenditure while expenditure was no more than 3.83 per cent in 1938 and 4.7 per cent in 1939. It is thus noteworthy that to maintain an all-volunteer force in being under current conditions, the United Kingdom is obliged to spend a disproportionately high percentage of its GNP on defence, a proportion that is greater than the European average.

At the same time, governments should not consider these issues simply in terms of fixed ideas about either the costs level or the scale and pattern of provision that is appropriate in a given area. On the contrary, because such an approach would ignore the essential business of resource allocation, politicians are today forced to strike a balance between the relevant defence needs of modern society and the real resource costs which are involved in meeting them. It is here that the economists' sense of opportunity costs looms larger and larger in the decision-making process.

A major controversial issue in this context is that of reconciling the competing and sometimes conflicting demands of defence and welfare. The decisions which have to be taken about resource allocation are in this case, as in the case of decisions about defence policy, essentially the expression of political choice. Although it may be fashionable from time to time to argue that policy decisions about defence are determined by the dominance within society of an all-powerful military - industrial complex, decisions about the level and nature of defence spending are primarily political decisions. Resource allocation is not initiated by some *deus ex machina*. It is not the axiomatic expression of inevitability. It is perfectly reasonable for any government, should it so wish, to prefer guns to butter. Conversely, a government can decide to reduce its defence expenditure to meet what it identifies as the satisfaction of more important social needs. The decisions which have to be taken are primarily decisions about the social allocation of scarce resources. These are choices between competing demands upon public expenditure in which strategic objectives as they are defined by the defence planner, have to be evaluated against the declared economic and social needs of modern industrialised society.

The ensuing problem, however, is that of the extent to which welfare goals are held by a given society to be more important than defence objectives. Hitherto, Western industrialised societies have significantly increased that proportion of their GNP spent on meeting welfare objectives. By 1970, for example, welfare expenditure in the Federal Republic of Germany had reached 19.5 per cent of GNP; in France the figure was 20.9 per cent and in the United States 15.3 per cent. In the United Kingdom, actual expenditure for the fiscal year 1977 - 78 on education, health and the social services, social security and housing amounted to 61.6 per cent of all public expenditure compared with the 11.5 per cent allocated to defence spending. In the Netherlands, the actual amount spent on welfare services has doubled every 4 years, until in 1975, for example, such expenditure totalled some 20 per cent of the GNP.

Such expenditures, when viewed in conjunction with declared political preferences, have encouraged the conclusion that the existence and growth of the welfare state is inevitable. It has produced throughout Western society a pattern of persistent deficit budget spending. What has now to be asked is whether the existing level of military expenditures can be maintained in the 1980s without limitations being placed on the current level of welfare spending. Alternatively, we have to question the effect of an increased defence expenditure upon the ability of a society to meet its welfare commitments. The exercise of political choice in this area clearly reflects preferences for the priority given to social or defence goals. The critical question may be the extent to which politicians are prepared to risk national security in their concern for social justice. Alternatively, we have to ask whether the implementation of an effective defence policy in the next decade will inevitably bankrupt the society which it is designed to defend.

In seeking answers to these questions we are faced with two specific problems. In the first place, much of the discussion which takes place is based on relatively simple equations. The price of a sophisticated missile system, for example, is evaluated against the national income of a developing country. New ships are identified with a failure to build hospitals or schools; the capital costs of technologically superior tanks are balanced against cuts in education spending or housing programmes. Such equations ignore the possibility that the cancellation of defence projects may not result in the building of new schools or in improved programmes of medical care. The debate at this level, moreover, suggests that when the success of a strategy of deterrence makes it difficult to establish criteria for the evaluation of the success or failure of adopted arms programmes, the symbols rather than the actualities of military expenditure assume an increased importance.

The second problem, however, reflects more fundamental issues. These increasingly assume a major importance in the culture and life of modern industrialised democracies. Put simply, we have to ask the question Who among the citizens of a country is prepared to take up arms in defence of that country? An initial response to this stresses the structural distinction which can be drawn between those countries which have adhered to a cherished principle of voluntary recruitment to the armed forces, and those which have retained a form of conscription. For the former, it would appear that a varying but limited proportion of the male population wishes to volunteer for the armed forces. In part, this reluctance may stem from the difficulty faced by national governments in convincing their citizens that a threat exists which necessitates the maintenance in being of the all volunteer force (AVF). In this context, it is interesting to note that the only European countries on either side of the Iron Curtain which do not have national service are the United Kingdom and Luxembourg. These governments, in common with the United States, are thus faced with the specific difficulty of recruiting personnel of a suitable quality. Increasingly, in Western society, this is part of a wider debate about a shift from labour to capital intensive force structures. For a variety of reasons, military equipments have become increasingly sophisticated, complex and expensive. If the defence budget cannot be increased, the costs of the new equipment are often met through a reduction in expenditure on personnel. The alternative is a shift to the purchase of less-advanced and less costly military hardware. Hitherto, such an option has been less than attractive to defence planners, and there is no reason to suppose that preferences in the 1980s will readily change. Yet if the adopted equipment is highly sophisticated and complex, the military must attract skilled specialists in competition with other employers to service the equipment. Where the military salary in particular is seen to be less than that available in comparable civilian employment because the defence budget is not increased, armed forces face the problem of recruiting and retaining these skilled specialists.

In seeking solutions to these problems, Western governments are faced with a number of seemingly intractable problems. If, for instance, they shift to a greater reliance on increasingly sophisticated technology, then they may have to accept that complex equipment cannot be readily operated by reservists. The primary difficulty here is that the force structure may be based on the assumption that reservists — including in the United Kingdom Territorial Army volunteers — will make up for shortfalls in regular recruiting. Yet these auxiliary and supplementary forces bereft of the intensive and continuous training available to 'regular' professionals, may not be capable of utilising fully high technology equipment.

A major problem, therefore, for the AVF continues to be the persistent difficulty of maintaining the established structure. In general terms, defence planners have done rather well. In the United States, for instance, there has been a reasonable degree of success in meeting annual recruiting goals even though force levels have declined somewhat since the first year of the AVF (1974). Even so, it is clear that the confidence of the Gates Commission in the potential ability of the AVF to recruit and maintain a larger force was somewhat misplaced. The force levels that are being maintained are barely 80 per cent of what the active component requires for its needs. Nevertheless, the AVF has been able to survive.

A more important consideration, however, is what has been done to obtain the numbers of volunteers for the AVF. The most obvious trade-off in any recruiting process is between quantity and quality. All things being equal, competition in the labour market means either the acceptance of recruiting shortfalls in order to maintain existing enlistment standards, or the reduction in enlistment standards in order to avoid incurring recruiting shortfalls in an already understrength active component.

In the case of the AVF, both courses of action have been adopted, albeit by different services and at different points in time. Generally, however, it is evident that the United States has not succeeded in making voluntary service sufficiently attractive in material terms to draw recruits from a broad cross-section of society. In the aftermath of Vietnam, recruitment has tended to be from narrow segments of society in both ethnic and educational terms. In particular, the presence of a growing number of blacks in the AVF is a sensitive issue, the resolution of which is likely to be very difficult. There are several aspects to this issue. One is that there is a very large difference in the degree of black representation in the officer corps and in the enlisted force. In 1979, for example, blacks constituted 32 per cent of the enlisted force but only 7 per cent of the officer corps. This draws attention to the social problems implicit in a situation in which a predominantly white officer corps commands a heavily black and partially resegregated enlisted force. Another concern reflects uncertainty over the political and military desirability of having an army which is heavily black. Yet another consideration is the moral desirability of allowing (or requiring) those who have profited least from American society to bear the brunt of defending it. Precisely how the United States will deal with this question is far from clear, but it is certain that it will not disappear of its own accord.

When faced with this dilemma of reconciling military manpower needs with the apparent reluctance of skilled specialists to volunteer for the military organisation, the military is forced to look for pragmatic solutions to the encountered difficulties. In the past, considerable emphasis has been placed on the advantages in terms of recruitment and retention of personnel of a rate of remuneration which compared favourably with civilian earnings. Thus in the United Kingdom in the late 1960s, the introduction of a military salary in accordance with the recommendations of the *Second Report of the National Board for Prices and Incomes* (1960) established the principle of comparability between earnings in the civil sector and in the armed forces. Subsequently, pay increases were governed by the findings of an independent civilian committee, the Review Body on Armed Forces Pay, which re-examined both pay and charges in the light of the principles laid down by the National Board for Prices and Incomes. One of the important economic effects of this was the way in which the review mechanism reinforced the organic linking of military and civil economic experiences. By comparison, the direct effects of government economic and social policies with the military sector put the military salary on a sound economic base inasmuch as wage costs were related to alternative civil earnings and work preferences.

The more questionable effect of such a programme of comparability, however, has been to raise even further the personnel costs of the armed forces. Moreover, we still have to question whether increases in pay will, in themselves, attract a desired number of recruits or persuade a specialist in mid-career to stay on in the military rather than return to civilian life. The continuing issue is whether the need to compete effectively in a labour market or the wish to establish comparability can be said to impose unacceptable demands upon budget allocation and thus detract from other defence programmes which involve major capital expenditure.

For those countries which wish to retain a system of conscription within their armed forces, the problems that are encountered are no less formidable. Conscription, it can be argued, becomes increasingly dysfunctional as a means of manning conventional force structure when its increased social costs are seen within a given society to be an unacceptable burden. Concomitantly, the budgetary advantages of conscription lose their attractiveness when economic costs increase as the rate of remuneration. This decline in the postulated advantages of conscription can also be seen where the conditions of service applicable to conscripts equate more closely to those of volunteer servicemen. More generally, however, the principle of conscription comes increasingly under attack as a generation evolves to whom compulsory military service is seen as a gross infringement of natural rights and a contradiction of the concept of democracy within a Western industrialised society.

The debate about the shape of defence in the 1980s is thus materially affected by the political, social and economic determinants of decision making. What this suggests is that politicians in the forthcoming decade will be forced to look increasingly at alternative force strategies.

ALTERNATIVE STRATEGIES

One solution to this problem of meeting contemporary manpower needs, therefore, has been hitherto to favour substitution policies. Two such policies have an immediate attraction. Firstly, military organisations can employ an increasing number of civilian personnel. The latter, in the 1980s, can be said to be an increasingly rational source of manpower in those occupational specialities where the need is for technologists rather than warriors, or where the demand is for pragmatic managers rather than charismatic leaders. Yet although the demand for enhanced civilianisation of military posts will continue to be both pressing and desirable, it may well be that we have already witnessed the limits of such civilianisation. Extended further, the continued replacement of servicemen by civilians becomes dysfunctional within the organisation where it raises basic questions about the very credibility of a military organisation, many members of which are civilians. Equally, civilianisation of appointments ultimately raises the question of What is military?, a question which implies that if few distinctions can be drawn between civilian and military, then there may be little, if any justification for the retention of a separate—and expensive—military organisation.

An alternative question is whether these manpower shortages can be offset by more radical structural changes such as the employment within armed forces of an increased number of women. In recent years, a considerable body of literature has evolved which seeks to consider critically the impact of such a change. Here, a central issue continues to be that of the equality/effectiveness debate, that is to say, it is the debate between those who analyse the structural change from the standpoint that military women should have equal opportunities with men in terms of command, promotion and job opportunities, and those who believe that the critical issue is the potential effectiveness of women in combat roles. What this debate tends to ignore, however, is the very considerable extent to which there is ample scope for the worthwhile employment of women in the armed services without placing them in combat roles. Ultimately, the only limiting factor on such utilising of women may be the question of the credibility of a deterrent force which employs women in an increasing number of traditional male roles. Nevertheless, the issues which have to be faced continue to be critical for force structures over the next decade: can women be used effectively in those areas such as the combat roles where the lack of male recruits may be most noticeable? Are women more expensive to recruit and train than male manpower in the light of the former's potentially lesser commitment to the military career? To what extent is the utilisation of women in the military dysfunctional in that their employment may reduce the credibility of armed forces as an effective means of responding to external threats? Is the balance of the costs of training and career possibilities between men and women in military organisations comparable with the costs and utilisation of men and women in other professions such as law, medicine or accountancy? To these and similar questions there are no simple answers, for evaluation often reflects value-judgements within a specific cultural context.

Yet answers must be sought, for one of the most persistent problems which will affect this manpower shortage in the future, is the effect upon recruiting of national demographic trends. These will materially reduce within the next decade the size of the age cohorts from which recruits to the armed forces are traditionally drawn. The overall picture for Western industrialised society therefore is one in which there is and will be, to an even greater extent in the 1980s, a steady decline in the number of males between the ages of 18 and 24. This is a persistent trend in modern society even though individual countries present variations in this pattern. The Federal Republic of Germany, in particular, seems to be less affected in the short term by the forecasted shortages of males in this age group. Nevertheless, if these trends are objective and irreversible in the near future, then the critical issue will continue to be one of identifying possible alternative strategies which serve as solutions to the manpower problem.

In looking at this problem, it is apparent that for the next decade governments will be forced to consider policies which may materially affect traditional preferences. For those countries where the adopted force structure continues to be based on the principles of conscription, a certain flexibility of choice may still be permitted. Thus, in mixed structures, which depend for their effectiveness on the recruitment of both conscript and volunteer personnel, shortfalls in recruiting can be partially avoided by changing the mix. An extension of the period of conscription, for example, may produce a quantitatively improved force structure. Alternatively, a government may shift towards a policy of universal rather than selective conscription. A third possibility is to improve the conditions of service for volunteers to such an extent that enlistment as a volunteer is to be much preferred to service as a conscript. In this context it is worth noting in passing that such improvements in conditions of service need not be limited to cash incentives or other extensive rewards. Deferred benefits in the form of early pension, post-service educational allowances, improved access to civil service appointments, and so on, may prove to be a successful inducement.

For the AVF the available options may be more limited. One major change of policy would be to revert to a modified form of conscription. The political and practical problems to which this could give rise are very considerable. A distinction, however, has

to be drawn between those arguments which reflect a highly sub-
jective and often prejudiced reaction to the concept of conscription itself and those arguments which are derived from an objective assessment of the advantages and disadvantages of such a
form of recruitment. In the former case, the force of reaction is
most marked, and in both the United States and the United
Kingdom we can identify a vehement opposition to the rein-
troduction of compulsory military service. This opposition reflects
strongly held internationalised values. It represents a variety of
opinions which range along a continuum that reflects at the one
end the view that military *per se* is immoral, and, at the other,
the conclusion that conscription is unfair since it places an unequal burden on the young male population.

These opinions are, of course, not only to be found in cases
where the AVF has already been established. They are equally
noticeable throughout Western industrialisation where even in
those countries with a long-established tradition of conscription,
we can identify a growing opposition to the retention of this
method of military recruitment. Thus in the Netherlands, attitudes towards the army changed drastically in the 1960s for a
number of reasons. In the first place, this could be attributed to
the disappearance, or at least easing of the cold-war complex.
This sense of international *détente,* which particularly affected
many of the younger generation, led to the feeling that enlargement of the military machinery was unnecessary and that defence
was a policy lacking in credibility. More recently the activities of
the conscripts unions (the VVDM and the BVD) epitomise a
substantial reaction to the maintenance of the conscript system.
Comparable attitudes could also be noted in France among the
comités des soldats, from conscripts in the Federal Republic of
Germany and more especially among young people in Scan-
dinavia.

Nevertheless, it is in those countries which have abolished the
draft that we encounter the greatest criticism of conscription as a
means of recruiting a military force. Studies of the true economic
costs of taking a 2-year age cohort out of the labour market, of
the impact within a military organisation of conscripts upon
training systems and, above all, of the very utility of short-term
personnel in a highly technological and sophisticated armed
force, lead to the conclusion that conscription has little to offer.

Nevertheless, notwithstanding the force of these and similar
arguments, and irrespective of the alleged difficulties which
would arise, the feasibility of, and possible necessity for, such a

radical alteration in traditional force structure cannot be dismissed out of hand. Firstly, the noted demographic trends may force
the United States and the United Kingdom to reconsider their
selected options despite their traditional preference for the AVF
structure. Secondly, the existing tendency within such a structure
to obviate manning and fiscal difficulties by making force reductions may have reached a point of no return. Within the AVF
reductions become unacceptable when the associated task limitation goes beyond a point where the military can maintain its
credibility both nationally and internationally as an effective
armed force. Thirdly, planners and politicians alike are faced by
the continuing dilemma that a modern society in a period of
limited resources balks at the cost of making the military sufficiently enticing to attract an adequate number of personnel. A
shortage of suitably qualified personnel then creates problems of
over-stretch, and the external efficiency of the armed forces may
be considerably reduced where these forces are insufficient to
meet a complex pattern of military roles. Yet if defence is
favourably treated at a time when other areas of public expenditure are being cut back, politicians, in particular, are reluctant
to tolerate the acute resentment which can emerge within society
as a reaction to such a pattern of resource allocation.

THE CITIZEN SOLDIER

What all of this suggests is that the time is ripe for a more
critical re-examination of the issues which have to be faced. One
aspect of this examination is already reflected in the analysis of
defence options and in the promotion of a more realistic debate
about the priorities upon which the allocation of resources to and
within defence depends. A second aspect of this is more concerned with wider social issues. Put shortly, this analysis focuses on
those alternative policies for defence which, irrespective of
whether existing recruitment is primarily based on the volunteer
principle, the conscript pattern or a mix of them, stresses the fundamental importance of the citizen soldier concept.

This is a concept which embraces three distinctive ideas.
Literally, it emphasises the tradition of the citizen army, a force
structure in which a special relationship between the armed
forces and the rest of society is confirmed by the organisational
and structural peculiarity of the military system. In Switzerland,
for example, the State is prohibited from establishing a professional army, a mercenary army or an army of conscripts for

anything other than training purposes. This leaves only a militia system if there is to be any at all. The peculiarity of this system, however, is that it does not create a reserve army. During their service, militiamen continue to be active members of the military organisation with all the attendant obligations and prerequisites. They are part of a close group of individuals who take up arms to defend the national territory, who sustain a civilian value system during military service, who bring supplementary skills into the armed forces and who readily re-adopt their civilian role on the completion of military service.

The second interpretation of the concept of the citizen soldier, however, emphasises the importance of the role of the individual as a member of the reserve or auxiliary force. This is that interpretation which, carried to the extreme, seems to reflect the Victorian belief that there is nothing done by the regular army which cannot be carried out more efficiently, more effectively—and more cheaply—by the reserve and auxiliary forces. Mor. precisely, it is a perception of military roles which recognises that the establishment of effective reserve forces not only provides a pool of skilled, trained and committed personnel, but also does much to close the gap between society and its armed forces.

The final interpretation of this concept extends further the boundaries of this relationship between armed forces and society. It extends it by stressing the importance within the next decade of an enhanced sense of civic consciousness. This sense is something more than the promotion of patriotism or the inculcation among citizens of a specific political ideology. Civic consciousness is essentially an awareness of individual responsibilities within the social and political framework, a responsibility which extends beyond the obligations of military service to embrace the concept of civic service. In short, the idea of the citizen soldier is linked with the idea of national service whereby the obligations of military service as they are implicit in conscription to the armed forces are paralleled by alternative yet complementary obligations of social service.

These alternative defence strategies attract considerable criticism. The general criticism which is frequently encountered is that the postulated suggestions lack reality. They suggest, it can be argued, solutions which are neither feasible nor realistic for they are derived from academic rather than practical questions. There are, however, a number of more specific criticisms. The Swiss militia model is thus questioned not only in terms of its legitimacy but also in terms of its postulated effectiveness in the

light of improved weapons technology. A growing imbalance between the weapons of mass destruction and the limited functions
of militia, invites critical evaluation of the proposed model.
Similarly, the perceived strategic and tactical shortcomings of the
reserves model are used to justify criticism of any proposal to
transfer resources — and responsibilities — away from regular armed forces. Even the more radical suggestion of developing some
form of a truly comprehensive national service attracts both
criticism and adverse comment.

Yet, the point to be stressed is that the question which remains
unanswered is whether in the course of the next decade Western
industrialised society can continue to afford armed forces in their
traditional form. If alternative strategies are to be discounted,
then we are left to re-examine the dimensions of that traditional
form. Part of such a re-examination necessitates the critical
analysis of the economic model. But an alternative approach ad-
dresses explicitly the question of public preferences. It advocates
a reasoned assessment of the political and social, as well as the
economic costs of continuing established military structures and
organisations. It is this assessment which finally reminds us that
the decisions to be made are the expression of political choice.
What is to be hoped is that in the complex world of the 1980s the
right choice is made.

An Anatomy of Defence Policy

ADMIRAL OF THE FLEET THE LORD HILL-NORTON, GCB

DEFENCE is a dynamic, not a static business, but the principles which lie at the heart of the formulation of defence policy do not change. It is a fact, and one much to be regretted, that these principles are frequently forgotten or set aside by those in whose hands responsibility for national defence resides, and too often for reasons which are short term in the historical perspective. It is, therefore, perhaps appropriate to look again at those principles, to set them out and to test them against the imperatives of the present and, in so doing, to draw out those threads in the tangled skein of politico-military affairs which have the ring of permanence.

Policy is one of the big words, widely used and frequently misused. Dictionaries offer seven or more possible meanings of it including 'cunning', 'prudence' and 'a system of administration guided more by interest than principle', and it may well be in some respects all of these; but on the whole we may settle in this article for the very simple definition—'a plan for action'. This allows attention to be drawn at the very outset to a crucial distinc tion, so frequently missed or misunderstood by many of those who should know better, which is that between the formulation of policy and its implementation. Plainly there is not much point in the first of those if the means or the will to do the second is lacking, and naturally the second stage cannot be achieved until after the first; but less plainly the actual process of implementation can hardly fail to influence the policy itself and so, it must be clear, a policy in so complex and diverse a matter as defence should be based on abiding principles, yet retain sufficient flexibility to be modified, if and when the surrounding circumstances are sufficiently compelling to demand it. But this is by no means to suggest that a coherent defence policy should be subject to frequent or major changes for, as these words hope to show, it is, above all, general stability which is perhaps the most important single feature of a successful policy in this field. That many defence policies lack this feature today and have sadly lacked it in the last

20 years the observed facts make clear enough, though to demonstrate these unpopular truths is not the main purpose of this exercise. It would certainly be possible to treat the whole subject in an abstract form, but this, though academically sound, would be bound to seem artificial, so that several references will be made to what has already happened in practice, as well as to what is still happening and some suggestions about what may happen in the future.

ELEMENTS OF DEFENCE POLICY

To deal first with the elements of defence policy: anatomy is also defined in dictionaries as 'the detailed analysis of anything', as well as 'a skeleton', and though the attempt is here made to deal with the former, the exercise can properly start by looking at and identifying the more important bones of the skeleton. As in the human body, so in defence, there are countless numbers of these, all interdependent and most performing a useful job, but clearly some are more basically important to the whole bodily function and these must be regarded as the essential elements of any policy, and are quite certainly essential to the formulation and subsequent execution of defence policy. They are, in fact, the big ones. They are also extremely simple and amount, briefly put, to examining the problem, deciding what to do about it, providing the necessary resources to do what has been decided and then, above all, sticking to it unless or until any of the variables should grossly change. This may seem, perhaps, rather too elementary a process for so grand a word, and listed so starkly would not—certainly on the surface—seem likely to lead to the award of many doctorates, but to the experienced practitioner it is realistic; and doctorates—or chairs—or the lease of presidents' or prime ministers' mansions—anxiously await the Minister or Chief of Staff who succeeds in completing this course successfully. Let us, therefore, look below the surface at these four elements just bluntly set out, which in practice really do comprise what policy is all about.

There is a crucial point to make before this process can begin, because the first quick look at the problem reveals, paradoxically perhaps, that there is no discrete 'thing' which can be identified as a defence policy—although lest the reader feels he may stop here he may be assured that if he perseveres he will be able to discern something which would answer to the name. Certainly for centuries and possibly for ever, but undoubtedly today, it is im-

possible to consider a nation's defence policy without simultaneously considering its policies for overseas affairs, economics,
industry and society in the broadest sense of home affairs. It is the
intimate linkage between these great affairs of State which bears
hardest on deciding what to do about the problem once it has
been identified then of providing the resources and then sticking
to the policy. This linkage is the very heart of government.

EXAMINING THE PROBLEM

Examining the problem must in the context of defence — by
which is meant the defence of the nation — start by a very hard
and careful and detailed look at the threat and not, possibly to
labour the point, only the military threat but at threats to all
those other elements of the body politic just mentioned which can
be posed by military means. Any threat, in this sense, is generally
accepted to be made up of capability and intention. The important points to note now are that military capability in these
sophisticated days takes, typically, about 10 years to create
because modern weapons systems take about as long as that to
build from the twinkle-in-the-eye stage to having them in the
hands of troops, and it takes about as long to tailor the entry,
training and career structures of the people who will have to fight
with those weapons systems. It is highly relevant to mention here
that the alarming growth and present power of the military
machines confronting one another in Europe have not arisen suddenly or recently but flow from plans (policies sound grander)
conceived at least 10 years ago and in many details earlier than
that. By contrast, intentions can never be known for certain and
they can change overnight. They are, indeed, likely to change as
those who wield the military capability change either through
political evolution or revolution or, more mundanely, by the due
process of age. It is also highly relevant to mention here that it is
an observed fact, as well as a likely hypothesis, that in the
Western democracies speculation (for it can never be more) about
intentions, in an understandable desire for a quiet and easier life,
is almost bound to be on the optimistic side. The misunderstood
and dangerous term *détente* and the so far unrewarding nature of
its pursuit, makes this clear enough, however eagerly sought it
may be on all sides. It seems reasonable, as well as prudent, in the
light of this very brief look at the components of the threat, to
suggest that the only responsible course for defence planners to
pursue is to base policy on the capability, rather than the intentions, of a potential aggressor.

THE SOVIET UNION

So in that light let us look briefly at the capability of the most obvious potential military aggressor, the Soviet Union and its satellites. First, because they are of a different nature, one must deal briefly with nuclear affairs, bearing always in mind that the use of nuclear weapons would almost certainly lead at once to the destruction of civilisation as we know it, and bearing also in mind that the best way of ensuring that they are never used is by the provision of adequate deterrence by conventional arms. Suffice it to say here, on this huge nuclear subject big enough for several long articles on its own, that only two main types need to be considered—the strategic and the theatre weapons; although recent advances in this horror technology have blurred what was previously a conveniently sharp line between them, and, thanks to Chancellor Schmidt, the term Euro-strategic has become both appropriate and fashionable. The two superpowers have approximate parity in strategic weapons, and each has a tenfold or hundredfold over-kill capability. In the process of 'examining the problem' of making defence policy as a whole, such esoteric criteria as throw weight, re-entry vehicles, launchers and the vulnerability either of platforms (this simple word in the newspeak means aircraft, ships, submarines, silos and the rest) need not detain us, but what does matter is that each of the superpowers has an invulnerable second-strike capability so that pre-emptive first strikes may, certainly for the present, be discounted. It should not be forgotten that the United Kingdom and France are also strategic nuclear powers with the ability to inflict what has been described as 'unacceptable damage' on Russia. China, too, has this power, and there are at least four other countries which might have it, and another larger number which, at least in theory, could develop it. In the balance of theatre nuclear weapons, sometimes and incorrectly called tactical, there is effective parity between East and West, though for what it is worth, and on the whole that may not be much, at the moment the West has a numerical and the Soviets a technological advantage. The importance of this intentionally superficial glance at nuclear affairs for the United Kingdom, and hence for its defence policy, is, of course, that although our nuclear arsenal is minuscule compared with that of the Soviet Union, the terrifying strategic power of it is, without doubt, adequate as an ultimate sanction should our vital interests be threatened and we once again stood alone as we did in 1940.

The conventional military capability which is available to any country can now be measured by a variety of means with greater precision, so that it is known how many guns and ships and aircraft and tanks and men and missiles are in its order of battle, and it is also known where and at what rates they are being built. Before looking in any detail at the sort of balance sheet which emerges, when taking the confrontation in Europe as an example, and as an integral part of the examination of the problem thereby posed, a word or two about the theology is necessary. While for many years it has been held that 'attack is the best method of defence' and this may still be true once war has started, the likely outcome of general war is today so terrifying that all defence resources must be directed towards preventing war ever breaking out. Thus it is an essential, and indeed the only really essential, feature of democratic defence policy to *deter* war. As the author has so often said in public, deterrence really is the name of the NATO game. This means, in a few words, creating in the mind of a would-be aggressor a fearful doubt that the risks are too high to be worth any likely gain. This can, and this is another essential principle, be achieved without attempting to match the threat man for man, tank for tank, aircraft for aircraft, ship for ship and so on. More than 50 years ago that great student of war, Captain Liddell Hart, propounded the notion that, certainly in the European theatre, a superiority of 3 to 1 was essential for successful attack to be likely, and even then it could not be assured, and this figure has never been seriously challenged. It can, of course, be varied up or down by surprise, or concentration, or superior weapons or braver or better trained men but, on the whole, it is a useful yardstick against which to assess the likely success of deterrence by conventional arms once the military balance sheet has been audited.

EAST - WEST BALANCE

How then do the East - West scales stand today? Figures are boring to read but a few need to be used here to give this aspect of the problem some meaning and sense of perspective. Put crudely, the Soviet Union deploys about 20 times as many men, about 30 times as many guns and 40 times as many tanks and 50 times as many aircraft and 10 times as many submarines as the United Kingdom does. They have 5 times the population and spend something like 3 times as much of their income — or more importantly 20 times as much in money or resources — as the United Kingdom does. So there can be no doubt that the British are not, and never could be, in the Liddell Hart league if alone, but happily

they are not, so it is more relevant to look at the corresponding
weights in the scales with NATO on one side and the Warsaw
Pact on the other. Here the West is inside the Liddell Hart
bracket in most respects, though not in all and, as can be
demonstrated, will not remain so comparatively well placed
unless some alarmingly adverse trends are at least arrested and
with determination reversed. On these bigger scales we find a
rough equality in manpower, and an advantage to the Warsaw
Pact of about 2 to 1 in guns, 3 in tanks, 1½ in aircraft and 3 in
submarines with a disadvantage of, perhaps, as much as 1 to 2 in
other effective maritime units. That sounds rather more hopeful
one may say, and so it is, but rather deeper thought must make
even those figures rather uncomfortable. For if comparisons are
examined of the rates of production of all these major engines of
war (and the less obvious ones are of a similar nature and a
similar importance to the total) it is clear that unless some urgent
action is taken Liddell Hart's ratio may quite soon be reached or
certainly come very uncomfortably close. For example, the Soviet
Union produces combat aircraft at a rate which would replace the
whole front line of the Royal Air Force every 6 months or a USAF
Wing once a month; they produce 7 or 8 of the most modern
tanks in the world a day, or enough to replace all those in the
British Army in 3 months or those in the whole US Army in a
year; they build nuclear powered attack submarines at least 3
times as fast as the British, the Americans and the French put
together. Similar daunting ratios run through the whole order of
battle in all three elements.

These are, certainly, other elements to be put into the conventional balance, but their weight is uncertain and can change
quite quickly as, for example, technological excellence, morale,
leadership and state of training. Senior officers whose business it
is to assess these intangible factors, would broadly conclude that
in most of them the West is today ahead. But quality, however
high, cannot indefinitely compensate for a gross disparity in
quantity, and since the time of Catharine the Great the Russians
have believed that safety really does lie in numbers — and not
without good reason.

Here, then, are what may be called the big bones in the
skeleton of the problem. But there are others which though of a
different nature must be given due weight in the examination of
the whole. First, the United Kingdom has residual responsibilities
even after the liquidation of our Empire, for which provision
must be made. They are small in comparison and demand cor-

respondingly small resources, but until political solutions have been found to relieve the commitments to defend, for example, Belize, Gibraltar, Brunei, the Falklands, Hong Kong and, within the very Kingdom's borders, that of Northern Ireland, some provision must be made to deal with them. And even if the threats are small compared with the threat in Europe just described, they will not simply disappear just because they are uncomfortable.

There are, too, some less-clear threats now emerging, which although posed by military capability—and thus, probably in the end only to be deterred (of if that fails countered) by military means—have in practice an economic or political effect first. These flow, obviously, from the events set in train 6 years ago by the rape of Angola by proxy Cuban forces, and to those which have followed in the Horn of Africa, in Vietnam and southern Arabia and, above all, in Afghanistan, and which, unhappily, it is only too easy to see extending elsewhere in Africa and in the Middle East and South-west Asia. It is probably no coincidence that all the areas mentioned straddle the sea lanes of communication on which the free countries of the World depend for their trade, and particularly for the energy and raw materials without which their economies would at once collapse. These must, therefore, be part of the whole problem.

For the formulation of defence policy one inescapable conclusion can be drawn already. No country in the West, not even the United States, can meet its gravest threat alone, nor the possible threat to its livelihood which may be posed in the future by events well outside the confrontation in Europe.

WHAT TO DO

Deciding what to do about it was the second of the four big bones identified in the skeleton of defence policy and should be tackled next. For the Western Europeans the first decision, rightly taken at intervals in their long history often as a matter of convenience, now becomes an imperative, and that is to seek sufficient strength to defend themselves by deterrence through an alliance. In fact they belong formally to NATO for this very purpose. Other countries in the Americas and South-east Asia and the Antipodes have special links, though none so formal as the North Atlantic Alliance. But it is much easier to perceive the need for such alliances or groupings of peoples of like mind who share similar hopes and fears than it is to agree on the actual language of the solemn treaties which give them effect. To return very briefly for a moment to what was said at the outset, the framework of such treaties must embrace areas much wider than the straightforward military alliances of a century or more ago in order to ensure that not only are military matters harmonised, but that the immediate consequences to national policies for external affairs, and the domestic economy, and social development, are not unacceptably distorted. The difficulties in such an enterprise are only too evident as, for example, in the fifteen nations which belong to NATO, where each of their non-military conditions vary as widely as they do between the United States and Luxembourg or Iceland, or when CENTO was formed between Pakistan and Iran and the United Kingdom, and in any alliance the whole community of interest must be covered if the military outcome is to be mutually tolerable, as well as achieving the aim of collective security. This is a large bone, though one which frequently does not receive as much attention as it should in the study of the anatomy of defence policy.

What next and what else, in the rather earthy phrase, must be done about it? Given that the first decision to rely upon alliances is right—and surely in the face of the facts so far retailed few would dissent from that—the next step must be to decide with whom to join forces. This has, of course, been done in Europe, indeed done over 32 years ago, but for academic integrity such an essential step in the argument should not be omitted. Of course the Western nations would wish to see as fellow members of their group those who share the important democratic notions, those who feel threatened by the same potential aggressors, those who can by geography or expertise or resources make an adequate contribution, and, perhaps more importantly, those who can be relied upon to do so. This done, what next? The defence policymaker must then immediately descend from precept to practice by getting in to the business of priorities. This, as those who have had to do it know very well, is extremely difficult—so difficult indeed that many actually funk it; more's the pity. For each country must, in the end, decide where its security stands in its own scheme of things, in the competition for scarce national resources; and each must decide what is his most appropriate subscription to the joint club and must also decide if he can afford to pay it; in this way national obligations must be related to international ones, and in the course of these connected but intellectually separate exercises each country must decide how best to apportion the defence budget between the separate armed forces. Surrounding and running through these complicated and interwoven threads is the need to be certain that the outcome of debate about them produces a coherent policy not only for the defence of the nation, but maintains the integrity of its total military, economic and political posture too. This is a complex undertaking and, as was also said at the outset, is a dynamic business in which theory and practice continually interact in a circular way, somewhat as those mathematical exercises of closer and closer approximations which lead nearer and nearer to the right answer but never to finality.

By way of illustrating some of the steps along the road whose broad direction is now becoming clearer, it may be said at once that the end product which is sought is sufficient power to deter attacks, on any scale, against the country or the allies it may have joined; and it is for precisely this reason that Article 3 of the North Atlantic Treaty states (in more formal language) that 'an attack on any one member will be treated as an attack on all'. But in that, or any other, alliance what sort of contribution should each member make? And how big should it be? Some countries are richer, some are better at making things, some are better at planning, some have special geographical locations or climates or difficulties of terrain, some by history and folk-memories are better soldiers than sailors or vice versa, and the catalogue could be much longer. This is what defence planners must carefully study, against the known capability of their potential opponents, and the need — to go back to Liddell Hart — to create forces which, in all the elements and throughout a threatened area, are seen to be capable of creating that fearful doubt which will stay the hand of potential opponents. Let us, for an example, look at the British contribution to NATO. Perhaps if they and their Allies had all suddenly arrived from outer space it might be different, but they did not — NATO started more or less where they all were at the end of World War II — and all the individual contributions flow to some extent from that. It is fortunate, but an accident, that each ally's contribution is tolerably well suited to its geographical, industrial, economic and political situation. Certainly for the United Kingdom, which has the largest navy in Europe (as well as being the third largest in the world), an army of 60,000 well-equipped and well-trained men permanently stationed in Germany and an air force of a similar size and nature. Even if the exercise had begun with a clean sheet of paper it is likely that the result, in the context of both the threat and of NATO, would not have been very greatly different. Whether that be so or not, the planner simply must lay out and deal consciously with all these factors in the process of what has twice been described as 'deciding what to do about the problem'.

PROVIDING THE RESOURCES

Turning from that second large bone of the skeleton, we come at once to the third, which is that of providing the resources to do what it has by now been decided is necessary. There seem to be three requirements, or elements, in this final assembly of the skeleton, of which the first is the political will (determination is better) to do it; the second is to examine more closely the constraints which make it difficult; and the third is whether it is, then, in practice, possible to implement the policy selected. Clearly, resources will never match what those responsible, and especially the chiefs of staff, would like, and this is one of the reasons why the whole enterprise must be a dynamic and circular one, of ever closer approximations if not to the very safest policy in military terms, at least to the policy which is in the best interests of the whole body politic.

Political will simply must come first, not only to provide and to continue to provide the necessary resources of manpower and their weapons systems, but to adopt attitudes which will proclaim the firm intention of the government to deter war, and, if that fails, to fight. This intention must be manifest not only to a potential aggressor but equally to those into whose hands the weapons are entrusted if deterrence is to be credible. It cannot be over-stressed that this is almost certainly the single most important ingredient of deterrence, and thus absolutely basic to both the formulation of defence policy and to its implementation. Government cannot, in the nature of modern society, either adopt or for long maintain this determination, unless it is required to do so by the people. It should, therefore, be (but regrettably more frequently is not) for the people to take an informed interest in defence matters. They have done so in the past and are likely to do so again, but it is one of the frailties of human nature that the longer peace continues the less interest in defence the general public takes, and this tendency is exacerbated in the democracies by a natural desire for a quiet and easier life, by the very high cost of arms today in competition with the rapidly escalating costs of the social services, and by frequent talk of détente. Wise governments would be well advised to do more than is habitually done in the democracies to inform public opinion of the essentials of the politico-military problem and their intentions for solving it, by way of ensuring that support for providing the resources is not withheld to the point where deterrence becomes insufficiently credible. In simpler words it is only the public who can demand and support the political will which must be the central feature of defence policy—and, indeed, of any policy.

What really are the constraints which may make the provision of the necessary resources more difficult? Some of them have been mentioned already in other terms. There are, of course, political constraints, some of them attributable to theology, or ideology which must be recognised, and they will clearly vary from country to country according to national habits. In a different sense, it is political constraints which to some extent create others, mostly in the field of national resource allocation, and any government must do a delicate balancing act to see that the whole body politic remains in scale. In its starkest terms, if more needs to be spent on defence, and national income is relatively fixed, on what should less be spent? If nothing can give, will the public support increased revenue? It is the author's view that they might be more ready to do so than they are often thought to be if they were better informed of what would be at risk if they did not. On what might be called the home front there are in any country very many people directly employed in the defence industries and as many in those related to them. Is this enough, too many, too few and what would happen to the rest of industry and to unemployment if these numbers were increased or decreased? Many countries make substantial profits across the exchanges by arms sales. Should they seek to increase this, and as a by-product probably get their own arms cheaper, or should they decrease this trade which some people believe to be immoral or at best destabilising and accept the loss of both foreign exchange and jobs? A significant number of the working population in most democracies is in the Forces, and carry with them even more civilians who are employed directly on defence administration. Is the number too many, about right, too few? What would they do which was more useful to their country if some were discharged, and would it be easier to meet defence commitments if there were more? These may be called second-order political constraints showing up in the fields of manpower, industry and the economy. The last group of constraints which demands mention is in the field of technology. Can any country still do it all? Is defence starving research into medicine, or mining, or alternative sources of energy, or transport, by deploying talent on their warlike disciplines; or is the spin-off from them a cheap way of doing research anyhow? What all these second-order constraints seem to have in common is that each of them makes it more rather than less difficult to provide the resources which ideally should be available to implement the defence policy which begins to emerge, but they are none the less part of its anatomy, none the less bones of the skeleton, for that.

So to conclude on providing the resources. At the very heart of the matter must lie the question 'Can it be done?' Surely there can be no country which claims to have a defence policy worthy of the name which would answer that question except with an unequivocal 'Yes'. This must be true except for those who believe that the constraints discussed are overriding, and some of them believe it sincerely, though others who profess it have less worthy motives. The dilemma, in fact, is strictly a matter of priorities, and there is no divine or natural law which would prevent any government making more resources available to ensure its people's way of life (and perhaps their very lives) if they really believed it was necessary. History shows that nearly every country has, at one time or another in its history, done exactly that.

There now remains only the fourth big skeletal bone which is, that having generated and recycled a defence policy, the crucial principle is to cling to it unless or until any of the surrounding circumstances grossly change, by way of emphasising that general stability is probably the most important feature of a successful defence policy. Stability in this sense must mean the creation and maintenance of continuity and coherence in all those elements here rehearsed which are under national control, just as much as in those of an allied nature over which a forceful national control can be exerted. There are, in the nature of the defence business, many matters, ranging from changes in the threat through changes in the economic situation to changes in what is technically feasible, to make the whole business a dynamic and not a static one, but it must, surely, be quite clear that a defence policy subject to frequent and arbitrary changes in the human and material resources made available to support it, would quickly become unmanageable.

As a tailpiece one may note that all around the world, at staff colleges and higher seats of defence learning, the students are told that the first two principles of war are to select the aim and then to maintain it, and they are then invited to consider what are described as the 'factors affecting the aim'. This is, in some degree, what has been attempted here in the effort to show that there is a clearly discernible anatomy of defence policy. It is to be hoped that the larger bones of the skeleton have also been identified with some clarity, and further that it is a complicated, delicate structure whose dissection reveals the total interdependence of the separate components. It is an immensely rewarding field of study, insufficiently understood, much less practised, today. It is also a field of endeavour where mistakes may be literally fatal.

Frank Cass

THE JOURNAL OF STRATEGIC STUDIES

Editors: **Amos Perlmutter,** The American University, Washington, D.C.
John Gooch, University of Lancaster

FROM THE EDITORS

No students of contemporary history and international politics can now ignore the importance of strategic studies. In some universities strategic centres have been established called Centres for 'International Relations' or 'Strategic Studies'. We felt that there was a clear need for a journal of strategic studies, since none existed in English, and hope htus to bring the subject into proper focus and concentrate the abundant material that has hitherto tended to be dispersed under other headings.

Frequency: Four times per year: March, June, September, December
Annual Subscription: Individual £18.00 Institution £27.50

ARMS CONTROL

Editor: **Ian Bellany,**   Centre for the Study of Arms Control and International Security, University of Lancaster
American Editor: **Coit D. Blacker,** Stanford University

FROM THE EDITORS

Arms control has moved in the past ten years from the wings to the centre stage of international affairs. Interest among scholars and students in security through arms limitation has risen in step with events, and a journal to provide an interdisciplinary focal point for their work has long been overdue. ARMS CONTROL is open to all whose study and research, within whatever discipline and from whatever perspective, enable them to make a contribution to arms control and disarmament studies.

Frequency: Three times per year: May, September, December
Annual Subscription: Individual £18.00 Institution £30.00

Frank Cass   Gainsborough House, 11 Gainsborough Road, London E11 1RS, England
& Co. Ltd.   Telephone: 01-530 4226   Telex: 897719

The Arms Trade and Arms Control

DAN SMITH

Dan Smith is the author of Defence of the Realm in the 1980s *and co-editor of* Protest and Survive

THE Stockholm International Peace Research Institute (SIPRI), which has specialised in reporting on the arms trade, its nature, extent and development, recently had this to say: 'There is no exact, reliable or even reasonable information as to the real value of the international arms trade.'[1]

Indeed, subjects in which the basic data are quite so unreliable as they are in this one are very rare. Apart from SIPRI, another major source of data on the arms trade is the US Arms Control and Disarmament Agency (ACDA); its estimate for the value of the global arms trade in 1977 of $16.7 billion compares to an estimate by a respected independent researcher of $120 billion.[2] This latter figure is the same as SIPRI estimates for the total value of all arms production worldwide.[3] Uncertainty about the overall value of the trade is repeated at a more detailed level. The US General Accounting Office in a 1979 study found major inaccuracies in State Department figures for US commercial exports,[4] while ACDA's estimates for British arms exports for 1975 - 77 are about half the value estimated by the British Government for those years.[5]

These remarks are a necessary preface to considering the arms trade. Before we start to try and understand it, we must first disabuse ourselves of the notion that we have any very sound empirical basis on· which to proceed. Yet this should not pre-empt the effort. As a subject of study, the arms trade includes the pro-

---

[1] *World Armaments and Disarmament: SIPRI Yearbook 1980,* Taylor & Francis, London, 1980 (hereafter *SIPRI*), p 57.

[2] *World Military Expenditures and Arms Transfers 1968 - 1977,* (US Arms Control and Disarmament Agency, 1979) (hereafter *ACDA*); R L Sivard, *World Military and Social Expenditures 1979, World Priorities,* WMSE Publications, Leesburg, Va. 1979.

[3] *SIPRI,* p 57.

[4] *US Munitions Export Controls Need Improvement,* US GAO, 1979.

[5] *ACDA,* Table III, compared to the annual *Statement on the Defence Estimates for 1975, 1976* and *1977.*

cesses by which most of the world's states equip their armed forces and an important part of the armament processes in the countries which export arms; its political, strategic and economic importance is virtually self-evident. Moreover, despite discrepancies in the basic data there is wide agreement about many salient features.

TABLE 1. MARKET SHARES OF EXPORTING COUNTRIES

A. ACDA estimates: World Market 1973 - 77	%	B. SIPRI estimates: Third World Market, 1970 - 79	%
United States	37.9	United States	45
USSR	32.8	USSR	27.5
France	6.3	France	10
United Kingdom	4.5	United Kingdom	5
Federal Republic of Germany	3.1	Italy	3
Czechoslovakia	2.8	Federal Republic of Germany	2.3
Poland	2.1	China	1.3
Italy	1.6	(Other third world exporters)	1.7
China	1.2	(Other exporters)	4.2
(Other exporters)	7.7		

Sources: *World Military Expenditures and Arms Transfers 1968 - 1977*, US Control and Disarmament Agency, 1979, Table IV; *World Armaments and Disarmament: SIPRI Yearbook 1980*, Taylor & Francis, London, 1980, pp 62 and 65.

Table 1 compares ACDA's assessment of the market shares of the exporting countries in the world market as a whole with SIPRI's estimate of market shares in export to Third World countries.[6] Although the period covered and the scope of the market reviewed are different, the leading positions in the 'league table' are the same. There is also general agreement about the main developments in the international arms trade during the 1970s. Firstly, it is agreed that the volume of the arms trade increased dramatically. ACDA estimates that in constant price terms the value of the trade almost doubled from 1968 to 1977 while, more vaguely, SIPRI states that 'the *spread* of major conventional arms increased four times as compared to the 1960s', and adds that the rate of increase was itself sharply accelerating as the decade

[6] However, a French estimate shows France taking a 16 per cent share of the world arms market: *La Croix* 26 August 1977, cited in A Grosser, *The Western Alliance*, Macmillan, London, 1980, p 293.

passed.[7] As part of this general increase, more sophisticated weapons are being exported to more countries: ACDA notes that in 1960 only 4 Third World states operated supersonic combat aircraft; by 1977 47 were equipped with them.[8] In consequence, recipients have also had a greater need for continuing technical assistance: in 1976, for example, there were about 10,000 Soviet and East European technicians in Third World countries; in 1978, though it never came to pass, it was estimated that by 1980 there would be 60,000 US contract personnel in Iran providing technical assistance; the Saudi Arabian purchase of the United States' F-5E fighter, regarded as a relatively simple aircraft, involves assistance from over 1600 personnel, while the same country's import of the more complex F-15 undoubtedly requires many more.[9] The transfer of technical expertise for the use of military equipment has been counterpointed by an increasing transfer of production know-how and capacity, often through the medium of licensing agreements.

Within this growing trade, ACDA and SIPRI both estimate that Third World countries provide about three-quarters of the demand. The shift in patterns of demand among these countries is well known: East Asian countries provide a much smaller share of demand according to ACDA (about 6 per cent in 1977 compared to 39 per cent in 1968), while the Middle East provides a much larger share (39 per cent compared to 12 per cent). Also significant is the increased share provided by African countries (about 17 per cent compared to 3 per cent), reflecting an increase in imports which ACDA estimates at over 1200 per cent by value.[10]

There have also been important shifts in the pattern of supply: most notably there are more suppliers. SIPRI estimates there are now 43 states which export major arms, while ACDA data show that from 1968 to 1977 just 14 states exported arms each year, but from 1973 to 1977 this figure was 25.[11] In other words, more states are becoming permanent arms exporters. Perhaps the most significant development here is that increasing numbers of the Third World states now export arms, a tendency which can be ex-

---

[7] *ACDA*, p 16; *SIPRI*, p 57 (emphasis added).

[8] *ACDA*, p 16.

[9] *SIPRI*, pp 63 and 68 - 69; see also *ACDA*, p 17.

[10] *ACDA*, pp 16 - 17; *SIPRI*, p 61 (*ACDA* states Third World countries account for 78 per cent of arms imports worldwide; *SIPRI* puts the figure at 74.3 per cent).

[11] *SIPRI*, p 63; *ACDA*, Table III.

pected to continue as arms-producing capacities take root in Third World countries. This has fed the process of intensifying competition in the arms trade even as the market has expanded. The efforts of West European countries have been a major influence here. According to ACDA figures, the share of the market taken by European NATO exporters has more than doubled since 1968, standing at about 20 per cent in 1977. At the beginning of the 1970s, only France and Britain were net exporters of arms; since 1973 they have been joined by Belgium (on a relatively modest scale) and Italy, and since 1976 by the Federal Republic of Germany (FRG). Even including Greece (a large importer which exports nothing) and Turkey (another large importer which exports very little), European NATO states as a group are major net exporters, a position which dates only from 1972.[12] Despite this competition, the United States and the USSR remain far and away the largest arms exporters. It would appear that Soviet prices are below those for equivalent Western equipment, and the credit terms are usually more generous.[13] In the United States a further important shift has taken place, with sales almost entirely replacing aid as the means of exporting arms. In the 1950s, over 90 per cent of US arms transfers went as grants; in the 1960s and through to 1973, 50 per cent of transfers were still grants; by the end of the 1970s, military assistance of this kind had been wound down and over 90 per cent of transfers are now sales by the US Government, with most of the remainder being commercial exports by private companies.[14] There is today, therefore, very little need to refer to the arms trade by the pseudonym of 'arms transfers'; with only small exceptions, the process is now genuine trade.

SIPRI comments that: 'The arms business is one of the fastest growing sectors within the world economy in monetary terms.'[15] This assessment would command general assent, and there is no reason to think it will be less accurate in the next few years. On current trends and plans a slackening in the arms trade as a whole seems unlikely, although it is possible that the expansion of the Third World market will slow, at least temporarily, because many recipients appear to have fully equipped if not over-equipped themselves.

[12] *ACDA*, Table III.

[13] *SIPRI*, p 64.

[14] Ibid, pp 66 - 68.

[15] Ibid, p 57.

ARMS CONTROL

The growth of the arms trade in the 1970s was met with widespread concern, most powerfully evidenced perhaps in the United States where opinion polls in the late 1970s consistently showed 50 per cent or more of those polled expressing opposition to arms exports as a general principle. Further, 'When respondents are asked about sales to specific countries, the proportion opposing weapon transfers rises dramatically for almost all potential recipients.'[16] Opinion may have shifted in the last couple of years along with other changes in the political mood in the United States, and it is possible that public opinion in the other main exporting countries was less anxious, but it is hardly surprising that the arms trade is viewed with such unease.

All issues involving arms and their potential or actual use should in any case call forth a morally and intellectually questioning response. This starting point is taken further in the case of the arms trade because of its association in many minds with the record of unscrupulous and often systematically corrupt and corrupting selling practices of certain companies.[17] Whether or not this association is fair to the majority of states and corporations involved, there is little doubt it contributes to producing a critical moral assessment of the arms trade as a whole. But concern about the arms trade need not only be directed at such issues.

The way states equip themselves militarily is always of major importance at a variety of levels. The effect of the arms trade is especially important among the less-developed countries, including those which are rich in resources or undertaking major industrialisation and thus are best able to build up their armed forces. With many of these states, their political, strategic and economic circumstances cannot for a moment be adequately understood without reference to the arms trade, to their or their neighbours' participation in it. These considerations create the need for a searching evaluation of the effects of the arms trade, and such evaluation produces a number of concerns. There is the issue of the militarisation of many states, and the effect of their import-based arms programmes on regional tensions and rivalries. It does not seem that equipping more and more states with more and more sophisticated weapons in ever greater quan-

[16] *ACDA*, p 16

[17] See A Sampson, *The Arms Bazaar*, Hodder & Stoughton, London, 1977, and D Boulton, *The Lockheed Papers*, Jonathan Cape, London, 1978.

tities produces a particularly pleasant picture of prospects for peace in the world. It does not seem that using resources in this way is the best use of them, at either national or global levels, when so many pressing needs cry out so urgently for more resources. To argue that the trade in arms is in principle no different from the trade in any other kind of product is to miss almost every salient feature of this particular trade — its products and their role for both suppliers and recipients, the nature of many of the major importing states and the way in which they may use their imports.

However, attempts to translate these concerns into effective action to control and limit the arms trade have hitherto been singularly unsuccessful. The major effort came from the largest exporter, the United States, with an initiative by President Carter in May 1977. The approach had three facets: restraint in US exports; negotiations with other major suppliers with a view to multilateral agreement on restraint; and encouraging regional agreements among recipients to restrain their imports. Diplomacy along these lines flourished briefly with US - Soviet talks, but had drifted into deadlock by the end of 1978, at the same time as doubts emerged within the Carter Administration about the wisdom of the policy. Little has come of the encouragement to recipients to restrain their imports, and there are strong grounds for doubting the effectiveness of the United States' self-imposed restraint in exports.[18] It is now clear that the Carter initiative has failed, and there is nothing around at the moment to take its place. At a time when the prospects for almost all varieties of arms control are hardly bright, the prospects for arms control in respect of the arms trade are exceptionally dim.

To some extent, this failure simply reflects the size and intractability of the problem. After all, there are very strong interests on both the demand and the supply sides of the trade with major political, military and economic investments at stake. The consequent resistance to any initiative for limiting the arms trade is bound to be far from puny. But it may also be the case that some of the difficulty here is due to a basic mis-specification of the problem. As I shall now go on to argue, this is an analytical rather than an empirical mis-specification, but it should be added that arms control is extremely problematic when the basic data are uncertain. Accordingly, any steps with lead to more reliable international data on the arms trade are unreservedly to be welcomed.

[18] *SIPRI*, pp 69 - 70 and 121 - 24.

The Importers

It is often argued that proposals such as the Carter initiative are inherently discriminatory against those states which find they can only equip their forces to the degree they think adequate by importing arms, other equipment and assistance. Who are the arms-producing states, it is often asked, to deny to other states the means for national defence? Now there is an element of speciousness in this argument which needs to be isolated out before we can properly proceed. First, it is simply naive to imagine that the arms trade is wholly made up of satisfying legitimate requirements for national defence; the trade also satisfies many other requirements—such as for domestic repression by some particularly repugnant régimes, for regional aggrandisement, and for the self-glorification of national leaders. Second, in the arms market, as in all markets, demand is never completely autonomous: if demand cannot be actually created by the exporters, it can nevertheless be given a nudge in the right direction, and enormous effort is put into this; whether the methods used to stimulate demand and win orders are above reproach or well below it, the desire to sell on the part of the exporters is at least as important in sustaining the trade as the recipients' wish to buy. Third, importing states are in any case denied certain types of equipment—most notably nuclear weapons—and the wisdom of this is widely acknowledged. Fourth, most exporters, including Britain, totally exclude certain potential importers on political grounds. Alongside these factors, however, there is an element which is certainly not specious. Most states, including most states that export arms, can only satisfy their perceived military requirements with the help of imports. Whether or not one thinks their perceptions are accurate or legitimate is not here at issue; what is at issue is that those perceptions grow from the situations in which states find themselves both nationally and internationally. To attempt to control the arms trade may therefore be, in a sense, to be diverted by the symptoms away from attending to the underlying problem—the situations in which states find themselves and the way in which their perceptions of those situations translate into requirements for armed force and thus into arms imports.

To this it can be added that an examination of the situations in which importers find themselves may reveal further problems. A state without arms-producing capacity which feels threatened by a neighbour which does have that capacity is bound to feel that control of the arms trade is an inappropriate form of arms control. In this sense, control of the arms trade risks not so much discriminating against Third World states as a whole as discriminating among them.

These arguments suggest that the appropriate object for arms control in relation to the arms trade is not the imports themselves, but the regional tensions and rivalries which create the demand for arms imports and the role of armed forces in those tensions and rivalries. From this perspective, the need is for regional agreements on security and arms control. Such agreements would affect the level of arms imports and thus act as a control on the arms trade, without agreements on the arms trade as such being needed. Perhaps the distinction can be illustrated by reference to Europe where both NATO and the Warsaw Pact have apparently agreed for many years on the desirability of reducing forces in Central Europe. It would not have seemed appropriate to any of the participants if the resulting Mutual and Balanced Force Reduction talks (MBFR) had begun by attempting to control arms imports in East and West Europe. The source of the arms is virtually a non-issue (at least as far as MBFR is concerned).

Of course, reference to the stalemated MBFR talks indicates that switching the focus of arms control away from the arms trade and onto tensions and deployed forces is no guarantee of success. But then, no arms control is guaranteed to succeed. The very factors which make meaningful arms control agreements such an urgent necessity also make them extremely hard to achieve. And it may be that some efforts at arms control are virtually guaranteed to fail if they address the wrong objects.

THE EXPORTERS

Where, however, does this leave the exporters? The perspective outlined above suggests that the main momentum for regional arms control agreements which would, as a by-product, act as controls on the arms trade, should come from the importing states. But this should not be taken to imply that the exporting states have no interest in and need pay no attention to such arms control. At the same time, it can be argued that if, as far as the importers are concerned, directing the attention of arms control at the arms trade itself derives from mis-specifying the problem, this is at least equally true when it comes to the exporters.

Here again, we must begin with empirical problems. Among the most irritating consequences of the weak data base is the difficulty of assessing the extent to which arms production in the main exporting states is dependent on arms exports. ACDA data for 1973 to 1977 suggest that in the United States an annual average of about 17 per cent by value of arms produced were exported; for the USSR, ACDA data suggest a figure of about 12 per cent — which is probably as good a guess as any.[19] Britain would appear to export an average of about 30 per cent of arms produced,[20] which is much higher than ACDA data suggest. SIPRI states that France exports 55 - 60 per cent of arms produced,[21] more than double the proportion suggested by ACDA data. In the case of Italy and the FRG ACDA data for 1973 - 77 suggest 17 and 10 per cent respectively as the export share of production, with the proportions rising at the end of the period. In view of the understatement in the case of Britain and possibly of France, these figures for Italy and the FRG should probably be increased quite sharply.

To the extent they can be trusted, these figures indicate a significant degree of dependence on exports to sustain military industry, especially in the case of West Europe, but for some industries the dependence is much greater. In France, for example, it has been estimated that three out of every four Mirage aircraft produced must be exported in order to maintain the profitability of the production line. In Britain, the aerospace, electronics and ship building industries show higher than average proportions of production destined for export, although the jolt given to the British tank industry when the Shah of Iran fell and his order for Shir Iran tanks fell with him was evidence of that industry's dependence on exports. The FRG exports a particularly high proportion of the submarines, frigates and fast patrol boats that it produces, while Italy is noted for aerospace exports (especially counter-insurgency aircraft and helicopters, often producing US-designed equipment for export), an increasing number of frigates and considerable quantities of small arms.[22]

The extent to which arms production of certain types is dependent on exports causes problems. In France, for example, there

[19] These figures are arrived at by taking data in *ACDA*, Tables I and III, and assuming 30 per cent of military expenditure is spent on equipment procurement. The same rough methodology produces the figures for Italy and the FRG.

[20] The necessary data are available in each year's *Statement on The Defence Estimates* from *1975* to *1980* as estimates of the coming year's procurement, exports and imports: *1975*, Cmnd 5976, pp 24 and 91 - 92; *1976* Cmnd 6432, pp 48 and 84; *1977*, Cmnd 6735, pp 33 and 71; *1978*, Cmnd 7099, pp 29 and 63; *1979*, Cmnd 7474, pp 29 and 67; *1980*, Cmnd 7826-I, p 82, and Cmnd 7826-II, p 8 and Table 3.1.

[21] SIPRI, p 75.

[22] Ibid, pp 79 - 81.

have been complaints in the army that new armoured personnel carriers have been designed with the requirements of desert warfare more in mind than the requirements of the French Army itself. Similarly, the land-mobile Crotale surface-to-air missile was being exported while the French Air Force was still waiting for its order to be fully met.[23] In Britain, there were similar complaints in the Army that its own requirements for modifications to Chieftain tanks took second place to export orders.[24] But such problems and complaints about them are themselves only reflections of a deeper problem, which the example of British tank exports illustrates. By the latter part of the 1970s Britain had pulled out of collaboration on a new tank with the United States and the FRG and had no requirement for a new tank until the late 1980s. In the meantime, the British tank industry would be kept in business by exports, and a major deal was arranged with the Shah of Iran who ordered 125 copies of the Shir-I (modified Chieftains) and 1225 Shir Irans equipped with Chobham armour. This appeared to be both a neat and a necessary way of keeping the British tank industry in business at little or no cost to the national exchequer until it was again required to meet British Army requirements. When the Shah fell in January 1979, the result was what SIPRI describes as 'an almost desperate sales drive' to stave off the collapse of the industry.[25] It was, or should have been, a grim warning of the potential consequences if military industrial policy comes to rely on the stability of an unpopular and repressive régime. It also illustrated the extent of reliance on exports of this part of British military industrial capacity.

Of course, it would have been, and still is, possible for the government to wind up British tank production and import its future requirements. But this would go against the long-established policy of sustaining the capacity independently to produce tanks as most other major items of military equipment. And it is this policy of maintaining a major degree of self-sufficiency in the production of arms which underlies the policy of promoting arms exports. So necessary is the latter policy to the former that one could say, assuming the complaints were accurate, that the French Army could not have had its new APCs nor the French Air Force its Crotales unless exports were given priority in development and production.

[23] Ibid, p 77.
[24] *The Times*, 2 May 1978.
[25] *SIPRI*, pp 98 - 99.

Accordingly, if emphasis is placed on self-sufficiency in military equipment, arms exports become an integral part of defence policy. This situation exists because in Britain and France, to an increasing extent in the FRG and Italy, and also in the United States and the USSR, the arms industries operate capacity which is surplus to national military requirements. Ironically, but not surprisingly, surplus capacity can co-exist with shortfalls in military industrial capacity; this is apparently a serious problem in the United States,[26] and will also affect Britain as it considers how to produce the submarines for Trident missiles and maintain production of fleet submarines.[27] The problem is that surplus capacity exists in the wrong sectors of the industry. But if the surplus is not sustained by exports, the profitability and existence of whole sectors of national military industrial capacity would be threatened, viz the case of the British tank industry. Maintaining capacity which is not required for national military purposes has become essential to maintaining the level of capacity which is required.

As well as the emphasis on self-sufficiency in military procurement, another side of the origin of this problem is in the arms industry itself—in its structural tendency to expand capacity as each new product succeeds another with ever-increasing sophistication and cost. With a policy of self-sufficiency, this tendency towards capacity expansion would impose intolerable costs in the absence of countervailing policies. One such policy is to export arms and, therefore, effectively to transfer abroad the costs of maintaining a military industrial capacity of the requisite technological scope.[28]

However, even as the promotion of arms exports functions in this way, as a part of defence policy, its effects are contradictory, creating problems of which some examples have already been mentioned. More important, of course, is the global problem to which discussion of the arms trade directs attention—the increasing militarisation of the international scene, the exacerbation of regional tensions and rivalries, the risks of further wars. While some opponents of the arms trade undoubtedly exaggerate its effect in starting wars and increasing tensions, many defenders of

[26] *Business Week,* 18 February 1980.

[27] It appears that the Ministry of Defence is not satisfied with the standards of all British submarine-building capacity: see *The Sunday Times,* 8 June 1980.

[28] The other main ways of countering the effects of capacity expansion have been industrial reorganisation, cancellations and international collaboration: for a discussion see my *The Defence of the Realm in the 1980s,* Croom Helm, London, 1980, chs 6 and 7.

the trade react with complacency. If the arms trade does not always cause the problems, it is undeniable that it can make a major contribution to making them worse. If arms exports as a part of defence policy are thereby an aspect of national security, they contradictorily diminish global security and thereby the national security of the exporting countries.

The economic effect of arms exports is similarly contradictory. In Britain it is estimated that arms exports provide about 75,000 jobs along with a positive contribution now standing at about £1200 million annually to the balance of payments.[29] This is clearly an economic benefit. But two points should be added. Firstly, the argument that these jobs and foreign income would be necessarily lost if there were no arms exports is not strong. The resources bound up in the production of arms — both the human and the inanimate resources — are extremely valuable ones which, with sensible planning, could be redeployed in other areas of manufacturing.[30] This redeployment could be a part of strengthening and renewing Britain's fast dwindling industrial base, which leads on to the second point. The contribution arms exports make to sustaining British military industry and defence policy is a contribution to sustaining an economic burden. The major resource cost of military spending is loss of investment in civil industry;[31] civil industry itself finds the necessary skilled personnel hard to come by, partly because so many are employed in military industry. It should have escaped nobody's attention that investment and skilled personnel are desperately required for the industrial and economic regeneration of Britain. High levels of arms exports make it seem possible for Britain to have a large capacity for military production and spend a relatively high proportion of national income on defence. Over the long run, this is an illusion.

DEMILITARISATION

From the discussion of the arms exporters, as from the discussion of the importers, it emerges that focusing concern on controlling the arms trade is to be tempted by the symptoms away from attending to the underlying cause. The policy of promoting arms

---

[29] Cmnd 7826-I, pp 81 - 82.

[30] D Smith (Ed), *Alternative Work for Military Industries*, Richardson Institute, London, 1977.

[31] R P Smith, 'Military Expenditure and Capitalism', *Cambridge Journal of Economics*, 1 (1) (March 1977).

exports is in one sense self-feeding—the more successful the policy is, the more exports are required to sustain the expanding surplus capacity; it would therefore seem that restraining arms exports could be a useful measure of arms control. But it only scratches the surface of the problem, and is unlikely to work at all if the causes of arms exports are left untouched. The arguments above suggest that if one were interested in limiting the overall levels of arms exports, what would actually be required is arms control agreements on the defence policies of the exporting states and on their arms industries. Such measures would have to be accompanied by redeploying industrial capacity to non-military uses in order to avoid either wasting valuable resources or retaining surplus capacity as a permanent pressure undermining the changes.

If, alongside such measures among the exporters, we consider the kind of arms control suggested earlier in the case of the importers, the process which emerges is one of global demilitarisation. This process would involve removing at least some of the military content of international relations, the policies of states, the international economy and national economies. The process as a whole can be broken down into a series of regional agreements on security, arms control and, where appropriate, redeployment of military industrial capacity. This is clearly a series of massive tasks which would be accomplished, if at all, over a long period of time; it would be a difficult and uneven process. But the alternative to undertaking these tasks is to watch and contribute to the further militarisation of the world. If there is any concern about the ill-effects of this, it ought to be clear that the time to tackle the problems is now when they are already bad enough, rather than waiting until they are much worse.

It is very evident that success cannot be guaranteed. To some, this may mean there should be no change in the policy of exporting arms to all comers except for a few states which are particularly disliked. The long-term perspective is all very well, but it is more likely that short-term interests will predominate. The argument is, of course, that if we do not sell arms, others will: as a prediction, it is strong; as a guide to policy, it is woefully weak. In Britain's case, one element of recovery from our own variant of the international recession needs to be a relative demilitarisation of the economy and industry, a major effort to use the talents and resources now bound up in military industry for restrengthening civil industry and technology. Following this path would include unilaterally reducing arms exports: so much the better.

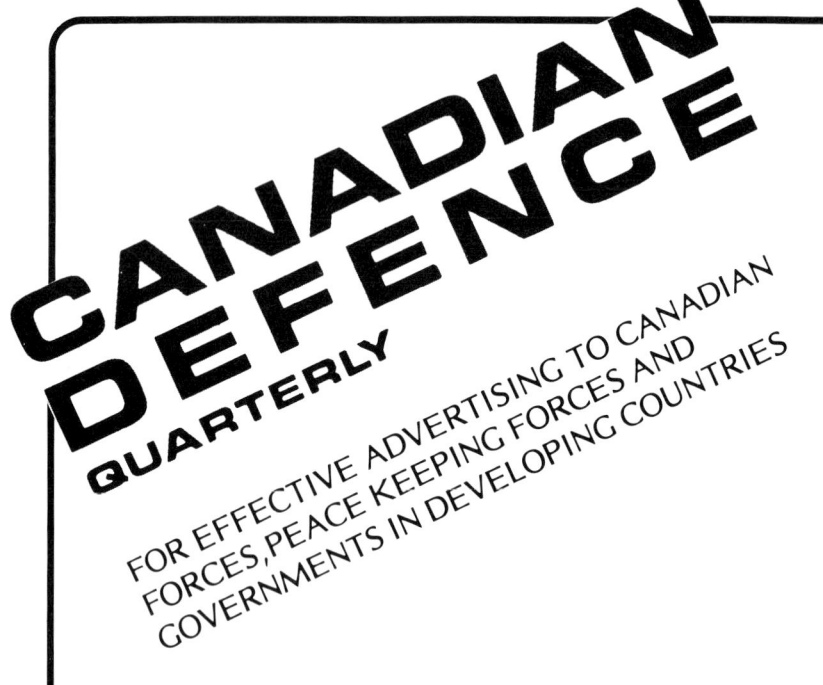

Our Common Defence for the Eighties

JOHN G TOWER

*United States Senator from Texas (Republican)
and Chairman of the Senate Armed Services Committee*

OVER three decades have now elapsed since the signing of the North Atlantic Treaty in Washington on 4 April 1949. The chronicle of each of these decades reflects the awesome degree of change the world has undergone through the 1950s, 1960s and 1970s. While our Alliance has matured against a backdrop of peace and general prosperity in Western Europe, the signatories of our treaty would surely be dismayed by the global turmoil and uncertainty which prevail as we move into the 1980s.

There is a broad consensus among informed Western leaders that unusually dangerous years lie ahead. The basis for this danger, however, now clearly perceived, is the looming threat of unrestrained Soviet military power. It is this power that holds Eastern Europe in bondage. It is this power that has deployed an army nearly 100,000 strong in brutal conquest of Afghanistan. It is this power that has established spheres of influence in various parts of the world and has seized upon opportunities to exacerbate tensions in Asia, Africa and Latin America. It is this power that through clandestine infrastructures, surrogate military forces and assumed management of native insurgencies, has sought to intensify and exploit social unrest and political instability.

These events and phenomena illuminate the vulnerabilities of the West. Our economies have grown increasingly interdependent and we rely heavily on sources of supply for energy and raw materials that are concentrated in areas outside our political control. This interdependence has at once hampered the economic resilience of the West and magnified the divergence of goals and the diffusion of power among many separate developing countries.

These vulnerabilities have become the focus of the Soviet régime as it has amassed a level of military power which exceeds any reasonable assessment of its defensive needs by several orders of magnitude. The result of this unprecedented build-up is the evolution of a spectrum of land, sea and air power capable of supporting the increasingly apparent global objectives of Soviet foreign policy.

Over the course of the past 15 years, our response as an Alliance to the threat has been woefully inadequate. We have permitted ourselves to become preoccupied with internal problems. We have allowed security policy to be influenced by domestic political considerations to the extent that we have failed to give priority to the funding of defence requirements. We have been dangerously naive and uncomprehending of Soviet intentions. We have demonstrated a singular inability to formulate within the Alliance a mechanism for crisis management. We have, therefore, fostered a clear impression of inability to respond to the Soviet challenge, thereby encouraging Soviet adventurism and Soviet-inspired exploitation of areas of instability.

The demoralising consequence that flows from unchecked Soviet aggression is the rising conviction that the Soviets can act with impunity. This ominous trend must be arrested lest it give added and irrevocable momentum to the Soviet drive for military supremacy and inflict fatal paralysis on the West.

Too often ignored or submerged in wishful thinking is the lesson of history that failure to prepare for conflict in response to a major challenge only invites conflict itself—or surrender.

As an Alliance, we must forge a common resolve to mount the strenuous effort demanded by the strategy essential to our response. We need examine only a few eloquent figures to realise what confronts us. The Central Intelligence Agency estimates that Soviet military expenditures presently exceed US military expenditures by approximately 50 per cent. In examining only the investment portions of these outlays, that is, the spending for procurement, research and development, and military construction, the Soviets have outspent the United States every year since 1971. The Soviet investment programme is about 90 per cent larger than that of the United States, which this year will spend about $50 billion less for investment purposes than will the Soviet Union. Even the total military investment spending for the NATO countries combined does not exceed the amount of these expenditures for Soviet military programmes.

Among numerous Soviet developments that have resulted from this enormous allocation of resources to the military, there are two which I believe warrant special attention. First, the Soviets have brought to an end the era of US superiority in strategic weapons. In 1982 we shall have lost our essential equivalence in strategic capability. Augmenting the Soviets' overwhelming conventional superiority along NATO's cental front is the growing disparity to their advantage in theatre nuclear (Euro-strategic) capabilities. Secondly, the Soviets have built a global navy capable of maintaining a sustained naval presence in any area of the world.

In their strategic forces, the Soviets continue to improve and enlarge their offensive nuclear capabilities, and there are no signs that these efforts are abating. While they have given predominant attention to their intercontinental ballistic missile forces (ICBMs), they have continued to diversify and improve the capabilities of their sea-based threat by commissioning new generations of submarines with longer-range submarine-launched ballistic missiles (SLBMs). The extended ranges of these new SLBMs will allow their submarines to operate in greatly expanded patrol areas. As a result, they will be more difficult to locate by our own anti-submarine warfare forces, and their patrol areas will be drawn in waters closer to the Soviet land mass than has been possible with previous submarines.

Across all of their strategic missile programmes, they continue ambitious modernisations incorporating increased throwweight, improved accuracy, more re-entry vehicles per missile, enhanced readiness, and better command, control and communications (C_3). It is evident that the more sophisticated Soviet ICBMs are especially suited for pre-emptively attacking our own strategic C_3 nerve centres and ICBM silos.

The Soviet bomber force has acquired a new dimension in the supersonic Backfire bomber, which is now being produced at the rate of about 30 per year. This versatile aircraft can, of course, serve in a theatre role as well as in an intercontinental role when refuelled. Soviet naval air forces make further use of the Backfire's capabilities in the anti-ship mission by equipping the bomber with long-range cruise missiles carrying either conventional or nuclear warheads.

An important but sometimes overlooked element in the strategic balance is the existence of a large and sophisticated Soviet air defence network, which far exceeds the capabilities of air defence programmes maintained by the United States and Western Europe. Civil defence, military and industrial dispersal, facilities hardening and survival training comprise the foundation of a significant passive defence programme in the Soviet Union.

Only a superficial review of the nature and direction of this build-up in Soviet strategic forces is needed to see how and where we have erred. The loss of American superiority in strategic forces occurred at a time when the United States was making a strenuous and good faith effort to bring arms competition under control through negotiated agreements with the Soviet Union. Today, while Soviet factories are mass-producing both land-based missiles and manned bombers, we in the United States have an open production line for neither.

ARMS CONTROL

It is thus that we must now reckon with a fate that our own actions have invited. Over much of the 1970s the United States chose to ignore reality. Our failure to negotiate from a position of strength has made meaningful arms control as elusive today as it was 10 years ago. The SALT I accord on offensive arms did not significantly impede the growth of the strategic offensive capacity of the Soviet Union. The SALT II proposal negotiated by the Carter Administration was an inequitable treaty which would have succeeded only in lulling the West into a false and dangerous sense of security. It would have permitted enormous increases in Soviet offensive strategic power, while restraining in a critical way many of our own programmes.

Nonetheless, it is important for our European friends to understand that the United States has not given up its commitment to real arms control. What we have given up under the Reagan Administration is our preoccupation with arms control as something we must pursue as an end unto itself. We now have an administration that will confidently develop a realistic approach to arms control by recognising its unavoidable prerequisites: a demonstrated ability and resolve to produce and deploy those forces and systems we must have. Only then, in my view, will we be able to engage the Soviets in negotiations that will yield actual and equitable restraints on arms. Of course, this new approach will require certain sacrifices to support a substantial increase in our expenditures to modernise our own strategic forces, and it will require close consultation within the Alliance itself.

As expected, Soviet resistance to this new direction in our arms control policy has already begun. Mr Brezhnev's recent appeal contained in his letters to leaders in each of the NATO countries heralds the predictable Soviet aim of dividing our Alliance on issues central to our common security. Leading his agenda is the disruption of our essential plan to modernise our theatre nuclear forces as agreed to in December of 1979. Indeed, our foremost imperative as an alliance today is to proceed with this vital modernisation programme to close the ominous gap which now exists as a result of Soviet deployments of the SS-20 missile and the Backfire bomber.

BACKFIRE AND SS-20 COVERAGE FROM SOVIET BASES

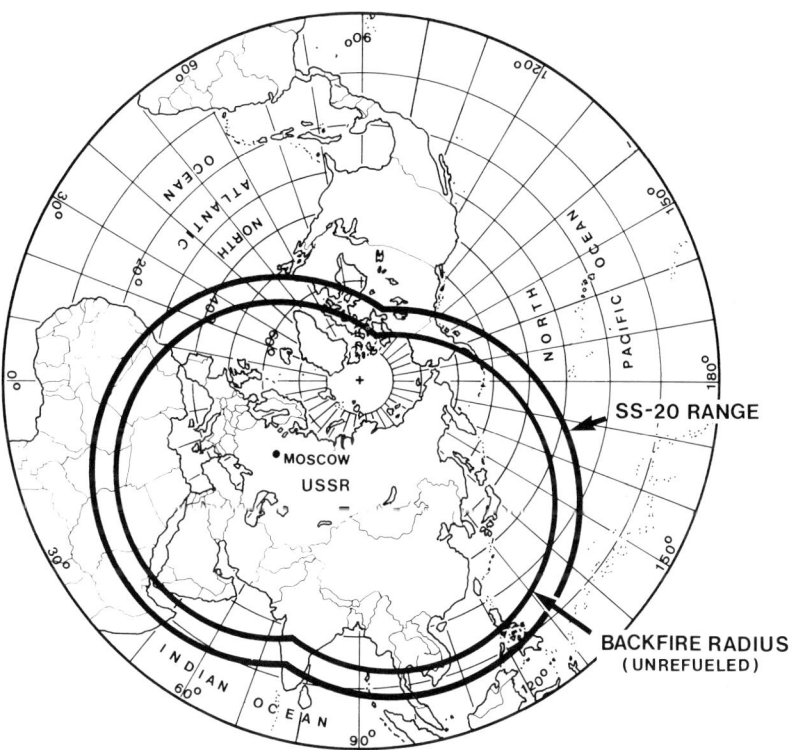

As we have now come to realise, the loss of US strategic superiority has substantially lowered the threshold of risk perceived by the Soviets and requires a higher level of preparedness for our allied conventional forces. This need is evident across the full range of our conventional capabilities. In an increasingly interdependent world that relies on vital sea lines of communication, the threat of Soviet naval power has become a highly visible instrument of Soviet political objectives which are no longer confined to the Eurasian land mass.

Under Admiral Gorshkov's aggressive leadership, the Soviet fleet has evolved from an essentially coastal defence force to an open ocean navy capable of projecting force at shores great distances from their own. The flexibility they enjoy in being able to concentrate superior force in a given area affords them a high probability of affecting the outcome of any naval confrontation. This flexibility is due to the fact that, unlike the allied navies, the Soviets would not be compelled to divert forces to vital sea control missions in time of crisis.

While the Soviets first concentrated on developing a seaborne, strategic nuclear strike capability and maintaining their defences of seaward approaches to the USSR, they have now become increasingly capable of meeting head-on with the US Navy in distant parts of the world. Their construction of large, offensively capable cruisers, vertical take-off and landing aircraft carriers, highly mobile logistics support ships, amphibious assault ships and advanced submarines is the product of the most concerted and determined build-up of naval power in the history of the world. In summary, their goal is to achieve maritime superiority and replace the United States as the predominant world sea power.

Let us remember that geography confers on the Soviet Union no requirement for importing vast quantities of raw materials by sea. Although their own agricultural system is chronically inefficient, they remain far more economically self-sufficient than any member of the Atlantic Alliance. This is the central fact which identifies the fundamental purpose behind the advent of a blue-water Soviet Navy: a threat to the very lifelines of the industrialised West and the ability to deploy naval forces to areas of regional instability around the globe.

These two developments—the loss of US strategic superiority and the advent of Soviet naval power on a global scale—are accompanied by many other initiatives which have enhanced Soviet military capabilities across the full spectrum of military power. It would be difficult to overstate the urgency of our gaining a comprehensive allied appreciation for the seriousness of this threat, for otherwise the decisions we must make to counter these developments in a decisive way may be difficult or impossible to achieve.

To this end, the United States is now embarking on a major effort to rebuild, revitalise and modernise the forces upon which our strategic and conventional deterrents depend.

I am confident that the Congress as well as the American people will fully support this enormous and necessary undertaking as a result of a growing recognition among our citizenry that the forthcoming decade portends times of great peril for free nations the world over.

THE REAGAN ADMINISTRATION

The Reagan Administration is now planning to increase overall US defence expenditures for the fiscal year to begin October 1981 by about 15 per cent in real terms over the level for the present year. This increase will be applied in several categories, four of which bear special emphasis.

First, we shall dramatically improve the readiness and sustainability of our existing forces. The new Administration is requesting the addition of over $11.5 billion for readiness improvements alone that had been rejected by the previous Administration. This increase will provide more training for combat units, additional spare parts to improve the reliability of aircraft and munitions needed to augment our reserve stocks. It will alleviate a severe maintenance back-log affecting aircraft in each of the Services and buy more missiles and torpedoes needed for our aircraft squadrons and ships.

We shall also provide necessary funds for our increased naval presence in the Indian Ocean and Persian Gulf areas and will improve upon our Rapid Deployment Force and its ability to respond to a challenge to our vital interests in the South-west Asia/Persian Gulf region.

Second, we shall improve our readiness by seeking to eliminate shortages in manpower that now hamper our ability to operate and maintain our conventional forces. This will entail additional outlays for our uniformed personnel as we work to recruit and retain the skilled manpower that today's sophisticated weapons systems require us to have.

Third, we shall step up our modernisation programmes across the board. For the Army, we will increase production of the M-1 main battle tank to a rate of 90 per month. We shall procure additional infantry fighting vehicles, towed howitzers, Blackhawk utility helicopters, armoured recovery vehicles, laser target designators and night vision sights for the Tow and Dragon anti-tank missile systems. We shall also restore our investment in the four-battalion Roland programme and further increase our inventories of the Patriot and Stinger air defence systems as well. Larger purchases of chemical agent alarms and modern communications equipment will round out this broad programme to increase the capability of our land forces.

For Navy modernisation (other than shipbuilding), we shall augment our production of ongoing aircraft programmes, including the A-6E, EA-6B, F-14, F-18, CH-53 helicopter and the P-3C anti-submarine warfare patrol aircraft. Navy missile procurements will also be increased for the HARM air-to-surface missile and the Tomahawk cruise missile.

The US Air Force will likewise be authorised additional funds to buy new aircraft and missiles at a more efficient rate than has been permitted in recent years. The total procurement of fighter and attack aircraft requested for fiscal year 1982 has been increased from 126 to 222, including additional F-15s, F-16s and A-10s.

We shall step up our production schedule for the E-3A airborne radar surveillance aircraft (AWACS), augment our investment in electronic warfare equipment across the board and enhance our force mobility by purchasing additional KC-10 aerial tankers and jet transport aircraft.

For our future strategic deterrent, the Air Force will undertake the development of a new manned bomber, and we are proceeding with the development of the MX ICBM programme to secure the land-based element of our TRIAD.

Finally, we shall begin immediately to build more ships. As was mentioned earlier, the commerce and industry of the industrialised West depends on our ability to control the seas. We must be able to defeat any potential adversary who threatens our access to the essential supplies of energy and raw materials that are distant from our own shores.

In this regard, the Reagan Administration has correctly identified the retention of naval superiority as an imperative. This is not an area of our defence structure that can tolerate the terms of equivalence or parity with the Soviet Union. We can no longer delay. We now face the consequences of having permitted our naval capability to deteriorate, and now we must move vigorously to restore it as a matter of highest priority. Accordingly, we shall begin next year to fund programmes for the construction of additional cruisers, frigates, attack submarines, amphibious ships and a new nuclear-powered aircraft carrier. We shall further undertake the reactivation and modernisation of two retired battleships and one retired aircraft carrier. Our future plans will provide for the maintenance of additional carrier task forces that will alleviate the strain imposed on the 12 carriers we are now able to deploy. We will equip these ships with improved anti-air warfare (AAW) and anti-submarine warfare (ASW) systems to counter effectively an increasingly sophisticated air and subsurface threat at sea. Our amphibious capability will be enhanced by improving our amphibious lift and modernising the equipment utilised by the Marine Corps in its Fleet Marine amphibious forces. It is clear that we must proceed with these efforts immediately in order to avoid placing ourselves in a position of unacceptable inferiority on the high seas.

This is an ambitious defence programme. It is promulgated simultaneously with President Reagan's plan to remedy the chronic economic problems that plague our nation. In order to achieve this goal, US Government spending in non-defence areas is being sharply curtailed, and many domestic programmes will be cut back and in some areas eliminated as our nation moves to live once again within its means. This emphasises the seriousness with which we view our responsibility to improve our military and naval capabilities as we mount the effort to rebuild and modernise our forces despite the economic difficulties we now face.

It is the intention of the Reagan Administration to reassert and restore confidence in American leadership in the area of collective security. But the tasks before us are too great for any one nation to achieve, and only if we act together will we as free nations muster the enormous resources at our disposal to provide for our common security. The focus of our collective efforts must be broad enough in the decade ahead to respond to contingencies in other regions of the world where our vital interests are at stake.

To this end, we must intensify our efforts to develop a collective understanding of how to plan and achieve this broader focus and how to manage our assets in more efficient ways than we have done in the past. Thus, not only must we all do more, but we must do so at a higher level of cooperation to achieve the maximum effectiveness from our new investments.

FUNDAMENTALS

We Americans realise, however, that for our strategy to succeed we must adhere to certain fundamentals in the execution of American foreign policy that have been lacking all too often in the past. These fundamentals have been publicly cited by

Secretary of State Haig as central to the conduct of foreign policy by the Reagan Administration.

First, we must act with consistency to retain the confidence of our allies and our friends around the world. We must not seize upon seemingly convenient and simple solutions to episodic distractions from our fundamental purpose within the Alliance.

Second, we must behave in a more reliable way with respect to our commitments in the international arena. Our adversaries cannot be expected to exercise prudence if they are able to observe fractures in our collective resolve or in our determination to act as circumstances require.

Third, we must balance the priority of our traditional commitments with a better understanding of certain developing countries and those regions where potential instability threatens vital Western interests. We can no longer consider the security of Western Europe in isolation from the rest of the world. We must recognise that the security of Western Europe depends more and more on what occurs beyond the defined boundaries of NATO. To concentrate our attention on the European central front to the exclusion of giving adequate attention to other critical areas would be foolhardy in the extreme. As has been observed many times before, where we cannot act as an alliance, we must behave as allies.

The pragmatism, cohesion and vision of our foreign policy will become more manifest as we address the challenges before us. As a major objective, we must enhance our security assistance programme, which presently lags behind the realities faced by many of our friends who do not have the means to safeguard mutual interests by themselves. It will greatly alleviate the demands we can expect to be imposed on our own forces if we work to develop the capabilities lodged in indigenous forces in countries supporting our common aims.

Today, we are presented with problems never visualised by those who created our Alliance that day in April of 1949. In the continuing process of adapting to an ever-changing world, we must all bear in mind that, as a successful Alliance, ours is a shared commitment and a shared endeavour. The challenges we face will require that all of us do more, and let no one doubt our determination and our ability to prevail.

Electronic components for defence equipment.

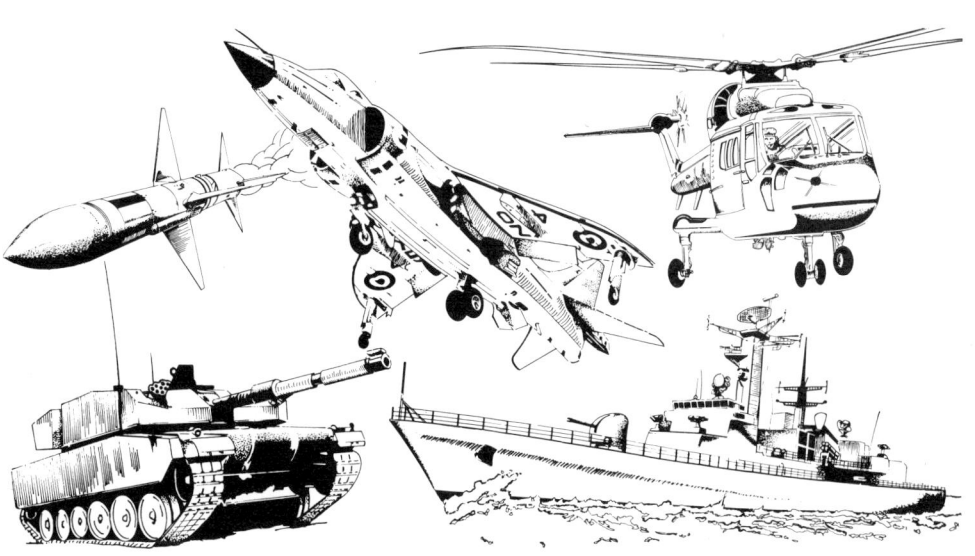

Mullard has the resources for the development and production of a wide range of electronic components for defence requirements, employing the most advanced as well as established technologies. Four of our factories have BS 9000 approval and three have been assessed by the British Ministry of Defence to quality assurance DEF STAN 05-21.

Infra-red detectors

Arrays and single-element infra-red detectors mounted in vacuum encapsulations are produced in quantity at Mullard's Southampton plant. The scale of production and depth of technology are among the best in the world.

For arrays, the principal material used is mercury cadmium telluride, additionally indium antimonide and lead sulphide are used for single-element detectors. We also offer TGS and Pyroelectric detectors.

Applications include thermal imaging, thermal detection and aerospace mapping.

Image intensifiers

Mullard offers a range of micro-channel image intensifiers covering most night vision applications. They are designed, developed, and manufactured at Mitcham, part of Europe's largest electro-optic capability.

Microwave components

Mullard is supplying microwave components or sub-systems for nearly every major military programme in the UK which calls for microwave capability. The Mullard Hazel Grove plant has one of the finest facilities in the UK for the design and production of microwave integrated circuits. Fixed-frequency and electronically tuned solid-state oscillators and mixer assemblies for frequencies up to 90 GHz are available and there is a full range of discrete microwave semiconductor devices.

Integrated circuits

Mullard leadership in ML specification bipolar integrated circuits is demonstrated by the Signetics range of 4, 8, and 16 K PROMs (programmable read-only memories). Leadership in fused-link technology is shown in the Signetics range of field-programmable logic arrays, semi-custom gate arrays, ROM (read-only memory) patches and the very advanced sequencer. Leadership in bipolar microprocessors resides in the Signetics 8X300, the world's fastest single-chip 8-bit microprocessor.

Mullard

MULLARD LIMITED, MULLARD HOUSE, TORRINGTON PLACE, LONDON WC1E 7HD. TELEPHONE: 01-580 6633. TELEX: 264341.
Mullard manufacture and market electronic components under the **Mullard, Philips** and **Signetics** brands.

Part II—Weapon Developments

Submersibles

FRANCIS BRUEN

The author is a retired Royal Navy Captain.
He is now a Director of Underwater Security Consultants Ltd

TRADITIONALLY all underwater vehicles have been developed for military purposes, and although they have only been an influence on marine warfare in this century their derivation goes back a long way. In 1620 Cornelius van Drebel is said to have constructed a submersible for King James I. It was operated by twelve oarsmen, with leather sleeves waterproofing the oar-ports and is reputed to have navigated the river Thames at depths of 12 - 15 ft for several hours. Even before that, Aristotle wrote of small 'diving bells', which were used by sponge divers down to depths of 75 - 100 ft.

More recently submersibles have been developed for scientific and research purposes, predominantly in the United States but also in most other countries with advanced technologies. During the last decade they have been extensively used in the North Sea in support of the offshore oil industry. Like all new industries the commercial underwater world has used ordinary terms to define special types and it is therefore advisable to give a few definitions which are used in this article and generally in offshore work.

Manned vehicles: this term applies to any vehicle whether or not it is connected to the surface by an umbilical or a tether, in which one or more men are carried in atmospheric conditions. When requiring a mothership in constant attendance for support but without any fixed connection to the surface, it is normally called a submersible. If no mothership is required it is referred to as an autonomous submarine.

Remotely operated vehicles (ROV): sometimes called unmanned, these are usually connected to the surface by an umbilical which provides a source of power to the vehicle and instantaneous communications in each direction.

Bells: the normal bell is used as a vertical transport vehicle to take divers from the surface to their place of work. When used in this manner the pressure of the working depth is the same both inside and out. Some of these are now fitted with a large window

and thrusters to provide horizontal movement. Under these conditions they are used for observation and the internal pressure is
maintained at 1 atmosphere. Thus they are similar to a tethered
submersible but lack the means of controlling their buoyancy.

By the middle of 1980 there were about 130 manned submersibles of which about 100 were operational. There were about 400
ROVs of which over 200 were military vehicles used in mine
countermeasure and made by a French firm.

To understand the reason for the use of these vehicles it is
necessary to consider the recent history of the oil industry in the
North Sea. Originally, drilling started in the south with the
search for gas. This was all south of 56°N and in relatively
shallow water (less than 50 m deep). The underwater support for
this work was supplied exclusively by divers and, although they
had limitations due to the tidal conditions, they met the requirements of the oil companies and were comparatively cheap.
When the monopoly buying power of the UK Gas Board made
the work unremunerative, the oil companies shifted their work
further north and searched for oil. The water here was deeper
and colder and the weather conditions inhospitable. The divers
were able to compete with these conditions, but less efficiently
and at much greater cost. The additional expense was caused by
three factors. The need to use a breathing mixture of helium and
oxygen, the necessity to supply a saturation diving spread which
can cost anything up to £1 million and the wages of the divers
which increase markedly with depth. While the diving industry
met the challenge, the sudden increase in the number of divers
led to a dilution of standards with an inevitable increase in fatal
accidents. These quickly became socially unacceptable, forcing
the oil companies to look for an alternative even though the divers
were still able to carry out the tasks.

The first alternative tried was the two-man observation
submersible. Although each manufacturer's product has variations, they are all somewhat similar. This is not surprising as their
method of work and the ambient conditions restrict the options
open to their designers.

A typical observation submersible has the following rough
overall dimensions: length 20 ft, beam 7 ft, height 8 ft: it weighs 7
tons in air, is driven by lead - acid batteries which are carried externally, has life support for the crew of two for 4 - 7 days and has
a normal maximum dive time of about 8 hours. It is fitted with a
large hemispherical window for observation and carries a low -
light television camera for recording data on videotapes. Two ex-

ternal manipulators are operated by the observer. The vehicle has the normal submarine's methods of controlling buoyancy and trim and is very manoeuvrable as it has vertical and athwartship thrusters in addition to the main propulsion. The air inside is cleaned by the removal of CO_2 and freshened by the addition of oxygen.

After each sortie the craft must be recovered by the mothership to replenish the compressed air and oxygen and recharge the batteries. Launch and recovery are carried out over the square stern of the ship using an A-frame which can tilt in and out as required. In order to deal with the relative motion, a heave compensation device is fitted to the main hoist and recovery is carried out with the mothership going slowly ahead while the submersible is hauled by a tow rope underneath the A-frame. The tow and the hoist ropes are both attached by a surface swimmer working from a Zodiac dinghy. So efficient are these systems that the limiting weather conditions are governed by the ability to launch and recover the Zodiac and by the need for the swimmer to work safely. This is normally taken to be a sea state of 6 although in an emergency a sea state of 8 has been achieved with an experienced crew. Originally, ships of opportunity were used as motherships but the increasing specialised need of submersible operation support eventually forced all operators to use specialised ships.

While these submersibles were useful and safe — there have been no fatal accidents involving submersibles in the North Sea — they were unable to do all the tasks performed by divers. Therefore, the next stage was the lock-out submersible which combined the versatility of the diver with the safety of the submersible. The largest of these lock-outs is the Taurus, which was built in Canada by International Hydrodynamics with dimensions of 34 ft length, 13 ft beam, 12 ft height and weighing 53,000 lb. While carrying out diving operations the crew consists of the pilot and diving supervisor in the forward compartment, which is kept at atmospheric pressure while the diving compartment, containing two divers, is pressurised to the working depth. It should be noted that Taurus is capable of submarine rescue as has been proved in trials with the RN. Mating is effected after fitting a special skirt round the diver lock-out hatch, which is in the keel of the submersible.

There are two main problems with these submersibles and these are that as all the lock-out diving is in more than 50 m depth there are the difficult requirements of keeping the divers warm and supplying them with a heliox breathing mixture. Warmth consumes power from the main lead-acid battery which has a restricted capacity. Some submersibles are fitted with a heat pump with reduces the drain on the battery but adds to the complexity. The heliox is stored in cyclinders under pressure but the submersibles have only a limited carrying capacity. There is one problem peculiar to Taurus. Due to her length and weight she is difficult to launch and recover, and consequently the maximum weather conditions in which she can be handled is reduced.

Lock-out submersibles have proved safe and are popular with the divers as they are in close proximity with their supervisor, ensuring readily available advice and support. The mothership requires additional handling facilities as after recovery the submersible lock-out compartment has to be mated with the saturation system in order to transfer the divers under pressure from the constricted lock-out compartment to the main chambers for rest and food. Lock-out divers have achieved good results, but it is essential that the submersible is positively controlled in depths before the divers leave the craft. This makes work on the bottom simple, but trying to work on structures is difficult and sometimes impossible. Another disadvantage is that the cost of operating a dedicated mothership is high, thus making the cost of hiring a lock-out diving spread uncompetitive in some cases.

ROVs are in general cheaper and for that reason were introduced. The commonest and the one that first appeared on the market was the Hydroproducts RCV 125. This was originally designed for the US Navy as an intelligence gatherer. Its method of deployment was from the submarine through a standard-size torpedo tube. This dictated its size and shape. It was designed to be positively buoyant so that in an emergency the umbilical could be cut and the vehicle would float towards the surface which it never reached because a hydrostatic switch operated a self-destruct device destroying the vehicle at a predetermined depth. In commercial use this positive buoyancy and lack of vertical power was a disadvantage as it was very difficult when deploying from the surface in conditions of swell to drive the vehicle down to its operating depth. For this reason it was modified by fitting it into a cage which was negatively buoyant and in which it was lowered to the operating depth and then flown out to the work site. It is now known as the RCV 225 and is used world wide.

There are many different types of ROVs and they vary considerably in size and capability. For instance, the FILIPPO is 65 cm high and 60 cm wide and long. It weighs 80 kg in air and is used for observation only. At the other end of the scale is CON-

SUB 2, which was made by the British Aircraft Corporation and is 12 ft long, 7 ft wide and 5½ ft high. It weighs 6500 lb and is capable of carrying a pay load of 1000 lb. While each manufacturer has his own method of construction, they are all somewhat similar with a combination of vertical, horizontal and athwartship thrusters and low-light black-and-white television cameras for navigation and work. Control from the surface through the umbilical is by a single operator using a joystick control and watching the relayed television picture. Although 90 per cent of the work is observation using tape-recorded television video pictures, other devices are carried and used for specific tasks.

The common feature of all systems is the use of an umbilical cable joining the vehicle to its controller on the surface which simultaneously is the biggest advantage and disadvantage of these systems. It provides substantial power and near instantaneous communications, but at the same time it is a potent source of drag and a ready method of entanglement. Like previously described systems, they can do many things but cannot yet do all the tasks that divers can do and are required to do. Also they have a poor record of reliability and many vehicles have been lost through a variety of reasons, of which entanglement and bad seamanship are probably the commonest.

Another form of device now being increasingly used is the one-man diving suit. These come in two main types, the JIM/SAM diving suit, which has been in use for more than 10 years and looks somewhat like the Michelin man as seen in advertisements. The man inside is at a pressure of 1 atmosphere and provides the power for movement and operating the arms. It cannot swim and is therefore basically restricted to bottom work. The other type is a single metal or GRP cylinder in which a man either stands or lies. Power is provided from an umbilical for thrusters and manipulators. The best-known types which are made in this country are called Wasp, Mantis and Spider. In the short time in which they have been in use they have proved safe and successful. They are sufficiently manoeuvrable to work inside offshore structures and the man in them is able to work in unpressurised conditions. Experience is limited, but it is thought unlikely that at present they will be able to do all the tasks carried out by divers.

There is one other class of vehicle to be considered that is in use and that is the bottom crawlers. They have been developed for the specific tasks of pipelines and cable burial and inspection. As their generic name implies, they are restricted to work on the sea bed and consequently have permanent negative buoyancy. Some are driven by wheels and others have tracks. Pipeline and cable burial is a misnomer as results are achieved by cutting a trench using either a water jet or dredge cutter, or a combination of the two, allowing the cable or pipe to drop into the trench by gravity and relying on the ocean to provide a covering. Under ideal conditions they carry out a satisfactory job, but their limitations are largely due to the very variable sea-bed conditions, which are difficult to assess prior to the vehicle being lowered to the bottom. Tyre pressures can be varied and so, to a limited extent, can the negative buoyancy of the vehicle, but even this does not always achieve satisfactory results. A further problem is to ensure that the vehicle does not roll over on hitting the bottom when lowered in deep water.

It is necessary now to describe the tasks that have to be carried out by these commercial vehicles and why. In late 1965 the jack-up barge *Sea Gem* collapsed in the North Sea with the loss of thirteen lives. As a result of the subsequent inquiry, various Acts of Parliament and regulations were issued. Basically, these require that all offshore structures must have a certificate of fitness and that this certificate must be re-issued every 5 years, which necessitates a complete re-survey. These regulations only apply to UK waters, but similar requirements are applicable throughout all North-west European waters. The recent accident to the *Alexander Kieland*, with a loss of 123 lives, has accentuated the need for thorough and meticulous inspection. The certificate of fitness covers the whole structure and all the equipment on it, but in describing the work required this article restricts itself solely to the underwater requirements.

A thorough inspection is required for the whole underwater structure with special attention being given to nodal points. The majority of the inspection work is visual but some nondestructive testing of welds is carried out. In addition, the cathodic protection is checked and voltage potential readings taken. The sea bed must be searched for debris and the feet or legs inspected for scouring. In addition, special attention must be given to the risers due to the high temperature of the oil inside them. This short description states what has to be done but not how. Inspection is predominantly carried out by low-light black-and-white television cameras with the information recorded on viedo tape for analysis ashore. Specific points of interest are photographed using black and white film, although increasingly colour is being used. Stereoscopic television is in its infancy and colour television has not been used mainly because sea water absorbs the different frequencies of coloured light unequally which leads to the green blue predominance of the colour. This is not, therefore, an accurate record and can cause inaccurate conclusions. Colour photography is used at very close range, which reduces the chance of error. This work is performed equally well by diver or vehicle.

Before this work can be carried out the structure must be cleaned to remove the marine growth. This is either algae and molluscs or other hard growth or a combination of all of them. Cleaning was originally carried out by wire brush or needle gun. Neither was very effective as the former is slow and laborious while the latter tends to hide the incipient surface cracks which the inspection is designed to find. Most cleaning is now done by water jet with the pressure adjusted according to whether the intention is merely to remove marine growth or to clean down to bare metal for weld inspections. The size of the task should not be underestimated and a few facts will explain this. A platform in 170 m of water will have 7000 m of steel members and a single nodal joint will have about 23 m of weld requiring inspection. It was estimated in 1977 that even then there were 1680 nodes in deep water north of 56° N with a total of 34 kms of weld requiring inspection.

Nondestructive testing is carried out using either magnetic particle or ultrasonic methods. It is generally agreed that the former is more reliable although neither system is as reliable under water as on the surface, and both are slow, requiring both skilled and patient personnel. At present only those vehicles using lock-out divers are capable of this work. Potential readings for cathodic protection inspection is achieved by driving a sharp probe firmly against the metal with the reading being recorded on the surface together with the exact position where the reading is taken. This work can be carried out by any type of vehicle.

Recently the small floating eyeball type vehicle has been used for diver support. It achieves this in four separate ways. It carries out reconnaissance in advance of the diver entering the water to decide what has to be done and where. Its illumination acts as a guide when the diver leaves the bell showing him where to swim to. It assists the diver supervisor on the surface to monitor the safety and competence of the divers and it supplies a movable source of light to assist them in their work. Only the smaller vehicles can be used for this work as larger vehicles with constantly working thrusters would be dangerous. This type of vehicle is not suitable for debris recovery or the inspection to check for bottom scouring. For these tasks a larger vehicle with manipulators and ability to carry small articles is required. Manipulators are very varied, with the single ones having only three degrees of freedom and a simple pincer grip to the very advanced manipulator made by GEC of America which has seven degrees of freedom and a force feedback control and costs about a $250,000. Some manipulators have their pincer replaced by a sucker plate to allow them to attach themselves to the large cylindrical struts of a structure. Most of these devices are worked by hydraulics using either hydraulic fluid or sea water to supply the power to the operating cylinders from a central electrical motor driving the hydraulic pump.

In addition to platform inspection, pipelines require inspection annually to check visually for damage or leaks and to ensure that, where scouring has occurred, they are still resting on the bottom. Where the pipeline is buried, the depth of pipeline must also be checked. In the Gulf of Mexico this work has been done by divers walking the pipeline. They are never used in the North Sea for this task as it is both dangerous and expensive. Here observation submersibles and the larger types of remotely operated vehicles are used exclusively. Where the pipeline is laid on the sea bed the work is done using low-light television cameras which provide a video tape record of the inspection. Each side of the pipe has to be photographed separately and the speed of advance is less than a knot. It is normal for one of the oil company's engineers to be in the control cabin when using a vehicle or in the submersible when using a manned craft. In addition to the visual inspection it is also necessary to record the magnetic strength along the line, and from this it is possible to calculate the efficiency of the cathodic protection which is invisible as the pipe is covered with a cement coat both to weigh it down and act as physical protection. When the pipe is intermittently buried the vehicle carries a pipe tracker which enables it to follow the line and also to record the depth to which it is buried beneath the sea bed. In the most advanced system a remotely controlled vehicle is fitted with two cameras on extreme ends of a boom to photograph both sides of the pipe simultaneously. It is also fitted with a pipe tracker which automatically sends signals to a computer which directs the vehicle movement both in direction and at a set height above the pipe. At the same time a high-frequency pinger is fitted on the top of the vehicle. This indicates the position of the craft relative to the mothership on the latter's bridge. The ship is fitted with dynamic positioning and the controls are set to maintain position on the vehicle's pinger. The whole system is completely automatic, and once the vehicle is switched to move, the ship follows automatically. It is a surprising feature that the author knows of no case where a bottom crawler has been successfully used for pipeline inspection. It does appear that to move over rough terrain, legs are best, and if you want to swim, a propeller or flipper is the ideal answer.

One of the tasks successfully carried out by vehicles is bottom survey. This requires not only a high standard of accuracy in plan but also in the ability to check depth and slope. This type of survey is required in two main types — planning pipeline routes and surveying small areas for the emplacement of jackets and choosing sites for exploration drilling. For small-area surveys an accuracy in metres is required, while for line surveys an accuracy of 10 - 20 m is required. This depends not only on the accuracy of navigation of the craft but also that of the mothership. In the North Sea accurate positioning is obtained by using Decca or, further offshore, astro-navigation. Two main methods of navigation are used by the underwater vehicle. Both are based on acoustic principles and are known as short- and long-base line systems. Because of the relative shallowness of the water the assumption is made that sound will travel in a straight line. The errors likely to occur because of this assumption are not appreciable and allowance is made for varying velocity due to temperature and salinity. In the short-base line system the phase difference of signals received by transducers in the mothership are measured, thus allowing the position of a transponder on the vehicle to be fixed. In the long-base line system, transponders are placed on the bottom and their position fixed by repeated passes of the mothership. An additional transponder is fitted to the vehicle and, by timing the receipt of signals in the mothership, the position of the craft relative to the transponders on the bottom is fixed. With this system it is also possible to alter the triggering of the transponders to allow the submersible to fix its own position relative to the sea-bottom transponders. It should be noted that accuracy can be considered in two forms: repeatability relative to a known position on the bottom such as a fixed structure, in which case the accuracy of positioning the mothership is immaterial, and geographical accuracy where the marrying of the accuracy of the surface ship's position to the sub-surface plot is important.

An inertial navigation system has been used in manned submersibles where very high accuracy is needed for such tasks as measuring damaged members of structures in order to make replacements. With this system, accuracies to the order of a few inches can be obtained but the system, which is made by Ferranti, has two disadvantages. It is expensive and in order to maintain the accuracy of the system it has to become momentarily stationary at intervals of 1 - 10 minutes depending on the accuracy required.

The above is a very short description of some of the commercial vehicles both manned and unmanned including brief details of what they are required to do and how they do it. There are also many other specialised vehicles such as underwater cranes, welding chambers and mobile habitats which have not been described for lack of space.

The future of any very young industry is always clouded in mist, but it does appear that this industry must be one of the growth points of the future for a variety of reasons. Oil and gas are increasingly being sought in ever deeper waters, and it is estimated that the majority of unknown oilfields are underwater. The oil industry will expand an increasing proportion of its budget offshore in exploration and this will require sub-sea support. While it has been proved that air breathing whales are able to dive to 3000 m, it is unlikely that man will ever reach these prodigious depths although his maximum capability is unknown. Under laboratory conditions he has dived to an assimulated depth of 660 m, but the problems of the high-pressure nervous syndrome and long-term effects have not been completely solved. The maximum depth which has been successfully carried out is about 1500 ft (46 m). The commercial cost at this depth is becoming prohibitive and only the best of the élite saturation divers will be capable of achieving it. The lack of diver support will not deter the oil industry but it will demand increased support and capability from the vehicle industry and, provided money is available, there is no physical reason why the industry should not meet the requirement. It will require coordination between the vehicle and oilfield equipment designers of which there is little sign at present.

The industry is very young and there are several avenues open for investigation which have not yet been developed. One obvious approach is the autonomous submarine which, like a military one, is capable of recharging its batteries in all weather conditions. A design for a craft of this type has been produced by both Kockums of Sweden and Gabler of the Federal Republic of Germany. The latter's design of about 100 tons and a crew of 11 would be able to operate, using conventional propulsion, submerged for 20 out of 24 hours and has life support submerged for a week. It would additionally carry up to 8 divers in saturation and be capable of sub-bottom coring to about 200 m. Also it would be capable of bottom survey and pipeline inspection. At present the design is marginally unattractive for financial reasons, but it does have the immense advantage of not being weather dependent, which in a winter emergency would be of inestimable advantage. Another device at present under development in academic establishments is the unmanned vehicle without an umbilical. This will require considerable preprogramming of its internal computer to deal with the unexpected, but is less likely to become entangled and with decreased drag will require less power for propulsion. As communication to and from the vehicle has to be acoustic, the quantity and speed of communication is restricted. Some feel that this is an example of a solution looking for a problem. What is certain is that the industry is so new that no avenue should be left unexplored at this stage.

Most of this article has dealt with vehicle support of the oil industry because this is where the money is and consequently the emphasis is on commercial development, but there are other fields where work in the future will require the support of underwater craft. The exploration of the hydrosphere is increasing in importance together with the need to carry out deep-sea mining which will necessitate underwater craft of many types. Recently the sinking of the *Salem* in unusual circumstances in 2000 fathoms (3656 m) has indicated the need to be able to survey wrecks and possibly salvage their cargo in deep waters. The future is fascinating and the industry is still in its infancy.

Strategic Weapons

LAWRENCE FREEDMAN

Dr Freedman is Head of Policy Studies at the Royal Institute of International Affairs

IN THE early 1970s it seemed that the future of strategic nuclear weapons was one of declining significance. A common view was that the offensive nuclear forces of both superpowers neutralised each other, and could therefore be of slight relevance in every-day international affairs. Given this, there seemed little point in adding to nuclear arsenals when the increments were so expensive. It was widely assumed that successive rounds of the Strategic Arms Limitation Talks (SALT), which got under way in the last months of the 1960s, would confirm the stability of the strategic relationship and diminish the stockpiles of nuclear weapons and their international role.

A decade later the picture is quite opposite to the one that had been expected. Nuclear weapons appear at the centre of domestic and international rows in both North America and Europe. New systems are being introduced by both superpowers and yet more are under development. SALT, and arms control in general, has reached a crisis point with its value seriously questioned in the United States.

The Reagan Administration contains many hawkish critics of SALT and advocates of greater US exertions in the strategic nuclear field. The eventual influence of their views remains to be seen, for there are many countervailing forces, including the anxiety of allies that arms control negotiations are not abandoned, and a variety of financial, technical, political and environmental objections to specific programmes. This, plus the character of the Soviet responses to the new US plans and the parlous state of SALT, makes for an extremely uncertain future. It is more difficult than it has been for many years to offer a forecast of the likely shape of the force structures of both sides by the end of this decade.

In attempting to assess the likely lines of development, it is important to keep to the fore the fundamental question of whether the strategic balance is likely to be seriously unsettled by any of these developments and, what if anything, this means for East-West relations.

The most fundamental feature of the strategic relationship has been that one superpower could not launch a nuclear attack against the other without risking retaliation in kind. It has been like this since the 1950s and it is the argument of this article that despite the current uncertainties it is likely to be so until the next century. Most developments over the past couple of decades have served to reinforce rather than undermine the stalemate. There has been a persistent belief in the possibility that a dramatic technical breakthrough might cause some decisive shift in the balance of advantage allowing the successful power to rescue its nuclear strength from the constraints on its use imposed by the nuclear strength of the adversary.

If one side did manage to achieve such a breakthrough, creating an ability either to destroy enemy forces in a surprise first strike or to shoot down an incoming attack, then the strategic relationship would be completely transformed. It would be possible to contemplate a victor in a nuclear war. For this reason, many surveys of developments in strategic weaponry are informed, implicitly or explicitly, by this prospect of a quantum jump, something equivalent to the first atomic bomb, or the movement from fission to fusion weapons, or from aircraft to ballistic missiles. One of the consequences of this preoccupation is a tendency to attribute an excessive significance to technological innovations. A developing asymmetry in one particular capability, say the capacity to attack hardened targets or to protect a portion of the population from fallout, may get presented as an historic shift in the international balance of power.

TECHNOLOGY AND CHANGE

In the United States the sensation of engaging in a desperate arms race, dominated by a rush to exploit the potential of new technologies, was at its strongest in the late 1950s. In 1957, when the Soviet Union was the first to test an intercontinental ballistic missile (ICBM) and then to launch an artificial earth satellite (Sputnik), there was near panic in Washington over being left behind. Yet the years since then have been marked more by incremental developments in nuclear weapons than dramatic breakthroughs, with plenty of advance warnings of innovations. Two current workhorses of the US nuclear arsenal—the B-52 bomber and the Minuteman ICBM Poseidon—are based on development programmes that were underway before Sputnik, while the Poseidon submarine-launched ballistic missile was developed in the mid-1960s and is still carried on submarines of a similar vintage. There have been major qualitative improvements on the earlier versions, but the link is still there.

Throughout their long service there have been rumours that these weapons were about to be superseded by systems representing wholly new concepts in strategic weapons. In the post-Sputnik excitement the next stage of development was presumed to be exotic space weapons with orbiting bombs and piloted spaceships and celestial battles. The moon was presented as the modern version of the 'high ground' beloved of warriors of old, control of which would allow for domination of the earth below. This was until doubts grew over the practicality of dispatching weapons hundreds of miles into space, where their reliability could not be checked and where their relationship to earthly targets would vary enormously. Eventually, the value of space was found in the wide coverage offered for surveillance and command and control satellites rather than in the launching of weapons against earth targets or in fighting rather futile battles against other spacebased systems.

Hopes of a great leap forward were then pinned on ballistic missile defences. This was seen as the inevitable next stage in the offence/defence duel which had begun with the attempts to obstruct the conventional air raids of World War II with radar and interceptor aircraft. The need was for a system that could provide early warning of a coming offensive force, track the progress of this force and then ensure that it was met by interceptor missiles. Actual interception presented less of a problem than the timely identification of targets and the prediction of their routes. Even when, by designing radar and computers of immense sophistication, these problems appeared close to solution, this achievement was thwarted by advances in offensive technology — manoeuvrability, decoys, chaff and most important of all multiple warheads. The programmes for constituting ballistic missile defence in both the Soviet Union and the United States, after making progress in the mid-1960s, had run out of steam by the end of the decade. In May 1972 the two countries agreed to a low ceiling of 200 ABM launchers each in the first treaty to come from the Strategic Arms Limitation Talks (SALT). This was reduced to 100 apiece in 1974. The American system was mothballed, although there are now moves to revive it (within the limits of the Treaty). The Soviet Union removed in early 1980 half of the 64 launchers protecting Moscow, apparently in order to replace them with an improved system.

This Treaty is still considered to be a major victory for arms control. However, it was only made possible by the low promise of the ABM programmes of the time. With greater promise, these programmes could have transformed the strategic balance by threatening to blunt the means of nuclear retaliation. The achievement of SALT I is therefore presented as removing this destabilising possibility while still quite hypothetical. It is not unduly cynical to note that if this possibility had been more than hypothetical the Treaty would not have been agreed. As we shall note below, a revival of interest in ABMs has led to the revival of interest in abrogating the ABM Treaty.

The experience with ABMs seemed to confirm that in nuclear exchanges the advantages would lie very much with offensive systems. These systems were both able to protect their own bases from pre-emptive attack, through hardening or mobility, and were able to reach and destroy any unhardened or immobile targets without serious interruption from defensive missiles.

The only qualification to this picture stemmed from the steady improvement in offensive technologies. These have been miniaturisation in nuclear warhead design and avionics, consequently lower yield-to-weight ratios and precision guidance combined with increased range, multiple warheads and soon mobility. The result is that it has become increasingly possible, and will be more so in the future, to concentrate attacks on specific targets. Even targets, such as ICBM launchers, protected by reinforced concrete able to withstand all but direct hits, have been rendered vulnerable by the attacker's ability to achieve, in effect, direct hits. This has created great interest, not to say an obsessive concern, with the vulnerability of one side's ICBMs to attack by those of the other side as well as an exploration of the opportunities for subtle nuclear tactics directed against specific targets.

Before examining these developments, one further point needs to be made on technological change and the strategic balance. Most weapons require about one decade for development and, if the programme is a success, can expect to stay operational for anything up to two decades after entering service. This allows some 30 years of a particular weapon's merits and demerits to be analysed and debated exhaustively. This is despite the image of a strategic relationship continually transformed and disrupted by rapid technological advance. By the time a new weapon actually becomes operational it is already a familiar part of the strategic landscape. Debate is often in anticipation of a coming capability rather than commentary on something well established.

It is arguable that the debate on the fitting of multiple independently targetable re-entry vehicles (MIRVs) to US ballistic missiles was not so thorough as it might have been prior to their deployment in the early 1970s, but speculation on Soviet MIRVs began in the US intelligence community 10 years before they were actually deployed in 1975. The first serious expressions of concern over the possibility of sufficient Soviet ICBM warheads to threaten all American ICBMs in a surprise attack were heard in 1967. Two years later this issue moved to the centre of American strategic debate, where it has remained ever since, yet the actual capability, though now in prospect, has still not been achieved by the Soviet Union. Cruise missiles provide another example of a system being the subject of considerable analysis, political argument and even international diplomacy, years before being proven in trials and prepared for deployment.

It is, of course, before full production and deployment that the key political decisions have to be made on any new system. Political debate often results in both the virtues and vices of a proposed system being exaggerated so that its actual arrival can be something of an anticlimax. The main point is that much of the strategic analysis consists of anticipation of what could be rather than reflection on what has been.

THE SOVIET BUILD-UP

The futuristic quality of many strategic studies can mean that projections for the coming period are often supported by inadequate analysis of past trends. One example of this is the common assumption that the 1970s saw the Soviet Union surging ahead in the arms race. An examination of the Soviet build-up does not support the view that it is far in excess of anything undertaken by the United States. In 1967 the United States reached force levels of 1054 ICBMs and 656 SLBMs, which it has maintained ever since. By contrast, the Soviet Union then had 460 ICBMs and 130 SLBMs. The Soviet ICBM force was already showing signs of rapid growth; 2 years later its number had more than doubled and soon it was well past the US figure. Its SLBM force took longer to show signs of growth, but it had doubled in size by the end of the decade and has grown steadily ever since. The 1972 SALT I Interim Agreement on Offensive Weapons put limits on this growth. The Soviet Union was to be allowed no more than

1618 ICBM launchers and up to 950 SLBM launch tubes on 62 modern submarines, though to be entitled to this number they would have to dismantle 209 old ICBM launchers. This defined the peak of the Soviet build-up. The USSR now only has about 100 more ICBMs than it had at the start of the decade. The real growth has been in SLBMs — of which it has now more than three times the 1970 figure.

Under the SALT II agreement, the two powers would be limited at first to a ceiling of 2400 strategic nuclear delivery vehicles (SNDVs), which will eventually be reduced to a total of 2250. This figure includes bombers, which were excluded from SALT I. This is an area of US superiority, with 347 operational bombers compared to 156. The main bomber the Soviet Union is producing at the moment is the Backfire which, though intended primarily for use in the European theatre, could possibly be used against the United States with the aid of refuelling. Though the US bomber force has been in a steady decline (the B-52 was first deployed in 1962), it has been given a new lease of life with the development of air-launched cruise missiles. At the moment the United States has only 2200 SNDVs as against the 2504 of the Soviet Union. the SALT II Treaty would therefore require cuts in Soviet force levels. These would probably come from the more obsolete sections of its bomber and submarine force.

Numbers by themselves are of less interest than weapons quality. Concern over the Soviet build-up has been directed at the many different types of modern weapons replacing obsolete models. Three new ICBMs, the SS-17, SS-18 and SS-19, each capable of carrying multiple independently targeted re-entry vehicles (MIRVs) have been introduced since 1974. Another type, the SS-16, which could be deployed in a mobile mode, has been tested and four more systems are being developed.

There is nothing particularly impressive about the variety in types of ICBMs. It reflects a Soviet preference for competitive programmes in contrast to American confidence in a design settled upon in an early stage in the development process. Furthermore, the fact that all but 54 of the US ICBMs have been known as Minuteman[1] should not obscure the fact that there have been three distinct models, each one a major improvement on the one before, and that the United States is now introducing a new warhead — the Mark 12A on 300 Minuteman III ICBMs — which will be even more powerful than the previous front-ends (3

---

[1] The 54 are the large Titan IIs, first deployed in 1962.

warheads of 340 kT as against 3 of 200 kT). Under the SALT II agreement, the two powers will be allowed 1200 MIRVed missiles, of which no more than 820 can be ICBMs.[2]

The United States still has more actual weapons — 9000 to 7000. However, the gap is narrowing and the lead and the US position is exaggerated by the number of individual weapons carried by its bombers and by SLBMs, while the Soviet strength resides in the more deadly warheads of its ICBMs.

ICBM VULNERABILITY

The growth in the number of Soviet MIRVed missiles could be seen as no more than an effort to catch up with the United States. It has been taken to be more ominous because of a basic feature of Soviet ICBMs as against US ICBMs: they are much larger. Throw-weight is the weight of the post-boost vehicle (warheads, guidance systems, penetration aids) that can be delivered over a given range. The Soviet SS-17 and SS-19 ICBMs have 3 to 4 times the throw-weight of the Minuteman III and the SS-18 has up to 10 times the throw-weight. The total throw-weight of all Soviet ICBMs and SLBMs' comes to some 10.0 million lb as against the comparable US figure of 4.2 million lb.

Aggregate throw-weight by itself does not mean very much. It certainly does not confer by itself any significant superiority on the Soviet Union. When the throw-weight equivalent for bombers is considered, that available to the United States is some 3 million lb, compared with 1.8 million lb in the Soviet Union. Throw-weight is best seen as an indicator of potential. Practical consequences depend on the efficiency with which the available space is used. The Americans have put a lot of effort into increasing the explosive yield for a given amount of nuclear material, and into the miniaturisation of the electronics contained in the missile nose-cone.

The most immediate consequence of high throw-weight is a high explosive yield. The Soviet Union can detonate explosions of some 25 megatons (Mt), that is equivalent to 25 million tons of TNT. This is a frightening prospect, but it is not a lot more frightening than being attacked by weapons of 1 Mt as nuclear explosions are subject to diminishing marginal returns. In terms of attacks on populations, the concentration of the populations of

---

[2] There is a higher ceiling of 1320 which is for the moment relevant only to the United States, of MIRVed missiles plus heavy bombers carrying air-launched cruise missiles.

both superpowers in a limited number of large cities, means that extra megatonnage confers no serious advantage.[3] If, however, the warhead can be split up through MIRVing, then a different sort of target structure can be attacked.

During the 1960s it was felt that placing missiles in submarines or hardened silos would keep them invulnerable. To be sure of destroying individual ICBM silos at least two attacking ICBMs would be needed, so the exchange ratio would be unfavourable. MIRVing initially did not help because the process involved a loss of accuracy and yield. With improvements in guidance systems, the most significant and persistent technological phenomenon of the 1970s, the capacity of even small warheads to destroy hardened targets was greatly enhanced.[4] The large size of the Soviet warheads means that they can each accommodate a number of re-entry vehicles of high yields that can individually threaten US ICBM silos without placing excessive demands on accuracy. Although the United States has been reinforcing its missile silos, this is more than compensated for by the gradual improvements in Soviet accuracy which now approach American standards.[5]

There is general agreement that the Soviet Union will soon be able to destroy virtually all of the US ICBM force in a surprise attack using a relatively small portion of its own ICBMs. The United States will not have a similar capability. Even when the Mark 12A front-end is in service, the match of warheads to targets will still not provide a complete counter-ICBM capability.

The SALT II Agreement was criticised in the United States for not dealing with this problem. During the SALT I negotiations the United States rejected restraints on MIRVing, as this was then an area of clear American advantage. In SALT II it was decided to regulate the number of missiles with a facility for MIRVing rather than the numbers of actual warheads. Neither the sub-

---

[3] As destructive power does not grow proportionately with yield, a better measure is equivalent megatonnage which is expressed as the two-thirds power of yields below 1 Mt and the square root of yields above 1 Mt. If the US bomber force was equipped with gravity bombs to the exclusion of Short-Range Attack Missiles (SRAM), then it would ensure that US equivalent megatonnage was greater than that of the USSR.

[4] The capacity to destroy hardened targets is known as lethality. This is directly proportional to yield 2/3 and inversely proportional to CEP^2. Circular error probable (CEP) is a measure of accuracy. This formula has the unfortunate mathematical property of creating an infinite lethality when CEP reaches zero. However, it does indicate the great sensitivity of lethality to improvements in accuracy.

[5] Despite its critical importance, little official information is released on accuracies of either Soviet or American ICBMs. Best public estimates suggest that the best Soviet missiles presently attain accuracies just above 1000 ft while the best US accuracies are measured in hundreds of feet and may soon be measured in tens of feet.

ceiling of 1200 for all MIRVed missiles or the sub-sub-ceiling of 820 for MIRVed ICBMs will prevent the eventual vulnerability of the US ICBM force. The US negotiators were able to point, with some pride, to a 'fractionation limit' which would prohibit putting more warheads on individual ICBMs than the current maximum, thus limiting the Soviet ability to fully exploit its throw-weight advantage.

The second complaint against SALT was that it inhibited the introduction of countermeasures which might alleviate this problem. Active defence of ICBM silos is ruled out by the 1972 ABM Treaty although there are now signs of a resurgence of interest in this option. Another favoured option, complicating the attacker's task by making the missiles mobile, is only limited by SALT II, but may be restricted in SALT III. A 3-year protocol to SALT II involved those problems where a definitive solution was yet to be reached. It permitted the development of a mobile system but not its deployment. Critics of SALT argued that the protocol would assume a status much greater than that of an interim measure and that its provisions would inevitably become part of SALT III, thus forever ruling out mobile missiles. Commitments made by the US Administration on the proposed M-X ICBM, as well as one passage in the Treaty, went against this assumption. The option of mobile ICBMs will remain open. If M-X falters it will be more because of domestic environmental and economic complaints than SALT.

Supporters of SALT point out that though the problem of ICBM vulnerability is not made any easier by SALT, it would be more difficult without SALT. As most defensive measures can be degraded by improvements in offensive capabilities, the uninhibited development of Soviet ICBM forces could overcome the obstacles posed by either greater mobility or active defences at a favourable cost to the attacker.

A MILITARY BREAK-THROUGH?

This question of comparative counterforce capabilities has become the cause of great anxiety. In a much-reported speech in Brussels in September 1979, Dr Henry Kissinger suggested it represented a fundamental change in the strategic situation of the United States and threatened the credibility of the nuclear guarantee. It is not self-evident that this need be so, particularly without complementary improvements in other Soviet capabilities.

There have been rumours of Soviet break-throughs in particle-beam technology that would permit an effective ballistic missile defence or at least serious interference with space-based support systems relevant to reconnaissance, navigation, command, control and communications. The possibilities for directing high-energy beams to targets instantaneously and with a 100 per cent destructive efficiency will command attention in the research laboratories of both superpowers. However, whatever the potential for the future, it is extremely difficult to see how energy could be generated in sufficient quantities, particularly if the system were space-based, how reliability could be ensured, or how the problems of covering large areas of space, tracking and identifying individual objects and overcoming a variety of possible (and cheaper) countermeasures could be overcome. Typically, in the enthusiasm for the concept, the promise is underlined while the obstacles are played down.

Nor does it seem likely that any Soviet civil defence programme will be able to reduce the impact of a nuclear attack to tolerable levels. The Soviet Union has taken civil defence more seriously than the United States, where the consensus opinion has been that protection against nuclear explosions can only be limited. Little could be done to spare most people the consequences of an all-out nuclear attack. The possibility of mass evacuation from cities has been mooted. There is no evidence of actual exercises in the USSR to assess the feasibility of this sort of operation. It is doubtful that the organisational and social problems created by mass evacuation to unprotected camps would be a sensible move in a nuclear crisis. The only form of mass civilian defence which might make some sense would be fall-out shelters, but only in the case of a limited attack not directed at cities.

Bombers and SLBMs are not expected to face the same vulnerability problems of ICBMs. Alert bombers can take off on warning and be recalled if the warning turns out to be false. ICBMs can also be launched on warning. This prospect might well weigh heavily with a Soviet planner contemplating an attack, especially as there is some evidence that they themselves are drawn towards this. As it would involve supreme dependence on warning systems to trigger a nuclear war this is not a policy to be encouraged.[6]

[6] Using a depressed trajectory missile from a submarine close to the United States it might be possible to attack bomber bases without adequate warning time for the bombers to escape. It has been suggested that this hypothetical capability would be an appropriate topic for SALT III.

Bombers, unlike missiles, face the problem of dense active defences. With defence suppression missiles, such as SRAM, and air-launched cruise missiles which, though individually vulnerable because of their slow speed, can saturate air defences or take detours, bombers will still represent a potent attacking force. Anti-submarine warfare has still a long way to go before it will reach a state permitting high-confidence attacks on large numbers of submarines. Those at port, however, are extremely vulnerable and this is an area of significant Soviet vulnerability because of the low percentage of its force on patrol at any time.

ESCALATION DOMINANCE

Neither superpower can escape the threat of the decimation of its society in a nuclear attack. Given this, what could be gained by attacking ICBMs without eliminating bombers and SLBMs at the same time? The suggestion is that what is lost is the capacity to respond in kind. Unlike bombers, which take time to reach their targets, and SLBMs, which were designed as counter-city weapons, ICBMs are a ready and reliable means of delivering rapid counter-force attacks. Deprived of his own ICBMs, a US President could not launch a comparable attack on the remaining Soviet ICBM silos. He would, therefore, be unable to demonstrate that America was prepared to engage in nuclear exchanges but wishes to avoid escalation to total nuclear war, because his only choice would be between launching a counter-city attack, probably resulting in retaliation in kind, and surrender.

The argument that ICBM vulnerability matters therefore rests on a theory of escalation dominance, in which it is assumed that the side which has the least to lose by each move up the escalatory ladder within a conflict expanding in scope and intensity, will be better able to impose its will on the other. The alternative perspective to escalation is that of the 'indivisibility of deterrence' which argues against the belief that a war in Europe could be controlled at any particular level of intensity. The deterrent effect comes through the risk of total war associated with any breach of the European peace. From this perspective the danger of theories of escalation dominance is that they treat different balances, be they in conventional forces, theatre nuclear weapons or counterforce capabilities, in isolation, exaggerating the opportunities for controlling a conflict at any particular level.

This has become a controversial issue in Europe because of the fear that the US plans to wage a 'limited nuclear war' confined to European territory. Disarmament groups on the Continent see this as the motive behind NATO's December 1979 decision to modernise its long-range theatre nuclear forces with ground-launched cruise missiles and Pershing intermediate-range ballistic missiles. The assumption behind the new NATO programme is that in a conflict it will find it easier to raise the nuclear stakes in a series of gradual moves rather than in a headlong rush to all-out exchanges and also the belief that mobile systems that can reach Soviet territory will dissuade the Kremlin from contemplating a pre-emptive attack confined to Western Europe. This second objective relies on Soviet planners not wishing to engage in area bombardment for risk of prompting an equally devastating retaliation, despite the fact that the new NATO missiles could be caught in such an attack. For a more comforting level of invulnerability the systems would need to be sea-based. This was considered to be too expensive and lacking the sort of political commitment gained by placing US nuclear systems on European soil. There remains some interest in the United States in a supplementary deployment of submarine-launched cruise missiles. At the moment the USSR has a marked numerical advantage in this area and is improving quality with the Backfire bomber and the MIRVed SS-20. The current position and possible future developments are summarised in Table 2.

The stage after long-range theatre nuclear weapons is considered to be counter-force attacks involving central strategic systems. It is not clear, however, that such attacks would be viewed as a discrete stage in the escalation ladder. The collateral damage resulting from an attack on US ICBM silos by existing types of Soviet ICBM would approach 2 - 20 million dead. This would be a catastrophe to dwarf anything in the American experience. The shock could induce all sorts of reaction, certainly including a full-blooded nuclear riposte. If it is believed that the United States would remain passive following such an attack, it is hard to accept that it would respond to a conventional attack on Europe, as NATO doctrine requires.

If any power should be alarmed by the vulnerability of land-based systems in the long term, it is the Soviet Union. Its strategic assets are concentrated in ICBMs—its most powerful and technically advanced weapons. Because of the warning time, US cruise missiles may pose it less of a problem than the growing component of the US ICBM force, which has a substantial hard-target capability, and the possible eventual deployment of counterforce SLBMs. The Soviet heavy bomber force is unimpressive and saved from total obsolescence by the lack of US air defences. There is evidence that Soviet submarines spend far less time on station than their American counterparts, and that the United States is well ahead on anti-submarine warfare techniques. The Russians have resisted American proposals in SALT to concentrate the arms competition in sea-based systems. This is not surprising, given their immense investment in ICBMs and the present inadequacies in SLBMs. Nevertheless, a switch of investment priorities to the sea-based deterrent by the Soviet Union in the 1980s is quite possible.

A NEW ARMS RACE?

Nevertheless, it is Americans who have become most preoccupied with the vulnerability issue and the question of whether comparative counter-force capabilities now provide the key to the strategic balance. The ideal weapon is now seen to be one which is both capable of attacking protected targets yet on a launch platform itself relatively invulnerable to attack. Obviously both sides cannot achieve both objectives at the same time. The attempt to do so could well be a recipe for an arms race.

Up to now it has been assumed that ICBMs offered high accuracy and high vulnerability, whereas SLBMs were exactly the opposite. Current US plans envisage improving the accuracy of SLBMs and the invulnerability of ICBMs.

The most difficult of these objectives is to improve the invulnerability of ICBMs. The design of a new missile—the M-X—with an impressive counter-force package of 10 MK 12A warheads has not caused serious problems. The major difficulty lies with the basing mode, which in addition to providing survivability must also be cost effective, environmentally tolerable and capable of verification in an arms control regime. By the end of the Carter Administration some 30 different proposals for basing had been evaluated, before settling on a system that will have 200 missiles on launchers moving between 4600 shelters, along interconnecting roadways. However, the Reagan Administration is continuing the tradition of an annual summer review of M-X basing. It has become worried at the prospective delays caused by environmental objections as well as the cost. A number of ideas, such as putting M-X to sea on a large number of small vessels, have been revived.

Meanwhile the new Administration is considering accelerating the pace of development of submarine-based force. At the start of the Reagan Administration 96 of the new Trident I missiles (with 8 warheads of 100 kt each) had been fitted onto 6 old Poseidon submarines, with another 6 of these submarines in various stages of conversion. A completely new type of submarine, the Ohio class, is being produced to carry 24 Trident I missiles at greater speed and less sound.[7] However, the first of this class is well behind schedule and the Pentagon is being forced to reconsider the advisability of such a large and complex submarine. It is also considering whether to move forward to the next generation SLBM—the Trident II—which, unlike the Trident I, could have a hard-target capability. A decision on this is likely within the next 3 years.

Finally, the new Administration is planning to reverse President Carter's 1977 decision not to proceed with a new manned bomber, the B-1. It was then felt that the extra lease of life provided to the B-52 force by air-launched cruise missiles would be sufficient. The new bomber will probably be a revised version of the B-1.

The likely Soviet response to all these moves is uncertain. In the past the USSR has on occasion developed unique systems, but these reflect distinct requirements rather than technological superiority (a good example of this is an anti-satellite satellite active testing of which resumed in early 1981, which is comparable to a type rejected by the United States in the early 1960s: the United States has been developing, but has not yet tested, superior systems). Any sense of overall superiority results from the greater number and larger size of individual systems. Its main technical effort over the past decade has been devoted to MIRVing, following a US example which it has been able to exploit to greater effect.

Little effort has been devoted to new forms of launch platform or basing. Harold Brown's last report as Secretary of Defense noted: 'We have been expecting the Soviets to develop a new long-range bomber for several years', but there is yet to be conclusive evidence. There has been a long-standing interest in mobile ICBMs. The SS-16 was developed in the mid-1970s but it does not appear to have been particularly impressive and deployment would be specifically prohibited under SALT II (though the two-stage version, the mobile SS-20 is now the backbone of the Soviet theatre force).

[7] The Trident I missile is to be purchased by Britain as the successor to its Polaris force.

The first of a new class of large submarines, the *Typhoon,* has recently been launched with a new long-range missile under development for its 20 tubes, making it comparable to the Trident system. Reports suggest a displacement of 30000 tons (compared with 19,000 for the Ohio class). The reason for this enormous size may be to accommodate a large propulsion unit to provide for greater speed and depth, which would suggest a continuing preoccupation with the quality of Western anti-submarine warfare capabilities.

All these uncertainties compound the political problems surrounding SALT. None of the possible technical developments discussed above would actually be halted by the prompt ratification of SALT II, which deals with quantity more than quality (except that it only allows for one new type of ICBM each). Even opponents of SALT seemed more concerned that the Treaty might lull the public into a false sense of security than over particular inhibitions on weapon development.

President Reagan has committed himself to persevering with the SALT process, and both sides are taking care not to take irreversible steps which would undermine the Treaty, so it cannot be written off yet. However, the delays already incurred will necessitate some adjustments to the SALT package before it can be resubmitted for ratification, and technological advances will not make an improved Treaty easy to formulate, if only because the advances now point to greater versatility and the blurring of the straightforward divisions between systems which make arms control manageable. The main barrier to SALT remains bound up with US domestic politics and the divisions within the Administration over whether to take SALT seriously. The Administration will certainly wish to have the broad lines of its strategic arms development worked out before it gets too involved in new negotiations.

All this uncertainty is creating much anxiety over the future. The continued difficulties with SALT the regular consideration of new systems and technical tricks on both sides and the arguments over doctrine and theories of limited nuclear war, have pushed the nuclear issue well to the fore of international politics in an unusually disturbing manner. Yet it is important to remember that despite all the expense and ingenuity devoted to nuclear weapons over the past decades, convincing answers have yet to be found to the problem of developing a nuclear strategy that offers the prospect of a decisive advantage and removes the risk of devastating retaliation. Given this, there is no reason to believe that the stalemate of the balance of terror is close to being broken.

TABLE 1. U.S. AND SOVIET STRATEGIC FORCE LEVELS

	1 January 1980		1 January 1981	
	US	USSR	US	USSR
Offensive				
Operational ICBM				
launchers a,b	1054	1398	1054	1398
Operational SLBM				
launchers a,c	656	950	576	950
Long-range bombers (TAI) d				
Operational	348	156	347	156
Others	225		223	
Force loadings g				
Weapons	9200	6000	9000	7000
Defensive h				
Air defense surveillance				
Radars	88	7000	91	7000
Interceptor aircraft (TAI)	327	2500	312	2500
SAM launchers	0	10000	0	10000
ABM defence launchers	0	64	0	32

a   Includes on-line missile launchers as well as those in construction, in overhaul, repair, conversion and modernisation.

b   Does not include test and training launchers or 18 launchers of fractional orbital missiles at Tyura Tam Test Range.

c   Includes launchers on all nuclear-powered submarines and for the Soviets, operational launchers for modern SLBMs on G-class diesel submarines: excluded are 48 SALT-accountable launchers on 3 Polaris submarines now used as attack submarines.

d   1981 figures exclude for the United States: 65 FB-111s, for the USSR: over 100 Backfires, about 120 Bison tankers, Bear ASW aircraft and Bear reconnaissance aircraft.

e   Includes deployed, strike configured aircraft only.

f   Includes, for the United States, B 52s used for miscellaneous purposes and those in reserve, mothballs or storage, and 4 B-1 prototypes: for the USSR Bears and Bisons used for test, training, and R&D.

g   Total force loadings reflect those independently targetable weapons associated with the total operational ICBMs, SLBMs and long-range bombers.

h   Excludes radars and launchers at test sites or outside North America.

i   These launchers accommodate about 12,000 SAM interceptors, some of the launchers have multiple rails.

Source: Secretary of Defense Harold Brown, *Department of Defense Annual Report for Fiscal Year 1982* (19 January 1981), p 53.

TABLE 2. US/NATO AND SOVIET LAND-BASED LONG-RANGE THEATRE NUCLEAR FORCES[a] STRIKE INVENTORY

Missile range/aircraft radius (km)		Weapons per system	1 January 1981				Mid-1980s (estimated)			
			Total launchers/ aircraft worldwide	Total launchers/ aircraft Europe[b]	Total warheads worldwide	Total warheads Europe[b]	Total launchers/ aircraft worldwide	Total launchers/ aircraft Europe[b]	Total warheads worldwide	Total warheads Europe[b]
Soviet										
SS–20 Launchers	4400	3	180	110	540	330	300 +[c]	f	900[c]	f
Backfire bombers[e]	4200	4[d]	65 - 70	40	260 - 280	160	150	f	600	f
Older missiles	1900 - 4100	1	400	400	400	400	50 - 200[g]	50 - 200[g]	50 - 200[g]	50 - 200[g]
Older bombers[e]	2800 - 3100	2[d]	450	350	900	700	400	300	800	600
NATO										
UK Vulcan Bomber	2000	-[h]	56	56	-[h]	-[h]	0	0	0	0
US F-111 DCA	1800	2[d]	360	170	720	340	330	170	660	340
US GLCM	2000	1	0	0	0	0	464[i]	464[i]	464[i]	464[i]
US Pershing II	1000	1	0	0	0	0	108[i]	108[i]	108[i]	108[i]

a   Systems with missiles ranges or unrefueled combat radii such that (a) Soviet systems can unambiguously hit targets in Western Europe from bases in the Soviet Union, and (b) NATO systems can unambiguously hit the Soviet Union from bases in Western Europe. Aircraft radii are illustrative for European missions.

b   Inventory normally based in Europe or within striking range of Europe.

c   Because of the continuing construction programme, the SS-20 force may be larger than estimated above.

d   Illustrative weapons load. Actual load would vary according to mission and type of weapon (ASM or bombs).

e   Strike-configured bombers and ASM carriers only. Does not include comparable numbers of Backfires and older bombers currently assigned to Soviet naval aviation.

f   Two-thirds of total worldwide inventory could be deployed against NATO.

g   The numbers shown reflect uncertainties about the future status of the force of older missile launchers.

h   Unclassified data not available.

i   After completion of LRTNF modernisation.

Source: Secretary of Defense Harold Brown, *Department of Defense Annual Report for Fiscal Year 1982* (19 January 1981), p. 66.

Weapon Development in the 1980s: Sea

ROGER VILLAR

Captain Roger Villar, formerly Captain of HMS Excellent *and Commodore (Intelligence), has been Naval Adviser to British Aerospace Dynamics since leaving the Navy in 1974*

THIS article is not intended as a complete review of naval weapons but rather to list today's current developments and their purpose in outline. Those who need more detail on specific weapons should refer to one or other of the specialist publications which cover these in considerable detail. The main areas covered here are anti-submarine, anti-air, anti-surface vessel and mine warfare together with naval aviation.

ANTI-SUBMARINE WARFARE

Anti-submarine warfare is the main concern of a majority of deep-water navies. The difficulties of detecting a submarine compared with a surface ship are such that the surface ship must always be at a disadvantage. Moreover, modern nuclear-propelled submarines may be so fast that, even when found, there is some difficulty in attacking them successfully.

Detection

Where once the prime method of detection was by active sonar, the main emphasis is now on passive sonars with much greater detection ranges, and with active sonars being used for final accurate location before an attack. There are, of course, many exceptions to this rule; some very powerful active sonars are at sea and, given the right circumstances, can achieve detection ranges of perhaps 20 miles or more—but the passive detections can have many times this range. Over and above all this, however, every means of detection yet found is so full of uncertainty, and so variable in performance depending on the conditions of the day and the characteristics of the target, that every available method has to be used in combination. If all information from all sources can be combined with advanced C_3, the total available is greatly increased; experiments using SATCOM and a shore-based computer have confirmed this.

SOSUS. Since the early 1950s America has been installing huge fixed hydrophone arrays on the edge of her continental shelf to cover the Atlantic in a system known as SOSUS (Sound Surveillance Under the Sea). The hydrophones are connnected to shore stations by cable and, being situated at some depth, can obtain very long-range detections indeed of any submarine making a reasonable noise — that is to say moving at some 8 knots or more.

It is fairly clear that over 30 years of work have enabled America to spread her SOSUS coverage over much of the Atlantic. Russia does not have the same access to the major oceans and, although she is known to have experimented with large buoys carrying passive hydrophones, it is probable that she has no coverage to compare with that of America although she may well have covered her own inshore waters as a defensive measure.

Passive towed arrays. For some years American nuclear ballistic missile submarines have had the BQR-15 passive towed array as a method of obtaining early warning of enemy submarines attempting trailing operations. That principle of towing hydrophones in quiet water astern is now being applied to other nuclear submarines and to surface ships. Long-range detections are certainly practicable from surface ships, and perhaps more from deep quiet submarines, although the precise figure varies from day to day with the water conditions as much as it does with the noise from surface shipping in the vicinity.

Ships so fitted require quiet water to get the best results and must therefore be clear of the main body of the fleet. Use of the towed array is not easy; nor is it the panacea for all ills which some think it to be. Sounds detected must be analysed by computer to distinguish them from the background noise and to identify the originating platform. Nor can towing ships steam fast because of the noise made and the consequent interference with detections. The passive towed array is indeed a major step forward in detection, but it does not do everything.

Sonobuoys. The standard sonobuoy in wide general use has been the passive Jezebel deploying its hydrophones at varying depths between 60 and 450 ft and being omnidirectional so that it does not give bearing information. Detection ranges of several miles have been achieved, and a pattern of buoys has been able to enclose a submarine so as to give approximate position and enable it to be followed by dropping further buoys.

More modern practice, however, is to use passive directional sonobuoys with variable depth hydrophones so as to achieve longer detection ranges and greater economy of use; detection ranges of 5 — 10 miles may be achieved, depending on the target and the conditions at the time. Nevertheless, passive sonobuoys, since they do not give range, do not generally allow the target to be fixed sufficiently accurately for a torpedo attack, and a directional active sonobuoy, with a detection range of 1 to 2 miles, may have to be used in the closing stages of an attack.

Both aircraft and helicopters use such sonobuoys. Analysis of the information which they provide is not easy and suffers from all the same difficulties as the passive towed array sonar and can only be resolved by a computer. Aircraft generally carry such a computer, but in helicopters the practice varies — the British Sea King and its replacement have full computer facilities enabling them to search autonomously for submarines; the American LAMPS III helicopter has to remain within high-frequency radio range of its parent ship so as to radio back the sonobuoy information for computer processing on board; smaller helicopters such as the Anglo-French Lynx do not have the capacity for such a computer and are not yet fitted widely with sonobuoys either.

Magnetic anomaly detectors. Magnetic anomaly detectors are carried by both aircraft and helicopters to detect the change in the earth's magnetic field caused by the presence of a submarine. Generally they are limited to about 1000 ft detection range although an experimental set detecting at 2000 ft has been reported.

Variable-depth sonars. Variable-depth sonars are carried by surface ships and can be lowered to some 200 ft to obtain detections below the layer. Those in use today operate at about 10 kHz but, although they penetrate beneath any normal layer, their sound path is still subject to all the vagaries of the ocean, and long detection ranges are seldom achieved. One French set is claimed to have a 25-km detection range, but that is the exception rather than the rule.

Hull-mounted sonars. Hull sonar development has moved more and more towards the high-power low-frequency set operating at around 5 kHz. Frequently such sets are mounted in the bows of a ship where they are as far as possible from the propeller noise and can then also operate in the passive mode; the outstanding example is the American AN/AQS-53 sonar fitted in the *Spruance* class destroyers which is capable of passive listening at slow speed, active transmission in the surface duct, and has sufficient power to operate in the bottom bounce and convergence zone modes whereby the beam may be directed downwards to reflect off the bottom or be bent up by the varying refraction of the sea at great depth until it comes to the surface again at some 15 — 20 miles' distance.

Smaller ships use smaller sonars, and it is general to mount them somewhat aft from the bow. Increasingly such hull sonars are being combined with variable-depth sonars.

Dunking sonars. Many shipborne helicopters are fitted with small dunking sonars which they can lower below the layer whilst they themselves go into an automatic low-level hover. After completing a search sweep, the helicopter moves on to another search area close by where it again goes into a low-level automatic hover. The performance of such sonars has not been published but may be expected to be not more than 2 or 3 miles because of their small size and high frequency. Nevertheless, they can be used by numbers of helicopters to set up a searching barrier or be used for final accurate location of a target prior to attack.

Weapons

The original weapon for use against the submarine was the depth charge dropped at first by surface ships and then by aircraft, but it suffered from the disadvantage that it took a finite time to drop to depth during which a submarine could evade, and this became more and more important as submarine diving depths increased. Moreover, surface ships lost sonar contact with a submarine during the final stages of an attack as it passed underneath the sonar beam, and this introduced further errors. Development therefore led to the ahead throwing mortar fitted in surface ships and capable of firing a pattern of charges to about a 1000-m range. Since the time of flight of these is fairly large, further development led to rocket launchers such as the Swedish Bofors 375 mm or the Russian MBUs which are still in service in large numbers.

Gradually, however, the homing torpedo has taken over; it is no longer so much a torpedo as an underwater guided missile which can be dropped by aircraft or helicopters or fired from ships and submarines. The air- and ship-launched are generally of light weight and 12¾-in diameter, whereas the submarine launched tends to be much bigger to fit a 21-in torpedo tube and have long-range performance against ships as well as submarines.

The lightweight torpedo is typified by the American Mark 46

which is in service with a number of navies. It weighs 230 kg and will be dropped within about 1000 m of a target, or fired from a ship's torpedo tube, to search in a circle round a preset position while it spirals downwards using either active or passive homing. Russian submarines now go deeper than expected when the Mark 46 was designed and have also been covered with anechoic coatings which reduce their sonar echoes. A Mark 46 development programme known as NEARTIP (NEAR Term Improvement Programme) has therefore been instituted to make some correction for this while a more modern torpedo is developed. America is thus engaged on the advanced lightweight torpedo which will take some years to come to fruition, while Britain has the Stingray in active development.

Some surface ships are fitted with missile systems which will drop a lightweight torpedo some miles away to attack a long-range contact. America uses the Asroc, which is an unguided rocket carrying the Mark 46 torpedo, or a nuclear depth bomb to about 11 km; Britain, Australia and Brazil use the Ikara which also carries a Mark 46 torpedo to about 20 km; France has her own 15-km Malafon, which is nearly obsolete; and Russia has both the 27-km Fras-1 carrying a nuclear depth bomb and the 55-km torpedo carrying SS-N-14. Asroc is relatively widely fitted but being outdated by the speed of modern submarines which allows them to steam outside the torpedo dropping area during the time of flight of the rocket. Ikara has in-flight guidance so as to compensate for the submarine movements and give an accurate torpedo drop; moreover, because of its longer range, relatively few ships need to be fitted as one can provide defence for many.

Modern submarine torpedoes are typified by the American Mark 48 and the British Mark 24 Tigerfish, which have respective performances of 46 km at 50 knots and 32 km at either high or low speed. Both weigh over 1500 kg and have performance against submarine and ship targets. They use wire guidance whereby the firing submarine transmits guidance signals derived from its own sensors until the final inbuilt acoustic homing guidance takes over. But torpedoes take a considerable time to run their full range and faster air flight weapons are already in the Russian fleet as the SS-N-15 and SS-N-16 which can be fired from submerged to carry either a nuclear warhead or a torpedo to a 36-km range. They probably, however, cannot make use of the full range against a submarine target because of the difficulty of obtaining accurate targeting information before firing at such a distance; it is one thing to fire a submarine torpedo down a line of bearing but another to achieve an accurate drop from which a torpedo has a good chance of acquiring the target itself.

Summary

Anti-submarine warfare is an expensive and difficult business. Although the modern torpedo is quite exceptionally efficient and lethal, it is complex and costly. But it is detection which is the most difficult problem of all and calls for a combination of many devices on many different types of platform. Each may be able to contribute some part of the story; none will give it all because sea and weather conditions are so unstable. America's experiments of transmitting all source information by SATCOM to a shore computer and then retransmitting it to ships in real time has brought an enormous step forward in available information, but it also points to the difficulty and expense of achieving success in this most difficult problem of all.

ANTI-AIR WARFARE

Air defence at sea is not quite such a difficult problem as anti-submarine because of the relatively greater ease with which radars can detect the target. Nevertheless, the difference is not very marked because missile targets are becoming smaller and smaller, with radar echoing areas down to 0.05 square metres, and are extremely difficult to detect at sufficient range for them to be engaged; electronic warfare makes the problem even harder to solve. The solution developed in the West has been a layer of defences, reaching from fighter aircraft aimed at missile launching aircraft, to long- and short-range missile systems, electronic warfare and short-range gun systems. Soviet developments seen today depend instead on high-capacity medium-range missile systems and short-range gun systems.

Fighter defence

The American Mach 2.4 Tomcat F-14 fighter is armed with 60-mile range Phoenix missiles and is capable of engaging up to 6 targets at the same time. It requires long-range warning from Hawkeye Airborne Early Warning aircraft and is an expensive and costly system. There is a limit to its effective range because of the difficulties of getting long enough warning of the enemy's

approach—probably something like 200 miles is the maximum
which is about the range at which the Soviets can now launch
their airborne missiles. As it is probable that the Soviet's missile
range will be extended in the future, even Tomcat may then be
unable to cope, and the shorter-range Sea Harrier, armed with
limited-range Sidewinder missiles, has little capability against
long-range missile-launching aircraft. Thus more and more
emphasis is being given to anti-missile missiles.

Area defence missiles

Area defence missile systems reach out to some 50—100 km
depending on their type. Both the British Sea Dart and the
American Standard missiles have such capability and can both
intercept and destroy attacking missiles provided only that they
get sufficient warning from their surveillance radars of small
missile targets. This need has led to the development of the
American Aegis system with the AN/SPY-1A radar—a phased
array radar built into a ships superstructure and weighing some
60 tons which is being fitted into the 9055-ton *Ticonderoga* class
destroyers costing about £400 million each. The British Sea Dart
has no such allied radar and will be in difficulties against the
smaller targets. The Russian approach has been to develop the
very high-speed Mach 5 SA-N-6 missile so that the very short time
of flight of the missile itself minimises the radar warning
required.

Point defence missile systems

Because of these difficulties of obtaining adequate radar warning, it is necessary to fit shorter-range systems into a large number
of ships. As yet few have been developed specifically to deal with
attacking missiles: the widely fitted Sea Sparrow and its derivative
of the Aspide/Albatros in Italy are largely intended to deal with
bigger and slower aircraft although they have some capability
against the bigger missiles. The British Sea Wolf has been
specifically developed to deal with attacking missiles but is as yet
at sea only in penny numbers. NATO is developing the 6S missile
system for wide fitting in small ships: few details have been released but it is believed to be a high-engagement capacity short-range
system which will not be in service before about 1990. Whilst
therefore the need and the possibility is there to fit point defence
missile systems, there are few at sea.

Short-range gun systems

Medium-calibre guns are fitted in a majority of ships and are extremely effective against aircraft targets as well as for shore bombardment and as a general purpose weapon. They have, however, little effectiveness against missiles; the damage caused by a medium calibre shell to a missile is insufficient to destroy it unless it explodes very close, and such small miss-distances have not yet been possible to achieve with any consistency. It may be that the development of an infra-red homing guided projectile will improve matters but the work in America is not yet concluded.

It is, therefore, more common to use a very high rate of fire small calibre guns under tight radar control aimed to hit and explode an attacking missile's warhead at 1000 m range or less, and such short range enormously simplifies the surveillance radar problems. Russia has installed such guns in many of her ships; America has the Vulcan/Phalanx 20-mm Gatling gun with a rate of fire of 3000 rpm; and Spain, Italy and Holland also have them under development. Typically, Vulcan/Phalanx uses high-velocity heavy-depleted uranium projectiles to give maximum penetrating power. Its tracking radar performs 'closed-loop' spotting whereby spotting corrections to the line of fire are applied as a result of measuring the miss-distances of the first rounds; it reacts automatically to a threat detected by its own surveillance radar; and it has achieved a satisfactory number of hits in extensive trials.

The doubt about such gun systems lies partly in their complexity, partly in a natural reluctance to wait to such a late moment before destroying an attacker, and partly in doubts as to whether modern warhead explosives will actually detonate when hit.

Electronic warfare

In air defence electronic warfare has two roles: firstly, to deny information to the enemy by, for example, jamming an aircraft surveillance radar; and, secondly, to put up false targets to decoy the enemy from the real one. Modern decoys are typified by the NATO Sea Gnat system still under development, which fires a mixture of chaff and an infra-red decoy either overhead or else all round a ship. In the former case, known as the seduction mode, a missile acquiring the ship will also acquire the decoy and, if the course of the ship can be adjusted to allow the two to drift gently apart, then the missile may follow the decoy if it is the larger of the two targets. In the latter, known as the distraction mode, decoys are fired to short range all round a ship so as to give a missile's homing head more than one target to think of.

Such a system has the merit of being cheap but is not easy to use. Particularly does the firing of the decoys require very critical timing, and this means a sophisticated surveillance radar and data-handling system. It is also difficult to simulate the enormous radar echoing area and infra-red signature of a large ship although a fast attack craft presents few problems. Finally, modern electronics in missiles may well be able to distinguish between the somewhat blurred response from chaff and the more clear-cut response from a ship's superstructure and hull.

Summary

Every type of defensive system thus has some short-comings no matter what its cost and sophistication. Necessarily, too, as attacking missiles get smaller and faster, more and more emphasis has to be placed on the shorter-range systems because of the difficulties of obtaining long-range radar warning. That difficulty has led the Soviets to develop a Mach 5 defensive missile to reduce the time of flight and the consequent radar warning required. It will not really be solved until something such as the laser damage weapon or the particle beam, which has the speed of light, is at sea.

There is yet an additional problem: what if the enemy uses nuclear warheads in his attacking missiles as is believed to be the Soviet intention? Attacking missiles must then be destroyed at some 15-km range or the explosions of their warheads could cause crippling damage. There is little possibility of achieving this without the speed-of-light weapon to assist.

ANTI-SURFACE VESSEL WARFARE

The anti-ship missile, launched from aircraft, ships and submarines, is the prime threat to surface ships. A majority of the missiles in the West have high subsonic speeds; the Soviets are largly supersonic with speeds of up to Mach 3. Western missiles commonly sea-skim; Russian missiles come in at various elevations ranging from a shallow dive of 1° or 2° to a very steep descent of perhaps 70°. Various methods of homing may be used either individually or in combination, and including active radar and infra-red, or even inertial in missiles with nuclear warheads since the terminal accuracy required is not so great. Russian missiles generally have the option of conventional or nuclear warheads, whereas Western missiles do not have the nuclear option.

There is no theoretical limit to the range of anti-ship missiles provided the target can be identified and located sufficiently accurately before firing. Both America and Russia use ocean surveillance satellites in combination with shore-based direction-finding stations and can obtain extensive worldwide coverage. The exact situation is hard to quantify but there is little doubt that the Soviets are more advanced in this field since they started on it in 1967. Such a system is generally adequate to locate ships but, because of the infrequency with which satellites pass overhead, is unlikely to be able to give up-to-the-minute targeting information, and long-range missiles will therefore be fitted with some device which either recognises the enemy by his radar and radio transmissions, or distinguishes friendly ships by their IFF, so as to take out any errors in the initial position given to it.

At shorter range the target can be identified and located by a helicopter or aircraft which can report back by data link. In one case, the Franco-Italian Otomat missile, the missile itself can be given guidance corrections in flight from a helicopter which is in contact with the target.

Current developments

Russia has the most extensive armoury of anti-ship missiles and has developed them gradually over a number of years. Her most modern missile is the ship and submarine launched SS-N-19 capable of a 500-km range at Mach 2.5, allied with over-the-horizon targeting from satellites and direction-finding stations, and is vertically launched—from submerged in the case of the submarine fit. Her longest-range air-launched missile is the AS-4 travelling 260 km at Mach 2 + from the supersonic Backfire bomber. At the other end of the scale she has the 55-km Mach 1 + SS-N-7 fired from a submerged *Charlie* class nuclear submarine in salvoes of 4, possibly 8, which is a particularly nasty threat because of the surprise effect of a salvo of supersonic missiles lofting out of the sea at short range.

The West generally has shorter-range and slower missiles. Many ships have the 45-km Exocet MM 38 which is being superseded by the 72-km Exocet MM 40. America has the 90-km Harpoon which can be fired from ships, aircraft and submarines; it is a particular advantage in the latter since it fires from a conventional torpedo tube and can thus be widely fitted, whereas the Soviet equivalent SS-N-7 requires special inbuilt launching tubes which restrict its fit. The shipbourne Otomat missile has up to a 200-km range; the American shipborne Tomahawk will have some 675-km.

Subsonic missiles do not, however, readily penetrate modern defences. NATO is therefore planning development of its own Mach 2 + missile which can be launched from ships, submarines and aircraft, but it is uncertain yet whether the project will go ahead and clear that it cannot reach fruition before the early 1990s.

Summary

There are great differences between the West and Russia in the Soviet emphasis on long-range and high-speed as well as in the use of nuclear warheads; equally Russia has developed over-the-horizon targeting to a fine art whereas it has only just begun in the West. Fast missiles such as the SA-N-6 are essential to get through modern defensive systems, yet there are few signs that the West is really setting about getting them.

MINE WARFARE

Mine warfare is the most cost-effective of all methods of fighting, yet less attention is paid to it than to most other forms of warfare. World War II statistics alone prove the point where the British laid 76,000 mines offensively, designed to sink enemy ships, at a cost of about £3000 each and 1 in 40 was effective. Today there is comparatively little effort being put into mining except in the Scandinavian countries and in Russia which has a stock of about 400,000 mines.

Mine laying can be of two types — offensive and defensive. Offensive mining is clearly designed to seek out an enemy in his own waters and aircraft are the normal and most successful method of laying, although America is reported to be developing a submarine-launched mobile mine which can be fired from a torpedo tube into an enemy harbour. Generally offensive mining is concerned with shallow water and ground mines, which can be effective in up to about 60 ft depth, are used with a variety of actuators — magnetic, acoustic, or pressure operated, or a combination of two or more of these.

In the West, defensive mining ranges from shallow-water

ground mines laid close to ports to confine entry to a single clear channel; controlled minefields such as in the Baltic straits; somewhat deeper water mines suitable for laying out to the edge of the continental shelf in order, e.g. to close the north-west approaches off Britain to enemy submarines; to even deeper water mines such as the Captor which can be laid in the G-I-UK gap to respond to passing Soviet submarines by releasing an acoustic homing torpedo. Russian development is not known accurately although they have a wide variety of mines and can certainly lay them in quite deep water with a majority of their ships and submarines being equipped for minelaying.

It is not too difficult to lay mines but it can be extremely difficult and very time consuming to sweep them. Moored mines are not too difficult — a simple wire sweep towed at a regulated depth between two ships will cut their mooring wires and allow them to float to the surface where they can be dealt with. Continental shelf mines in fairly deep water will have to be moored to the bottom so that they can float near enough to the surface to sense their target, whether or not they subsequently release a charge to be propelled upwards to hit it. This, however, requires a deeper wire sweep than for the conventional type of moored mine, and Britain has therefore developed the EDATS (Extra Deep Armed Trawler Sweep) system. Nevertheless, the difficulty with such deeper-water mines is the greatly increased area in which they can be laid, and therefore the effort which is needed to clear a channel which can run for many miles.

Ground mines can be dealt with in various ways depending on their type. In the waters of up to about 60 ft depth in which they are effective, acoustic and magnetic mines can be actuated by towing a suitable noise maker or a double L-sweep in which a heavy current is pulsed rhythmically to create a magnetic field. Pressure mines cannot be so swept and have instead to be found and destroyed where they lie. This has brought in the minehunter concept in which a largely non-magnetic ship operating extremely quietly, so that it does not actuate magnetic or acoustic mines, is equipped with a special sonar. Such ships are known as minehunters and will steam at 3 — 4 knots while they search and, when they find a mine, will send out a dinghy with a diver, or a remote-controlled vehicle such as the French PAP 104, to lay a counter-mining charge. The process takes at least 20 minutes for each contact and many of them will be biscuit tins and the like.

Non-magnetic grp minehunters have been developed in Britain, France, Holland, Belgium and Italy. America concentrates on helicopter sweeping instead using a towed noise maker or double L-type of sweep and is developing a helicopter-borne minehunting sonar.

The first problem which mining brings is the enormous effort required to find them particularly when they can now cover so much deeper water and area than before. A modern minehunter of the British 700-ton *Hunt* class costs £25 million; no nation has enough minehunters to keep all its ports open against even a small mining effort; generally they will be able to keep no more than one clear; and many nations do not have any sophisticated minehunters at all but rely on the older minesweepers with sweeping gear but no hunting sonar. Secondly is the problem of yet deeper water particularly if mines such as the American Captor can lie on the bottom where they cannot be reached by a wire sweep nor found by a sonar which is limited to about 60-100 ft depth. Nevertheless, technically the means do exist to counter a majority of the known Soviet mines, or will do so in the next few years—it is the considerable finance and manpower and numbers needed which makes the mining threat so dangerous.

NAVAL FIXED-WING AVIATION

Conventional fixed-wing aviation is an enormously expensive business particularly if it is developed to the level of the American 91,400-ton *Nimitz* and her modern aircraft. The cost of that one ship, together with her aircraft and weapons, is very nearly the whole of the annual budget for Britain's Royal Navy. In the *Nimitz* it incorporates air defence from the Hawkeye airborne early warning aircraft and the Mach 2+ F-14 Tomcat fighter with 60-mile Phoenix missiles which can engage six targets at the same time; the A-6 and A-7 squadrons for long-range strike; the more general purpose Phantom F-4 multirole fighter to be succeeded by the F-18; and the S3A Viking maritime patrol anti-submarine aircraft. For some years America has been the only exponent of such a sophisticated system although Russia is now building a 60,000—70,000-ton aircraft carrier, and France is building two nuclear-powered carriers to replace her older *Clemenceau* and *Foch.*

A large part of such air power goes to defend the fleet, and it must be questionable, in view of the comments under the anti-surface vessel warfare section, just how effective it will be in the future as anti-ship missile launching ranges increase when they are already at about the limit of the engagement range of the

F-14 and Hawkeye combination. Air power is nevertheless of prime importance in projecting naval strength world wide since it can reach far out over land and sea, and it is primarily for that role, but with a limited air defence capability, that some nations are looking at the vertical/short take off aircraft.

There are two—the Sea Harrier adopted by Britain, Spain (in a modified AV-8A version) and India; and the Russian Forger Yak-36. The two aircraft are much the same size, with equivalent aerodynamic performance of high subsonic speed increasing to just over Mach 1 in the dive, and some two-thirds less weight than the F-14 Tomcat. Otherwise they differ substantially with the Yak-36 having two engines for lift and one for thrust as opposed to the Sea Harrier which has one engine and vectored thrust nozzles. The difference is substantial in that Forger can take off vertically or from a full conventional run but cannot achieve the short take off of the Sea Harrier—and it is that short take off, particularly when combined with the upward thrust of the ski-jump ramp, that gives additional aerodynamic lift to increase the maximum weapon load. The Sea Harrier is thus fitted with a full AI radar; Sidewinder short range air-to-air missiles which will be replaced by longer-range missiles when they become available; and will soon have the Sea Eagle 100-km anti-ship sea-skimming missile; and the options of guns, bombs and rockets. The Yak-36 has a range-only radar, short-range air-to-air missiles, and a lesser load of guns, bombs and rockets.

Where conventional fixed-wing naval aviation has just about reached its limit with the *Nimitz,* the Sea Harrier has considerable potential either in an increased lift big wing, or by development of a plenum chamber burning engine to make it supersonic. Its future is as yet uncertain and confused between the British defence budget, which has little spare cash, and the American Marine Corps, who have adopted the basic RAF Harrier in a version known as AV-8A and are developing it to a big-wing version known as the AV-8B. It is the start of a new road and one which many nations may be able to afford; it would be good to see it go further.

WS 25/Seawolf anti-missile system

ea Dart Surface-to-Air missile system

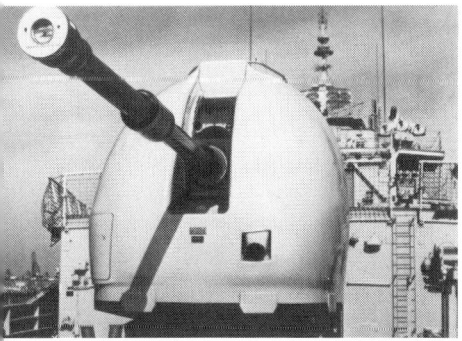

5in Mk8 Gun

4. FH70 155mm Field Howitzer

5. BBC/Corvus Chaff Protection system

Future Trends in Maritime Warfare
—NATO and the Warsaw Pact

ROGER VILLAR

Captain Roger Villar, formerly Captain of HMS Excellent *and Commodore (Intelligence), has been Naval Adviser to British Aerospace Dynamics since leaving the Navy in 1974*

TODAY'S trends in maritime warfare are dictated largely by the superpowers for only they have the immense resources needed to exploit modern technology widely and deeply. There is no doubt that both have a very wide field of modern technology available to them and, whilst the United States may have the most advanced capability, Russia has a very adequate base and is even ahead in some respects. But it is the direction in which they have chosen to exploit their technology which is of most interest since the available field is widening so fast that even the superpowers cannot afford to exploit every avenue. Indeed, as the cost and complexity of modern weapon systems escalate, they are finding that they must almost choose between several fundamentals, and smaller nations with lesser resources have an even more difficult choice.

Both the United States and Russia have chosen different directions—sometimes running together, but more often widely divergent. Russia has chosen to develop her maritime power to project her strength whilst still keeping NATO at bay; she has a dynamic and forward-moving maritime strategy. The United States has chosen to support NATO in a largely defensive role and, although she is now urgently increasing her naval spending, has little left over with which to project her power and influence.

Yet that is perhaps to talk about conventional war. The nuclear threat overhangs the conventional scene at all levels and again there are differences in the way the two superpowers look at it. The West seeks to deter nuclear war; Russia would no more initiate nuclear war than would the West but she plans on using the threat of her nuclear power quite deliberately. And it is worth looking in more detail at the relative attitudes of the two in this respect before discussing conventional war.

THE NUCLEAR DETERRENT

The philosophy of the maritime element of the nuclear deterrent appears superficially much the same between NATO and the Soviet Union, but there are differences in emphasis. NATO's philosophy is not to strike first, but instead to maintain a strong reply which the Soviet Union cannot take out in a pre-emptive attack. In consequence great emphasis is placed on the submarine-launched ballistic missile and on maintaining its invulnerability to a first strike. Because the United States is so concerned at the dangers of nuclear war, she also endeavours to maintain her conventional forces at a high level to match every conventional move by the Soviets so that the onus of escalating to a nuclear exchange, or of backing down, is placed on them.

Russia, too, aims at a secure deterrent and believes that NATO and the United States are more aggressive than is in fact the case. But she aims also for a considerable superiority of nuclear power since she hopes to frighten the United States so much that she will inhibit even her lower level conventional actions and she will thus be able to get her way with the minimum of trouble. She plays a considerable game of world politics which includes such matters as civil defence — the studies which have been announced show that in a nuclear exchange the United States might lose 150 million people whereas Russia, with her considerable civil defence measures to aid her, would lose no more than 10 or 20 million. That sort of study gives Russia confidence in her nuclear power.

United States development has led from the early 1200-mile-range Polaris, which was soon improved to a 2500-mile range, to the 2500-mile Poseidon with increased penetration capabilities and more warheads, to today's 4000-mile Trident. Her submarines have not been declared to NATO but have remained as a national asset under the control of the President. Her development philosophy has been based on maintaining effective penetration and hitting power through MIRVing and on keeping the invulnerability of the submarine through extending the missile range — every additional mile gives an extra 15,000 square miles of ocean in which a submarine can hide and makes the Soviet task of finding them well nigh impossible.

As well as this, however, the possession of an independent deterrent in Britain and France enormously complicates the Soviet calculations. If they gain a superiority over the Americans, can they guarantee that Britain and France will react in the same way? These two independent deterrents have tremendous value over and above that which appears superficially.

Russian development has followed broadly similar lines but with the differences of emphasis already noted. It is at least arguable that her early developments were directed against the reinforcement shipping in the Atlantic rather than against the United States mainland at all. Whatever may be the truth of that, it is clear that the 11,750-ton Delta III submarines, with their 5000-mile missiles, are capable of dealing with a majority of the United States mainland without even leaving their home waters. Why Russia should therefore go for the 30,000-ton *Typhoon* submarine with a new missile is not entirely clear—but possibly she felt that the Delta III was too threatened even in her home waters by United States submarine operations and she wanted the greater invulnerability which she would obtain from a submarine with a very-long-range missile which could operate in much of the world's oceans and be clear of NATO's fixed Atlantic anti-submarine defences. It is one more step in her search for nuclear superiority.

CONVENTIONAL WAR

In conventional terms, as in nuclear terms, the two main fleets have developed differently and are now in widely divergent paths. Let us look first at how the Soviets have developed and the reasons for their doing so.

Soviet development

Admiral Gorshkov became Commander-in-Chief of the Soviet Navy in 1956. At that time it was a largely coastal defence force although it had plans for a considerable expansion and was, for example, aimed at a force of 1200 submarines. Those plans, however, came to nothing because the main problem at that time was considered to be defence of the Homeland against nuclear attack by United States bombers and emphasis was given to the land forces.

Gorshkov, however, continued a programme, which must have started well before he took office, which was aimed at defence of the inshore waters of the Homeland and also directed against the United States strike carrier fleet cruising in the Norwegian Sea. Rather than embark on a programme of aircraft carriers to match the Allies, he relied on the anti-ship missile—many small inshore boats, the *Osas* and *Komars,* were built with a main armament of Styx SS-N-1 anti-ship missiles; a new class of destroyer, the *Krupny,* and of cruiser, the *Kynda,* also appeared with anti-ship missiles; emphasis was also placed on nuclear submarines armed with anti-ship missiles and some of the conventional submarines were also armed similarly.

No sooner had these craft appeared than the scene shifted with the United States introduction of the Polaris missile which moved the main nuclear threat further offshore. Thus the Soviets embarked, on the one hand, on an anti-submarine navy designed to search out these Polaris submarines. They built the large *Kresta* and *Kara* class of anti-submarine cruiser and the helicopter carriers *Moskva* and *Leningrad;* they accelerated their building programme of nuclear attack and cruise-missile-carrying submarines and directed them against NATO's Atlantic lifeline; and their own submarine-launched ballistic missile developed from the early *Golf* and *Hotel* class submarines to the nuclear *Yankees* with a 2500-mile missile.

But as the Americans extended the range of their submarine-launched ballistic missiles even further, it became more and more impracticable for the Soviets to seek them out with surface ships and they did not attempt to do so seriously with their submarines. As they, too, extended the range of their own ballistic missiles with the 5000-mile SS-N-18 in the Delta III class submarines, they increasingly found they were able to operate them close to their own waters where they needed the minimum of protection. That anti-submarine emphasis therefore appears to have ended about 1968 with the introduction of the 43,000 *Kiev* class carrier — primarily configured with anti-submarine helicopters although necessarily building continues with the normal roll-over effects. Building programmes cannot be changed as quickly as policies.

But in the course of this more open ocean deployment, the Soviets had made a number of advances which placed prime emphasis on the anti-ship missile. They have today a wide range of anti-ship missiles in service with ranges of up to 500 km and speeds of up to Mach 2.5 or greater. They have a very comprehensive and efficient ocean surveillance system, based on shore direction-finding stations and satellites, with aircraft and submarines and intelligence collecting ships linked in, which is progressing to give them real time information for units at sea. With their departure from the close support of the Homeland they have developed sophisticated surface-to-air defences based on missiles, but with small calibre rapid-fire guns as a back-up. Their command and control facilities are excellent although perhaps somewhat over-centralised. And they have a complete range of advanced and capable weapons and a continuous rolling programme of development.

That change of policy in the late 1960s is only just becoming apparent. It shows itself:

(a) The 32,000-ton battlecruiser *Kirov* with 500-km SS-N-19 Mach 2.5 supersonic anti-ship missiles and Mach 5 surface-to-air missiles.

(b) The 24,000-ton *Oscar* submarine with 500-km SS-N-19 anti-ship missiles.

(c) The building of at least one 60,000 — 70,000-ton aircraft carrier which seems likely to be operational about 1985.

(d) The 42-knot 2000 + ft depth *Alfa* submarine.

(e) A growing range of afloat support ships headed by the 36,000-ton *Berezina* capable of supplying both fuel and ammunition.

(f) Three new classes of cruiser which have not been identified positively but are likely to appear shortly.

(g) The 30,000-ton *Typhoon* class of submarine with nuclear ballistic missiles.

There can be no doubt whatever what this is all about. It is the first time that the Soviets have begun to develop a fleet for worldwide operation rather than being merely reactive to NATO's developments. Although they have been deploying ships overseas in increasing numbers for the past 20 years, they have not until recently specifically designed their ships for this purpose. It is a most significant change in their maritime purpose, and undoubtedly it is a most expensive one. When it began, perhaps about 1970, the Soviets did not feel themselves under particularly severe threats at home; they could afford to emphasise their Navy and their expansionist policies. Today, however, they have to face two fronts — to the West a NATO whom they regard as potentially hostile and aggressive whatever NATO itself may say; to the East is China. Even the Soviet Union does not have limitless resources; maybe it will now be driven to changing its strategy once again to support the land forces. But as yet there is no sign that this is happening and all eyes are on the Navy. What, then, may we see?

The Navy is now emphasising all arms. It will have the strike carrier; the very large offensively armed submarine; and the powerful battlecruiser. It has to go with this sophisticated weapons both designed to keep it afloat during air and missile attack, and also to operate offensively. Its submarines have never made great efforts to carry out operations against Western ballistic missile submarines, and the 42-knot *Alfa* is probably designed as an attack submarine with the prime task of defending the fleet against other attack submarines. Its great superiority in speed and diving depth is likely to make it most effective. A task group composed of the new carrier, the *Kirov*, the *Oscar*, and one or two *Alfa* class submarines, would be most difficult to destroy.

Soviet anti-ship missiles have, very largely, the ability to carry nuclear warheads. If these are detonated at about 15 km from their target, they will cause sufficient over-pressure to put any existing ship out of action. Defence against them therefore becomes almost impracticable; the Soviets have a most powerful offensive force.

The *Typhoon* is still something of an enigma but is clearly capable of operations far from home away from NATO's existing anti-submarine defences in the Atlantic such as SOSUS. Whereas NATO's forces have hitherto been able to mount operations against nuclear ballistic missile firing submarines in the Atlantic, it is unlikely that they will be able to find the *Typhoon* which will be able to operate in much of the world's oceans. Thus the Soviets are now obtaining what, in their eyes, is the invulnerable and undetectable deterrent, as well as massive conventional naval strength.

American and NATO development

NATO began in 1949 as an organisation of free nations banding together to defend Europe against the Soviet threat. It established an area north of the Tropic of Cancer in which an attack on one member would be considered an attack on all. Although it had overwhelming maritime superiority, the whole Alliance was, by its nature, defensive, and the tasks which it then set itself are basically unchanged today. In essence they were:

(a) Control of the Mediterranean.
(b) Closure of the Baltic and Black Sea exits to prevent those two Soviet fleets from getting out into the open.
(c) To escort reinforcements and resupplies (Re/Re) coming across the Atlantic from the eastern North American seaboard.
(d) To make early reinforcement of the northern flank in Norway where the border is common with Russia not far from the main fleet base at Murmansk.

(e) To reinforce the southern flank in northern Greece where it is only a few miles from the Bulgarian border.

In addition, as already discussed, an early task for the US strike carrier fleet was to provide the nuclear deterrent operating close to Russia in the Norwegian Sea area. That has since been overtaken by the development of Polaris and Poseidon and was a US national commitment rather than a NATO task, although both were viewed by the Russians in much the same light.

NATO's main task is undoubtedly in the Atlantic where the Re/Re commitment consists of transporting 1.5 million men by air and 12 million tons of stores by sea during a time of tension prior to war, and thereafter supplying Britain and Europe by means of 1000 ship sailings a month from the eastern American seaboard—implying 13 large convoys always at sea with the fastest ships sailing independently. Its basic maritime strategy can best be described in terms of that Atlantic area.

The main strength in the Atlantic is provided by the US and British fleets with the addition of units of the Netherlands fleet; the French position is far from clear. They operate a forward defensive policy, stationing forces as close as possible to Russia where they stand the best chance of defeating them before they get close to the main Atlantic Re/Re line. So far as possible, all forces are coordinated closely together with advanced C_3 but complete integration is not possible because of national differences of equipment fit.

The first line of defence is the G-I-UK gap. Here British aircraft based in Scotland and US aircraft based in Iceland can deal with enemy surface ships and submarines before they get into the Atlantic. Hunter killer submarines will be stationed well forward to deal similarly with Soviet submarines; and it is hoped in the future to be able to lay deep-water Captor mines in the G-I-UK gap to close it firmly to Soviet submarines. Aircraft carriers will also operate as far forward as possible but are unlikely to work too close to the G-I-UK gap until the air threat has been minimised.

The main Re/Re supply line runs south of the Azores partly outside the range of present Soviet bombers based in the north but still within range of submarines throughout. With the defences mentioned in the G-I-UK gap there is little chance of Soviet surface ships getting out unless they can do so before war breaks out; equally, attacking aircraft will have to run the gauntlet of the G-I-UK defences and it is expected that they will be decimated. But submarines may not only get through, but are also the easiest to pass through in the period of tension leading up to a war. NATO planning therefore puts first priority on anti-submarine warfare; second on anti-air warfare; and last of all on anti-surface vessel strike.

The development of ships and weapons to fill this role has not been so dynamic as in Russia, probably because the role itself has been very largely static since 1949. The main core of the surface forces is the aircraft carrier which has steadily grown bigger and bigger until the 91,400-ton *Nimitz* with her embarked aircraft and weapons virtually costs as much as the whole British naval budget for one year. Nuclear attack submarine development has been one major improvement and Western submarines are quiet and efficient and armed universally with the 100-km Harpoon anti-ship missile. But that development aside, all the emphasis has naturally gone on to defensive measures which have reached their nadir in the *Nimitz*, the *Ticonderoga* Aegis-equipped air defence destroyer, and the enormous anti-submarine effort. There are, for example no offensive supersonic anti-ship missiles, nor any that reach more than 100 km with the exception of the Tomahawk cruise missile adaptation which is not yet in service.

A highly significant modern trend is nevertheless the emphasis which is being placed on all these ships and submarines operating as one coordinated whole. The development of the NAVSTAR satellite system enabling ship, submarines and even aircraft to measure their positions accurately as well as their heights and course and speed combines with the JTIDS relative navigation system to enable every unit of a force to relate itself to all others and to be identified positively from the shore. The further development of ocean surveillance, even though it lags behind the Soviet's own development, will one day enable good plots to be held of all surface ships, whilst all source reporting of submarines will vastly improve that picture also. The United States is moving towards a position from where complete information will be available to shore and to all units at sea on the totality of the maritime picture, and as that progresses it will move the command more and more to the land rather than to the tactical commander at sea.

Summary

One can say with certainty that the Soviets are offensively minded and configured whereas NATO has increasingly become defensively minded. The level of technology is better in the West but the level of offensive thinking and development is much more marked in Russia. Moreover, NATO's strategy has remained defensive whereas Russia's has been reactive and aggressive and is now moving out deliberately into the open oceans. On both sides, however, there is a far greater integration of forces at sea than before with a greater emphasis on C_3; the Soviets have yet to learn this fully, whereas the United States has practised it for many years and is moving towards the close integration of major and widely dispersed forces at sea.

Navies, however, have many purposes and uses. It would seem that the Soviets are aiming to achieve nuclear superiority to such an extent that the United States and NATO will feel unable to take any actions even in the conventional field, and also to be able to dominate an area of sea with massive and impregnable power as much as to prevent NATO from carrying out the Re/Re task. At the other end of the scale their Navy has many peacetime uses for spreading their power and influence. It is a powerful tool for achieving the Soviet's political ambitions but it is only one of a number of tools which are available. It needs to have a power to intervene on land with an amphibious warfare capability and to combine with economic and political warfare and other methods of fighting in order to achieve the Soviet's overall political aims. It is the power of the Navy to intervene on shore, and to combine with economic warfare—with placing a stranglehold on NATO—which is here of most interest.

AMPHIBIOUS WARFARE

Amphibious warfare gives a country a power to intervene decisively on land. During World War II it developed as a science of the assault over the beaches which reached its peak in the Normandy D-day landings with an 'initial softening up bombardment followed up by paratroop landings behind the enemy lines accompanied by direct assaults over a beachhead. Within NATO its use has largely died since then except for the need to reinforce the southern and northern flanks in a hurry during a time of tension preparatory to a war. With the withdrawal of the British from the Mediterranean and continuing differences between Greece and Turkey, the organisation for reinforcing the southern flank is in some disarray but that for the northern flank in Norway is extant and continually practised.

But even here there is no call in NATO's doctrine for an opposed assault. British and Netherlands Marines are required to be landed with comparatively light armament during the period preceding a war and then to hold a narrow strip of mountainous and difficult terrain close to the sea to prevent the Russians from moving south. Some 2 weeks after they have landed the US Marine Corps will move in, but will have to cross the Atlantic first. In consequence, few new techniques have had to be developed although there is steady training in arctic warfare methods; and there is little amphibious specialised shipping available in the early days.

Indeed, within NATO amphibious warfare techniques are kept alive and moving only by the US 185,000 strong Marine Corps who have developed new methods of making a rapid opposed landing and have a considerable force of specialised shipping at their disposal. The Marine Corps places emphasis on speed, surprise and deception, and is a fully integrated force with its own aircraft, helicopters and landing craft as well as tanks and assault weapons. Only the ships are provided by the Navy and include five 39,300-ton *Tarawa* class of landing ship dock carrying helicopters, Harrier V/STOL aircraft and landing craft which will soon be replaced by 165-ton hovercraft to carrying troops right up a beach at high speed; 27 dock landing ships ranging from 11,000 to 18,000 tons; 2 17,000-ton command ships; 5 18,600 ton-cargo ships; 2 17,000-ton transports; 23 tank-landing ships; and a host of smaller craft. Their technique is to use the Harriers for initial strike and these can subsequently make use of ill-prepared landing sites when a beachhead has been captured. In order to achieve speed, over two-thirds of a landing force will move in by helicopter using vertical assault techniques; and the troops will then follow up by hovercraft with their tanks and artillery. It is a highly impressive and efficient force, highly trained, integrated and well capable of making its presence felt world wide.

The US capability is now being extended by the Rapid Deployment Force designed to increase the speed with which troops can intervene in far-distant quarters of the world. Its prime strength will consist of 5 pre-positioned ships which will carry the armaments, and a new development of heavy-lift aircraft to get the troops out there quickly. Initially it will be deployed in the vicinity of Diego Garcia and carrier battle groups will be detached to support it when necessary. In this fashion the Americans hope to make up for their lack of foreign bases.

Soviet techniques have primarily been directed at NATO's northern flank and the Baltic exits. They have some 15,000 specialised naval infantry who, unlike the US Marine Corps, are tasked merely with preparing the way for the Army to move in behind them, and they are thus no more than very fit, highly trained, motorised infantry equipped with light amphibious tanks and anti-tank weapons. In the northern flank they need to move in behind NATO's forces to outflank them; in the Baltic they are equipped with hovercraft which can make a quick surprise landing on, for example, the Danish islands before the defences have had time to prepare themselves. Thereafter a Russian merchant fleet under tight government control is sufficient to ensure that there will be transport to bring in the Army back-up.

That task has not hitherto demanded any very large ships and the biggest has been the 4500-ton Alligator tank-landing ship. In 1978, however the 13,100-ton *Ivan Rogov* dock-landing ship appeared; not as big as the US *Tarawa* class but with a capacity for 700 naval infantry and up to 40 tanks as well as supporting vehicles and also 3 assault vehicles in the dock. The building rate is slow — only two have been reported so far — but it may be indicative of a future move further overseas and there are also some reports that the new Soviet cruisers may have bigger guns than the 76 mm which has been hitherto universal and may therefore be acquiring a shore bombardment capability. In no way does this Soviet amphibious capability match, or begin to match, that of the US Marine Corps, but it is certainly a significant strength, nevertheless, and beginning to acquire a distant water capability.

ECONOMIC WARFARE

The Soviets themselves are not truly vulnerable as yet to economic warfare. Their land covers an enormous area with tremendous potential resources. They are short of only one or two essential minerals and can stockpile these without difficulty. They have for the moment sufficient of their own oil. Today the West could wage economic warfare against the Soviet Union only because of the deficiencies of their system which makes them import grain and high technology — and though the Soviets and their occupied countries may have to tighten their belts considerably, it is not likely that they would starve. Shortage of oil may be a major factor in the mid-1980s and could force them to competition with the free world, and perhaps to using force to obtain it, but that has not come yet.

NATO, however, is potentially much more vulnerable. Its economies depend on extensive worldwide trade. The world's merchant fleets have grown sevenfold in deadweight tonnage since NATO was founded; there is a massive and continual flow of goods in which much of the world is inextricably intertwined and interdependent. The Soviet merchant fleet joins in this flow but is not a significant part of it — it forms only 4 per cent of the world's whole and is much more important to the Soviet Union as an earner of foreign exchange than it is to the free world.

Moreover, NATO is short of many of the essential minerals for its life and economy. The prime mineral, of course, is oil; 40 per cent of the world's oil comes from the Arabian Gulf; no NATO nation is self-sufficient. Even in the United States a 10 per cent dependence on oil imports in 1966 rose to 20 per cent by 1976. In Europe the equivalent figures were 47 per cent and 56 per cent. And though NATO's nations maintain some 90 days' stockpiles, these could soon run out at wartime rates of usage. Oil comes from many places apart from the Arabian Gulf — from Venezuela, from Libya, through the Mediterranean, from the North Sea. The opportunities to interrupt the flow are legion.

Several attempts have been made to analyse NATO's dependence on other mineral supplies from overseas but have failed to be precise because of the immensely complex nature of trade. NATO generally uses 50 per cent more minerals than it produces and imports the remainder largely from the Third World. About 5 years ago (and the position will not be significantly different today) the EEC imported nearly 100 per cent of its nickel, manganese, chromium, cobalt, molybdenum, titanium and vanadium amongst others; the United States was less heavily dependent on outside sources of supply although still significantly so. And although NATO is not dependent on Soviet supplies, it is noteworthy that Russia and South Africa between them hold over 90 per cent of the world's platinum, over 80 per cent of the gold, 65 per cent of the vanadium, over 50 per cent of the chrome and so on. South Africa is important if the Soviet Union is not.

But whilst NATO may be thus dependent on supplies of minerals from overseas, although the full extent to which it will be vulnerable in war is difficult to analyse, the supplying countries are equally dependent on NATO for the continuance of their own economies. Thus over 80 per cent of Bolivia's export earnings come from metal ores; 75 per cent of Zambia's from non-ferrous metals; over 45 per cent of Malaysia's from rubber and tin. Moreover, all these are carried in a number of different nations' merchant ships. Thus any attempt to interrupt that trade would have very widespread repercussions throughout the world; economic warfare in that sense cannot be directed at NATO alone.

And it is noticeable that, whilst the Soviet Union has made numerous attempts to extend its influence overseas, it has not succeeded in any country which has been tied in to this invisible net of international trade with the possible exception of Cuba—which it is in consequence supporting at the rate of about $8 million a day.

Finally, NATO is nearly enough self-sufficient in food although there are particular shortage categories—coffee and tea for example. But with these exceptions it can manage provided it can distribute what it has amongst its nations. That means, of course, bringing it across the Atlantic to Europe from America in a continuous flow. For example, NATO produces 98 per cent of its consumption of edible oils and fats, but European NATO produces only 50 per cent of what it requires.

So of all the possibilities, the only ones to which one can point with certainty are those of interrupting the oil supply, or the Re/Re lines across the Atlantic in war. Unless Russia intends to take on the world, she is unlikely to have much success in interrupting the other sources of supply and supply lines in peace. While her mighty and growing fleet may have the power to dominate large areas of ocean, it must be questionable whether it would be worth its doing so without the Soviet Union being able to bring to bear the additional economic factors which would make such an intervention a long-term success. And the Soviet Union is too stretched with its present commitments, and too backward and poor commercially, to be able to do so. The danger remains one of full war rather than peacetime operations. It also is one of the fight for the oil on which NATO is now totally dependent on overseas supplies, and where Russia may have to look to the same sources within a few years.

THE ROLE OF THE SMALLER NAVIES

Only the two superpowers have the strength and resources to be able to develop navies which are up to date with today's technology in a major sense, and already we have spoken of the difficulties of them following all that technology has to offer—the expense is just too great. The smaller countries have an infinitely more difficult problem and of necessity have to choose more carefully what to do. None can afford the 32,000-ton battle cruiser of the Soviets nor the 9055 ton Aegis-equipped *Ticonderoga* of the Americans or its 91,400-ton *Nimitz*.

What they choose to do depends fundamentally on the role which they select. Two classic and opposite examples are the British and the French. The British have chosen to support the Americans in the Re/Re task in the Atlantic and are closely allied with them. For many generations they have emphasised quality rather than quantity—quality has been their watchword and so has lack of money. The result must be seen in today's Navy where the type 42 air defence destroyer—as a classic example—is equipped with the British-developed Sea Dart missile system, but the money was not available at the time this was developed to work on a sophisticated surveillance radar. Thus the 965 radar now in use is virtually obsolete and, although it is to be replaced one day with the newer STIR radar, this in no way matches the American Aegis. Nor does the ship today meet the postulated threat of the future; her successor has been planned as a ship of half the size again with two Sea Dart systems as well as two Sea Wolf systems for self-defence. The trend is always to bigger and bigger and thus to more and more expense; as the expense mounts, so does the search for quality reduce the quantity whilst itself remaining inadequate; and the British fleet is reducing some 15 per cent in numbers in the next decade.

The French fleet does not subscribe to the Re/Re task but more to maintaining an offensive intervention capability overseas as well as maintaining its own deterrent. Hence it maintains a force of nuclear ballistic missile-firing submarines and is developing nuclear-attack submarines; it also has two aircraft carriers and plans to replace them with its own design of a nuclear-propelled aircraft carrier. But with these exceptions its general run of ships are small with relatively unsophisticated armament because the money is not there and it does not have the same stringent defence requirement which the British, with their Atlantic role, must follow.

Other navies have clearer-cut roles. The German, Danish and Norwegian navies are clearly devoted to guarding the narrow exits of the Baltic with the Norwegians also guarding their coastline further north, and the Germans showing a continual national desire, never quite fulfilled, to get further out to sea. The Italian fleet strengthens the Mediterranean; the Greek and Turkish fleets do the same when they are not arguing among themselves; the Dutch keep a big fleet for their small size and largely support Britain and the United States in the Atlantic.

And around the world, and outside of NATO, are a large and growing number of smaller navies which increasingly have greater power with the introduction of the fast missile armed attack craft. There are 780 of these worldwide; they are sophisticated warships with many of the facilities for command and control and coordinated working together of the larger destroyers and frigates but without their defences against missile attack nor their anti-submarine capability. They are no more than offensively designed craft which can control a nation's offshore waters out to some hundreds of miles provided the weather is not too difficult and they do not meet with sophisticated attack themselves.

Overall it is a considerable and uncoordinated ragbag of fleets which follows no common policy; the ships are as different as are the weapons. The serious commonality only exists in the sharing of the Atlantic Re/Re role by the American, British and Dutch, in which the Americans provide the carrier fleet but the British and Dutch have more than half of the surface escorts between them.

TODAY'S PROBLEMS

Today's problems may therefore be summed up as two major alliances, each resting on a superpower, which follow different policies. Each has the capability to take what modern technology has to offer, but each is following a different line. Nevertheless, there are sufficient commonalities for each to be able to contain the other at the moment. Inevitably, however, this will be less and less true if the lines continue to differ and new and different weapons are developed.

Today there is a problem in the Arabian Gulf with both Iran and Iraq at war. There are no other major indigenous navies in the Gulf; yet 200 tankers a day used to pass through the Straits of Hormuz and to a large extent probably still do so. In order to protect this trade, which is international and, for example, of more importance to Japan than it is to Europe, although still fundamental to both, there is a large US squadron based on two aircraft carriers supported by two British and three French warships. An almost equal number of Soviet warships is in the area, probably based at Aden and Socotra and the Dahlak Islands in the Red Sea. It is worth noting that the oil trade does not go to Russia yet, although they have thought fit to put a considerable number of ships close to the oil route. The main impact of their presence, however, is to make the Americans think very carefully before they intervene to deal with any interruption to the oil trade — it is something of a stalemate — for all their power they are relatively helpless unless very hard pushed.

But the smaller navies are not so inhibited. Oman, at the entrance to the Gulf, has a very small fleet, but all the power to intervene if she wishes since neither the United States nor Russia would be able to stop her for fear of the other. Britain could do much the same were her ships not becoming increasingly specialised to the North Atlantic Re/Re role. So could France with a more offensive interventionist fleet.

One significant trend of maritime warfare is, therefore, to the spread of power to the smaller navies provided they are prepared to take advantage of it. It may be only a temporary phenomenon — the Soviet and American fleets are relatively evenly balanced at the present — but once let the Soviets get clearly superior power and they will intervene themselves if need be.

THE FUTURE

The face of maritime warfare has already been revolutionised by the missile and the development of sophisticated launching platforms — not least of all the nuclear submarine. A most significant factor in this has been the development of over-the-horizon targeting from satellite surveillance and direction-finding networks. Technology has led the Soviets to their well-nigh undefeatable combination of *Kirov*, *Alfa* and *Oscar;* the Americans to their *Nimitz* and *Ticonderoga* and advanced Los Angeles submarines. It is inevitable that this technological advance will continue — it is unlikely to achieve any sudden major break-throughs — development seldom follows that road but it does achieve remarkable advances little by little through constant and continuous work. When the Soviets introduced their first anti-ship missiles in the 1950s they were not new — the Germans had had them some years earlier — but they were technological developments of what had gone before and as such they revolutionised maritime warfare.

It is the country which manages this slow and steady and continuous research and development which may well take a commanding lead. The particle beam, for example, could make a ship well-nigh invulnerable to missile attack and revolutionise its role and capabilities; the *Alfa* class submarines with their

42-knot capability could well be the forerunner of yet faster submarines which will be able to outrun any opposition. And regrettably Russia spends far more, perhaps twice as much, on research and development as does the United States.

One can therefore point the trend of maritime warfare today but not tomorrow. Today they are towards a greater integration of forces of all types of advanced and complex C_3; in Russia to the missile and in the United States to the aircraft carrier. Russia is offensively and expansionist minded; the United States defensive, at least in its NATO role. And some resolution of the roles and equipment of the smaller navies, particularly the British, would be of inestimable value.

FIRE CONTROL – NO LONGER HIT OR MISS.

The Lasergage LP7 is the most advanced military handheld laser rangefinder currently available. Fire control is fast and accurate, to achieve surprise – indeed estimated first round hit probability is 80%.

The LP7 is precise – with a ranging capability of ten kilometres and an accuracy of 5m.

It is compact – the size of standard 7 x 50 monoculars and light – weighing only 2.0kg.

Reliable and inexpensive, because of the simplicity of the design the LP7 is essential

equipment for forward observation officers and mortar fire controllers. It can be mounted on an angle measuring tripod and night observation devices for distance measurement at night. The range is numerically displayed and there are multiple target indicators. Unwanted targets, on the other hand can be eliminated using the minimum range control.

The LP7 is in production for the British, NATO, and other armies, and is being evaluated by many military authorities throughout the world.

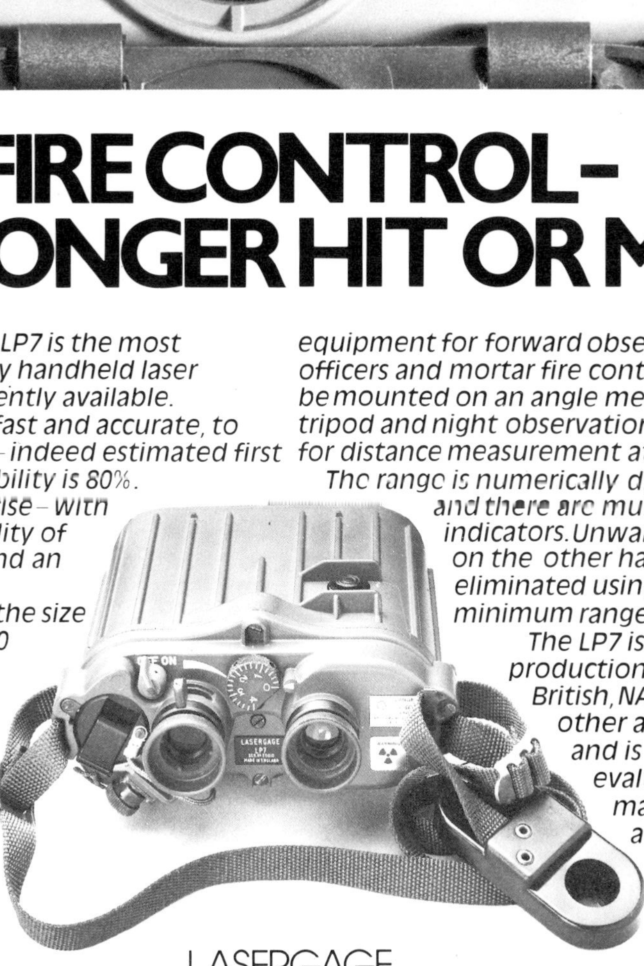

LASERGAGE

LASERGAGE LIMITED, NEWTOWN ROAD, HOVE, EAST SUSSEX BN3 7DL, ENGLAND.
TEL: (0273) 70341/723639. TELEX: 877062.

LASER RANGEFINDERS OF THE HIGHEST PERFORMANCE AND RELIABILITY FOR USE WITH
INFANTRY WEAPONS · ARTILLERY WEAPONS · ANTI-TANK WEAPONS · ARMOURED VEHICLES · COMBAT AIRCRAFT · NAVAL SYSTEMS

THE
ARMY QUARTERLY
AND DEFENCE JOURNAL

A *rmy Quarterly* is the longest established of the world's military journals. It was first published in 1829, only fourteen years after the defeat of Napoleon.

Editorial Policy

A *rmy Quarterly* publishes the best military writing: in each issue the special team of correspondents contribute articles on land and air warfare, maritime affairs and new weapons and equipment. Leading military experts from many countries write on defence policy, nuclear warfare and international affairs.

Many eminent figures of the past wrote for the magazine. Lawrence of Arabia, for example, wrote about the Arab Campaign for the October 1920 issue and the journal has published articles by many famous soldiers of the last hundred years. Sir Winston Churchill, Lord Montgomery, Lord Slim and Sir Basil Liddell-Hart all wrote for *AQ*. The journal is now edited by Major-General C. H. Stainforth, CB, OBE, and the team of regular correspondents includes Major-General J. D. Lunt, CBE, MA, Dr. R. L. Clutterbuck, CB, OBE, MA, PhD and Vice-Admiral Sir Ian McGeoch, KCB, DSO, DSC.

An International Journal

O ne reason for the journal's international reputation lies in its catholic approach; the contents cover a wider field than that which is usually found in a professional journal.

In addition to current military affairs covered by the correspondents, the journal includes contributions by military historians. Each issue also includes a Digest of World Defence News and more than 330 news items were published in 1980. It is the only journal to publish each January the full Command Staff List of the British Army. In 1978 the "*AQ* Diary" joined the other regular features: this chronological picture of military events covers the previous three months. Finally, there is an important Book Review Section.

Army Quarterly in Microfilm

I n 1977, complete sets of microfilm of all issues since 1920 became available from Newspaper Archive Developments Ltd. a subsidiary of *The Times* newspaper group. *Army Quarterly* joins their list of world famous newspapers and journals selected for microfilming as being the best in their field.

Army Quarterly associated publishing

O ther titles are published from time to time in The Defence Forces of the World series. Produced in close co-operation with the ministries of defence concerned, books have been produced for the governments of Austria, Finland, Sweden, Switzerland and Australia. Others are planned for West Germany, Pakistan, Japan and Norway.

How to subscribe

Army Quarterly is published four times a year and each issue contains 128 pp plus an 8 pp photographic section. You can subscribe by completing the form below and sending it with your cheque.

Annual Subscription £16.00   *Single and back issues £4.50*

Address your subscription application and cheque to

The Subscriptions Manager
1 West Street, Tavistock, Devon PL19 8AD England

Weapon Development in the 1980's: Land

IAN V HOGG

Ian V Hogg is Military Correspondent for Defence *magazine*

ARMOURED VEHICLES

The year under review has seen some significant moves in the continuing attempt to obtain some sort of parity between NATO and Warsaw Pact armoured forces. So far as NATO is concerned, any such parity must be on terms of superior quality to overcome superior quantity; recent American intelligence estimates that the Soviet Union produces upwards of 2400 MBTs every year, to which must be added production from factories in Czechoslovakia, Poland, Romania and possibly North Korea. An estimate of future production, recently made by a firm of American analysts, indicates that Soviet bloc tank production in the next 6 years will outstrip the West by 95 per cent. At the last information, production was of the T-72, but by this time we ought to assume that the T-80 has begun to replace it on some production lines. Very little is known in the West of the T-80; it is assumed to be of much the same appearance as the previous T-64 and T-72 types (since the Soviets appear to have reached what they consider to be an optimum shape) though rather heavier. It is expected to be armed with the same 125-mm gun as the T-72, if only to simplify ammunition supply, and it is expected to have some form of improved armour protection. Whether this will be laminated compound armour, that type known in the West as Chobham armour, or whether it will be a more conventional spaced-plate armour, we cannot say. If the Soviets continue to put their faith in ballistic shaping—curved and sloped plates, 'turtle-back' turrets—then laminated armour is unlikely unless they have devised a method of forming it into compound shapes.

The US Army has begun taking delivery of its M-1 Abrams MBT, of which 462 are scheduled for delivery in the fiscal years 1979—80. A further 569 in FY 1981 and 720 in FY 1982 are called for, the ultimate requirement being for 7058. According to the

budget request, the unit price in FY 1981 will be $1,815 million
giving a total of $12,810 million for the total programme if the
price stays the same, plus an undisclosed amount for spares. But
the likelihood of costs remaining static is remote; in the last fiscal
year the cost of the M-1 programme is said to have increased by
20 per cent.

At present the Abrams is armed with the standard 105-mm
gun, but agreement was reached with Germany to fit the 120-mm
Rheinmetall smoothbore gun in future production. Ratification
of this agreement is due to take place late in 1981, and the gun to
go into production tanks in 1984. But ratification looks like
becoming a political football; Congress has said that development
of the 120-mm can continue only if the Army can show that it will
save $600 million, and it has also cut the entire $62 million programme for development of a common (US — German) 120-mm
barrel. It blamed this on the Army's 'serious affordability
program in procuring weapon systems hardware' and also pointed
to the reluctance of the Bundeswehr to buy the US-developed
120-mm gun ammunition. In the hopes, no doubt, of regaining
some of its expenditure, the US Army submitted the Abrams for
consideration by the Dutch Army, but they elected to buy the
German Leopard 2, even though it is rather more expensive at an
estimated $2.2 million. The Abrams is now the subject of Swiss
interest since they are seeking a new MBT and have abandoned
their own development programme, but even if they agree to buy,
it will be several years before the US Army's immediate
requirements are filled and outside orders can be supplied, and
by that time the cost would have increased considerably.

The British Army, seeking a replacement for Chieftain, had
been working on a projected MBT-80 for some time, but the
Iranian revolution precipitated something of a crisis. The Royal
Ordnance Factory, Leeds, was about to begin production of 1225
Shir 2 tanks for Iran when the Shah was deposed and the contract
went up in smoke. Shir 2 was an advanced design, with Chobham
armour, a 120-mm rifled gun, a sophisticated fire-control system
and a Rolls-Royce 1200 bhp engine. The problem which then
faced the British was whether to continue production of the Shir 2
for the British Army, to replace Chieftain, in which case the
MBT-80 would be cancelled (since it was financially
impossible to have both tanks) or to abandon the Shir 2 and await
the completion of the MBT-80 design. The latter course, attractive as it was, would mean that the labour force at Leeds would
have nothing to occupy them for some long time, since MBT-80

was no further forward than the project definition stage. Moreover, its programme was slipping and its anticipated in-service date was rapidly moving towards the early or middle 1990s. The decision was therefore taken to drop MBT-80, begin low-priority planning of MBT-90, and build 200 Shir 2s for the Army under the name Challenger.

Meanwhile, evidence that private enterprise was not entirely dead was presented in the summer with Vickers' introduction of their new Valiant MBT. This is primarily aimed at the export market, for countries whose tactical needs and purses do not extend to tanks of the Shir 2, Leopard 2 or Abrams class. Valiant has a welded aluminium hull and a welded steel turret, both overlaid by Chobham armour to give additional side and frontal protection. Main armament is the 105-mm L-7 gun, but a second Universal turret has been designed which will allow either the 105-mm L-7 or the Rheinmetall 120-mm smooth-bore gun to be fitted. Various fire-control options are available to suit the purchaser; the basic pattern is the Marconi SFCS-600 pattern, with the gunner and commander using laser rangefinding and electro-optical sighting aids. The combat weight is in the order of 43 tonnes. It has been the object of considerable overseas interest, and at the time of writing is understood to be under evaluation (in competition with the French AMX-32) by the Greek Army.

The AMX-32 MBT is the French contender for overseas sales. It uses the same engine and hull as the French service AMX-30 but has additional armour protection and modified suspension. The turret is of new design, mounting the GIAT 105-mm gun, and a new GIAT 120-mm gun is offered as an alternative. Both these guns fire APFSDS rounds capable of defeating the NATO heavy target at ranges in excess of 5000 m. We understand that Saudi Arabia, Malaysia and Greece have all expressed interest in this design.

That the export market is by no means a constant one is borne out by recent developments in Brazil. South America has bought tanks from more industrialised countries for many years, but in the last decade the Brazilian heavy engineering industry has expanded and has produced a series of effective armoured cars and APCs. Now there are moves into the tank field; Bernardini have modified a number of elderly American M5 light tanks by up-armouring and re-gunning with a French 90-mm weapon, and 60 of these, known as the X1A2, are in course of production for the Brazilian Army. The company has then gone on to design a completely new tank, the X-30; final details are not completed, but it is said to be in the 30-ton range and is to be armed with a high velocity 105-mm gun.

The Bundeswehr has begun taking delivery of the Leopard 2, 1800 of which will eventually be supplied by 1986. In addition, the Netherlands have ordered 445 to replace their Centurion and AMX-13 models. Belgium and Switzerland have also expressed interest, and there are hopes that Turkey and Greece may select it. Meanwhile the Leopard 1 continues to serve; over 4500 have been built, including some 720 built under licence by OTO-Melara of Italy.

Sweden has a record of springing surprises on the rest of the world ever since the advent of its revolutionary S-Tank; development is now under way of a new MBT for the 1990s, a consortium having been formed by Bofors and Hagglund & Soner, the former being responsible for the armament and fire control and the latter for the hull and running gear. It has been suggested that the new design will have a three-man crew, be armed with a 120-mm gun, have high mobility and survivability, and generally be a technical *tour de force* as was the S-Tank. It is known that several unconventional solutions are being explored; one current test-bed is a German Marder MICV chassis mounting a remote-controlled 105-mm gun in a pod above the hull, dispensing entirely with the conventional type of turret.

ANTI-TANK WEAPONS

Since the MBT is accepted as being the spearhead of present-day military forces, it follows that a great deal of effort is being put into developing weapons to counter them. This is particularly so in the NATO countries, since they cannot hope to develop parity with the Warsaw Pact forces, and much of NATO's tactical planning revolves around the use of infantry-manned or airborne anti-tank weapons. The British Army is developing LAW-80, a portable, shoulder-fired rocket weapon similar to but bigger than the current 66-mm LAW. This is being developed in production form by Hunting Engineering and is unusual in that the launch tube carries a five-shot integral aiming rifle, firing a special observing bullet which is ballistically matched to the flight of the rocket. A collimating sight is fitted to the launcher, and the operator sights, fires the aiming rifle until he obtains a strike, and then fires the rocket.

The need for an aiming rifle doubtless stems from the low velocity generally attained by rockets and hence their curved trajectory, which means that relatively minor errors in range estimation can lead to missing the target. An alternative approach to this problem has been put forward by Israeli Military Industries with their Picket launcher. This uses a supersonic rocket stabilised in flight by a gyroscope which senses changes in flight attitude and corrects them by a thrust vectoring system in the jet efflux. This gives a very short and flat trajectory so that no range estimation or correction is required, and very little aim-off for moving targets. The maximum range is said to be 500 m and the time of flight to that range no more than a second.

The US Army has developed its own replacement for the 66-mm LAW, known as Viper. As with the earlier weapon, the replacement is a free-flight rocket in a telescoping tubular launcher; the rocket is 70-mm calibre but has an improved motor giving a velocity of 280 m/sec and an improved hollow charge warhead said to be capable of penetrating 400 mm of homogeneous armour.

The Bundeswehr has been using the PzF-44 Lanze for several years; this is virtually a modernised version of the wartime Panzerfaust. It is about to be replaced by the Armbrust launcher, a one-man device with an unusual method of operation. Armbrust is a recoilless launcher, and the usual method of operation for these is simply to allow some of the propellant explosion to vent to the rear and thus counterbalance the forward ejection of the missile. In Armbrust, however, the explosion takes place between two pistons; the forward piston ejects the hollow-charge missile, and the rear piston ejects a counterweight in the form of several thousand flakes of plastic material. As the two pistons reach the ends of the launch tubes they lock into sealing collars. Thus none of the explosive gases is released to the atmosphere and very little noise is emitted; it is claimed that the noise of firing is no more than that of a pistol shot, and there is none of the danger connected with the normal rearward blast of a recoilless weapon. Indeed, it is claimed that Armbrust can be fired from inside a building. After firing, the launch tube is pressurised and somewhat hot, though not dangerously so, and anyway it is immediately discarded. The effective range against armour is 300 m but an anti-personnel projectile with a range of 1500 m is also available.

The only other recoilless launcher undergoing evaluation at present is the Italian Folgore, a powerful 80-mm weapon with a range of 1000 m against tanks. It fires a hollow-charge, fin-stabilised projectile and is equipped with an electro-optical sight,

though a simpler optical sight is available for shoulder-firing.
Most development work in the anti-tank field is being directed
into missile research. At present there is much debate over
proposals for a US—European agreement for development of the
forthcoming generation of anti-tank weapons under a 'family of
weapons' concept. The proposed deal would have the Americans
develop the medium-range (up to 2000 m) weapons and the Europeans the long-range (up to 5000 m) weapons, with common procurement of the results throughout NATO. Objections have been
raised to this idea in Europe on the grounds that developing only
two weapons will make the Soviet development of countermeasures that much easier; having a diversity of weapons
available would make their countering more difficult and would
also allow a golf-bag approach to the different types of Warsaw
Pact armour likely to be encountered. There are also suspicions
among European manufacturers that the Americans would evade
the spirit of the agreement by updating some of their existing
long-range weapons instead of buying whatever the European
side of the programme produced.

Current development, irrespective of this US—European programme, is devoted to two prime objectives; firstly, to improve
existing warheads since it is claimed that those in service today are
no longer capable of penetrating the frontal armour of the newer
Warsaw Pact tanks, and, secondly to develop the third-
generation of anti-tank missiles, those with fire-and-forget
automatic homing guidance. Manufacturers, while ready to
admit that they are working on third-generation models, are
understandably reluctant to say very much about them; we know,
for example, that Bofors are working on their RBS-56 Bill, but
apart from a non-committal photograph, nothing has been
divulged. The Euromissile consortium (Aérospatiale,
Messerschmitt-Bolkow-Bloehm and British Aerospace) have said
that they are directing their research into three areas: top
attack, in which the missile is aimed over the tank and dives down
from its flight path to strike the thinner top armour; direct
attack, in the conventional way; and over-flight attack in which
the missile passes over the tank and discharges its warhead
downward. From these styles of attack, various warheads
requirements appear, and as well as the normal (though constantly improved) hollow charge, work is being done on multiple
hollow charges and on self-forging fragment warheads, which
appears to be the latest name for the Schardin plate effect.

Methods of guidance for fire-and-forget systems are of infinite variety, but only a handful appear to show any practical promise. Among these are infra-red and millimetre-wave guidance, laser beam riding, active homing on laser-illuminated targets, and, apparently most promising, passive homing using infra-red focal-plane arrays, millimetre wave radar or television relying on background/target contrast. The only certain thing in this uncertain business is a universal belief among manufacturers that whatever the solution adopted, the cost of the third-generation missile will be considerably more than that of the second-generation types.

While the battlefield up to 5000-m range is thus receiving a good deal of attention, equally as much is being devoted to the development of methods of attacking armour at even longer ranges by the use of remotely delivered armaments. One of the first such devices was the American Copperhead 155-mm projectile which can be guided to its distant tank target by a laser designator, the reflections from which are picked up by the sensors in the projectile and cause it to be steered to impact. The American WAAM (Wide Area Anti-armour Munitions) programme gave birth to this device, and others are now in the course of perfection. SADARM (Sense and Destroy Armour) is another gun-fired device, initially for the 8-in howitzer, later to be configured for the 155-mm howitzer. The projectile contains three SADARM sub-munitions, each consisting of a radiometric sensor, a self forging fragment warhead and a parachute. It is an over-flight attack weapon, the sub-munitions being ejected from the carrier shell over the target area. They then descend by parachute with a slow rotation which allows the sensor to scan the ground beneath so as to distinguish the 'cold' sky reflection from a tank from the 'warm' reflection from the ground. Once a target is detected, electronic circuitry determines its position vis-à-vis the rotation of the sub-munition and fires the warhead at an appropriate time and attitude, discharging the self-forging slug into the top of the tank.

A similar sensor is used by STAFF (Smart, Target-Activated, Fire-and-Forget), a 155-mm shoulder-fired missile. This is launched at a range of 1-2 km to pass above the target at a height of about 30 m. The sensor detects the target, tilts the weapon into the right attitude and then fires a self-forging fragment.

More random in their effect are numerous carrier projectiles, from artillery or from field rockets, which discharge quantities of mines into areas of tank concentration. The new Multiple

Launch Rocket System (see below) has, for its third development phase, a programme now known as the NATO Terminally Guided Weapons (TGW) system which is intended to produce a suitable carrier warhead for the rockets, containing some form of self-guiding smart sub-munition.

FREE-FLIGHT ROCKETS

The free-flight artillery rocket has seen something of a revival in the past few years, and 1980 saw the US Army take the decision to adopt the Vought MLRS (Multiple Launch Rocket System) for service. This type of weapon has been developed in order to try to develop a heavy counter-battery system capable of neutralising enemy tube and rocket artillery, and two contesting designs, by Vought and Boeing, were thoroughly tested before the Vought system was chosen. The equipment consists of self-propelled launcher on a tracked chassis, capable of carrying 12 rockets. These are 227 mm in diameter and are supplied in a sealed launch pod container of 6 rockets in individual glass-fibre launching tubes. This unit is simply loaded into a metal framework on the tracked carrier, and this frame, bearing two pods, is then elevated and trained in the requisite direction. The rockets are then fired out of the pod unit, the empty unit discarded, and a fresh unit reloaded. The rocket has a range of some 30 km and carries about 600 anti-personnel sub-munitions in the warhead. The first phase of this programme involves supplying the US Army with its basic requirements. After this a joint programme by the United States, the United Kingdom, France and Germany will develop a warhead carrying scatterable anti-tank mines, while the third phase (referred to above) is the TGW programme of guided anti-tank sub-munitions.

French collaboration in the MLRS programme will probably mean that two systems which have been under development in France for some years will not now be contemplated for French Army service, though they may well be offered for export. These are the 'Rafale' 147-mm rocket and the RAP-14 140-mm rocket, both of which offer multiple-tube launchers on various truck mountings. Rafale has a maximum range of 30 km and multiple sub-munition warheads for anti-personnel or anti-tank use. RAP-14 uses a conventional warhead and has a range of 20 km.

The Italian Army has not, so far, expressed formal interest in the MLRS programme, and is believed to be currently evaluating an Italian system, the Firos developed by SNIA-Viscosa. Firos-25 uses a 122-mm rocket with a range of 25—27 km. Warheads available include conventional high explosive and a number of sub-munition options for anti-personnel or anti-tank attack. Firos-6 uses a 51-mm rocket with a range of 6.5 km and a number of conventional HE, hollow-charge, smoke and similar warheads. Both types use multi-tube launchers which can be mounted on a variety of vehicles.

SMALL ARMS

The NATO small-arms trial, to determine the cartridge which will be the standard for the forthcoming generation of weapons, appears to have decided that the 5.56 × 45-mm cartridge offers the optimum package of advantages, though there is still some debate about the best bullet to adopt. The trials indicated that the Belgian SS109 bullet, which uses a compound lead—steel core and weighs 4.0 g, gave the best all-round performance, penetrating a standard American steel helmet at a 1200-m range. Several manufacturers and commentators have taken to referring to the SS109 as NATO Standard though as yet we have seen no official notification of such a decision. Unfortunately this bullet, being somewhat longer than the American M-193 pattern, which has been the standard in this calibre for many years, requires a steeper twist of rifling in order to stabilise it adequately, and it functions best in a weapon with the barrel rifled at 1 turn in 32 calibres. Almost all existing 5.56-mm rifles use a twist of 1 turn in 55 calibres, and thus adoption of the Belgian bullet would demand either completely new rifles or, at best and almost as expensive, re-barrelling of existing ones. The American services, with an estimated 1.3 million 5.56-mm rifles in use, are understandably concerned about this. For their part, the US Army put forward a bullet of their own in the trial, the XM-777. This is also a compound core bullet but shorter and lighter than the SS109 and it performs best in a barrel rifled at 1 turn in 41 calibres. Moreover, it can be fired from 1/55 barrels with satisfactory, if not optimum, results. At its best it is not so good as the SS109, but it is likely that the XM-777 will be adopted as a compromise solution.

So far as the British Army is concerned the bullet question is of little material consequence. Their Enfield-designed 4.85-mm rifle and light machine gun were designed from the start with the realisation that the 5.56-mm cartridge was likely to be the chosen one; indeed, the British 4.85-mm cartridge used the 5.56-mm case, necked down to take the smaller bullet, so that rebuilding the British weapons to 5.56-mm calibre, in any desired twist of rifling, is not a problem.

Unfortunately, however, it seems that the final words have not yet been spoken over this vexed question. The Federal Republic of Germany's interests are now urging that a decision should be withheld until their 4.7-mm caseless cartridge and its associated rifle have been subjected to prolonged trials scheduled for 1984. This design is quite revolutionary, and the Germans are convinced that once it is perfected it will make the conventional 5.56-mm cartridge obsolete overnight. It is doubtful, though, whether the other members of the NATO Alliance would be willing to defer their re-equipment for yet another 3 years; it is also doubtful whether they would be willing to face the economic consequences of either buying a German rifle and its special ammunition or designing, under licence, their own equivalents.

The Bundeswehr has also raised objections to the proposed adoption of the 5.56-mm cartridge as a machine gun round, claiming that it has insufficient power in that role. In this they may be right. It is generally accepted that the squad light machine gun needs to be effective at somewhat longer ranges than the rifle. It is also vital, on today's battlefield, to have a machine gun which is capable of delivering a powerful armour-piercing bullet and of using a long-ranging tracer, and neither of these requirements is easily satisfied by the small physical dimensions of the 5.56-mm bullet. It should be remembered that when the US Army unilaterally adopted the 5.56-mm calibre in the 1960s, they retained the 7.62 × 51-mm cartridge for their machine guns on the grounds that the 5.56-mm was not suited to that role. Now, however, the US Army is on the point of adopting a 5.56-mm weapon as their squad light machine gun, having conducted a long trial on three competing designs and having decided that the Fabrique National's Minimi should be further developed for the role.

It is to be regretted that the Americans have a lamentable history of making the wrong choice at critical moments and then contradicting themselves later. In the 1950s they refused the British 7-mm intermediate round on the grounds that it was insufficiently powerful, and forced through the adoption of the 7.62 × 51-mm, which was no more than the contemporary .30 in US service bullet fitted into a slightly shorter case so as to pay lip service to the concept of more compact ammunition. Having done this, they then adopted the 5.56-mm round, lighter and far less effective than the refused 7-mm design. Now they are attempting, once again, to force through a second-best cartridge for rifles and a worthless cartridge for machine guns, all in the holy name of standardisation. Some years ago both British and American (and probably other) designers were working on a variety of 6/7-mm cartridges, any one of which would have given us a better solution than the 5.56-mm, a design which has very little development potential left in it (as the NATO trial showed). We believe that some British opinions were not in favour of the 4.85-mm design, indicating a preference for a 6-mm or 6.5-mm solution, but it looks very much as if fashion took over and the current mania for micro-calibres has overcome ballistic commonsense.

The supporters of micro-calibres have had their hands strengthened recently by news of the Soviet adoption of a 5.45-mm version of the Kalashnikov rifle, the AK-74, followed by the RPKS-74 squad light machine gun. In our view this does not strengthen anybody's case; the Soviets are no more infallible than anyone else, and they have been known to make mistakes before. Nevertheless, the Soviet design shows some interesting features, notably an airspace in the bullet nose, between the steel core and the gilding-metal envelope. The core is surrounded by a lead sheath which terminates in a short lead plug at the nose of the core. This form of construction would appear to be aimed at putting the centre of gravity well back which, allied with a twist of rifling of one turn in 26.9 calibres, will endow the bullet with good stability. It has been suggested that the effect of the bullet's construction will be to cause it to topple on striking, giving it severe wounding power, but we are inclined to disagree with this, since the rapid twist of rifling argues against the marginal stability needed for satisfactory toppling. American studies indicate severe damage caused by the bullet when fired into soap and gelatine blocks, the usual way of checking wounding ability, but we venture to suggest that these results may well be due to the inertia effect of the bullet core moving forward in the jacket, a result analogous to that obtained with some types of false-tipped hunting bullets in the past. Whatever the mechanism, the construction of the bullet makes it obvious that the Hague Convention on exploding bullets is a dead letter.

Humanitarian considerations are also said to have played their part in the selection of the new Swedish Army rifle, the FFV890C, which is currently undergoing evaluation trials in Sweden and Switzerland. This is, in fact, a slightly modified version of the

Israeli Galil 5.56-mm assault rifle, and the most significant change has been in the rifling which has been tightened to 1 turn in 41 calibres. With the usual type of 5.56-mm bullet this would give over-stabilisation and a reduction in wounding capacity, and this is said to have been a deliberate choice in view of the many objections to the wounding ability of the 5.56-mm bullet in 1/55-rifled barrels. In fact the Swedes have also developed a bullet of their own, similar to the Belgian SS109, which with the new twist of rifling will give better stability and accuracy.

The Austrian Army has now commenced re-equipping with a 5.56-mm rifle known as the Steyr AUG (Armee Universal Gewehr). As the name implies, it can be tailored to any requirement — as assault rifle, carbine or light machine gun, the only change being in the length and weight of the barrel. The weapon is very space-age in appearance, with a stubby stock, large trigger-guard which takes the whole hand, raked carrying handle-cum-optical sight, and exposed barrel. Apart from this latter part, the remainder of the weapon is in plastic material, even to the transparent magazine. The receiver locks into the plastic body, and the bolt travels on two guide rods within it. The barrel is locked into the receiver by interrupted threads and can be removed by a folding hand-grip-cum-carrying handle. The mechanical arrangement is a bullpup design, with the bolt more or less alongside the firer's chin and the magazine behind the pistol grip. In spite of its futuristic appearance it is a robust and accurate weapon and has attracted much interest; as well as the Austrian Army at least one African country has bought the weapon and others are expected to follow suit.

SUMMARY

The foregoing has been a brief commentary on some of the more interesting weapon developments and trends which have come to our notice during the past year. There are, of course, other developments and fields which we have not mentioned; artillery, for example, has shown nothing really new in this period, though we have no doubt that things are happening behind the scenes and we shall have something to say next year. The development of fin-stabilised discarding-sabot anti-tank ammunition continues apace, but 1980 has seen no really significant announcements. Undoubtedly the threat of Warsaw Pact armour is the principal design incentive at the present time, though some European commentators incline to the view that American intelligence circles are painting the worst possible picture in their estimate of the difficulty of penetrating the next generation of Soviet tanks. This may be so, but on the whole it may be no bad thing since it might lead to a qualitative leap in anti-armour effectiveness which will see us safely into the 21st century. As must be obvious, we are not entirely in agreement with the selection of 5.56 mm as the NATO standard calibre for small arms, though we can but hope that time will prove us wrong. What we fear, in all phases of weapon development, is the siren call of technological wizardry which seems to have more appeal than cold tactical sense. Present-day attitudes seem to favour seizing on a novel weapon and bending the Army's tactics to suit, rather than deciding what the tactics are to be and then bending the technology to fit the perceived task. If the players cannot make up their minds as to how the game is to be conducted, they will only have themselves to blame if they are holding the wrong club when the time comes to drive off.

230

Two wooden shoes the same?
Forget it!

For centuries the Dutch have used wooden shoes. So you can take it for granted that we know what we are talking about. Wooden shoes can be made from the same willow tree, according to the same specifications and dimensions by good craftsmen, but still they differ. So do the customers – we all know that.

The same applies to ammunition. For over three hundred years Eurometaal has been involved in the production of conventional ammunitions. We know that here, also, there are differences.

Take our highly sophisticated 8 inch howitzer shell: completely centrecally forged without internal turning operations, which gives you unique ballistic characteristics and only one weight class. Think about your logistics! Our internally developed process for

HE filling, recognised world wide, supplies you with excellent wall adhesion, structure and density.

Utmost care in heat treatment processes in connection with an upgraded steel quality, results in the best quality in existence. Modern numerically controlled lathes and a high standard of control are a guarantee of a constant level of quality.

Is it, therefore, so strange that many armed forces and arsenals are asking us for assistance? That is also the reason that our 8 inch shells differ from others. Ask our users – they will agree.

EUR◉METAAL
a cornerstone of modern defence

P.O. Box 419 / 1500 EK Zaandam / Holland.
Telephone 075 - 504911 / Telex 19303.

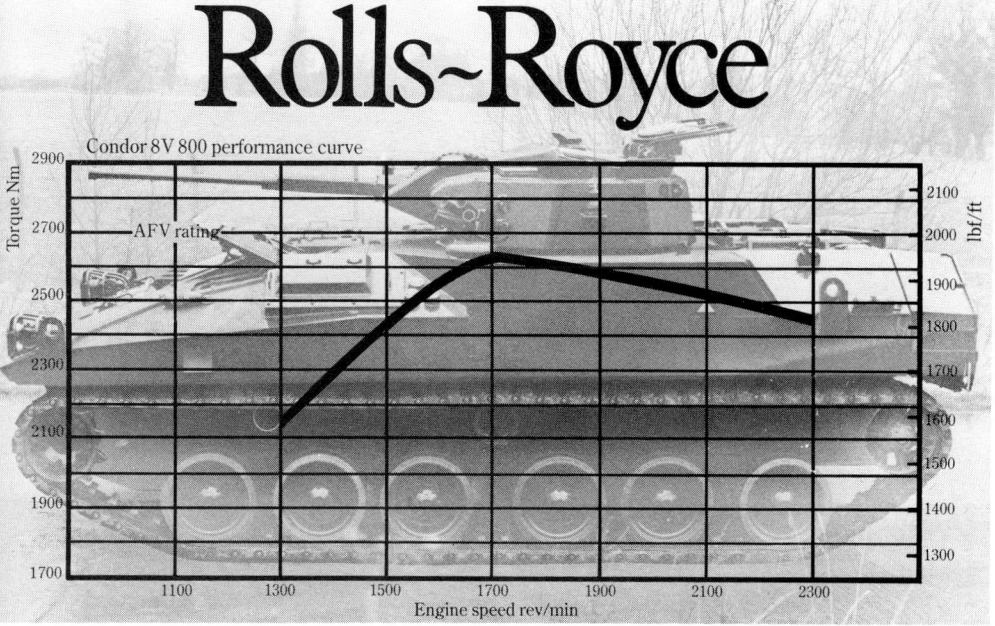
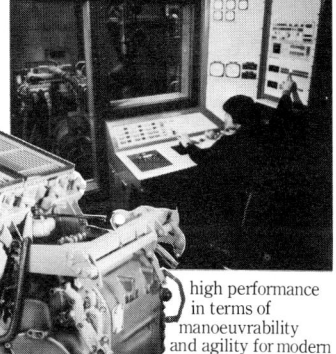

Trends in Land Warfare: Infantry Support Vehicles

IAN V HOGG

Ian V Hogg is Military Correspondent for Defence *magazine*

IN THE better part of 40 years which have passed since the practice of carrying infantry into battle in armoured vehicles began, it seems surprising that we are no nearer a consensus of opinion about what may be the optimum design for such a vehicle. The diversity of types ranges from simple wheeled 'troop taxis' to complex armoured vehicles which, at first glance, seem to be trying to supplant the main battle tank with some new tactical concept. This is, therefore, perhaps as good a time as any to look at the history of the infantry support vehicle, consider what is currently being done and contemplate the direction in which future development might go.

In fact the idea of carrying troops into battle in a protected vehicle is as old as the idea of the tank itself. One of the first projects embraced by the Admiralty Landships Committee in 1915 was an articulated tracked vehicle capable of carrying a 50-man trench-storming party through the barbed wire and obstacles to deposit them inside the German defences. Had it not been for the mechanical problems posed, this might well have come into being. Later the Mark IX tank was devised for the same task, to carry either 50 men or 10 tons of stores, but only 3 were completed before the Armistice and so the idea was never put to the test of action.

During the inter-wars years the principal train of thought on armoured vehicles was directed to developing the tank, and very little time was spent on any other sort of vehicle. Moreover, the attitude in those days was that the infantry were amply served if they had good boots, a rifle and a shovel; until the middle 1930s the most that was done for them was to outfit them with a decent light machine gun. Some desultory experiments took place with motor infantry, but these formations usually consisted of the nearest infantry battalion rounded up and transported in the cargo vehicles of the nearest supply truck company. There was little or no attempt at developing specialist vehicles or developing a dedicated force of infantry trained in appropriate tactics. The trucks trailed behind the tanks and simply acted as taxis to deliver the infantry into a position from which they could form up and advance on their feet in the traditional fashion.

But in the middle 1930s the spectre of the machine gun was resurrected and the question arose of how to move the infantry's light machine gun—which was the base of fire for the infantry section—across bullet-swept ground and into a position from which it could provide covering fire for the advance of the rifle component of the section. This led, in Britain, to the Bren gun carrier, a lightly armoured and nimble vehicle which eventually found its niche as a general-purpose cross-country tractor for loads as diverse as the 3-in mortar, flamethrowers or the artillery forward observer. It was, though, too small to lift a complete infantry section, and it seems to have had very little effect upon tactics.

At much the same time the German Army was approaching similar questions from a rather different direction. Their path led them to consider the mobility of a cohesive force of armour and infantry, the infantry being carried along in order to be deployed when the tanks came up against an obstacle. This led them to the adoption of lightly armoured half-track carriers which had sufficient speed and cross-country ability to keep up with the tanks; and from this came the Panzergrenadiers—troops specifically trained to work closely with armour.

Thus by the early 1940s two disparate schools of thought had arisen around the employment of motor or mechanised infantry; either they were plain ordinary foot soldiers moved by motor transport to a convenient point from which they would fight in the normal way, or they were troops trained to operate with their own tanks and carried on to the objective (if the situation allowed) or, at least, as close to the objective as possible, relying on armour to protect them *en route*. To some degree, this distinction is still apparent.

Although the German Army never achieved the level of mechanisation it wanted, and the Panzergrenadiers never received the amount of half-tracked armour that was planned, their use of armoured troop carriers led other people to contemplate the same thing. The Americans had the White and International half-tracks; the British Army would probably have ignored the idea but for the peculiar circumstances which surrounded Operation Totalise, the breaking of the German defensive lines across the

Caen—Falaise road in 1944. The forward German line was heavily laced with artillery, machine guns and mortars, and a second line, almost as strong, lay some 4 miles behind. Tactical surprise, in respect of either the objectives or the direction of the attack, was out of the question, and Lieutenant General Simonds, commanding the 2nd Canadian Corps, decided that the only solution was to carry the infantry through the first line, in the wake of the assaulting tanks, to sufficient depth so that they would actually be among the German gun and mortar positions before going into action. This meant that the infantry had to be adequately protected by bullet-and splinter-proof vehicles.

As it happened, the three field artillery regiments of the 3rd Canadian Division were on the point of exchanging their self-propelled M-7 105-mm Priest howitzers for towed 25-pdr guns. The 105-mm weapons were badly worn, and so permission was obtained for the howitzers, mantlets and ammunition racks to be removed, and armour welded over the front opening. An *ad hoc* workshop detachment, code-named Kangaroo, performed the conversion on 76 Priests, from which came the name Kangaroo to describe the finished vehicle. The task was completed barely 24 hours before the attack was to begin, and after a brief rehearsal the initial attack went in exactly as planned, the protected infantry being delivered well inside the German defended zone. Unfortunately, after that the operation slowed down and eventually ran out of steam, but the initial use of armoured carriers (as the Kangaroos had been officially termed) was a success.

It was so successful, indeed, that by September 1944 the Canadian Army had formed a special Kangaroo unit, the 1st Canadian Armoured Carrier Regiment, using converted Ram tanks, of which plenty were available. These were used in the taking of Boulogne, and the success of this operation persuaded the British to follow suit and convert another 120 Ram tanks into carriers; the 49th Royal Tank Regiment was redesignated the 49th Armoured Personnel Carrier Regiment and operated these vehicles until the end of the war. This was probably the first official recognition of the term Armoured Personnel Carrier (APC).

In post-war years the development of the APC began in earnest, and it took two separate forms—wheeled and tracked. The first to produce a wheeled vehicle were the Soviets, with their BTR-152 series, which was disclosed to the rest of the world in 1950. This was a simple open-topped vehicle based on a standard 6 × 6 truck chassis protected by a maximum of 13.5 mm of armour. Eventually a number of improvements were added; centralised tyre pressure regulation, roof covers, infra-red driving aids and so forth, and in spite of now being over 30 years old a large number of these basic vehicles is still to be found in Soviet satellite countries. The body has twin doors at the rear of the hull, with various possible arrangements of seating which will permit up to 17 men to be carried in addition to the driver and the vehicle commander. Although some specialist versions have been produced mounting heavy machine guns for anti-aircraft use, the vehicle does not normally carry any other armament than a light machine gun for the vehicle commander's use, while the occupants can only join the fire fight by standing up and shooting over the sides. In other words, the BTR-152 is little more than a battle taxi.

The other line of development was begun by the American Army when they produced their first tracked APC, the M-39. This had actually begun as a command and reconnaissance vehicle in 1944 and was little more than the M-18 tank destroyer with turret and gun removed. In reality it was no improvement on the Kangaroo conversion, though it was later enhanced by putting top hatches on the body and calling it the M-44 APC. But the result of all this was an ungainly monster which, even though it could cram in 27 men, was an inviting target to drive around the battlefield. It was rapidly abandoned in the early 1950s in favour of the purpose-built M-75 APC. This had a boxy superstructure but was smaller and carried only 12 men. It was a satisfactory vehicle in many respects, but it suffered from being built largely of tank components (for commonality of supply) and was therefore more complex and expensive than was justified by its performance and role. It was, in its turn, rapidly superseded by the M-59 which, though similar in weight and appearance, was designed to use a large proportion of commercial components so as to be cheaper.

Britain, at this time, opted for a wheeled solution; more by luck than good management it obtained a vehicle well suited to its eventual role. The original idea was a vehicle to carry the troopers of an armoured reconnaissance regiment, but by the time the Saracen appeared, internal security was the prime task, particularly in Malaysia and East Africa, and the requirement was for an armoured carrier which could move rapidly along roads or tracks. For this purpose wheels were perfectly adequate and, in addition, there was the psychological bonus that to most people a wheeled military vehicle is simply an armoured car, whilst anything on tracks is a tank with all the emotive overtones of repressive Colonialism, Imperialist domination and excessive force.

Saracen was a six-wheeled troop-carrier which differed from most previous attempts in that it was custom-built for the task in view rather than being made-over from a commercial truck chassis or a redundant tank. Although expensive in comparison with such extemporisations, it proved to be an economy in the long run, since the vehicle was far more resistant to wear and damage than any commercially based model could have been; there are several cases of Saracens having a wheel blown off by a mine and continuing on their mission, something which no truck chassis would withstand.

The Saracen became a pattern for other designers, and one of the first to follow were the Soviets, who turned away from the BTR-152 type of design and produced the BTR-60P, an eight-wheeled APC with amphibious capabilities.

The first version was open-topped, with cross-seats for 16 men in the troop compartment; the driver and commander sat in front, the commander was provided with a pintle-mounted heavy machine gun, and two light machine guns were fitted on the sides, to be used by the passengers. An innovation was the provision of firing ports in the hull sides so that some of the occupants could fire rifles or sub-machine guns without exposing themselves; the remaining passengers either played no part or had to stand up and fire their personal weapons over the side. In the event of inclement weather the open top could be covered with hoops and a canvas tilt. The occupants entered and left the vehicle by means of small doors on each side; rear entry was not possible because the vehicle's twin engines filled the rear of the troop compartment.

This was succeeded by a slightly better model, one having an armoured roof with hatches. Driver and commander each had an entry hatch, a third hatch behind them allowed someone to stand and fire the machine gun, and there was a fourth hatch over the rear of the troop space. On the debit side the doors were removed so that entry and egress were solely via the roof hatches. Such an awkward method of dismounting troops under fire could not last, and the final version of the BTR-60P reverted to using side doors and added a small turret for the machine gun.

It was thus apparent that by the early 1960s the Soviets were looking at their APC not merely as a taxi but also as a form of fighting vehicle. Three roof-mounted machine guns, plus three firing ports along each side, allowed a useful amount of fire-power to be used, but while this sounds good on paper one is entitled to ask whether it is quite so good in practice. Photographs of these vehicles on manoeuvres indicate the machine gun operators are exposed from the waist up, which suggests a limited life expectancy; moreover, the value of haphazard rifle fire, delivered through ports, sighted by periscopes, from a vehicle bounding across rough country, must be very suspect indeed. On arrival at the objective the awkward method of exit, either by roof hatches or by small side doors, precludes rapid deployment of the occupants and presents the enemy with a series of easy targets. Nevertheless, the Soviets appear to be well satisfied with it, and it is widely used by Warsaw Pact and other Soviet-influenced armies. The Czechs though, having a tradition of sensible military design, rejected the BTR-60P after a short trial and developed their own equivalent. It, too, is an eight-wheeled vehicle, very similar in appearance to the Soviet design, but with differences in detail which, in most people's view, makes it a more effective vehicle. The engine compartment is moved from the rear to a position just behind the driver and commander, separating them from the troop compartment which now has double rear doors. Varying numbers of roof hatches will be found, depending upon the date of production; firing ports are provided in the rear doors and in the hull sides. Originally no armament was fitted; then the Polish Army adopted the design and put a machine gun on a shielded pintle mount; after this the Czechs fitted a small machine-gun turret; and, finally, the Poles adopted a larger turret with two machine guns.

The only other country to essay a wheeled APC at that time was the Netherlands, which saw the DAF YP-408 into service in 1964. This, too, was an eight-wheeler, with the engine at the front, driver and commander behind (the latter with a pintle-mounted machine gun) and 10 infantrymen in the troop compartment. This had twin rear doors, each with a firing port, and six roof hatches which, when flung open, gave an open-topped compart-ment. About 750 of these were built, but there has never been a really convincing explanation of what the Dutch had in mind when they adopted them; in spite of the rear-firing ports and the roof machine gun, they were no more than transporters, and quite a large proportion of those vehicles in service are actually variant models to perform such roles as ambulances, command posts, radio vehicles, cargo-carriers and mortar tractors.

This adaptation of the basic infantry carrier to perform specialist tasks is common to every army, and it has to be admitted that once a suitable basic vehicle is in production it makes economic sense to adapt it to other tasks where possible rather than build special vehicles in small numbers. But what needs to be guarded against is the danger, particularly prevalent in British design history, of taking a good single-purpose design while still on paper and then adapting and re-adapting it so as to fit the basic production vehicle for as many tasks as possible with as little modification as can be achieved. The result of this approach is often a multipurpose vehicle which fails to live up to its promise in any one facet of its employment.

These three vehicles — Saracen, BTR-60P and YP-408 — saw the demise of the wheeled APC for military combat use for some time, and in the middle 1960s this virtually meant its demise for any military use whatever. Its revival will be deferred for the moment; what became the 'mainstream' of APC development, the tracked carrier, will be dealt with first.

The first tracked APC to appear was a regression to the 'made-over tank' idea, though carried out in an intelligent manner. The Soviets took their existing PT-76 amphibious tank chassis and lower hull and built a new armoured superstructure on to it. This placed the driver and commander at the front of the forward-located troop compartment; behind them, cross-seats accommodated 20 infantrymen. Behind the troop compartment was the rear engine and transmission compartment, on top of which it was possible to load cargo or light anti-tank weapons. Some models had a side door to the troop compartment, but for most of them the only way in or out was over the side. No firing ports were provided, and the only vehicle armament was a pintle-mounted machine gun on the forward edge of the troop compartment. A later version gave full overhead armour protection, entry and exit being by two roof hatches. Some versions of this type have been seen with two firing ports on each side.

The amphibious capability of this BTR-50P (which was first seen in 1957) made it an extremely agile vehicle but, as with previous Soviet designs, the need to enter and leave over the side or through two restrictive hatches meant that the actual deployment of troops left a good deal to be desired. The Czechs set about rectifying this, as they had already done with the wheeled vehicle, and their OT-62, whilst still resembling the BTR-50P, shows numerous improvements in detail. The troop compartment is covered and provided with hatches; doors in each side of the hull improve entry; the hull front is formed into two projecting bays at each side of the centrally placed driver, one of which is for the vehicle commander and the other for the squad machine gunner. A later version placed a small turret on top of this second bay; the Poles went one better and put their twin-gun turret on top of the troop compartment. The Czechs also put in a supercharged engine to give the vehicle greater power and speed.

At much the same time as the Soviets must have begun developing the BTR-50P the American Army had decided that they needed an APC which could be air-lifted. This led to the development of aluminium armour and the eventual production of the M-113 APC which appeared in 1960. This was petrol-engined, and it was soon replaced by the M-113A1 which had a diesel engine. Since then something like 70,000 have been built in the United States and under licence in Italy, and there is scarcely a country outside the Soviet bloc which does not have some M-113s somewhere in its military inventory.

The M-113 in its basic form is a box on tracks, with a sloping front; the driver sits at the left front and has the engine on his right; the troop compartment can carry 10 men, and the vehicle commander has his own cupola and machine gun in the centre of the hull. Entry and exit are by a bottom-hinged, hydraulically operated ramp-door in the rear face of the hull. By erecting a splash vane on the hull front, the vehicle is instantly prepared for amphibious operation. Since the basic vehicle is so simple, an infinite number of variant models have been produced or converted; everything from Pershing missiles to recoilless guns, vehicle repair equipment, bridges, radars, anti-aircraft guns, at one time or another practically every conceivable weapon or device has been applied to the M-113 with varying degrees of success. But for all that, it has remained a simple carrier, with no inherent fighting ability.

A very similar vehicle, developed at much the same time, was the British FV-432; at the time of its inception it was called Trojan, but out of consideration for a moribund motor-car the name was dropped by authority, though many soldiers still use it. This appeared in 1963 and is generally similar in concept to the M-113; the armour is steel instead of aluminium, so that it weighs about 4 tons more; entry is by a side-hinged rear door; and, like the M-113, it has room for a 2-man crew and 10 infantrymen. It, too, has spawned innumerable variants, most of which failed to survive the prototype stage.

Other tracked APCs of the period included the Austrian

Saurer, which carried 8 infantrymen and mounted a heavy machine gun on the roof, with roof hatches and entry by rear door; the French AMX-VCI, 10 passengers, 2 rear doors, firing ports, roof-mounted machine gun; the German SPz-12-3, 8 infantry, roof hatches, roof-mounted machine gun; and the Yugoslav M-60, with rear doors and firing ports for the 10 infantrymen inside.

Whatever anyone else thought, the German Army were far from satisfied with their Schutzenpanzer, and as early as 1959 they had begun to think ahead. Basing their requirements on their extensive experience of mobile warfare on the Eastern Front in 1942 – 44, one prime demand was that the occupants had to be able to fight from the vehicle. A complex armament specification was also laid down, and in the event it was to be 1971 before these vehicles saw service. Nevertheless, they must be rated as the first of the new generation of APCs, vehicles with such a greater potential that they coined a new term — the Mechanised Infantry Combat Vehicle (MICV).

The resulting vehicle, which took the better part of 10 years to develop, was 'Marder', a highly sophisticated and extremely expensive vehicle which set new standards. The box body carries the driver and engine at the front; behind this the troop compartment holds 6 men and has ball-mount firing ports on each side, with a periscope for each man. Between the driver and passengers are the 2 gunners; above them is the turret which carries a 20-mm cannon and a co-axial 7.62-mm machine gun. On the left of the turret are 6 smoke dischargers, and at the rear of the hull is a remote-controlled 7.62-mm machine gun. The turret is also provided with a white/infra-red searchlight. Entry and exit is by a bottom-hinged ramp-door at the rear of the hull.

The 20-mm cannon is ingeniously fed by three separate ammunition belts, so that three distinct types of round are ready for instant use and the commander can select, according to his target, HE, AP, or tracer. Marder is fully NBC-protected, and although not completely amphibious it can ford without preparation, but with the aid of a snorkel, depths up to 2.5 m.

The basic trouble with Marder is simply that it is too good for what it sets out to do; what was asked for was a vehicle that would transport troops and carry armament, and to pay £300,000 + for that seems a trifle excessive. Moreover, 28.2 tons, 600 bhp and a height of 2.85 m also seems to be excessive in order to carry 6 infantrymen to their objective. These are all objections which have been advanced to Marder, but there is the suspicion that they will be heard less frequently when full details of the next generation of MICVs become apparent. Production of Marder was completed over 5 years ago, and the specification is such that they will remain highly effective MICVs for at least the next decade; since they were built, manufacturing costs have greatly increased, and it is a matter for speculation whether anyone will succeed in producing a better vehicle, or even as good a vehicle, at a lower price. Current estimates for the new American MICV (of which more later) run at about £180,000, but this is probably a highly optimistic figure. Only time will tell, but it seems that the Bundeswehr will have the last laugh here.

While Germany was producing Marder another improved APC or 'near-MICV' appeared in Sweden. This was the Pbv-302, a boxy vehicle carrying 10 men plus driver and commander/gunner, and armed with a 20-mm Hispano-Suiza cannon in a turret. The passengers could open roof hatches and use their personal weapons if necessary, and the vehicle was fully amphibious. Since its adoption by the Swedish Army, the makers (Hagglund & Soner) have suggested modifications to convert it to full MICV standard; these include replacing the 20-mm gun with a 25-mm weapon, fully stabilised and with power operation, and changing the seating arrangements and superstructure profile so that the occupants could fire from side ports.

France now adopted an MICV in the AMX-10P, which replaced the earlier AMX-VCI. This was an aluminium-armoured, fully amphibious vehicle carrying a crew of 3 (driver, commander and gunner) and 8 infantrymen. The main armament was a turret carrying a 20-mm cannon and a coaxial 7.62-mm machine gun; the cannon had dual feed allowing instant selection of HE or AP projectiles. Various sighting options have been provided to cover day or night shooting, a searchlight is carried and there are smoke dischargers. Strangely, for a vehicle specified as an MICV, the infantry have no firing ports in the sides; there are two in the rear ramp-door, however.

After all this activity, nobody was surprised to see the Soviet Army adopt an MICV in 1967, but what did surprise them was the armament. The BMP-1 lifted the MICV specification into a new stratum, though whether it is in fact as effective as it looks is another question entirely.

As before, the Soviets began with the suspension and chassis of the PT-76 amphibious tank, placing a new superstructure upon it. They then added a turret in which was a 73-mm smooth-bore low-pressure gun and, on top of the gun's recoil cradle, a mounting rail for a Sagger anti-tank guided missile. Eight infantrymen are carried in a cramped compartment at the rear, entered by rear doors; each man has a hull firing port and a periscope. This party also has an RPG anti-tank rocket launcher and an SA-7 anti-aircraft missile launcher, both of which, it is claimed, can be fired from open hatches. Perhaps they can, but one would not wish to be inside the vehicle when it was done.

Weighing 12 tonnes and capable of 55 km/hr on roads, with 40 rounds for the main armament and 5 Sagger missiles, the specification is formidable. But specifications do not fight battles. The question is whether the vehicle is as formidable as its paper promise. On balance it is probably not. So far as one can ascertain, the gun is a re-hash of a 1944 German design, firing a fin-stabilised hollow charge projectile with rocket boost. According to an American source the hit probability against an MBT is 50 per cent at 800-m range, falling rapidly to 25 per cent at 1300 m, when fired from the halt. Being fin-stabilised it will be highly susceptible to cross-winds; being rocket-boosted and fired from a short, smooth-bored barrel its consistency and accuracy are doubtful. The Sagger missile is also open to criticism, but this question will be dealt with a little later on, since it is one which affects several other prospective MICVs. On balance, it seems that the BMP-1 looks more formidable than it really is.

It might be said here that there would be nothing new in this; the Soviets have a long history of bluffing the West with fearsome-looking weapons. In the 1950s various 31-cm and 40-cm self-propelled guns were trundled across Red Square on various occasions, causing a great deal of disturbance in Western intelligence circles; practical artillerymen considered various constructional aspects and dismissed them as nonsense, but they remained as bogeymen for a long time before being finally discredited.

By the beginning of the 1970s, therefore, the position was that the Germans and the Soviets had two true MICVs; the French had a near-MICV and the rest of the world was using APCs with varying degrees of combat capability. There were three lines of approach open; to go for an MICV at full speed; to sit down and carefully think out what the role of the infantry was to be and then to design a suitable vehicle for that role; or to do nothing until everybody else had played their hand. This latter course is an admirable way of saving money in the short run, but it tends to get expensive when the inevitable crash programme is called for; there is also the danger of being left behind. But however logical these three options might sound, in fact a good deal of subsequent development seems to have fallen somewhere in between them.

As might be expected, the Americans had a head start. In 1967 they had gone to the makers of the M-113 and asked them to develop an MICV from that vehicle. The result, called the 'Armoured Infantry Fighting Vehicle' (AIFV) appeared in 1970 and was a workmanlike job. The basic M-113 body had been converted by sloping the roof over the troop compartment to allow provision of two firing ports with periscopes on each side and one at the rear in the bottom-hinged ramp-door. On top was a turret mounting a 25-mm Oerlikon cannon with a coaxial 7.62-mm MAG machine gun. The vehicle was fully amphibious, and an additional layer of laminated steel armour gave good protection. Weighing 13 tonnes, it could move on firm ground at 60 km/hr and in water at 6 km/hr. But the US Army refused it; it was then sold in considerable numbers to the Dutch Army and later to the Philippines and Belgium. In 1972 the US Army, after reviewing various fresh designs, issued a new set of specifications and gave a development contract to the FMC Corporation who had built the M-113 and the AIFV.

At about this time there was also a development programme afoot for an 'Armoured Reconnaissance Scout Vehicle', but this was cancelled; as a result, the requirements embodied in this scout vehicle were merged with those in the MICV specification, which did not help the designers, and a completely new specification was drawn up calling for main armament of a 25-mm cannon, a TOW anti-tank missile, adequate armour protection and an amphibious capability. This new concept became the 'Fighting Vehicle System' and two models were demanded, the XM2 Infantry Fighting Vehicle (IFV) and the XM3 Cavalry Fighting Vehicle (CFV). The basic difference between the two was that the CFV would not have firing ports, would carry only 5 men, and would carry a motor-cycle in the crew compartment; primarily, it was to be a scout and reconnaissance machine. The IFV was to carry a crew of 3 plus 6 infantrymen, with 6 firing ports, a 25-mm Hughes Chain Gun and coaxial 7.62-mm machine gun in a power-operated 2-man turret, and, on the side of the turret, a TOW missile launcher.

In 1978 the programme ran into trouble when the US General Accounting Office criticised the design for being slower than the XM-1 tank; higher (thus easier to see and hit) than the XM-1; noisy and smoky because of its diesel engine, in comparison with the gas turbine-driven XM-1; and less well protected than the

XM-1. On the whole, one had the impression that they were criticising the IFV because it was not an MBT. There were also complaints about the projected cost — £183,200, whereas the M113 had cost only £47,000. Comparing the prices of the XM-1 tank and the earlier M60 tank, the GAO complained that the price of the MBT had merely doubled, while the price of the MICV/APC had quadrupled; they seem to have overlooked the fact that in comparing the IFV with the M-113 they were comparing apples with bananas. The complexity of the IFV's armament alone guarantees a higher price, without taking into account other mechanical improvements and before allowing for inflation. In addition the GAO originally calculated the XM-1 at $1.47 million per copy; latest indications are that this has, in the ensuing 3 years, escalated to £2.2 million per copy. It is doubtful if the IFV cost has risen in the same proportion.

In spite of various alarums and excursions, the IFV/CFV programme has managed to survive, largely, one suspects, because nothing better is in sight and also because the US Army is determined to adopt a tactical organisation which is predicated upon the co-existence of the XM-1 tank and the XM-2 IFV, the two to work in harmony. Latest indications are that the IFV should reach the hands of troops some time in 1982.

The latest word in the tracked MICV field was the announcement late in 1980 that the British Army is to purchase between 1800 and 2000 MCV-80 MICVs from GKN-Sankey, the first vehicles to be in service in 1986. The total programme cost is said to be £2000 million which, even allowing for development costs, suggests that the unit price is going to be in the same area as that of Marder. Full details of the MCV-80 are not yet available at the time of writing; for example, it is not known whether entry is by ramp-door or double doors. But it is apparent from published drawings and photographs that there are roof hatches but no firing ports; that there is a 2-man turret with a 30-mm Rarden gun and coaxial machine gun (though these may yet be changed for 25-mm and 7.62-mm Hughes chain guns); and that there will probably be no amphibious capability. Eight infantrymen will be carried, and there will be full NBC protection. Inevitably, drawings of a number of variants have been published, including an engineer vehicle with bulldozer blade, a recovery vehicle with crane, a surveillance radar vehicle and several different turret options; a French company has even discussed the possibility of fitting the hull with a twin 30-mm cannon anti-aircraft turret. The thought is inescapable; how much was the basic MICV concept altered in order to provide a compatible platform for all these adornments?

That brings us to more or less the latest state of the tracked MICV/APC story; it would be as well now to step back and see what happened to the wheeled APC in the same period. In the 1960s the wheeled solution was more or less abandoned for tracks, certainly in the major armies, and for some years very little happened, though a number of manufacturers still continued to produce designs for wheeled APCs. Then in the late 1960s/early 1970s the demand for internal security vehicles began to grow, and the wheeled APC found a new role; or, rather, re-discovered the role which the British Army had pioneered with Saracen.

Most of these designs were private ventures, and among the earliest was a range of vehicles by the Swiss firm of Mowag. Their Roland was a 4-wheeled vehicle for 6 men, with well-shaped armour and a remote-controlled machine gun in a small turret; Grenadier is similar, but larger, carrying 9 men; their later Piranha came in a number of configurations, with 4, 6 or 8 wheels, carrying from 9 to 14 men, armed with anything from a light machine gun to a 90-mm cannon. Eventually their 6-wheeled version, mounting an American turret with 2 machine guns, entered Canadian Army service as the Grizzly. This has a 3-man crew and carries 6 infantrymen; the troop compartment has vision blocks and firing ports, but entry is by a narrow door and the interior is extremely cramped. Various members of the Mowag range have been adopted by police and security services throughout the world.

GKN-Sankey, the British company who built the FV-432 APC and who are now to build the MCV-80, developed a small 4-wheeled armoured vehicle specifically for internal security work. This, the AT-104 was a simple design, based very much on existing commercial components for the running gear, and could carry a crew of 2 and 9 passengers. It has protection geared to its intended role; the armour resists small-arms fire and the floor and underbody are reinforced for protection against mines. It was followed by an improved model, the AT-105 with more protection, more manoeuvrability and a more powerful engine, and recent news is that a number are being bought by the British Army for use in Northern Ireland to supplement their ageing Saracens.

One of the most widely distributed private venture designs is that of the American company Cadillac Gage. Their Commando appeared in the early 1960s as an armoured car, but it was soon modified into an APC form. There are, by now, so many variant models tailored to specific roles that it is difficult to select any one of them and call it the standard, though that appellation might be said to apply to a version carrying 9 passengers and mounting a simple machine-gun turret. The vehicle is liberally provided with vision and firing ports for the infantry, and has doors at the rear and on both sides. Other variants mount different armament options up to a 90-mm gun.

Whether or not these private venture vehicles had any effect on the policies of the major armies is uncertain, but it seems that the cost of tracked APCs certainly had its effect, and the wheeled vehicle suddenly found itself back in favour as a combat equipment. France, in the late 1960s, decided that the tracked AMX-10P MICV would be confined to fully mechanised units and that a wheeled APC would be developed for the rest of the infantry as a cheaper and equally suitable vehicle. This resulted in the Renault/Saviem VAB design which first appeared as a 4-wheeled vehicle in 1974. This was a mid-engined design, with the driver and commander at the front, a passageway past the engine unit to the troop compartment in the rear, and a light machine gun mount for the vehicle commander. Ten fully equipped infantrymen could ride in the troop compartment, entered by 2 rear doors, and each side of the hull had 3 firing ports. The VAB is fully amphibious, being propelled in the water by steerable jet units. A number of variant models followed, turning it into an ambulance, repair vehicle, command vehicle and so forth, and different anti-tank missiles have been experimentally mounted. An improved version is the VAB/VCI which has an additional pair of wheels to turn it into a 6 × 6 configuration.

The Bundeswehr had, in the middle 1960s, expressed a requirement for an 8-wheeled armoured reconnaissance vehicle and for 4 × 4 and 6 × 6 armoured cargo carriers. The programme became extremely involved, but out of it appeared, among other things, the Transport - panzer 1, a 6-wheeled armoured carrier which appears to be all things to all men. It was basically configured as a cargo carrier or APC, with room for 10 passengers, but more recent information seems to indicate that it is unlikely ever to be used in the APC role, most of the production having been earmarked for specialist applications such as surveillance radar carrier, anti-aircraft command vehicles, NBC vehicle and so forth. Since the basic design carried no armament and there are no firing ports, its role cannot be more than that of a battle taxi.

Lastly in this discussion of vehicle types and development, we should perhaps mention the Israeli Merkava MBT, which has trailed a quite splendid red herring among the world's armies. This tank was first revealed in 1977, and the most startling feature was that the engine and transmission were placed in the front, leaving a space at the rear of the hull into which 6 (or 10, according to some reports) infantrymen could be carried. This immediately opened up all sorts of tactical speculation; now the infantry actually accompanied the tank as members of the crew as it were, to be deployed wherever the tank commander required their services. The MICV/APC was annulled at one swoop, since now the MBT could perform all the duties of armoured vehicles within the striking force, acting both as the gun carrier and the infantry carrier. Several pyramids of theory are erected on this troop compartment but they have shown a tendency to collapse in recent months, since it now seems apparent that the entry to the rear compartment is a narrow door scarcely able to allow a fully loaded infantryman to squeeze through and that the purpose behind the rear door and interior space is not to carry troops but to load and carry pre-packaged ammunition re-loads. This, in its own field, is as revolutionary as the troop-carrier idea, since it means that an MBT can be re-fuelled and re-ammunitioned in about a third of the previously best time, but it leaves the MICV/APC discussion exactly where it was before.

The great imponderable in this argument is the actual performance of these vehicles in combat, something which no number of exercises will ever answer. The prize example of this is the performance of Soviet BMPs in the 1973 Arab-Israeli war. They were handled by the Egyptians in accordance with received Soviet doctrine, being driven straight up to the Israeli positions. The use of the vehicle's machine guns and the weapons of the troops inside did not have very much effect on the Israelis, while the closer the APCs came to the prepared infantry positions, the better targets they became; and as the troops attempted to disembark they became the focus of intense small-arms fire. Another defect noted was that an APC, when hit by any sort of gunfire capable of piercing the armour, inevitably caught fire and incinerated the occupants before they could get out. Their failure to get clear of the vehicle was probably assisted by the confining effect of the overhead armour upon any missiles getting into the body; solid projectiles would ricochet, while explosive projectiles would be confined within an armoured box which would enhance their destructive effect.

As a result of these experiences, the Soviets, after a long and agonising debate, have now laid down that when delivering a deliberate attack the infantry will be disembarked as close to the objective as possible but in locations covered from the fire of anti-tank weapons and small arms. From there, the infantry attack goes in on foot in the traditional manner; the BMPs would, probably, take up hull-down positions and use their fire-power as additional covering fire for the assaulting troops. On the other hand, once the momentum of an armoured thrust has got under way, there is every reason to suppose that the MICVs would simply sweep forward against villages and minor opposition, hoping to bounce out the defenders before they could collect their wits.

Another point which emerged from the Yom Kippur War was the disparate opinions about the relative positions of armour and infantry in battle; some commanders placed their entire faith in armour, using it not only as a spearhead but also as the back-up, while at other times the infantry were put in first with the armour following. The one mix that seems to have been abandoned, at least in the initial stages of the war, was the balanced armour—artillery—infantry battle group.

This leads to the question of just how the infantry—armour mixture is to be put together and used in the future, for until this basic matter is satisfactorily resolved there can be no discussion of what might be the best infantry support vehicle. In the past the British Army has set its face against earmarking specific infantry formations for the armour-accompanying role; every battalion has been expected to take its place in whatever type of formation in which Whitehall has seen fit to place it. The Soviets, on the other hand, having the better part of 2 million men to play with, have been able to develop specialised motor rifle divisions who are trained to accompany 'their' tanks and are practised in the tactics involved. There are arguments on both sides; the British, with an all-regular force, can take the time to give a wide-ranging variety of training to their infantry so that battalions are equally skilled in all sorts of tactical operations. The Soviets, relying largely on conscripts, doubtless find it more profitable to hammer just one sort of tactic into the man's head during his relatively short stay in the army.

Perhaps more important than the minutae of tactics is the more fundamental question of whether the infantry and armour should stay as separate entities or whether they should become an integrated force. This conjures up such ghosts as Fuller's 'Tank Marines' and Liddell Hart's 'light car skirmisher companies', and with them the fears that long-standing infantry and cavalry regiments might lose their autonomy. And for anyone who is familiar with the regimental system, particularly as it is applied in the British Army, there is a great deal of sympathy with such fears. But it is not necessary to go to the sweeping lengths advocated by the theorists of the 1920s; there is no need to do any more cap-badge changing. All that is needed is the recognition that henceforth armour and infantry (and artillery, too, for that matter) must no longer train in their own separate ways, meeting perhaps once a year for a week or two of combined manoeuvres, but must work together constantly so that each knows the other's mind, his possible reactions to any situation, his capabilities and his limitations. It has been a species of this sort of reasoning which has led the US Army to specify the XM-1 tank and XM-2 IFV as coadjutors, giving them similar performance so that they will stay together in battle. Whether, having got both these vehicles into service, they will actually brigade them together and proceed to train them inseparably, remains to be seen.

Assuming then that a suitable tactical purpose can be determined, what parameters must we now look for in the vehicle? Since it is, at bottom, an armoured vehicle, it must conform to the three basics — fire-power, protection and mobility. In addition, and specific to this role, it must have room for the occupants. Perhaps this latter requirement ought to come first since it poses the very basic decision of whether to make a convenient size of vehicle and then tailor the infantry squad to fit, or whether to decide on the optimum size of squad and then make the vehicle large enough to accommodate them. This latter is obviously the more sensible course, but some designs of the past, notably some Soviet designs, give cause for thought. If the design is, as has been done by the Soviets, tied to an existing vehicle substructure (in this case the PT-76 tank chassis), then by the time the mechanical components, the turret, ammunition, radios and other vital items have been fitted, what space is left is given to the troops, and this automatically governs the size of the squad. Admittedly, the automatic rifle and its enhanced fire-power has permitted a reduction in squad size, but an NCO and 7 men seems to be cutting things rather fine. The Americans have cut it even finer in the IFV with an NCO and 5 men. The amount of equipment expected to be deployed by an infantry squad today means that these 5 will be burdened like pack-mules, and if one man gets shot there is an instant 20 per cent reduction in force strength. Perhaps the reasoning is that the vehicle crew, with their cannon and machine gun, can replace the squad light machine gun as the base of fire, providing the covering fire for the foot soldiers to move beneath. It is doubtful if this theory would stand up to the test of battle; the squad commander needs to be on the ground with his men, and he needs to have complete control of all the elements of his squad, deploying them as he sees fit. While the cannon and machine gun of the MICV are very reassuring, the fact remains that they can hardly be moved around the battlefield as easily as 2 men and a light machine gun used to be. Indeed, if the battlefield is so dangerous as to warrant the use of an MICV in the first place, there is little chance that, once closed up to the objective, the MICV will be able to move at all until the infantry on foot have taken out the enemy's weapons. One can also foresee the day when the squad commander sits tight in the MICV and transmits his orders to the squad by personal radio, and when that happens the battle will be as good as lost.

While on the subject of the occupants, some physiological factors, which are rarely spoken of by the MICV enthusiasts should be mentioned. Firstly, there is the very real problem of motion sickness. This is akin to seasickness and appears to be more provoked by wheeled vehicles than by tracked due to the large wheel movements and softer suspension. Some vehicles are worse than others; one French wheeled APC is said to reduce the occupants to near-hospitalisation after half an hour across rough country. The avowed object of the APC/MICV is to deliver a group of highly motivated fighting soldiers into a position from which they can assault the enemy; a collection of walking wounded is hardly likely to provoke fear in the defenders.

Closely allied to this is the question of disorientation. A party of men is locked up in a box, their view of the outside confined to the restricted angle of view of a periscope or vision block, through which Salisbury Plain, the Luneberg Heath, the Steppes or the Sahara Desert look much the same. The vehicle twists and turns, stops and starts, and then suddenly it stops, the doors are flung open, and the troops leap out. Where to? They are usually trained to fan out in the direction in which the vehicle is facing, but it does not require much imagination to see that there are bound to be occasions when the driver finds it advantageous to stop with his front not necessarily pointing towards the enemy. Thus the squad will dismount and rush blindly off in the wrong direction. If, on the other hand, they stop to collect their wits, they are likely targets. They are, moreover, in strange country with no immediate chance of orienting themselves with the map; nor can they be certain what their objective may be. Some years ago the Americans tried putting a tank driver into the turret, giving him a contra-rotating seat so that he always faced forward, no matter where the turret was aligned. Even this man, with probably the best field of view, the best chance of orientating himself and knowing what was going on, was found to become disorientated after a very short time, and the experiment was abandoned. How much worse will it be for the sardines in the back of an APC!

Of the mechanical attributes, there are several areas for discussion. Protection: this has to be carefully balanced between what is desirable and what is practical. What missiles must the MICV be proofed against? In the past the standard rifle bullet and the artillery shell-splinter have been the chosen yardsticks, and so long as the APC was merely being used to shift troops from here to there, then they would appear to be satisfactory. But if the MICV is to be used as some sort of assault vehicle, moving around with tanks, what then? It cannot, obviously, be given protection to the same level as the front face of an MBT, which is what the American General Accounting office seem to have been demanding. Economics and mechanical considerations prevent this. But if it is to move in company with MBTs it will come into the target area of enemy anti-tank weapons of all types, and with manpower being the Achilles heel of NATO, there is a good incentive for the enemy to turn his heaviest weapons on to the MICVs instead of the tanks. MICVs cannot be expected to stand up to, say, 120-mm APFSDS projectiles or the major guided missiles. Perhaps the best idea is to revert to the principle employed years ago in warship and fortress design, and select a degree of protection which will hold off attack from weapons of equivalent power to those you carry. Even so, 25—30-mm APDS is now commonplace and will require a sizeable thickness of plate to stop it. The answer to this may lie in the application of compound armour, though so little firm fact has been published about this material that it is difficult to offer any practical suggestions about its possibilities in an MICV application.

Armament is the reverse question to that posed above; in this case the question is what is the proposed target? The Soviets, with their 73-mm gun and Sagger missile appear to be prepared to engage MBTs. Most other designs rely on 20—30-mm cannon, presumably to cope with other MICVs and such lightly protected targets as armoured cars and reconnaissance vehicles. This looks like a sensible approach, but there have been opinions voiced that the current fashion for cannon solutions is no more than a fashion and has not been well thought through. If the sole purpose of the MICVs armament is to attack other armoured vehicles, then the high-velocity cannon has merit, but, it could be said that the prime requirement for the MICV weapon is the support of the infantry squad, and for this the high-velocity cannon is useless. It is marginal against any sort of field fortification and its flat trajectory means that it has no beaten zone and is ineffective against entrenched men. The high explosive shell is less effective than the average hand grenade, and the piercing shell will not go through much reinforced concrete. If the MICV is to be part of a mixed force of MICVs and MBTs, then it must be the task of the MBTs (and possibly of lighter tanks and tank destroyers) to protect the MICVs from the major threats, so that the MICV's anti-armour capability comes second to its suppressive fire capability.

In this context one should perhaps question the current crop of APC- and MICV-mounted anti-tank missiles. The Soviets started this with their BMP—Sagger combination, and there is the feeling that subsequent combinations have been a matter of keeping up with the Ivanovs. It is, of course, very comforting to know that, *in extremis,* any MBT which happens to get in the way can be dealt with. But in the present state of missile development it is necessary for the vehicle to stop, fire and remain stationary for a period of time while the missile's flight is controlled. The Israelis, in 1973, soon got the measure of this, and showed that by directing small-arms fire at the controller he can frequently be distracted sufficiently for him to miss. Moreover, while he is controlling the missile the vehicle gunner (or commander) cannot attend to any other duty, and there may well be other things requiring his urgent attention. A stationary MICV firing a missile is, firstly, a prime target for every MBT in the vicinity and, secondly, is not attending to its business, which is delivering the infantry to its objective. One is reminded of the American experience with tank destroyers in 1944—45; these were supposed to use their mobility to reach positions from which they could ambush enemy tanks. But in far too many cases they took the bit between their teeth and tried to play at being battle tanks, with fatal results. If the commander of an MICV gets similar delusions of grandeur and starts tank hunting, the armour—infantry team will be ruined before it begins. As and when the third generation of fire-and-forget missiles makes an appearance, then perhaps this assessment can be modified, but at present the addition of an anti-tank missile to an MICV seems to have several drawbacks.

The only specification regarding mobility is the necessity to be able to keep up with the tanks. On the face of it this would seem to be a simple enough demand, since we are talking about a lighter vehicle, but it must be borne in mind that the smaller MICV cannot afford the space for the massive engines normally carried by tanks. It will be recalled that the General Accounting Office complained that the XM-2 IFV could not keep up with the XM-1 MBT, and an examination of their comparative power-to-weight ratios is instructive. The XM-1 has a figure of 28.1 bhp/tonne, while the XM-2 has 23.45 bhp/tonne. Power-to-weight ratios are not the whole story, and we would like to see some comparative torque figures, but even so, the comparison is useful. The vehicles' respective speeds on hard surfaces are quoted as 72 km/hr and 66 km/hr, and transmuting these figures into cross-country performance suggests that the tank will outrun the IFV at any time. The explanation for all this lies in the fact that the tank, for twice the weight, has three times the power of the IFV. This, though, should be capable of being overcome; what is needed is the resource to develop an engine tailored to the MICV application instead of simply taking whatever engine appears suitable from stock. We know this is a policy of perfection, but if (as in the British case) £2000 million is being invested, it is spoiling the ship for a ha'porth of tar not to include a suitable engine in the programme. Moreover, the investment in the engine would not necessarily be entirely chargeable to the MICV, since such an engine would doubtless find applications elsewhere. What is adding to the MICV's cost today is not so much the basic hardware of body, tracks, engine, transmission and gun, but the peripherals—the fire-control system, sophisticated night vision and sighting equipment, stabilisation for the main armament, radio and data transmission equipment, navigational devices, NBC filtering, laser rangefinders and designators, infra-red search-lights and a host of similar expensive extras.

Having thus given the MICV/APC something of an airing, perhaps we can make some sort of a summary.

Firstly, there has to be a firm understanding of how infantry are to be used in conjunction with armour, what sort of mix is to be employed, what sort of tactics are to be used, what size of squad should be employed. Only when these fundamental questions have been satisfactorily answered can the choice between MICV and APC be made.

If, as seems likely, the MICV is to be preferred, then the basic parameters of protection level, mobility and fire-power must be decided before the designer as much as sharpens his pencil.

What is the dividing line between APC and MICV? The tacit assumption nowadays is that if the vehicle has its own armament and firing ports for the occupants, then it is an MICV, but is this, in fact, a reasonable distinction? Should, perhaps, tactical function be looked at as a distinction? But to do that it is necessary to have a firm understanding of what the infantry's tactical functions, in conjunction with armour, are to be, which leads back to the first proposition above. Perhaps there should be some official delineation of what constitutes an APC and what an MICV. The answers would be instructive, and, perhaps, widely divergent. And the effort of producing such answers might concentrate a few minds and make them think harder about some of the aspects of design and employment which have been sketched out here. There is, after all, an old maxim to the effect that one reaches the right answer if care is taken to ask the right question in the first place.

The armament of the MICV needs closer examination. It appears that several current armament mixes are put in simply because they are available and not because anyone has given any reasoned thought to the matter. The first step in this is to decide upon what the primary target is to be, and the desire for an anti-armour capability must not be allowed to stand in the way of adequate supporting fire for the infantryman. In this connection, it would seem that the French development of 60-mm and 81-mm gun-mortars is worth investigation.

The temptation to add an anti-tank missile capability as part of the vehicle's fire-power should be examined closely and weighed against the possibility of giving the infantry squad a portable launcher. Milan (to quote but one example) is perfectly satisfactory as a ground weapon and can be easily concealed; but to plant the same apparatus on top of an MICV and then expect the controller to expose himself through the roof while he fires it is fatuous.

Above all, the twin temptations of (a) adapting an existing vehicle or chassis, and (b) extrapolating innumerable variant models for economy's sake must be firmly resisted.

Looking around the world's APC/MICV scene at the moment, one thing seems to be apparent, and that is the paralysis in infantry thinking which has been brought on by the advent of mechanisation. Unless and until the infantry makes the basic decisions on what size the infantry squad is to be, how they are to be used in conjunction with armour and what their tactical role is to be, then there is no hope of producing a satisfactory vehicle to carry them and assist them in their chosen role. Every MICV so far seen (in the West at any rate) seems to exhibit far too many elements of compromise. If only somebody, somewhere, would bang on his desk and say '*This* is how my infantry will operate, *this* is how they will be armed, and *this* is how they will be transported. . .', then we might get an answer. It might not necessarily be quite the right answer, but it will be a good deal more right than some of the suggestions presently being touted.

DATA TABLE. INFANTRY SUPPORT VEHICLES

Vehicle	Type	Class	Crew	Infantry	Armament (mm)	Amphibian?	Weight	Engine	Speed	Range
Argentine										
VCI	T	MICV	3	7	20	No	27.0	D 720	72	850
Austria										
STEYR 4K7FA	T	APC	2	8	12.7	No	14.8	DT 320	65	525
SAURER 4K4FA	T	APC	2	8	12.7	No	12.5	D 250	65	370
Belgium										
SIBMAS	6×6	APC	3	9	30	Yes	15.0	DT 352	115	1400
BDX	4×4	APC	2	10	7.62	Yes	10.7	P 180	100	900
COBRA	T	APC	3	9	20	Yes	6.5	D 143	80	600
Brazil										
URUTU EE-11	6×6	APC	1	14	20	Yes	13.0	DT 174	95	600
China (PRC)										
TYPE 63	T	APC	4	10	12.7	Yes	12.5	D 180	50	400
Czechoslovakia										
OT-64	8×8	APC	2	15	14.5	Yes	14.5	D 180	90	700
OT-62	T	APC	2	18	14.5	Yes	15.0	DT 300	60	450
Finland										
VK	6×6	APC	3	10	?	Yes	9.0	D 115	40	?
France										
AMX-VCI	T	MICV	3	10	20	No	15.0	P 230	65	350
AMX-10P	T	MICV	3	8	20	Yes	14.2	DT 280	65	600
VAB/VTT	4×4	APC	2	10	7.62	Yes	13.0	D 235	90	1000
VAB/VCI	6×6	APC	3	8	20	Yes	14.2	D 235	90	800
VXB-170	4×4	APC	1	11	7.62	Yes	12.7	D 170	85	750
VCR/TT	6×6	APC	3	9	20	Yes	7.0	P 140	110	950

Vehicle	Type	Class	Crew	Infantry	Armament (mm)	Amphibian?	Weight	Engine	Speed	Range
France (cont)										
VCR	4×4	APC	2	10	7.62	Yes	7.1	P 140	100	950
M-3	4×4	APC	2	10	7.62	Yes	6.1	P 90	90	600
Germany (FRG)										
MARDER	T	MICV	4	6	20	No	28.2	D 600	75	525
TPz-1	6×6	APC	2	10	—	Yes	16.0	D 320	85	800
SPz-12-3	T	MICV	3	5	20	No	14.6	P 220	60	275
HWK-11	T	APC	2	10	7.62	No	11.0	P 211	65	325
CONDOR	4×4	APC	3	9	20	Yes	9.8	DT 168	105	500
TM-170	4×4	APC	2	12	7.62	Yes	9.5	DT 168	100	650
UR-416	4×4	APC	2	8	7.62	No	7.6	D 120	85	650
Italy										
IAFV	T	MICV	3	6	20	Yes	11.6	D 215	65	550
CM-6614	4×4	APC	1	10	12.7	Yes	8.5	DT 160	100	700
Japan										
TYPE 73	T	APC	3	9	12.7	No	13.5	D 300	60	350
TYPE 60	T	APC	4	6	12.7	No	11.8	D 220	45	250
Netherlands										
DAF YP-408	8×8	APC	2	10	12.7	No	12.0	DT 165	80	500
Portugal										
CHAIMITE	4×4	APC	2	9	12.7	Yes	7.3	P 210	100	1000
COMMANDO	4×4	APC	3	5	12.7	No	4.8	P150	110	600
South Africa										
RATEL	6×6	MICV	3	7	20	No	17.0	D T ?	105	?
Spain										
BMR-600	6×6	APC	2	10	7.62	Yes	13.0	D 305	100	900
Sweden										
Pbv-302	T	APC	2	10	20	Yes	13.5	D T 280	66	300

Vehicle	Type	Class	Crew	Infantry	Armament (mm)	Amphibian?	Weight	Engine	Speed	Range
Switzerland										
TORNADO	T	MICV	4	6	25	No	20.5	D 500	70	600
PIRANHA	4 × 4	APC	2	7	7.62	Yes	7.8	P 216	100	700
PIRANHA	6 × 6	APC	3	9	25	Yes	9.6	D 300	100	600
PIRANHA	8 × 8	APC	3	11	25	Yes	12.5	D T 325	100	750
MR-8	4 × 4	APC	2	5	—	No	8.2	P 160	80	?
GRENADIER	4 × 4	APC	1	8	20	Yes	6.1	P 202	100	550
ROLAND	4 × 4	APC	3	3	7.62	No	4.7	P 202	110	550
United Kingdom										
FV-432	T	APC	2	10	7.62	Yes	15.2	MF 240	55	425
SARACEN	6 × 6	APC	2	10	7.62	No	10.2	P 160	75	400
FV-4333	T	APC	2	10	7.62	No	10.0	D 180	?	?
AT-105	4 × 4	APC	2	8	7.62	No	10.7	D 164	95	500
AT-104	4 × 4	APC	2	9	7.62	No	8.9	P 134	80	600
CENTAUR	½-T	APC	3	8	7.62	No	6.3	P 156	80	?
FV-1611	4 × 4	APC	2	6	7.62	No	5.8	P 120	65	400
SHORLAND	4 × 4	APC	2	6	7.62	No	3.5	P 91	95	350
USSR										
BTR-40	4 × 4	APC	2	8	7.62	No	5.3	P 80	80	300
BTR-152	6 × 6	APC	2	17	7.62	No	8.9	P 110	75	600
BTR-60P	8 × 8	APC	2	16	14.5	Yes	9.9	P 180	80	500
MTLB	T	APC	2	9	7.62	Yes	11.9	D 240	60	400
BTR-50P	T	APC	2	20	7.62	Yes	14.2	D 240	45	400
BMP-1	T	MICV	3	8	73	Yes	12.5	D 280	55	300
United States										
XM-2 IFV	T	MICV	3	6	25	Yes	21.3	D T 500	65	500
AIFV	T	MICV	3	7	25	Yes	13.7	D 264	60	475
M-113A1	T	APC	2	11	12.7	Yes	11.2	D 215	65	475

Vehicle	Type	Class	Crew	Infantry	Armament (mm)	Amphibian?	Weight	Engine	Speed	Range
United States (cont)										
M-59	T	APC	2	10	12.7	Yes	19.3	P 254	50	170
M-75	T	APC	2	10	12.7	No	18.2	P 295	70	185
COMMANDO	4 × 4	APC	3	9	20	Yes	9.8	D 200	90	800
RANGER	4 × 4	APC	2	6	7.62	No	4.9	P 180	115	475
AM-301	4 × 4	APC	3	9	25	Yes	11.4	D T 270	115	850
Yugoslavia										
M-960	T	APC	3	10	12.7	Yes	9.5	D 140	50	400
M-980	T	MICV	3	8	20	Yes	12.0	D T 276	70	500

Type: T = Tracked; 4 × 4, 6 × 6 or 8 × 8 indicates wheeled.

Class: the description APC or MICV is that given by the makers or users.

Armament: the weapon shown is the principal weapon; there may be additional machine guns.

Weight is in tonnes; speed in km/hr; range in km.

Engine abbreviations: P = petrol; D = diesel; MF = multifuel; T = turbo-charged. Figure gives bhp.

Several countries employ APCs listed above but under different names:

China (PRC): Type 56 is Soviet BTR-152.
Type 55 is Soviet BTR-40.

Poland: SKOT APC is Czech OT-64.

Egypt: WALID APC is locally manufactured copy of Soviet BTR-40.

Eire: TIMONEY APC is same as Belgian BDX.

Romania: TAB-70 APC is Soviet BTR-60.

Weapon Development in the 1980s: The Air

F W THOMPSON

Air Commodore F W Thompson, CBE, DSO, DFC, AFC, BSc, RAF (Retd) left the RAF after a distinguished career to join the aircraft industry. He has recently retired from British Aerospace Dynamics where he was Director of Air Weapons

THERE is no doubt that air forces have lost none of their significance in this age of advanced technology and missiles. However, as Mr Geoffrey Pattie, the Under Secretary of State for the RAF, recently stated: 'many old assumptions will have to change if we are to maintain the country's air strength in the face of rising costs and increasing pressure on the defence budget'. This is a problem faced by both the NATO powers and the Warsaw Pact countries alike. No one should be in any doubt about the crucial importance of air power in any future conflict. It is significant that the Soviet military planners have vastly increased spending on new aircraft and air weapons. In fact they are now believed to be spending between 10 per cent and 20 per cent of the GNP on defence and of this expenditure, air power accounts for 45 per cent. This is well in excess of the expenditure on the widely publicised 'blue-water navy'. The expenditure of air power has now been increased in real terms by twice that on the Soviet naval and ground forces combined and now amounts to something between £17 and £30 billion. The rest of the Warsaw Pact countries are spending some £3 billion per annum on air power, giving a Warsaw Pact investment of between £20 and £33 billion per annum.

Against this the NATO powers spend on average about 30 per cent of their defence budget on their air forces and even this is not uniformly spread. For example, the United Kingdom spent twice as much on providing air defence for its own blue water navy as it did on its defence of the United Kingdom. The combined expenditure of the European NATO powers on their air forces is less than £6 billion per annum. It is true that the United States and Canada spend a further £17 billion but probably not one-third of this can be realistically attributed as directly available to NATO.

It is obvious, therefore, that unless the NATO powers can maintain a real advanced capability in terms of technical standards, inspired tactics and training methods, the Warsaw Pact will easily subdue the NATO air forces by sheer weight of numbers. It is essential, therefore, that the quality of the NATO equipment and air crew must be considerably better than those of their opponents. The Warsaw Pact countries can muster almost twice as many aircraft as could be mounted by the NATO countries in defence of the Central European front. What perhaps is even more dangerous is the continuing assumption that in any future confrontation the initial strike would be at the Soviets' initiative. Time and again the immense advantage gained by the side which strikes first has been demonstrated. The classic example from World War II was the Japanese strike against Pearl Harbor.

AIR FORCES AVAILABLE TO THE NATO COUNTRIES

Air power can be divided into three main roles: maritime support, participation in the land battle and defence of the Homeland base. Within NATO, each country will see the need for a different balance between these roles although they all will share the same basic objectives. It is this differing balance between the roles that makes standardisation so difficult.

Maritime activities

The United Kingdom deploys a considerable part of its RAF strength in the maritime role in support of the NATO commands in the Channel and the North Atlantic areas. Even its Nimrod AEW aircraft are largely used in support of NATO although these do remain under national command. France, although not a member of the NATO military organisation, remains in very close association and has a considerable although somewhat dated maritime air force. The Federal Republic of Germany (FRG), Holland, Norway and Italy have a smaller involvement although they all participate, and are building up their helicopter squadrons. In Italy the maritime role is covered by the Italian Navy.

Participation in the land battle and defence of the homeland

For the Central European members of NATO the air forces deployed in the land battle must also play an essential and decisive part in the defence of the Homeland. Unlike the United Kingdom, where at this time home defences leave much to be desired, Norway, Holland, Belgium, the FRG and Italy rely on the somewhat dated F104 for both defence and interdiction. The first three have now embarked on a re-equipment programme in the joint F16 consortium. The FRG has several Phantom squadrons for defence and ground attack purposes. All these countries are supported with NATO Nike Hercules and Hawks for AA purposes. In common with the RAF, the FRG Phantoms and the Italian F104s will in due course be replaced by the Tornado. In the main this will provide multipurpose ground attack and interdiction facilities, but the RAF will also have the ADV version giving a very advanced defence fighter capability.

Most of these countries have some transport capability, but generally this is limited, the most extensive being in the RAF and the Italian Air Force. Only the United Kingdom and France maintain a flight-refuelling capability and this is limited in the United Kingdom to 3 squadrons of Victors and in France to a few C135Fs. This field of operation can not be left without mentioning the RAF Harrier squadrons which provide extremely good flexibility in operation and very quick redeployment.

Portugal, although a member of NATO, contributes no squadrons to the Alliance. Greece was a member of the 6th Allied Tactical Air Force, but at this time is still withholding support as a result of the rift with Turkey over Cyprus. During this period of duress, the Greek Air Force has in fact been built up considerably, and when she resumes active cooperation with the NATO air forces she will be able to play a more active role. Turkey is also committed to the 6th Allied Tactical Air Force and is also a member of CENTO. The most important Turkish role is the provision of bases for USAF operations and, since the Greek withdrawal from NATO military operations, the availability of these has been constantly under question. The Turkish Air Force has 2 squadrons of F4Es and 6 squadrons of F5A/B, 5 squadrons of F100 Sabres and 4 squadrons of F104s. It also is equipped with 6 squadrons of Nike Hercules and so can play a very useful role in this most vulnerable area.

The United States and Canadian participation in NATO

The United States is, of course, the dominant member of NATO and as such operates some 10 wings of F4s, F111s and F15s in Europe. The United States also provide airborne early warning and transport support. In addition, the USAF maintains a quick reinforcement force in the United States and this is supported by an extensive air-refuelling capability. In the near future the United States will have a force of cruise missiles deployed in Europe and this should greatly enhance the NATO capability to react to a Soviet advance. In the United States, the USAF Tactical Air Command provides a very potent defence capability. Available are 16 wings averaging 72 aircraft each and mainly equipped with F4s, although some F111s, F15s and F16s are included. For the United States the maritime role is covered by the USN with both carrier-borne and land-based forces. Canada keeps 3 squadrons of F104s based in Europe. She is currently looking for a replacement for her home defence and may well choose a general purpose aircraft such as the F16 or F18 which could also be used in Europe. In the maritime role she has some ageing Argus maritime patrol aircraft used entirely in the North Atlantic theatre. She also has a small force of Trackers and Sea Kings but, again, these are not available to NATO.

Neutral countries in Europe not members of NATO

The NATO line-up cannot omit reference to certain countries who, although not members of the organisation, are generally regarded as favourably dispersed to the Western powers. In particular, Sweden, Austria and Switzerland should be considered. Sweden has a most important strategic situation including a common frontier with the USSR. Although firmly committed to a nonaligned role, her Viggens and Drakens could provide a most important bonus towards holding the northern flank of NATO. Austria and Switzerland would undoubtedly resist any encroachment onto their territories. This would provide a most useful block to Soviet advance in the south, but beyond this no active participation in defence of NATO can be expected.

NATO strategic attack capability

Of all the NATO air forces only the USAF maintains a capability of reacting strategically to a Soviet offensive. The USAF B52s are capable of striking deep into the USSR and the deployed ICBMs could strike in a pre-programmed programme against most Russian targets of importance. In the United Kingdom the deterrent role of the RAF has been transferred to the Royal Navy. Tactical nuclear strike can be made by the RAF

F4s in RAF Germany and also by the FRG Pershing missiles. The French Air Force is the only one in Europe which maintains a strategic nuclear capability. Her SSBS squadrons and the 'Force de Frappe' are capable of striking at most of the important targets in the USSR. In addition her Mirage IIIEs and Jaguars are equipped to carry tactical nuclear missiles.

AIR FORCES OF THE WARSAW PACT COUNTRIES

Against the above NATO air forces must be considered the very large number of aircraft available to the Warsaw Pact countries. The German Democratic Republic (GDR), Poland, Hungary, Czechoslovakia, Romania and Bulgaria, are all very much under the influence of the Soviet Union which is capable of exercising overall coordination in any war. The Soviet Union itself keeps tactical aircraft based in all these countries. The Warsaw Pact countries have a distinct advantage over NATO in that they mainly operate similar types of equipment. Although there is much friction between these satellite countries and their Soviet masters, the NATO countries would be ill-advised to think that this would prevent effective collaboration should the Soviet Union decide to launch an attack.

The GDR has 6 fighter squadrons equipped with MiG 21s and these are supported by batteries of SAM 2 and SAM 3. Poland has the largest air force in the Warsaw Pact outside the Soviet Union. It is the only country in the Pact to have a larger air force than that of the Soviet Air Army stationed within its boundaries. The Polish Air Force is technically very well advanced and is supported by a fixed-wing naval air force. The bulk of the Polish Air Force consists of MiG 21s although it does have some SU 7s, LiM 5s and IL 28s. The Czechoslovakian Air Force has two roles — air defence and the support of ground force. It is the only Warsaw Pact air force which is not entirely of Soviet creation. However, most of its equipment is of Russian design. This comprises MiG 15Fs, 17s, 19s and 21s although quite a number of these have been built by the Czech industry under licence.

Hungary has the smallest Warsaw Pact air arm, mainly devoted to support of the Army although it also contributes to the Warsaw Pact air defences with interceptors and SAM batteries. The Soviet Union, however, maintains upwards of 200 combat aircraft in Hungary including some MiG 27s. There are also believed to be more than 100 MiG 21s. Romania remains somewhat isolated from the rest of the Soviet block and gives a high priority to home defence. The main types available to the air force are MiG 21Fs although there are a few Mig 21PFs with a limited all-weather interception capability. In Bulgaria the air force is mainly under direct Army command. It has some 100 MiG 17s and there is a growing number of MiG 21s for use as interceptors or in the fighter/bomber reconnaissance role. In addition there are now some MiG 23Es.

Air forces of the Soviet Union

The Soviet Union itself has massive forces covering the strategic role with bombers, ballistic missiles, and from naval submarine-launched missiles. New designs of equipment are constantly being introduced although it is probably true to say that these systems are still behind those of the Western powers in terms of sophistication. The air forces of the Soviet Union are well capable of launching an attack on any of the NATO countries, including the North American continent. It possesses a very large interception force of advanced SU 11s and 17s. There is also a good electronic warfare capability. For long-range operations there is a large tanker force, and this is matched in the Soviet Army with a large number of close-support aircraft and helicopters.

The nonaligned countries of Eastern Europe

These are Albania and Yugoslavia. It is not thought that either of them present any threat to the NATO powers despite their communist régimes. The Albanian Air Force is one of the smallest in Eastern Europe and is completely integrated with the Albanian Army. The Yugoslav Air Force plays an important role in the country's policy of independence both from the Warsaw Pact and from NATO. It is equipped with a mixture of Western, Soviet and domestically developed and manufactured aircraft. It is certain that it would stubbornly resist any infringement of Yugoslav territory despite its association with Comecon.

THE INITIAL PHASE OF AN EAST–WEST CONFLICT

As already stated, it is generally thought that the initiative in any war would be taken by the Warsaw Pact countries. Russia might seek to dominate the West by destroying the Atlantic bridge between America and Europe, then go for a quick military success in Europe before reinforcements could arrive. It is considered that our current resources in the eastern Atlantic and the Channel are adequate to meet the Soviet threat. In any event a sea campaign would merely be a means to an end which could be achieved more quickly and effectively by a direct assault on land. Air power would play a vital role in blunting the main Russian thrust on land in the Central European region.

To be effective in this role it is essential that the NATO forces are provided with good intelligence on any pending attack and good information on size and direction once the attack has started. It is most unlikely that normal intelligence sources would fail to give good indication of an increasing probability of attack. This would permit NATO to be brought to a satisfactory standard of readiness. However, a high degree of readiness can only be maintained for relatively short periods. The airborne early warning (AEW) forces and the NADGE chain would give useful indications and might certainly be expected to raise the alarm if an advance was actually started. But the scope of the AEW forces must of necessity remain limited. Their effectiveness might well be degraded by enemy electronic warfare both land and airborne. Fortunately reconnaissance by satellite is now a steadily growing capability.

The flexibility of air power

The interplay between offensive and defensive forces is the essence of air warfare. On the one hand, offensive forces must endeavour to surprise, evade, deceive, confuse and frustrate the efforts of the opposing defences in every way possible. On the other hand, the defensive forces must aim to make the attacker's task as difficult as possible by posing the maximum number of threats to him, forcing him to disclose his intentions and to expose himself to defence weapons as early and as frequently as possible. They must deny the attacker tactical and operational freedom of action to the greatest possible extent. In World War II, for example, fighter aircraft operating in the tactical role could make repeated low-flying passes and expect to survive and kill personnel and destroy tanks with their rockets and 20-mm cannons. Improved defensive weapon systems with their better armour and much-improved ground air defence capability invalidate this form of attack. Improved offensive aircraft flying at high subsonic speeds find target detection and line of sight aiming impractical except from high angles of descent. This leaves them too exposed to the defences, and in any case such tactics are dependent on the cloud base. On the other hand, low-level and very low-level attacks using cluster bomblets create very difficult navigation target acquisition and weapon-release parameters. It is necessary, therefore, to examine the capabilities of the opposing air forces to see if the numerical disparity can be balanced by superior technical capability.

Maritime operations

Tactical reconnaissance is undoubtedly the major task for the air forces in this role. The available NATO maritime aircraft, together with those of France, can probably provide adequate cover in the North Atlantic and Channel areas to ensure that the Warsaw powers could not achieve a major break-through. The situation in the Mediterranean and the Indian Ocean has changed dramatically over the past few years, but even here USN air forces are probably able to provide adequate cover of Russian movements. It is not likely that any of these maritime air forces will be used directly to strike against major naval units. The US Harpoon weapon system and the British Sea Eagle system do, however, give them a good stand-off strike capability against smaller vessels and fast patrol boats. They will have to face up to increasing harassment both from the enemy defensive aircraft and from ship-launched missiles. Already, in fact, ship missiles are available which not only have the capability of destroying aircraft but can be used to destroy missiles launched by those aircraft.

Maritime surveillance can be effected by satellites, but these must of necessity be flexible in use. The Soviet Union is already known to launch satellites to cover NATO exercises, their orbits being changed as necessary to keep them over the ships. For general overall search when targets have not yet been identified, their sensors fitted into the satellite must search a wide area to compensate for the time taken for the satellite to come back to the same place on the globe.

In this maritime satellite field it is probable that the Soviet Union is better equipped than the United States. Satellites are particularly useful in gathering electronic information. Nearly all radars, data links, WHF, VHF or microwave transmissions have straight-line paths. Consequently a receiver 100 miles or more up in the atmosphere can detect the signals over a very great distance. AEW aircraft can also take advantage of this phenomenon. Other sensors used by maritime reconnaissance aircraft include cameras, infra-red line scan and radar.

Cameras can be installed in the aircraft or in a detachable pod to give flexibility to the use of the aircraft. They can be used for vertical, forward or sideways oblique shots and can be made to cover a field of view from horizon to horizon. Panoramic views of high resolution can also be provided. The cameras can be linked with the aircraft computer to give accurate correlation of the recorded data in time and space.

Infra-red line-scan equipment is in many ways similar to the optical equipment. It makes use of the infra-red radiation from the ships or from ground sources in lieu of the visual light used by the cameras. At present such equipment normally converts the infra-red signal for processing on a standard photographic film. The newer equipment now becoming available can give instantaneous information on a TV screen in the aircraft or utilise a data link to pass the information directly to a ground or ship-borne station. Direct television with or without image intensification can also be used to give direct information.

All these equipments do have limitations particularly in very low visibility and cloud. Consequently they must be augmented by radar scanners which are generally regarded as all-weather devices. Radar does not give positive identification but when the data is matched with other intelligence this is not a major limitation in the maritime role. It is most unlikely that the equipments available to the NATO powers have any major superiority over those available to the Soviet forces. However, it is more likely that it will be a case of the NATO powers looking for the Soviet fleet than vice versa.

For the other maritime role, anti-submarine, the aircraft has lost some of its importance. Increasingly, this task will have to be taken over by killer submarines and other naval units. However, aircraft such as the Nimrod and Atlantique still have an important role to play and do carry the most sophisticated equipment. Radar is still of importance against the diesel-engined submarines and modern radars can detect the smallest exposure of a snort mast. However, this is not effective in the case of nuclear-powered submarines which can patrol at great depths and at high speed and can also remain submerged for many days at a time. The aircraft can still monitor the movement of these with sonar devices planted either as static barriers or laid as a special location pattern where other intelligence indicates the presence of a submarine. More flexibility still can be found by the use of helicopters carrying dunking sonar although these are usually part of the naval forces. Magnetic anomaly detection has also lost

most of its potency since it has a limited range of about 1000 ft
and hence only useful against submarines at very modest depths.
The Soviet Union has probably got a smaller and less-
sophisticated maritime air force than the NATO powers but,
again, it is more likely that the NATO powers will be looking for
Soviet submarines than vice versa.

Support and participation in the land battle
    This is regarded as the primary role of the Warsaw Pact coun-
tries and generally of the European members of NATO. It can
encompass many aspects from direct attack against tanks and
armour to much more deep penetrations against the enemy bases
and headquarter organisations. Transport support both for
actual troop movements and for logistic purposes is also a most
important role of the air force in the land battle. Faced with
surface-to-air missiles, Mach 2 interceptor fighters, radar-
controlled anti-aircraft gunfire, modern systems of camouflage
and very sophisticated ECM methods, the ground-attack aircraft
has a formidable task in delivering its weapon load. Present
techniques are to fly as low as possible to keep beneath the radar
screen and to take advantage of ground clutter against air-to-air
weapons. Usually only one pass at the target will be possible and
the probability of detecting a moving target will be very low. In
fact without the modern computers now fitted to aircraft, the
task would be impossible.
    If the task is to attack a static target, such as a base complex,
then the sortie can be pre-planned. Modern navigation equipment gives a very good chance of finding the target. The basic
standard navigation relies on some form of inertial platform based
on accelerometers to detect motion in the three planes. The information provided is converted by highly specialised electronic
computers to give heading, track and ground speed. Each time a
positive fix is obtained by visual sighting, radar or other means,
the system can be updated. Since, however, it is based on
gyroscopes it will drift between fixes. In some ground theatres
more sophisticated ground systems such as Omega may be
available. These can give very active fixes from a lattice work of
hyperbolic lines based on a series of VHF beacons. Clearly these
beacons have to be located very accurately and so it is difficult to
maintain this type of coverage over a fast-moving battle front.
    Alternatively the aircraft may carry its own doppler system.
This consists of three high-frequency radar beams transmitted

from the aircraft at an angle to one another. As the aircraft passes over the ground, frequency changes are caused in the beams and by comparing these changes, ground speed and drift can be obtained. When this information is fed into the aircraft computer it can be used to give a constant update of the aircraft position or can be used to produce a rolling map presentation. Like the inertial platform it is based on data from gyroscopes and so needs updating from time to time.

Radar remains a very important part of the aircraft equipment for search ahead, to give a maplike presentation and to provide moving target indication either for attack purposes or self-defence against fighter attacks. Also in many modern aircraft radar can provide ground avoidance or automatic terrain following — essential for the high-speed low-flying attacks. Radar has some disadvantages. Firstly, many radars in the older aircraft including the early F4s cannot adequately penetrate ground clutter and so cannot detect targets either on or near the ground and hence the aircraft is unable to illuminate these for its semi-active weapon systems. The later F4s, the F15, F16 and Tornado do not suffer from this limitation. Radar also gives the ground defences early indication of approach and where target illumination is concerned indicates the point of attack. Ground defences make use of this using the radar illumination to provide a homing beam for SAMs. To overcome this disadvantage of the radar system we can adopt a purely passive system for target detection such as infra-red.

Forward-looking infra-red (FLIR) can produce a very good picture of the ground ahead of the aircraft without giving advance warning of its approach. It can be used by day or by night and in marginal weather conditions such as thin fog, light rain or industrial haze. It is, however, severely limited in heavy rain or cloud. Since it reacts to heat emissions it not only produces pictures similar to TV but can also indicate whether, for example, aircraft engines on the ground are hot or cold, whether oil or petrol tanks are full or empty or whether power supplies are live or dead. It can be used in association with a laser range-finder and target indicator to provide boresight illumination for a laser homing weapon system. The central aircraft and air data computers are essential for the processing of the received information. This is turned into readily readable presentations such as on a roller map or for head up display (HUD) purposes.

Tactical ground attack

For this purpose we cannot use the pre-planned sortie except to get the aircraft into the general area of probable targets, such as an advance of armour. Furthermore, tactical targets other than large formations of tanks or headquarters complexes are virtually impossible to find from low-flying aircraft. Consequently some form of target indication is necessary. If the tactical situation permits a Forward Air Controller (FAC) can illuminate the desired target with man-portable laser illuminator. The laser reflections from the target can then be used either by the aircraft laser-finder giving a direct alignement presented on the pilot's HUD or used as a homing beam for a laser homing weapon. If no FAC is available, then the aircraft laser range-finder can be used to designate the target as well as providing range and direction information. The great disadvantage of this mode is that the aircraft must continue to illuminate the target until weapon impact. Thus tactical freedom is greatly reduced and vulnerability considerably increased. Alternatively, a second aircraft could be used to illuminate the target allowing the weapon carrier to regain its freedom of manoeuvre. However, this is not considered a very desirable situation since it not only requires the coordination of the flight of two aircraft but also still leaves the illuminating aircraft exposed during the flight time of the weapon.

Air defence

The enemy will certainly try to deny the NATO forces the use of safe bases from which to mount a counter-offensive. The Warsaw Pact will give great importance to the attack on NATO bases in Europe and the United Kingdom. It is essential, therefore, that these bases are defended at the greatest range possible so that as many enemy aircraft as possible can be destroyed or frustrated before they are in a position to launch their weapons. At this time we can expect these attacks on bases, at least where defences are likely to be met, to be made at low level, the intention being to penetrate the defences below the SAM's radar horizon and within the ground clutter returns of the air defensive fighters. As stated earlier, this not only presents the attacker with a very difficult task but also makes it difficult for the air defences to locate and identify the target and then attack successfully. The later F4s and F111s have a capability of penetrating ground clutter. The F15 and Tornado will not only be able to do this but also will be provided with a track while scan mode permitting the launch of more than one missile at a time. It must be expected that at least some of the enemy aircraft will survive the first attack be it from aircraft or SAMs. Hence the defensive fighter must be able to manoeuvre quickly to get in a second shot and then have adequate manoeuvre capability both from the aircraft and weapon systems point of view to join in a melée end play situation.

It must be assumed that the Warsaw Pact defensive fighter will adopt similar tactics against any counter-attacks the NATO forces may decide to mount. In this they would probably have an advantage of working nearer to their own bases and prepared defences, but the airborne equipment may at this time not be so sophisticated as that available to the NATO powers.

Vertical lift aircraft

Helicopter gunships have been used by both the United States and the Soviet Union. It is not clear if they would have a major role to play in a European land battle. If they were extensively used there is no doubt that the Warsaw Pact forces would not only considerably out-number the NATO units but would be as efficient if not even more so than the NATO opposition. The RAF Harriers do provide a most useful quick deployment force, and although the available numbers are limited, they could produce a favourable situation, at least locally.

Tactical air-to-surface weapons

Weapons with some form of guidance have now almost completely replaced free-falling bombs, rockets and other missiles with ballistic trajectories. All the devices used for aircraft navigation and location can be adopted for use in missiles. Microcomputers are available which can be incorporated to fulfil all the functions of the aircraft computer. At the same time they can provide the flying commands necessary to get the missile to its target. There are four main types of self-homing missiles or bombs.

(a) *Anti-radiation homing.* This is where a missile has a receiver which detects the enemy radar, locks on to it and uses its beam for homing. This type of homing is, of course, only applicable when the enemy radar is actually transmitting. Of course, if it is an aircraft detection radar or a SAM guidance radar, it is useless to the enemy unless it is in fact radiating. Examples of this type of missile are the US Shrike, Standard and

HARM with ranges in excess of 25 km; and the French AM39. The Soviet Union has the Kennel and the Kelt which have quite a long range but are probably only for use against shipping. Modern missiles and bombs can be fitted with mercury circuits so that they continue homing on the last-known bearing during short breaks in transmission. However, if the breaks are more than, say, 30 sec, the probability of the missile picking up the radiation signal when the radar again becomes active is small. Again many ground radars are now fitted with sophisticated ECCM devices such as frequency agility which make this anti-radiation homing most difficult.

(b) *TV homing.* TV missiles can be produced which home on-to the visual picture transmitted back to the aircraft. These will not work at night or in very low visibility. Existing weapons generally rely on an operator examining the TV picture and then directing the missile through a command link. In general these are only suitable for sore-thumb targets, particularly ships. Examples are the British French Martel and US Walleye. Alter-natively, techniques now exist which allow TV weapons to lock on to contrast differences received from the target and home in autonomously. The difficulty here is that no positive identifica-tion of the target under attack is provided. The US Maverick used this type of homing.

(c) *Infra-red homing.* Here the missile relies on the infra-red (heat) emissions from the target. These are purely passive homers and give no indication of attack to the enemy. Infra-red heads can be substituted for TV, or radar homing heads on the missile giving the possibility of a mixed load. The only known version is the Norwegian Penguin of which an air-to-surface version of the ship-to-ship missile is being developed.

(d) *Semi-active radar homing.* Instead of relying on the signal transmitted by the ground radars, the target can be illuminated by the aircraft radar and the reflected signal used to generate homing commands. This method, however, does have several disadvantages. The aircraft has first to find and identify the target and then maintain the illumination throughout the whole of the missile flight, thus greatly increasing its vulnerability to the enemy SAMs whilst at the same time proscribing its own manoeuvrability. Furthermore, many aircraft radars cannot find and illuminate targets through ground clutter. Nor for that matter can many of the missiles themselves home through ground clut-ter. The only known missile system in this category is the British Sea Skua, which at present is limited to the anti-shipping role.

Active Radar

To avoid some of the above limitations the missile can be made to provide its own radar transmissions. This permits the aircraft to 'fire and forget' i.e. to break away immediately after missile launch. These are ideal over sea where generally only an isolated target is being attacked. Over land, however, it is difficult to pick out the target through extensive ground clutter. Furthermore, the power which can currently be generated in a missile system is extremely limited and therefore the range available for active radar homing is generally quite small. To overcome this some form of mid-course guidance (initial or semi-active) might be adopted, but this obviously increases the attack problem and detracts from the active radar advantages. The FRG Kormoran has mid-course initial and terminal active radar homing; the French AM39, which is under development as a version of Exocet; the Italian Otomat is also an air-launched version of the ship-to-ship weapon and the Swedish RBO4E, which is in service with the Swedish Air Force, all make use of active radar homing.

Other forms of guidance

More naval forms of guidance are being developed although little detail of the function of these has been released. DME, which is used by the United States for guided bombs, relies on ground-based equipments to give missile to target range by triangulation. It can be used for all-the-way homing, using a command link as for mid-course homing being replaced in the terminal phase by other means such as active radar. Millimetric radar can be used in an active or passive mode. It works on very high frequency transmissions in the 35-GHz or G4-GHz bands.

This type of homing offers many attractions and can be used in all weathers. It can also provide a target recognition capability. However, at this time there is no known weapon system in service with this type of homing.

Balance of development

As already stated there is no known reason why the Warsaw Pact countries cannot match Western development in any of these homing techniques. However, from the information available it seems that most Soviet missiles are designed for long-range use against sore-thumb targets such as shipping or transmitting radars. Against this NATO is known to have at least

24 systems making use of a full cross-section of the techniques described.

Bombs and Rockets

As noted above, these are in general unsuited for use in a highly defended area such as Europe but will still have some role to play. Both bombs and rockets are cheap compared with missiles and a much greater load of explosives can be carried on each sortie. However, delivery is most inaccurate and if the attacking aircraft wishes to stay below the radar screen, target recognition becomes well nigh impossible. Possible methods of overcoming this are to use guided bombs or some type of dispensers releasing a large number of guided bomblets. These would have no propulsive power but would have a means of being steered onto the target. This would be based on one of the above homing techniques. The bomb dispenser could be loaded with bomblets where homing and warhead characteristics were specially suitable for, say, attacks against runways or massed armour. In the latter case, some of the bomblets could be made to home onto the radiating SAMs whilst others could home onto the infra-red signature of individual tanks. In both cases it will be necessary for the dispensing aircraft to penetrate to the general area of the target and so be exposed to the enemy defences. In due course it is possible that the dispensers could be given a capability of flying to the target area after release from the parent aircraft. Cluster bombs are already in service such as the British BL755. Later introductions might include fuel air explosives where a cloud of vapourised particle is dispensed from a cluster of bomblets and then exploded by detonators released from the bomblets by small grenades. This can give a high-pressure wave over a very large area. Hence accuracy of delivery is not vitally important. Another new bomb is the British JP-233 designed to cause huge craters in runways with an associated pattern of delayed mines to interfere with runway repair activities. No details of equivalent Soviet bomblets and dispensers are available.

AIR DEFENCE

In order to attack any enemy intrusion at the earliest possible stage, the NATO powers have developed an efficient early warning system. This should indicate the size and direction of the attack in adequate time to alert and man the defences. This NADGE radar chain stretches from Norway to Turkey and is augmented by a network of ground observers. The radar system is automated as far as possible and, via a series of computers, gives details of the attack, indicates the best defensive weapon system to use, and also sites and landing fields for take-off and return to base. This latter takes into account the refuelling state, the recommended flight plan and the anticipated fuel consumption. The major problem is, as ever, one of identification. This is done by interrogating the radar with a coded signal (IFF) but it is far from foolproof. The NADGE system also suffers from the fact that it gives little coverage to the NATO southern flank, particularly in view of the considerable Soviet build-up in the Mediterranean. Furthermore, it can only detect low-flying aircraft at very short range.

These shortcomings are to some extent covered by the ground observers, but these two systems together do not, by any means, provide 100 per cent coverage. For this reason the airborne early warning system provided by AWACs and in the northern area by the British Nimrods has been introduced. These can give upwards of 200 miles warning on low-flying aircraft. The problem is that overland they detect all moving targets and so have to be set to ignore anything moving at less than 90 mph. Over the sea this setting is lowered to about 15 knots. The aircraft are very expensive both to provide and to maintain, and hence availability must always be limited.

Surface-to-air missiles

The main NATO European defences are provided by the now obsolescent Nike/Hercules and Hawk systems. The former, relying on radio command guidance, is used for high-altitude interception up to a 140-km range. The latter being a semi-active radar system is mainly used against medium altitude and low-flying targets out to some 35-km range. These systems are scheduled to be replaced by Patriot, which is reported to operate against both high and low targets with a range intermediate between the Nike/Hercules and Hawk. This new system uses both command guidance and semi-active terminal homing. In the United Kingdom the RAF aerodrome defences still rely on Bloodhound II. This is an old system with medium range and using semi-active homing. Its performance against both high- and low-flying targets is limited.

For the defence of point targets such as airfields, mobile low-level SAMs are required. A considerable selection of these is available to the NATO powers. Typical examples are Rapier made by British Aerospace, and Roland II produced by Aérospatiale and MBB and under licence in the United States. In addition to these vehicle-mounted weapons, there is a considerable number of man-portable weapons such as the US Redeye and Stinger and the British Blow Pipe. These use either infra-red, optical or laser homing. Fast crossing targets present a most difficult sighting problem, and detection range against low-flying targets is severely limited by physical obstructions. A target coming in at 50 m is unlikely to be detected in time to give more than some 15 sec for activation.

The USSR and the Warsaw Pact countries are particularly well equipped with most efficient SAMs ranging from SAM 1s, 2s, 3s, 4s, 5s and 10s. The first two rely on radio command guidance. The SAM 3s and 4s use semi-active radar, SAM 5 infra-red and the SAM 10s active radar. They thus provide a very formidable combination. They are available in large numbers and will undoubtedly provide a very formidable opposition to NATO aircraft.

Interceptor aircraft

Aircraft continue to be one of the most satisfactory means of air defence. They can be used both against the initial penetration and also in a melée situation which might develop as some of the intruders evade the first attack. The initial attack will usually be under ground control from the operational centres. The possibility of using data link control directly from NADGE is still under investigation. Speed, rate of climb and manoeuvrability are vital characteristics for the defensive fighter. Although the F104s, the F4s and the Lightnings are now inferior to the latest Soviet types, they still have a considerable interception capability when armed with the latest guided missiles. This should be adequate to deal with the new Soviet bombers such as Backfire and fighter bombers such as Fencer and Flogger. NATO will certainly require improved performance aircraft such as the F15, the Tornado ADV and the F16 (should the latter be equipped for air defence). Foxbat will be faster than anything in service with the NATO forces.

Air-to-air missiles

As already stated the performance of current interceptor fighters, attacking bombers and fighter bombers and ground-attack aircraft is such that guided missile armament is essential to successful defence. The interceptor fighter must be able to deal with an intruding stream of bombers, be able to turn and attack a second time and capable of participating in a mêlée situation. Manoeuvrability of the aircraft and flexibility of the weapon system are therefore of the greatest importance. Ideally all weapons should be of the 'launch and forget' variety giving the aircraft full freedom of manoeuvre after launch either to break off and evade or to attack a second and possibly a third target. The objective is to maximise the chances of a successful shot whilst minimising the defensive fighter's exposure time per shot.

Apart from TV and anti-radiation homing, all types of guidance discussed under tactical air-to-surface missiles can be used for air-to-air missiles. Even anti-radiation can be used as an ECCM measure. At this time only infra-red gives a real 'fire and forget' capability. Furthermore, being entirely passive it is difficult, although not entirely impossible, for the enemy to produce countermeasures against it. However, infra-red missiles are not satisfactory in cloud or heavy rain. Infra-red missiles can be made to be self-launching— that is, the pilot is only required to press an 'enabling' button and then the missiles are launched automatically when the signals presented to the heads give maximum chance of successful interception.

A major problem is caused by sun or cloud reflection and, unless this is solved satisfactorily, some form of pilot override is essential. This greatly detracts from the self launch capability; greatly increasing the reaction time because of the need to generate an audio or visual indication of 'lock-on target'. As far as is known only in the British Red Top weapon has this problem been successfully solved.

The other problem is for the head to deal with 'sight line spin' that is, the effects of rapidly changing aiming angles particularly associated with crossing targets. Current infra-red missiles are quite capable of dealing with head-on targets, particularly if the target speed is high, but the older weapons are restricted to the tail chase situation. Infra-red missiles can give either a 'shoot-up' or 'shoot-down' capability providing the design of the head is capable of dealing with direct or reflected sunlight and providing the infra-red signal of the low-level target is sufficient to attract the missile head away from other ground heat sources.

Both Warsaw Pact powers and NATO countries have infra-red missiles in their inventories but it is believed that the UK missiles are further advanced than those of Soviet or US design.

Semi-active radar missiles

These have exactly the same capability as similar air-to-ground weapons. Identification of targets is generally more easy than in the air-to-ground case, providing satisfactory IFF can be given. In the case of low-flying targets it is essential that both the aircraft radar used to direct the illuminating beam and the missile are capable of detecting targets through ground clutter. We have noted the limitation of radars in the earlier intercepts. In the case of the missile only the British Skyflash is known to have this capability. The versions of the US Sparrow now in development should also be capable of use in a 'shoot down' situation.

As already mentioned, the other limitation of the semi-active radar missiles is that the attacking aircraft must continue to illuminate the target throughout the missile flight. This creates a major if not impossible problem in close combat or melée situations, and also in the case where the interceptor and the target have a very considerable altitude difference. It also means that in general only one target can be engaged at a time. This last limitation should be overcome with the introduction of aircraft radars having a 'track whilst scan' capability such as in the F15 and Tornado ADV. Apart from the advantage of the British Skyflash missile in the shoot-down situations, there is thought to be little to choose between the NATO and Soviet missiles.

Long-range missiles

The concept of an air-to-air missile which could be launched at really long range and at targets with considerable up or down altitude differentials is very attractive. The missiles would be launched at targets in excess of a 100-mile range and many thousands of feet in height differential. With such weapons, combat patrols could be carried out at normal economical cruise height and also the immunity given to low-flying targets could be considerably reduced. Unfortunately, we again come up against the target identification problem. Unless one is prepared to adopt an 'open-sky' policy, the value of such long-range missiles must be considerably limited if not, indeed, prohibited. The United States has such a weapon, the Phoenix, now in service with the USN F14s. With this system multiple launches (subject to IFF) are possible and as many as 6 missiles can be launched in quick succession against 6 different targets. The weapon performance is, of course, entirely proscribed by the capability of the radar in the launching aircraft both in detection range and look up/look down capability. The Soviets are believed to have both Ash and AIR D missiles in this category although the attributable ranges are considerably less than those for Phoenix.

Warheads

At this time all air-to-air weapons use high explosive warheads with proximity fuses. These latter may be infra-red or radar activated. Accurate homing and fusing are essential if such warheads are to guarantee a kill, since the amount of HE which can be carried is limited. However, quite small damage in the right area can totally disable an aircraft. In order to improve the kill probability, the expanding rod has been adopted in most of the later missiles. Focused fragmentation and multishaped charges have also been introduced. The warhead requirement is, of course, in inverse ratio to the homing accuracy. Even a .303 bullet can totally frustrate an intruder missile providing it can be delivered with absolute accuracy. Given such accuracy, future missiles may in fact become real 'hitches' and be able to dispose of the HE warhead altogether, relying entirely on their own mass and kinetic energy.

SUMMARY

It is certain that at this time the Warsaw Pact countries will be able to outnumber the NATO forces in all operational roles. Although the NATO countries have weapon systems of greater sophistication and technical capability, it is doubtful if these advantages are adequate to redress the balance of numbers. Furthermore, unless the Western powers are prepared to increase defence spending appreciably, these advantages are likely to be rapidly eroded. President Reagan has indicated an increase in the US defence budget but the other NATO powers are inclined to reduce rather than increase defence expenditure in real terms. Even with a real determination by NATO to invest in defence, it is probable that the Warsaw Pact will have a superior capability in all air force activities. Even an immediate increase in defence spending would leave the NATO forces lagging in the immediate future, although if correctly directed, it might redress the balance in, say, 10 years' time by major improvements in technical sophistication.

STRATEGIC STUDIES

Future Trends in Airborne Weapons Systems

F W THOMPSON

Air Commodore F W Thompson, CBE, DSO, DFC, AFC, BSc, RAF (Retd) left the RAF after a distinguished career to join the aircraft industry. He has recently retired from Aerospace Dynamics where he was Director of Air Weapons

GENERAL TRENDS

Any examination of future trends in weaponry has to be based on an analysis of the primary driving forces, likely development in the threat and in both economic climate and political will. The advances of Western technology in the military field will clearly be constrained by these factors in relation to the availability of funds for research and for development and production of new equipment, but, in addition, the type of weapons that are required will be modified by the balance in quality and quantity between the forces of the East and West.

It bears repetition that the Warsaw Pact enjoys considerable numerical advantage over NATO both in ground and air forces, not least in the vital Northern and Central European theatres. Even now it would be essential for NATO air forces to attempt to redress the balance on the ground, both by direct offensive and by providing air cover, in the face of superior numbers of aircraft mostly dedicated to air combat. Nevertheless, there is no sign of any slackening of the relentless build-up of Warsaw Pact forces, a build-up of numbers which is increasingly being accompanied by markedly greater quality. Indeed, the build-up might appear to be self-perpetuating as the Soviet Services carry increasing political weight as they expand. The difficulties of redeployment into civilian work in the Eastern Bloc and the inevitable drop in living standards which would ensue must make the prospect of a reversal in the present trend very unattractive to Soviet military men. For whatever the reason the Soviet build-up seems certain to continue for some years yet.

Against this, Western nations are still sliding deeper into recession with little sign of improvement. This has the effect of reducing the collective GNP and at the same time sapping the political will to allocate a sufficiently high proportion of it to defence. The end result seems likely to involve pruning of front-line forces while also cutting back both research and development of equipment which might still provide adequate capability in the future.

In summary, we face the prospect of increasing East to West imbalance in the numbers of both air- and ground-borne fighting machines due to the West's financial and ideological inability to match the Warsaw Pact's military expenditure. The only hope for containment appears, therefore, to lie with the development of weapons which can provide greatly increased fire-power at the same or less cost than existing ones. This, then, has to be the pattern for future Western weaponry in the foreseeable future. Improvements in technical performance and reliability must play their part in this, but the aim must be effectiveness against large numbers at low cost rather than technical wizardry for its own sake.

Weapon systems, i.e. aircraft plus weapons, will have to be designed from the outset with low cost as a major aim. One such avenue to lower cost will be to design complete integrated weapon systems to take the most advantage of individual system performance as a contribution to the whole. We shall no longer be able to afford the over-designing inherent in piecemeal developments put together as completed items.

Nowhere will the advantages of integration be more pronounced than in respect of electronic warfare, i.e. countermeasures and counter-countermeasures. The sheer density of threats to aircraft penetrating the Central European theatre will necessitate rapid, accurate but economical response to ensure survival. With the pilot already heavily loaded, such instant but efficient management of countermeasure power and disposables will only be achieved by close integration of systems for detection and response aided by at least a degree of automation. Here again, low cost should be achievable by careful tailoring of the system to the task and even by adjusting tactics to favour lower cost systems.

The major influence in recent years in civil electronics, large-scale integrated circuitry and the microprocessor has yet to make its full impact on the military scene. It is an industry which thrives on quantity production, and military requirements do not bear comparison with the vast commercial market. Furthermore, military demands are more stringent, particularly in respect of environment. However, perhaps the biggest factor is the length of the development cycle for complex weapons, those currently in production were designed while integrated circuit electronics was comparatively in its infancy. What is certain, however, is that this technology will have a profound effect on military electronics and nowhere more so than in aviation. The vast increase in computing power in lower weight, volume and cost could revolutionise airborne weapon system performance and may be the major instrument in providing the badly needed increase in fire-power at minimum cost.

AIR DEFENCE

In Europe NATO interceptor aircraft are outnumbered by their Warsaw Pact counterparts by 5 to 1. Although this high figure is in part due to a difference in equipment balance in the two opposing air forces, there remains a 2 to 1 ratio even when all operational tactical aircraft are included. High fire-power has to be the aim.

In the context of air defence, high fire-power implies carriage of large numbers of air-to-air missiles, each with high performance and multitarget engagement capability together with the ability in the aircraft to make optimum use of its weapons in a severe environment. Advancement of ECM and ECCM installations and techniques will be fundamental. There will be much to be gained by relating tactics to the hardware from the onset to avoid the cost and weight penalties of over-design, although flexibility must always remain a great asset against a superior force which is also largely dictating the very nature of the battle by initiating the offensive.

Reduction in the size, mass and installed drag of air-to-air weapons is an obvious route to increased weapon loads. Without doubt, advances in technology, particularly in electronics packaging and miniaturisation, will be capable of considerable, even dramatic, reductions in weight and size of future air-to-air weapons for a given performance. It may be necessary, however, to tread a careful path between small, simple weapons in quantity and the temptation to build in the greatly increased complexity which will be possible, albeit at a size and, more significantly, cost premium. However, current advances in technology are such that the small weapon of the future may still greatly out-perform existing hardware.

Integration of missiles and aircraft, preferably at the design stage, is likely to be another powerful factor in increasing weapon load. Mechanical integration can reduce installed drag, which is usually a greater embarrassment than weight, while functional integration can reduce missile complexity by delegating more of the normal missile functions, particularly during the acquisition phase, to the parent aircraft.

A large weapon load will be of little use unless the total weapon system is designed to enable it to be brought to bear on the threat.

The problem of target identification beyond visual range, particularly in the dense EW environment expected in any European conflict remains and may continue to remain essentially unresolved. Indeed, even reliable target detection in this environment will require greater sophistication, most probably by the coordination of multiple passive and active sensing devices, electro-optical and radio, with automatic processing and threat assessment.

The net effect of these difficulties will be to require rapid reaction, agility and high speed from the missile system. 'Fire and forget' capability will be essential. Target information may be late and require the missile to take out targets widely spaced in altitude and azimuth with little or no dynamic assistance from the launch aircraft. At the opposite extreme, targets may be seeking a measure of mutual protection in close formation, requiring the missiles themselves to discriminate and ideally to attack them selectively.

It is clear that in order to extract the maximum advantage of high fire-power against greater numbers, the exchange of fire should be achieved without getting drawn into close combat.

Once at close quarters, it is almost impossible to disengage without first destroying your opponents, but, even more significantly, numbers become more crucial. Superior numbers, even of inferior aircraft, are likely to become dominant. Future Western airborne weapon systems are therefore likely to be designed to bias engagements away from close combat.

It does not follow that future Western aircraft will not carry close combat weapons. For one thing the necessary qualities of such weapons—rapid response, agility, high thrust (for manoeuvre) and all aspects of engagement capability—will equip them well for a major role in the many-target, short- to medium-range engagement; a missile with the power of thrust to execute major manoeuvres will have a considerable range potential in a low manoeuvre engagement. Also it may prove impossible to avoid getting caught in close combat without giving ground if the opponent seeks it.

An impressive capability of aircraft and missile in close combat may be necessary for survival but also may serve to deter the opposition from engaging in it—although admittedly the logic of the latter comment is somewhat ambiguous.

High aircraft agility and thrust-to-weight ratio has been a recent trend towards close combat capability in fighter aircraft design, and this may be expected to continue. Fully active control will lead to increases in agility and to controlled flight in dramatic incidence attitudes in the interests of weapon delivery. A trend to all digital electronics based on LSI techniques will facilitate this and provide great assistance to the pilot by work-load reduction due to sensor coordination, computation, data presentation and automation.

There is great potential for improvement in short-range missile capability relative to current hardware. Enhanced agility, high off-boresight angle (between launch direction and target), all aspect engagement and reduced reaction time will greatly increase firing opportunities both in single and multiple combat; off-boresight angles of up to and even in excess of 90° should be achievable if tactics require it and cost permits. Indeed, it is conceivable that, in time, increases in missile performance could render close combat unattractive to either combatant—provided, of course, each carries close combat missiles.

One of the perennial problems for the pilot in close combat has been that of estimating, in a high stress situation, important target parameters with sufficient accuracy to ensure launch of his missiles within their successful firing zone. In the past many apparent missile failures have been for this very reason, and the problem still persists. The great computing power which will be available in future aircraft is likely to be harnessed to this problem. Potential targets can be assessed for the threat they present and missile success predictions made by rapid computation of simplified mathematical models of one's own and of hostile missiles. The information could be presented as a simple priority and go/no go indication or could provide the basis for fully automated missile firings.

STRIKE/INTERDICTION

The task of attacking vital targets in the area behind the battle zone also raises the problem of numerical supremacy of Warsaw Pact forces, although here the emphasis moves to their ground-borne anti-air weapons. The density of overlapping anti-air firepower, which the modern Soviet ground forces carry with them, is now well known and the effectiveness of these weapons, even to the limited standard they are prepared to export, has been demonstrated.

Future years will probably see both improvement in quality and increase in numbers of such weapons with a bias to quick reaction and low altitude effectiveness. Both the forward edge of the battle area (FEBA) and areas around vital targets will be formidable obstacles for penetrating aircraft. In addition, Soviet interception aircraft will increasingly be given a look-down/shoot-down capability further to deny today's relative safety in flying ultra low and fast.

What, then, will be the West's response to these developments? Currently two main routes for future development seem to lie in the balance, although in the cause of compromise both may well be followed in the shorter term. Essentially, the possible adoption of pilotless, stand-off weapons for the penetration of heavily defended areas offers an attractive alternative to pressing home attacks with manned aircraft. To extract the most advantage the stand-off range would need to allow launch from west of the FEBA since this is a major threat area. Possibly the logic might even lead to ground launch, although, as discussed below, there are obvious advantages in air launch.

The technology developed for the nuclear cruise missile points a clear path for the development of conventional warhead weapons for interdiction. Small, very low-flying weapons may have a higher survivability than manned aircraft and by using terrain following and scene-matching techniques still be very accurate over the target area. Either unitary or multiple bomblet warheads could be carried and laid with great accuracy.

The arguments for SOMs versus manned penetrating aircraft centre mainly around total system operational costs to achieve the tactical objective, but a major factor must be the saving in that most valuable of commodities—pilots. Current indications, however, are that against the anticipated high attrition rates the SOM will provide the more cost-effective solution. The attrition rates are a powerful factor in the analysis.

Given sufficient range capability in the SOM, ground launch, or even ship launch, becomes an alternative possibility; air launch, however, shows a number of advantages. Air launch offers a high degree of operational flexibility and quick reaction, together with the ability to optimise trajectories (hi-hi, hi-lo, lo-lo), to suit the prevailing conditions. None of these could be achieved so readily with ground launch. The operational airfield from which the launch aircraft operates shares risks which are no different from those expected for main aircraft attack, and the vulnerability of the launch aircraft in flight can be minimised by tactics and flight profile. Fixed sites for ground-launch missiles are vulnerable to enemy reconnaissance, allowing the positioning of SAM sites to attack the missiles early in flight. Mobile ground launchers require considerable logistic support both in men and materials and are still vulnerable.

The enemy could still react to position his defences in the same time scale as the launch sites are moved. Further, all ground-launched missiles require boost motors, adding to their cost.

In the short term SOMs will probably be launched from strike aircraft: not only will these be in existence, but the option for manned penetration remains open. In the longer term larger load-carrying aircraft may prove more effective, but it may be necessary for the role to be designed as an option from the outset. Studies for conversion of existing cargo aircraft do now show it to be cost effective.

There is certainly much scope for improving the survivability of manned aircraft in a penetration role, and much attention to this is expected, particularly in the shorter term. Specialised weapons for defence suppression could enable 'safe' corridors to be cleared through the defences both for penetration of the FEBA and in the target area. A sophisticated mix of ECM and 'shoot back' weapons may enable the aircraft to combat successfully the ground missile sites, although the complexity of ECM and weapon mix and the high threat density would inevitably require integrated computer-managed systems in order to ensure instant threat evaluation, response and — just as important — economy of dispensable stores.

Against the look-down/shoot-down interception aircraft, the interdiction will require a high-performance self-defence weapon with good range, agility and off-boresight capability.

Although it is sometimes taken for granted, the survivability of the SOM itself needs careful evaluation and protection. Current cruise missile concepts rely on stealth and ability to fly under defences, a freedom which could be rapidly eroded by improvements in defensive systems. Consideration must be given to maintaining SOM survivability in future generations, either by speed or by carrying its own defences in the form of ECM and perhaps shoot-back missiles.

BATTLEFIELD SUPPORT

The primary role of strike aircraft in the battlefield will continue to be the attempt to redress the numerical balance in armoured fighting vehicles. The Warsaw Pact currently enjoys an advantage of over 2½ to 1 in main battle tanks in Northern and Central Europe, and there is nothing to suggest that this will decrease in the foreseeable future.

Air cover must also be provided to a greater extent than currently if NATO forces are to have adequate daytime mobility, but this is the province of the air defence fighter.

The strength of Warsaw Pact air defence systems over the battlefield is again a major factor placing a severe limitation on flight time over the area. In order to make any inroad into the sheer number of WP tanks, high fire-power rapidly employed is essential. Before that fire-power can be effectively employed, significant advances in avionics will be required. In difficult conditions tanks will need to be identified rapidly and accurately with little assistance from the pilot who will be otherwise heavily loaded. Hope may lie in multisensor systems combining electro-optical devices with radar, long wavelength and millimetric, the latter offering potential for all weather operation.

An alternative approach to direct-fire weapons are the indirect systems which have been gaining favour in the United States although Europe seems much less enthusiastic. The approach is to saturate the area around a known tank concentration with smart bomblets and mini-missiles. It relies heavily on intelligence of tank concentrations and the discrimination capabilities of the miniature guidance/detection systems but minimises exposure of the launch aircraft.

The helicopter armed with anti-tank weapons appears to offer an alternative to the fixed-wing aircraft in the battle zone, but its much lower speed and greater vulnerability when exposed probably points to a complementary role rather than an alternative. The fixed-wing aircraft will have greater speed of response and flexibility of target selection.

Reduction of the second echelon forces may prove to be the most important role of air attack. Major problems here relate to intelligence of movement and concentrations. It will be essential to develop systems to provide data on this area which are not stale before they can be acted upon. Speed will be of the essence in provisioning and processing data and in the subsequent strike if the disposition of targets is to be accurately anticipated.

MARITIME

In their sea and naval air forces the Soviet Union has placed a

major emphasis on very long-range missile capability and
multiple-launch platforms. It deploys impressive fleets of modern
ships and aircraft armed with stand-off weapons having ranges
measured in hundreds of kilometres. They are known to favour
saturation attack tactics against which a purely defensive posture
is unlikely to prove fully effective. Soviet development in this
capability is likely to be 'more of the same or better', i.e. a greater
number of launch platforms with similar and higher performance, speed, accuracy, countermeasures, etc.

To predict future Western developments, one must first
analyse the current capability and the scenario likely to be
fought.

In the event of a major East—West war, troop and material
reinforcements would have to be brought from North America to
Europe by sea. The ships would be particularly vulnerable to
attack by Soviet submarines, surface ships and naval aircraft. The
task of the Royal Navy would be to protect this shipping in the
North Atlantic and particularly in the area between Iceland,
Norway and the Faeroes.

Ships of the North Atlantic Fleet would be supported by
Nimrod, Phantom, Tornado and Sea Harrier aircraft. The
primary objective of the Nimrod aircraft will be to maintain
surveillance of the movements of Russian submarines. The
AWACS version of the Nimrod will similarly keep watch on the
movements of Russian naval aircraft and surface ships. Neither of
these aircraft is currently armed. Both are vulnerable to air
attack by long-range fighters and to Russian surface-to-air
missiles.

Neither currently has the capability to attack any enemy aircraft or surface ships they may detect, nor can Nimrod currently
attack submarines, though the air-launched Stingray torpedo
should facilitate short-range attacks in the future.

The Fleet is subject to air attacks from Bear, launching long-
range missiles and directing missiles from surfaced submarines
and ships. Air defence against the launching and surveillance aircraft would currently be provided by Phantom and Tornado aircraft flying from Leuchars in Scotland. These aircraft are currently armed with four Skyflash and two Sidewinder missiles. The
aircraft must fly CAP above the Fleet, but after their long flight
out their endurance on patrol is low.

In the future, Tornado will be armed with Sea Eagle to supplement the ship-borne Exocet surface-to-surface missiles. These
weapons are basically defensive. They can attack ship borne

weapon systems and may immobilise the Russian ship, but are unlikely to sink any but the smallest craft.

In the near future, Sea Harriers armed with air-to-air missiles will supplement the longer-range air defence. Point and area defence of the Navy is provided by Sea Wolf and Sea Dart missiles.

Future development of airborne naval armament must be directed to provide a more effective strike capability against the Soviet launch platforms both in the air and on the sea to pre-empt the saturation attack or at least to force it to be mounted from extreme range. If the stand-off weapons have to be launched at extreme range and any update from surveillance aircraft can be denied, then the spatial and timing coordination required for a saturation attack will not be achievable and the accuracy of individual missiles will be severely degraded.

Because of the numbers involved, high fire-power must clearly be an important future trend, but in the maritime case this will need to be allied to long range. In the interests of range and flexibility, the airborne weapon system offers clear advantage, but the use of land-based aircraft appears to be less than ideal in terms of initial response time and endurance on patrol. The VSTOL aircraft, Harrier and future developments of it, appears to offer a much more effective solution in the longer term. They will, however, need to be deployed in sufficient numbers and be armed with suitable light weight but long-range missiles.

There are problems in providing such VSTOL aircraft with a really high-speed capability, although in such long-range engagements average speed will be important. The objective will be to attack the enemy launch platforms before they release their weapons. It may be more cost effective to place the onus for the high average speed on the guided missile. Developments in compact ramjet motors are being geared to the provision of high velocity and long range within compact dimensions.

Anti-ship weapons are inevitably going to be much larger than air-to-air weapons if only because of the need for a large warhead. High fire-power with such weapons entails a large launch platform or at least a large load carrier. Strikes against ships are going to be at least as important as against air targets, and air launch offers very desirable increase in range and flexibility. Sadly, economic constraints in the United Kingdom may limit the deployment of suitable aircraft in adequate numbers apart from land-based aircraft such as Nimrod or Tornado.

BROAD CONCLUSIONS

In all of these scenarios the most important future trend has to be to counter the numerical supremacy of the Warsaw Pact with equipment that the West will be able to afford. Basically this must mean a search for much higher fire-power but at no greater cost than current systems. At the same time survivability of systems has to be enhanced in the face of great odds.

A major key to this is likely to be the impact of large-scale integrated electronics on airborne weapon systems, but this will need to be accompanied by intelligent application of strong determination to develop low-cost designs.

Towards a Grand Strategy for Global Freedom
FOREWORD BY LORD HOME OF
THE HIRSEL KT, PC
Edited by Geoffrey Stewart-Smith   £5 or $10

They Mean What They Say
A COMPILATION OF SOVIET STATEMENTS
ON IDEOLOGY, FOREIGN POLICY AND THE
USE OF MILITARY FORCE
by Ian Greig   £5 or $10

The Price of Peace
A PLAIN MAN'S GUIDE TO CURRENT
DEFENCE ISSUES
by Brian Crozier   £1 or $2

The Struggle for Freedom
A BRITISH CONTRIBUTION TOWARDS THE
FORMULATION OF A GRAND STRATEGY
FOR THE DEFENCE OF THE FREE WORLD
by Geoffrey Stewart-Smith   £3 or $8

The Ultra-Left Offensive against the Multinational Companies
MOSCOW'S CALL FOR WORLD TRADE
UNION UNITY
by Ian Greig   £3 or $8

Inside the KGB
AN EXPOSE BY AN OFFICER OF THE THIRD
DIRECTORATE
by Alexsel Myagkov   £3 or $8

The Communist Challenge to Africa
AN ANALYSIS OF CONTEMPORARY SOVIET,
CUBAN AND CHINESE POLICIES
by Ian Greig   £3 or $8

SEND FOR A FREE CATALOGUE
Foreign Affairs Publishing Co. Ltd.
139 Petersham Road, Richmond, Surrey TW10 7AA

The Far East: Notes on Maritime and Air Forces

GENERAL

The region described as the Far East is a huge area stretching 5000 miles north and south from China to Australia, and 4500 miles west to east from Thailand to New Zealand. The peoples who inhabit the area number more than 1450 million including 1000 million in China. The standard of life and levels of industrial development vary tremendously across the region and within societies. Japan is looked upon as an industrial giant; Taiwan and South Korea have made great strides; and Singapore and Malaysia continue to develop economically. The importance of internal stability of individual countries is obvious but, equally, good relations between states will be the key to continued progress. There are problems to be faced in the resolution of disputes over rights to fishing and sea-bed resources. The free passage of seaborne trade is of particular significance in an area which has a history of piracy and smuggling. Japan is almost wholly dependent upon oil from the Arabian area, and a measure of the general shipping commitment is the fact that Singapore sees one ship every 12 minutes day and night throughout the year. The USSR has acquired a considerable role in Far Eastern commerce with Europe through the development of her merchant fleet and the capacity of the Trans-Siberian Railway. It has been thought appropriate, therefore, to discuss briefly the capabilities of the navies and air forces in the region.

REGIONAL AGREEMENTS

An important factor bearing on the current capabilities and potential developments of many of the armed forces of the Far East is the political circumstance of their origin and of their likely future support. Many aid programmes have already been, and new ones will no doubt continue to be, involved in these matters. A number of bilateral and multilateral agreements, which link many of the countries concerned with some of the more powerful

BD' - U

countries of the East and West, form part of the equation. Before, therefore, looking at the present status and possible future of individual forces it will be beneficial to make a brief review of the overriding political and financial factors.

The United States has had bilateral defence treaties and agreements with Australia, Indonesia, Japan, Taiwan, the Republic of Korea (South) and the Philippines. The agreement with Taiwan lapsed on 1 January 1980, although some arms supply and production arrangements continue. Under several other arrangements in the region the United States provides military aid on either grant or credit basis to Indonesia, South Korea, Malaysia, the Philippines and Thailand, and also sells military equipment to many countries, notably Australia, Japan and South Korea. The United States has major bases in Japan, South Korea and the Philippines.

The 1973 Diego Garcia Agreement between the British and American governments provides for the development of the US naval communications facility on the island into a US Naval Support Facility. This is now being objected to by the Government of Mauritius.

The Soviet Union has treaties of friendship, cooperation and mutual assistance with Bangladesh, Mongolia, the Democratic People's Republic of Korea (North) and Vietnam. Military assistance agreements exist with Sri Lanka.

Australia has supplied defence equipment to Singapore and Indonesia and has a defence aid agreement with Malaysia.

In July 1977 Vietnam and Laos signed a series of agreements which contained military provisions and a border pact and appeared to have covered the stationing of Vietnamese troops in Laos. A similar series of agreements seems to have been negotiated between Vietnam and Kampuchea following the recent change in the ruling régime in the latter country.

In 1955 the South-East Asia Collective Defence Treaty brought the treaty organisation (SEATO) into being. In 1975 the SEATO Council decided to phase the organisation out and it was formally closed on 30 June 1977.

Australia, New Zealand and the United States are members of a tripartite treaty known as ANZUS, which was signed in 1951 and is of indefinite duration. Under this treaty, each country agrees to act to meet a common danger in the event of an attack on either metropolitan or island territory of any one of them or on armed forces, public vessels or aircraft in the Pacific.

Five-power Defence Arrangements, relating to the defence of

Malaysia and Singapore and involving Australia, Malaysia, New Zealand, Singapore and Britain, came into effect on 1 November 1971. These arrangements stated that in the event of any externally organised or supported armed attack or threat of attack against Malaysia or Singapore, the five governments would consult together for the purpose of deciding what measures should be taken jointly or separately. Britain withdrew her forces from Singapore (by 31 March 1976) except for a small contribution to the integrated air defence system. New Zealand troops remained, as did Australian air forces, in Malaysia.

The Association of South-East Asian Nations is not a military organisation: its objectives are essentially economic, although it has declared that it wishes South-East Asia to be recognised as a zone of peace, neutrality and freedom, free from interference by outside powers. Its five nations — Thailand, Malaysia, Singapore, Indonesia and the Philippines — cover a vast area, over 2000 miles from north to south and 3000 miles from west to east, in the heart of the Far East. They have over 20,000 islands with some 260 million people and many thousands of miles of coastline. ASEAN occupies the major strategic portion of all at the centre through which a great volume of shipping must pass. It is also an important source of raw materials. The Association has already established a favourable reputation for its economic progress, and estimates of the economic prospects of the member states are very hopeful.

POLITICO-STRATEGIC FACTORS

The most significant strategic factor is the change in the maritime balance of power. Three elements have contributed to this change; firstly, the enlargement of the Soviet Navy's capability for worldwide deployments; secondly, the diversion of US naval forces to the Indian Ocean; and, thirdly, the withdrawal of the Royal Navy's resident contribution to the free world navies in the area. The Soviet deployments are not only more versatile in character, but are also drawn from a navy which has been rapidly increasing in numbers. By contrast, the US Navy's carrier task forces are found from naval resources which have been considerably reduced in recent years.

The ideological dispute between Soviet imperial communism and the People's Republic of China is a major influence on the mainland. Vietnam is a thorn in China's side and a spectre of aggression looming over the peaceful development of ASEAN.

New relationships are being forged between China and the West, but the problem of Taiwan remains an irritant in relations with the United States. Economic support for Vietnam is one of the drains on the feeble Soviet economy in addition to the arms transfers which are the only form of aid in which the USSR indulges. The parallel case is Cuba, and it is a sinister thought that the two principal surrogates of the Soviet Union lurk on the borders of her principal rivals. A quirk of history is the renewed Russian naval presence at Cam Ramh Bay 75 years after the visitation before the Battle of Tsushima.

One other ingredient in the politico-strategic situation is the Islamic revival. Without magnifying the prospect of Moslem unity versus the world, the strength of Islamic influence in the Far East area cannot be disregarded. For example, the Soviet action in Afghanistan, US policies in the Gulf area and Western relationships with African states are likely to be viewed with particular attention.

Australia

The Royal Australian Navy has a personnel strength of 16,000 including the Air Arm. It consists of 6 *Oberon* Class submarines, 1 aircraft carrier, 11 destroyers/frigates and a small number of MSMV and patrol craft.

The Royal Australian Air Force has a personnel strength of 21,000 and consists of 2 SR squadrons of F111s, 3 interceptor squadrons of Mirage 1110, 2 maritime reconnaissance squadrons, 5 transport squadrons which include C130 and DHC-4 aircraft, and Chinook and Iroquois helicoptors.

The economic importance of Australia is growing very rapidly although the population is still small for such a large territorial area. Her defence needs are difficult to assess, but it seems likely that Australia may wish to play a larger role in the politico-strategic affairs of the Indian Ocean. The significance of the security of seaborne commerce will command increasing attention.

Brunei

The naval element of the Brunei forces is provided by the Royal Brunei Malay Regiment 1st Flotilla and consists of Waspada fast attack craft and Perwira coastal craft, some river craft and some amphibious vessels.

The air element consists of a small number of fixed and rotary wing transport/communication aircraft.

China, The People's Republic of (PRC)

The naval forces of the PRC have a personnel strength of 360,000 including the Air Arm. It consists of 80 patrol submarines, 19 destroyers/frigates and no less than 800 fast attack craft. There is a small force of MCMV, considering the possible mine warfare tasks, and a number of landing ships and craft.

The Air Force has a personnel strength of 400,000 and consists of about 400 bomber aircraft of Soviet origin and over 4000 fighter aircraft including Soviet and US types. There is a large transport force. Fighter defences are supplemented by a small number of SAMs and a very large number of AAA pieces.

The conflict of ideology with the Soviet Union and the need to restrain the ambition of the Kremlin leaders and their supporters in Vietnam call for strong defence dispositions by the PRC. The economic situation and the strength to develop the necessary industrial strength make it unlikely that the PRC can afford to modernise and increase the equipment of her forces in the immediate future. The maritime situation in the China Seas will be of particular interest in maintaining freedom of action.

Indonesia

Indonesia occupies a position of crucial strategic importance stretching 3000 miles across the sea approaches to the Far East. Her navy has a strength of 39,000 and consists of 4 submarines, 11 frigates, 12 missile or torpedo armed fast attack craft and 24 patrol craft. There is a considerable amphibious capability and a small naval air arm of 2 maritime squadrons, including Nomads and a number of helicopters.

The Indonesian Air Force has a personnel strength of about 25,000 and consists of 3 FGA squadrons, a Coin squadron of OV-10F Bronco aircraft, a transport force of mixed composition and 2 helicopter squadrons of Bell 2043 and Pumas. A considerable number of operational and training aircraft is on order together with more Pumas.

It is to be hoped that the current trend to seek aircraft for the re-equipment of the force from free world sources will continue. UK Hawk trainers are among aircraft on order and F16 and F5G are possible acquisitions from the United States.

Japan

The size and character of the Japanese Self-defence Forces is dictated by the continuing thrust of post-war policy, and the proportion of the GDP devoted to defence remains below 1 per cent. Nonetheless, the Maritime Self-defence Force has a strength of about 54,000 including the air arm, and consists of 13 submarines, more than 50 destroyers and frigates, together with a strong force of minesweepers and patrol craft.

The Air Force, although limited by the Peace Treaty, is potentially one of the most powerful in the region. It has a personnel strength of 44,000 and consists of 13 FGA and interceptor squadrons, including F1 and ATF-86F aircraft. There is a reconnaissance squadron of RF-AE aircraft, 3 transport squadrons of 7S-11 and 30 C-1A, and 11 training squadrons. The search and rescue wing consists of 23 MUD-2, 8 T-34A and 34 helicopters. More fighter aircraft are on order and 4 AEW are among other fixed and rotary wing accessions which are understood to be planned. There is a comprehensive air defence ground environment including 6 SAM groups equipped with Nike J missiles.

Pressure is likely to be kept up to encourage the Japanese Government to take a larger part in the defence of free world maritime interests.

Kampuchea

Kampuchea has no air forces at present, and the status of naval forces is uncertain.

Korea—Democratic People's Republic (North)

The North Korean Navy has a personnel strength of 27,000 and consists of 15 submarines, 4 frigates, 27 large patrol craft armed with missiles or guns and about 300 other patrol craft armed with guns or torpedoes.

The Air Force has a personnel strength of 47,000 and consists of 3 light squadrons of 85 IL-28 aircraft, 30 FGA squadrons, including 340 MiG-15/-17/-19 aircraft and 20 SU-7, 12 interceptor squadrons with 120 MiG-21 and 50 MiG-19 types. The force includes a transport element of fixed and rotary wing aircraft of Soviet origin.

Soviet influence, interest and aid is likely to keep the North Korean forces up-to-date with equipment and training.

Korea—Republic of (South)

The South Korean Navy has a personnel strength of more than 40,000 including the Marine Corps and consists of 17 destroyers/frigates of wartime or early-post war US origin. There are 18 large patrol craft, some armed with SSM, 6 corvettes and 8 AACM(V). In addition, the force includes 20 other coastal patrol craft and about 20 landing ships and craft.

The Air Force has a personnel strength of 33,000 and consists of 16 FB squadrons, 4 equipped with 60S-4 D/E aircraft, 10 with 220F-5A and 2 with F-86F aircraft. There is a reconnaissance squadron of 12 RF-5A, and an ASW squadron of 20S-2F, a mixed helicopter SAR squadron. There is a fixed-wing transport force and a mixed force of over 50 helicopters. F16, 55E and F5F fighters are on order together with more transport aircraft and helicopters.

The influence, instead of support, of the United States is likely to keep the South Korean forces up-to-date with equipment. The economic situation in the Republic may make it a source of envy to its neighbour but augurs well for the inhabitants.

Laos

The situation of the riverine force which has served the Laotian Government is uncertain.

The Air Force consists of 1 FGA squadron, 20 Coin aircraft, a transport force and a mixed force of helicopter transports and gunships.

The strategic position of Laos makes it a likely candidate for Soviet attention as a base for activities against China and in the South Asian Peninsula area generally.

Malaysia

The Royal Malaysian Navy has a personnel strength of about 6000 and consists of 2 frigates, 14 missile and gun attack craft, 22 large patrol craft, together with some MCMV and landing ships.

The Royal Malaysian Air Force has a similar personnel strength and consists of 2 FGA squadrons, 2 Coin squadrons, 1 maritime reconnaissance squadron, 3 transport squadrons and 5 helicopter squadrons including Sikorsky S-61A4 and Aérospatiale Alouette III. MBB BO-105 helicopters are reported to be on order.

The importance of Malaysia in the South China Sea and its approaches and the moral influence of the kingdom in conjunction with that of the Republic of Singapore suggests that the efforts of United Kingdom, the United States and Australia will be concentrated to assist in maintaining economic progress and internal stability.

The Philippines

The Navy of the Philippines has a personnel strength of 22,000 including 7000 marines and consists of 10 frigates of war-time US origins, 11 corvettes and 15 large patrol craft. There is also a large number of other patrol craft and landing ships and craft.

The Air Force has a personnel strength of 17,000 and consists of 3 FB squadrons of Northrop F-5A, 3 Coin squadrons, 1 SAR squadron and a helicopter squadron of Bell UH-1H. There are also 6 transport squadrons, a liaison squadron and a mixed force of helicopters.

The United States retains its base rights in the Philippines and is likely to encourage the development of maritime capabilities in the forces in the area against the growing Soviet naval threat.

Singapore

The naval forces of Singapore have a personnel strength of 3000 and consist of 12 missile or gun armed attack craft, 2 minesweepers and 6 LSTs.

The Air Force has a strength of about 4000 and consists of 2 FR squadrons, 2 FGA, 1 AD squadron, 1 Coin squadron and squadrons for SAR, transport and training.

Singapore occupies the key position at the entry to the South China Sea and is of high importance in politico-economic terms.

Taiwan

The naval forces of the Republic of Taiwan have a personnel strength of 35,000 and consists of 2 ex-US Guppy submarines, 33 destroyers/frigates of US origin, 3 corvettes and 10 fast attack craft gun and missile types. There is a large force of landing ships and craft and 14 MCMV.

The Air Force has a personnel strength of 67,000 and consists of 12 squadrons of fighters including 200 Northrop F-5A/E aircraft, 1 reconnaissance squadron, 3 interceptor squadrons of

Lockheed F-104G, 1 maritime squadron including Grumman S-24 Trackers, 1 SAR squadron and a substantial transport force. The equipment of the Taiwanese armed forces bedevils relationships between the People's Republic of China, the United States and Western Europe. The Netherlands are in difficulties over the projected sale of submarines and the new US administration is under firm warning about possible equipment sales to Taiwan.

Thailand

The Royal Thai Navy has a personnel strength of 20,000 and consists of 6 frigate, 6 missile fast attack craft and 21 large patrol craft. There is also a strong force of landing ships and craft and a small minesweeping force. The maritime air squadron contains Grumman S-2F and HU-16B.

The Royal Thai Air Force has a personnel strength of 43,000 and consists of 3 FGA squadrons of Northrop F5s, 7 Coin squadrons, 1 reconnaissance squadron, 3 transport squadrons including C-47 and C-123B aircraft, and more than 120 helicopters of mixed types.

Thailand, not for the first time, finds herself confronted by bellicose neighbours and a continuing Communist terrorist insurgency problem. Free world support is likely to be forthcoming, not least from her partners in ASEAN who have a particular interest in the security and stability of the kingdom.

Tables

TABLE 1 – Principal Ship-to-Ship Missiles

Name	Country	Length (metres)	Launch weight (kg)	Guidance	Range (km)	Speed	Remarks
Exocet MM38	France	5.2	735	Active radar homing Sea-skimmer	42	0.9 Mach	Fitted in RN and many other navies
Exocet MM40	France	5.65	850	Active radar homing Sea-skimmer	70+	0.9 Mach	Recent development. Tube launched
Otomat	France/Italy	4.46	770	Mid-course update and active radar homing Terminal sea-skimmer	180	0.9 Mach	Fitted in Italian and some other navies. Improved version reported under development named Briareo
Gabriel 1	Israel	3.35	395	Beam riding with active(?) radar homing or optical. Sea-skimmer	25	0.7 Mach	
Gabriel 2	Israel	3.35	490	Probably similar to Gabriel 1	36	0.7 Mach	
Gabriel 3	Israel	3.8	560	Active radar	36	Subsonic	Iranian Navy only, but also used as helicopter-to-ship missile
Sea Killer 2	Italy	4.7	300	Beam riding. Sea-skimmer	25	Transonic	
Penguin 1	Norway	3.0	340	Infra-red homing	30	0.8 Mach	
Penguin 2	Norway	?	?	Similar to Penguin 1	35+	0.8 Mach	
RB O8A	Sweden	5.73	900	Active radar homing	200?	0.85 Mach	Used for coast defence. Obsolescent
RBS 15	Sweden	4.35	770	Active radar	100	0.9 Mach	Under development for Spica class fast attack craft
SS-N-2	USSR	4.6	2275	Active radar homing	40	Subsonic	Fitted in Osa and Komar fast attack craft and Kildin destroyers. Latest versions SS-N-2B (Once known as SS-N-11)
SS-N-3	USSR	11.0	4420	Mid-course command update and active radar homing	300?	1.5 Mach	Both surface ships and submarines

TABLE 1 — *continued*

Name	Country	Length (metres)	Launch weight (kg)	Guidance	Range (km)	Speed	Remarks
SS-N-9	USSR	9.15	Large	Mid-course command update and active radar homing	270	1.5 Mach	Nanuchka class only
SS-N-12	USSR	?	Large	Probably similar to SS-N-9	450	Believed supersonic	Both surface ships and submarines. Successor to SS-N-3
SS-N-14	USSR	?	Large	?	55	?	Anti-submarine torpedo carrying missile with probable anti-ship capability
SS-N-19	USSR	?	Large	Probably active radar	500	2 Mach	Fitted in *Kirov* battlecruiser and *Oscar* submarine
Harpoon	USA	4.57	656	Active radar homing Sea-skimmer with terminal climb and bunt	90	0.9 Mach	Fitted in USN and many other navies
Tomahawk	USA	6.25?	1200?	Active radar homing	500	Subsonic	Still in development

TABLE 2 — PRINCIPAL SUBMARINE-TO-SHIP MISSILES

Name	Country	Length (metres)	Launch weight (kg)	Guidance	Range (km)	Speed	Remarks
Exocet SM 39	France	?	?	Probably similar to Exocet MM 40 using active radar homing	?	?	Reported development of Exocet probably just starting
SS-N-3	USSR	11.0	4420	Mid-course command update and active radar homing	300?	1.5 Mach	Surface launch only
SS-N-7	USSR	6.7	?	Probable active radar homing	55	1.5 Mach	Submerged launch from *Charlie* class submarines
SS-N-12	USSR	?	Large	Probably similar to SS-N-3	450	Believed supersonic	Surface ships also. Successor to SS-N-3
SS-N-19	USSR	?	Large	Probably active radar	500	2 Mach	Fitted in *Kirov* battlecruiser and *Oscar* submarine
Harpoon	USA	6.40	1051	Active radar homing. Sea-skimmer with terminal climb and bunt	110	0.9 Mach	Fitting in USN and RN

TABLE 3—PRINCIPAL SUBMARINE-TO-SUBMARINE MISSILES

Name	Country	Length (metres)	Launch weight (kg)	Guidance	Range (km)	Speed	Remarks
SS-N-15	USSR	?	?	?	35	?	Probable nuclear warhead. May also carry torpedo instead and then known as SS-N-16
Subroc	USA	6·40	1,786	Inertial pre-programmed	46–55	1+ Mach	Nuclear warhead. Operational 1965 and successor being considered

TABLE 4—PRINCIPAL SHIP-TO-SUBMARINE MISSILES

Name	Country	Length (metres)	Launch weight (kg)	Guidance	Range (km)	Speed	Remarks
Ikara	Australia	3·45	?	Radio command	24	?	Carries homing torpedo. Modified versions in service in RN and Brazilian navy
Malafon Mk 2	France	6·13	1,473	Radio command	15	0·7 Mach	Carries homing torpedo
FRAS-1	USSR	?	?	Inertial?	27	?	Probable nuclear warhead
SS-N-14	USSR	?	?	?	55	?	Carries homing torpedo
Asroc	USA	4·7	435	Ballistic	10	?	Carries Mk 46 homing torpedo or nuclear depth bomb

TABLE 5—PRINCIPAL SURFACE-TO-AIR MISSILES

Name	Country	Length (metres)	Launch weight (kg)	Guidance	Range (km)	Speed	Remarks
Masurca Mk 2	France	8·60	1,817	Semi-active radar	45	2·5 Mach	In Colbert, Suffren and Duquesne
Crotale Navale	France	2·90	78·6	Command to line of sight	18	2·3 Mach approx	
Aspide	Italy			Italian development of the Sea Sparrow missile to fire from the Albatros shipboard system			
NATO 6S	NATO			Collaborative study programme by a number of European NATO countries			
SA-N-1 (Goa)	USSR	6·71	?	Radio command?	30?	2·0 Mach	Adaptation of army weapon
SA-N-2 (Guideline)	USSR	10·58	2,230	Radio command?	45	3·5 Mach	Adaptation of army weapon
SA-N-3 (Goblet)	USSR	6·1	535	Semi-active radar?	55	1·5 Mach?	Adaptation of army weapon
SA-N-4	USSR	3·2?	?	Possible semi-active radar or infra-red homing	15?	2·0 Mach	Widely fitted in USSR navy
SA-N-5	USSR	1·5	14·3	Infra-red	10	1·5 Mach?	Naval adaptation of army SA-7
SA-N-10	USSR	7·0	?	Active radar homing	55	6·0 Mach?	
Seacat	UK	1·49	62·5	Radio command	5	Subsonic	
Seaslug Mk 2	UK	6·0	1,965	Beam riding	45 +	2·0 Mach +	
Sea Dart	UK	4·36	540	Semi-active radar homing	30 +	?	
Seawolf	UK	2·00	78	Command to radar line of sight	?	2 + Mach	
Standard SM-1 (MR)	USA	4·57	590	Semi-active radar homing	18 +	Mach 2 +	
Standard SM-1 (ER)	USA	8·23	1,060	Semi-active radar homing	55 +	Mach 2·5 +	
Standard SM-2 (MR)	USA	?	?	Semi-active radar homing with mid-course command guidance	35 + ?	Mach 2 ?	Designed for Aegis system
Standard SM-2 (ER)	USA	?	?	Semi-active radar homing with mid-course command guidance	90 +	Mach 2 ?	Designed for Aegis system
Talos	USA.	9·53	3,175	Beam riding with semi-active radar homing	120 +	Mach 2·5	Obsolescent
Terrier	USA	8·0	1,400 approx	Beam riding or semi-active radar homing	35 +	Mach 2·5	Being replaced by Standard
Tartar	USA	4·6	680	Semi-active radar homing	16 +	Mach 2	Being replaced by Standard in USN but fitted in a number of other navies

TABLE 6 — NATO's PRINCIPAL TACTICAL NUCLEAR MISSILES

Missile	Numbers deployed in Europe	Range in Miles	Warhead	Remarks
Pershing	90	400	Nuclear or HE	72 deployed by W. Germany. 18 by US. More accurate Pershing II under development with much longer range
Lance	60 +	75	Nuclear or HE	36 deployed by US. Remainder by UK, Netherlands, Belgium, W. Germany
Pluton	100	France 75	Nuclear	In service in France

TABLE 7 — WARSAW PACT'S PRINCIPAL TACTICAL NUCLEAR MISSILES

Missile	Total numbers	Range in miles	Warhead	Remarks
Frog (various Marks)	600	45	Nuclear or HE	Unguided rocket. Was used by Egypt and Syria in Yom Kippur war
Scud A		85	Nuclear or HE	Unguided rocket with radio command for ordering motor cut off
Scud B	200	170	Nuclear or HE	Inertially guided. There may be more than one type of Scud B
Scaleboard	100?	500	Nuclear	Reputed to carry a 1 MT warhead. Inertially guided

Note. Frog, Scud and Scaleboard are being replaced by new SSM with greater ranges — SS-21, SS-22 and SS-23.

TABLE 8 – MODERN BATTLE TANKS

Model	Country	In service with	Max speed (km/hr)	Max range (km)	Main Armament (mm)	Year Produced
M60 A1	USA	USA Italy Australia Iran Austria Israel	48.3	449	105	1961
M60 A2	USA	USA	50	595	152	1973
M48 A2	USA	USA Germany Greece Norway Turkey Spain Jordan Taiwan S. Korea Pakistan	51.5	257	90	1952
M48 A3	USA	USA Israel Vietnam	51.5	464	90	1964
M1 Abrams	USA	USA	72	450	105	1980
Leopard 1	W. Germany	W. Germany Belgium Italy Netherlands Norway	65	580	105	1965
Leopard 2	W. Germany	W. Germany Netherlands	68	500	120	1980
Pz 61	Switzerland	Switzerland	55	300	105	1965
Pz 68	Switzerland	Switzerland	60	300	105	1971
Chieftain	UK	UK Iran	48	500	120	1965
Vickers Mk 3	UK	India Kuwait	53.5	483	105	1963
Centurion	UK	Egypt Australia Denmark Israel Canada Iraq India Jordan Kuwait Lebanon Netherlands Switzerland Sweden S. Africa	34.6	185	105	1948-60 (Different marks)

TABLE 8 — *continued*

Model	Country	In service with	Max speed (km/hr)	Max range (km)	Main Armament (mm)	Year Produced
Vickers Valiant	UK	—	60	600	105/120	—
AMX 30	France	France Libya Spain Greece	64.4	600	105	1966
AMX 32	France	—	65	520	105/120	—
Strv 103B	Sweden	Sweden	50	340	105	1967
TAM	Argentine	Argentine	75	550	105	1980
Merkava	Israel	Israel	?	?	105	1979
T 10	USSR	USSR	45	220	122	1957
T54/55	USSR	USSR Poland CSSR E. Germany Cuba Egypt Algeria Finland Syria China Romania India Israel Hungary N. Korea Yugoslavia Morocco Zimbabwe	50	620	100	1949
T62	USSR	USSR Bulgaria CSSR E. Germany Egypt Poland Romania Syria	48	400	115 (smooth bore)	1965
T64	USSR	USSR	50	—	125 (smooth bore)	1975
T72	USSR	USSR Poland Czecho- slovakia	50	—	125 (smooth bore)	1977

TABLE 9—WESTERN ANTI-TANK MISSILES

Missile	Country	Description	Max range (m)
Vehicle or Ground Mounted			
ACRA	France	Gun launched. IR beam riding. Under development	3,000
ENTAC	France	Wire guided. Jeep mounted. In service	2,000
Harpon	France	Wire guided using semi-auto IR. Vehicle or helicopter mounted. In service	3,000
SS11 B1	France	Wire guided. Vehicle or helicopter mounted. In service	3,000
SS12	France	Wire guided using semi-auto IR. Vehicle or helicopter mounted. Larger warhead than SS11. In service	6,000
HOT	France, Germany	Wire guided using semi-auto IR. Vehicle or helicopter mounted. In service	4,000
Shillelagh	USA	Gun launched. IR command guidance. Vehicle or helicopter mounted. In service	?
TOW	USA	Wire guided using semi-auto IR. Vehicle or helicopter or ground mounted. In service in many countries	3,750
Hellfire	USA	Fire and forget missile. Laser guided. Vehicle, helicopter or ground mounted. Under development	?
Swingfire	Britain	Wire guided. Vehicle or ground mounted. In service	4,000
Man portable			
Vigilant	Britain	One man, wire guided, ground launched. In service in many countries	1,375
Bantam	Sweden	One man, wire guided, ground launched. Can be mounted in vehicles or helicopters. In service	2,000
Cobra	Germany	One man, wire guided, launched directly off the ground. In service	2,000
Mamba	Germany	Similar to Cobra but improved performance. In service	2,000
Milan	France, Germany	One or two men, wire guided, using semi-auto IR. Ground tripod or shoulder launched. In service	2,000
Mosquito	Italy	One man, wire guided, ground launched. In service	2,300
Sparviero	Italy	One man, IR guidance. Ground launched. Under development	3,000
Dragon	USA	One man, wire guided, shoulder launched. In service	1,000

TABLE 10 — PRINCIPAL TACTICAL GUIDED AIR-TO-SURFACE WEAPONS

Weapons	Country	Guidance	Range	Remarks
Bullpup	US	Radio Command	11 km	Two versions A and B. A is in use in USN and many NATO nations. B is larger and has a range of 17 km
Maverick	US	TV self guidance	22.5 km	For use against hardpoint targets. In service. IR homer in production. Laser homer under development
Shrike	US	Anti-radiation homing	12 — 16 km	For use against ground radars. In service
Standard	US	Anti-radiation homing	25 km +	For use against SAM radars. In service
HARM	US	Anti-radiation homing	?	Improved Shrike and Standard missile. Under development
Harpoon	US	Active radar homing	90 km +	Air launched version of ship-to-ship missile. Under development
Walleye	US	TV	12? km	Unpowered glide bomb. In service
Hobos	US	The name given to all unpowered glide bombs guided by TV or by lasers. Many are being developed under the PAVEWAY programme		
Tow	US	Described under Table 9		
Hellfire	US	Described under Table 9		
Hounddog	US	Inertial	15 km	Strategic thermonuclear
Sea Skua	Britain	Semi-active radar homing	20? km	For use by helicopters against fast missile boats
Kormoran	Germany	Inertial Nav. Active radar or passive IR homing	40 km	Primarily an anti-ship missile. In production
HOT	France Germany	Described under Table 9		
Penguin	Norway	IR homing	12 — 16 km	Air launched version of ship-to-ship missile. Under development
Martel	Britain and France	Two types — anti-radiation homing and TV guidance	30 km +	In service in Britain and France
Sea Eagle	Britain	?	?	Anti-ship missile. Under development
AS11	France	Wire guidance with optical tracking	3 km	In service
AS12	France	Wire guidance with optical tracking	8 km	In service
AS20	France	Radio command with optical tracking	8 km	In service in many countries

TABLE 10 — *continued*

Weapons	Country	Guidance	Range	Remarks
AS30	France	Radio command with either optical or auto IR tracking	12 km	Missile can be launched by one aircraft and controlled by another. In service in many countries
AM39	France	Active radar homing	45 km	Air launched version of Exocet ship-to-ship missile. Under development
Marte	Italy	Radio command with radar/ optical tracking	25 km	Air launched version of Sea Killer ship-to-ship missile. Under development
Otomat	Italy	Active radar homing	40 km	Air launched version of ship-to-ship missile
RbO4E	Sweden	Active radar of anti-radiation homing	20 — 29 km	In service in Swedish Air Force
RbO5	Sweden	Radio command	12 km?	In service in Swedish Air Force
Kennel (AS-1)	USSR	Beam riding or radio command with active radar or anti-radiation terminal homing	90 km	Probably for use against shipping
Kipper (AS-2)	USSR	?	180 — 210 km	Probably for use against shipping
Kangaroo (AS-3)	USSR	?	Estimates vary between 185 and 650 km	Carried by the Bear bomber. Probably now obsolescent
Kitchen (AS-4)	USSR	Probably inertial Nav with terminal radar homing	Estimates vary between 300 and 800 km	
Kelt (AS-5)	USSR	Probably anti-radiation homing	180 km	Probably for use against shipping
Kingfish (AS-6)	USSR	Probably inertial	200 km?	Fitted in the Backfire bomber and Badger
Kerry (AS-7)	USSR	Nav with terminal radar homing	10 km?	Fitted in the Su-19 Fencer fighter-bomber

TABLE 11 — AIR-TO-AIR MISSILES

Missile	Country	Homing	Range	Remarks
R530	France	Either a semi-active radar or an IR head can be fitted	18 km	In service in France and other countries
Super 530	France	Semi-active radar?	35 km	Higher speed and longer range. Not yet in service
Magic	France	IR	7 km	A close-combat weapon. In service in France and other countries
Shafrir	Israel	IR	5 km	In service in Israel and perhaps two other countries
Aspide	Italy	Semi-active radar	Medium	Coming into service in Italy. Can also be used in the ship-to-air and ground-to-air role
Aam 1	Japan	IR	7 km	In service
Aam 2	Japan	IR	?	Under development
Firestreak	Britain	IR	Short	In service with RAF and other air forces
Red Top	Britain	IR	Short	In service in RAF
Sraam	Britain	IR	Short to very short	Close-combat weapon test vehicle programme
Sky Flash	Britain	Semi-active radar	Medium	In service with RAF and Swedish Air Force
Falcon	US	Semi-active radar or IR	11 km	A number of different versions available, some with SA homing, some with IR

TABLE 11—continued

Missile	Country	Homing	Range	Remarks
Genie	US	Unguided	9.6 km	Nuclear warhead. In service
Phoenix	US	Semi-active radar with terminal active radar homing	163 km	Mainly used by USN
Sidewinder	US	IR	10 km	A number of different versions, now all IR homing, are in service
Sparrow III	US	Semi-active radar	25 km	In service in USAF, RAF and various NATO air forces
Alkali	USSR	Semi-active radar	6-8 km	Fitted in MiG 19, MiG 17, SU9
Anab	USSR	Either a SA radar head or an IR head can be fitted	8-10 km	Widely fitted in USSR
Ash	USSR	Either a SA radar head or an IR head can be fitted	30 km	Fitted in Fiddler long-range aircraft. Two versions
Atoll	USSR	IR	5-7 km	Similar to the US Sidewinder. In service
Awl	USSR	Believed that either a SA radar head or an IR head can be fitted	Medium?	Fitted in MiG 23
Acrid	USSR	Either SA radar or IR	37 km +	Fitted to Foxbat
Apex	USSR	Either a SA radar head or an IR head can be fitted	30 km	Probably fitted in the MiG 23
Aphid	USSR	IR	Under 8 km	Close-combat weapon. May be fitted in the MiG 23

TABLE 12—PRINCIPAL FIGHTER/INTERCEPTORS IN NATO EUROPE

Aircraft	Type	Engines	Max. speed	Main air-to-air weapons	Remarks
Lightning	Single-seat fighter	2 × 7,420 kg RR Avon 301 turbojets	Over Mach 2	2 Red Top (or Firestreak) missiles 48 rockets	In service with RAF
Phantom II F4E	Two-seat interceptor tactical interdictor	2 × 8,120 kg GE J79-GE 17 turbojets	Mach 2·4	4 Sparrow III and 4 Sidewinders	In service with RAF and USAF
Starfighter F104G	Single-seat interceptor, tactical strike	1 × 7,165 kg GE J79-GE 11A turbojet	Mach 2·2	Up to 4 Sidewinders	In service with German, Dutch, Danish, Italian, Belgian Air Forces
Mirage V	Single-seat fighter-bomber	1 × 6,200 SNECMA Atar 9C turbojet	Mach 2·1	2 Sidewinders	In service with Belgian Air Force
Freedom F5	Single-seat lightweight fighter	2 × 1,850 kg GE J85-GE 13 turbojets	Mach 1·4	Up to 4 Sidewinders 2 × 20 mm guns	In service with Dutch Air Force
F15	Single-seat air superiority fighter	2 × 11,340 kg Pratt & Whitney F100-FW-100 afterburning turbo-fans	Mach 2·5+	Up to 4 Sidewinders 4 Sparrow III	In service with USAF
F16	Single-seat advanced combat fighter	1 × 11,340 kg Pratt & Whitney F100-PW-100 afterburning turbo-fan	Mach 2+	2 Sidewinders	Coming into service USAF and in the Air Forces of Belgium, Denmark, The Netherlands and Norway

TABLE 13 — PRINCIPAL TACTICAL SURFACE-TO-AIR MISSILES

Missile	Country	Guidance	Range	Remarks
		LONG AND MEDIUM RANGE		
Nike/Hercules	US	Command	140 km +	Main high-level air defence missile in Europe
Hawk	US	Semi-active radar	35 km	Main medium and low-level air defence missile in Europe
Improved Hawk	US	Semi-active	35 km	Improved data processing and performance against low-level aircraft
Sparrow III	US	Semi-active radar	40 km	Used in other nations' systems such as the Italian Spada. Not yet in service
Patriot	US	Command and semi-active radar	Long	Under development to replace Nike and Hawk
Bloodhound II	Britain	Semi-active radar	80 km +	Used by RAF for defence of airfields in Germany and the UK
Gainful (SAM6)	USSR	Command	30 km	Used by Egyptians in latest Middle East war. Semi-active radar homing
Ganef (SAM4)	USSR	Command	70 km	In service with Russia
Goa (SAM3)	USSR	Semi-active radar	30 km	In service in Soviet Army and Navy
Guideline (SAM2)	USSR	Command	50 km	Used by Egyptians in latest Middle East war

TABLE 13—*continued*

Missile	Country	Guidance	Range	Remarks
		CLOSE RANGE		
Crotale	France	Command IR missile gathering	8.5 km	In service in France and as Cactus in S. Africa and as Shahine in Saudi Arabia
Roland II	France, Germany	Command with auto radar aiming	6 km	In service in France and Germany. Now bought by America
Indigo	Italy	Beam riding or command. Optical or IR tracking	10 km	In service in Italian Army
Rapier	Britain	Command with optical or radar tracking	5.5 km	In service in British Army. Also sold to Iran, Abu Dhabi, Oman, Australia
Tigercat	Britain	Command with optical tracking	4 km	In limited service with overseas air forces
Chaparral	US	IR homing	4 km?	In service in US Army. Uses a modified Sidewinder missile
Redeye	US	IR homing	3 km	Shoulder launched. In service
Stinger	US	IR homing	?	Successor to Redeye. Production begun 1981
Saber	US	Laser-tracking	3 km	Under development
Blowpipe	Britain	Command with optical tracking	3 km?	Shoulder launched but also fitted in vehicles, ships and submarines. In service with the British Army

TABLE 13 – *continued*

Missile	Country	Guidance	Range	Remarks
		CLOSE RANGE		
RBS70	Sweden	Laser beam riding	5 km	Tripod launched
Grail (SAM7)	USSR	IR homing	3.5 km	Used with success by the Egyptians in latest Middle East war. Shoulder, ground or vehicle launched
Gecko (SAM8)	USSR	Command	10 km	Vehicle launched. 4 Missiles to each vehicle
Gaskin (SAM9)	USSR	IR homing	6 km	Vehicle launched. 4 Missiles to each vehicle. Larger version of SAM7

Part III

Defence Literature of the Year

ROBIN STEPHENSON

A SELECTION of titles in the field of defence studies published during the last 12 months. The works are listed under broad subject headings, bringing together material dealing with specific topics and, in some cases, various aspects of defence in a particular geographical area.

AIR POWER

EMERSON, D E, *TSARINA: User's Guide to a Computer Model for Damage Assessment of Complex Airbase Targets* (RAND Corporation, Santa Monica, Ca, 1980), N-1460-AF.

HALLEY, J J, *The Squadrons of the Royal Air Force* (Air-Britain, Tonbridge, 1980), £12.50.

HUSCHKE, R E, RAPP, R R, and SCHUTZ, C, *Military Weather Calculations for the NATO Theater: Weather and Warplanes*, VIII (RAND Corporation, Santa Monica, Ca, 1980), Reports Series R-2401-AF.

JANE'S, *All the World's Aircraft 1980—81* (Jane's, London, 1980), £40.00.

PFALTZGRAFT, R L and DAVIS, J K, *The Cruise Missile: Bargaining Chip or Defense Bargain?* (Institute for Foreign Policy Analysis, Cambridge, Mass, 1980), $3.00.

POLMAR, N (Ed), *Strategic Air Command: People, Aircraft and Missiles* (Stephens, Cambridge, Mass, 1980) £8.95.

AFRICA

INTERNATIONAL DEFENCE AND AID FUND, *The Apartheid War Machine: The Strength and Development of the South African Armed Forces* (International Defence and Aid Fund, London, 1980), £0.50.

JASTER, R S, *South Africa's Narrowing Security Options* (International Institute for Strategic Studies, London, Adelphi Paper No 159, 1980), £2.00.

MARTIN, D and JOHNSON, P. *The Struggle for Zimbabwe* (Faber, London, 1980), £7.50.

SAMUELS, M A, *Africa and the West* (Westview Press, Boulder, Colorado, 1980), $16.50.

SELASSIE, BEREKET HABTE, *Intervention and Conflict in the Horn of Africa* (Monthly Review Press, New York, 1980), $15.00.

ARMED FORCES

COHEN, E A, *Commandos and Politicians* (Frank Cass, London, 1981), £12.50.

COFFEY, K J, *Strategic Implications of the All-Volunteer Force: The Conventional Defence of Central Europe* (University of North Carolina Press, Chapel Hill, NC, 1980), $15.00.

CORDIER, S S, *Calculus of Power: The Current Soviet-American Conventional Military Balance in Central Europe* (University Press of America, Washington, DC, 1980), $7.50.

DEWS, E, *NATO Inland Transport as a Potential Rear-Area Target System. Lessons from German Experience in World War Two* (RAND Corporation, Santa Monica, Ca, 1980), N-1522-PAE.

DEWS, E, *POL Storage as a Target for Air Attack. Evidence from the World War Two Allied Air Campaign against Enemy Oil Installations* (RAND Corporation, Santa Monica, Ca, 1980), N-1523-PAE.

FORSTER, T M, *The East German Army: The Second Power in the Warsaw Pact* (Allen & Unwin, London, 1980), £12.00.

GERAGHTY, T *Who Dares Wins* (Arms and Armour Press, London, 1980), £8.95.

HAGEN, L S, *Twisting Arms: Political, Military, and Economic Aspects of Arms Co-operation in the Atlantic Alliance* (Center for International Relations, Queens University, Kingston, Canada, 1980).

JOHNSON, A R, DEAN, R W, and ALEXIEV, A, *East European Military Establishments: The Warsaw Pact Northern Tier* (RAND Corporation, Santa Monica, Ca, 1980), Reports Series R-2417/1-AF/FF.

LOVELL, J P, *Neither Athens nor Sparta? The American Service Academies in Transition* (Indiana University Press, Bloomington, Indiana, 1979), £10.50.

MENAUL, S, *Countdown: Britain's Strategic Nuclear Forces* (Robert Hale, London, 1980).

NAILOR, P and ALFORD, J, *The Future of Britain's Deterrent Force* (International Institute for Strategic Studies, London, Adelphi Paper No 156, 1980), £2.00.

SOHLBERG, R, *Analysis of Ground Force Structures on NATO's Northern Flank* (Rand Corporation, Santa Monica, Ca, 1980), N-1315-MRAL.

WISE, R A *et al, A Model of Vehicle Activity in the Warsaw Pact Tactical Rear During a Conventional Attack against NATO* (RAND Corporation, Santa Monica, Ca, 1980), N-1495-AF.

ARMS CONTROL AND DISARMAMENT

BARNABY, F, *Prospects for Peace* (Pergamon Press, Oxford, 1980), £4.75.

BERTRAM, C, *Arms Control and Military Force* (Gower Publishing Co, Farnborough, Hants, Adelphi Library, vol 3, 1980), £9.50.

HOAG, M W, *Forward-based Nuclear Systems in NATO in Historical Perspective: Lessons for SALT III* (RAND Corporation, Santa Monica, Ca, 1980), Papers Series P-6426.

HUMPHREY, G J *et al, SALT II and American Security* (Institute for Foreign Policy Analysis, Cambridge, Mass, 1980).

HUSSAIN, F, *The Future of Arms Control,* Part IV, *The Impact of Weapons Test Restrictions* (International Institute for Strategic Studies, London, Adelphi Paper No 16, 1981), £2.00.

IMAI, R and ROWEN, H S, *Nuclear Energy and Nuclear Proliferation: Japanese and American Views* (Westview Press, Boulder, Colorado, 1980), $17.00.

KELIHER, J G, *The Negotiations on Mutual and Balanced Force Reductions: The Search for Arms Control in Central Europe* (Pergamon Press, Elmsford, NY, 1980), $25.00.

PAYNE, S B, Jr, *The Soviet Union and SALT* (MIT Press, Cambridge, Mass, 1980), $19.95.

POTTER, W C, *Verification and SALT: The Challenge of Strategic Deception* (Westview Press, Boulder, Colorado, 1980), $20.00.

QUESTER, G H, *Navies and Arms Control* (Praeger, New York, 1980).

RECORD, J, *Force Reduction in Europe: Starting Over* (Institute for Foreign Policy Analysis, Cambridge, Mass, 1980), $6.50.

SMITH, G, *Doubletalk: The Story of SALT I* (Doubleday, New York, 1980), $17.95.

STOCKHOLM INTERNATIONAL PEACE RESEARCH INSTITUTE, *The Non-proliferation Treaty: The Main Political Barrier to Nuclear Weapon Proliferation* (Taylor & Francis, London, 1980), £3.00.

STOCKHOLM INTERNATIONAL PEACE RESEARCH INSTITUTE *World Armaments and Disarmament: SIPRI Yearbook 1981* (Taylor & Francis, London, 1981), £19.00.

WALDHEIM, K, *Building the Future Order: The Search for Peace in an Interdependent World* (Collier Macmillan, London, 1980), £8.50.

WINKLER, T, *Nuclear Proliferation and the Third World: Problems and Perspectives* (Graduate Institute of International Studies, Lausanne, 1980).

ASIA

GIBERT, S P, *Northeast Asia in US Foreign Policy* (Sage Publications, Beverly Hills, Ca, 1979), £2.20.

FUKUYAMA, Y F, *The Future of the Soviet Role in Afghanistan* (RAND Corporation, Santa Monica, Ca, 1980), N-1579-RC.

FUKUYAMA, Y F, *The Security of Pakistan* (RAND Corporation, Santa Monica, Ca, 1980), N-1584-RC.

GIRLING, J L S, *Thailand, Society and Politics* (Cornell University Press, Ithaca, NY, 1981), £15.00.

HENDERSON, W D, *Why the Vietcong Fought: A Study of Motivation and Control in a Modern Army in Combat* (Greenwood Press, Westport, Conn, 1979), £11.95.

LEIFER, M, *Conflict and Regional Order in Southeast Asia* (International Institute for Strategic Studies, London, Adelphi Paper No 162, 1980), £2.00.

MARWAH, O and POLLACK, J D (Eds), *Military Power and Policy in Asian States: China, India, Japan* (Westview Press, Boulder, Colorado, 1980), £9.00.

NEWELL, N P and NEWELL, R S, *The Struggle for Afghanistan* (Cornell University Press, Ithaca, NY, 1980), £9.00.

O'LEORY, G, *The Shaping of Chinese Foreign Policy* (Croom Helm, London, 1980), £13.50.

PRINGLE, R, *Indonesia and the Philippines: American Interests in Island Southeast Asia* (Columbia University Press, New York, 1980), £16.60.

SAYEED, K B, *Politics in Pakistan: The Nature and Direction of Change* (Praeger, New York, 1980), $21.95.

SOLOMON, R H (Ed), *Asian Security in the 1980s: Problems and Policies for a Time of Transition* (Oelgeschlager, Gunn & Hain, Cambridge, Mass, 1980), $20.00.

ARMS PROCUREMENT

ANGUS, R, *Collaborative Weapons Acquisition: The MRCA (Tornado) Panavia Project* (Center for Defence Studies, University of Aberdeen, 1979), £2.00.

GANSLER, J S, *The Defence Industry* (MIT Press, Cambridge, Mass, 1980), $19.95.

GREENWOOD, D, *The Polaris Successor System: At What Cost?* Center for Defence Studies, University of Aberdeen, 1980).

KOISTINEN, P A C, *The Military Industrial Complex: A Historical Perspective* (Praeger, New York, 1980), $18.95.

LONG, A and REPPY, J, *The Genesis of New Weapons: Decision Making for Military Research and Development* (Pergamon Press, Elmsford, NY, 1980), $22.50.

MILLER, S E, *Arms and the Third World: Indigenous Weapons Production* (Programme for Strategic and International Security Studies, Geneva, PSIS Occasional Papers, No 3, 1980).

DEFENCE ADMINISTRATION AND POLICY

HER MAJESTY'S STATIONERY OFFICE, *Defence in the 1980s: Statement on the Defence Estimates* (HMSO, London, 1980), £4.00.

FREEDMAN, L, *Britain and Nuclear Weapons* (Macmillan, London, 1980), £12.00

HAGEN, L S, *Twisting Arms: Political, Military and Economic Aspects of Arms Co-operation in the Atlantic Alliance* (Center for International Relations, Kingston, Canada, 1980).

HARKAVY, R and KOLODZIEJ, E A (Eds), *American Security Policy and Policy Making: The Dilemmas of Using and Controlling Military Force* (D C Heath, Lexington, Mass, 1980), £15.50.

HOEBER, F P, *Arms, Men and Military Budgets: Issues for Fiscal Year 1981* (National Strategy Information Center, Washington, DC, 1980), £5.25.

KORB, L J, *The Fall and Rise of the Pentagon: American Defence Politics in the 1970s* (Greenwood Press, London, 1979), £13.50.

PIERRE, A J, *US Defence Policy in the 1980s* (Daedalus, Cambridge, Mass, 1980), $4.00.

ROHERTY, J M (Ed), *Defence Policy Formation: Towards Comparative Analysis* (Carolina Academic Press, Durham, NC, 1980), $14.95.

SCOT THOMPSON, W, *National Security in the 1980s* (Institute for Contemporary Studies, San Francisco, Ca, 1980), $8.95.

SIMONS, W E, *NATO's Interacting Models of National Mobilization,* (RAND Corporation, Santa Monica, Ca, 1980), Papers Series P-6482.

EUROPE

ALEXIEV, A, JOHNSON, A R, and WIMBUSH, S E, *If the Soviets Invade Poland* (RAND Corporation, Santa Monica, Ca, 1980).

BLAZYNSKI, G, *Flashpoint Poland* (Pergamon Press, Elmsford, NY, 1980), $39.50.

CURRY, J L, *The Polish Crisis of 1980 and the Politics of Survival* (RAND Corporation, Santa Monica, California, 1980).

DAWISHA, K and HANSON, P, *Soviet—East European Dilemmas* (Heinemann Educational, London, 1981), £14.95.

EIDLIN, F, *The Logic of 'Normalization': The Soviet Intervention in Czechoslovakia of 21 August 1968 and the Czechoslovak Response* (Columbia University Press, New York, 1980), $20.00.

FISCHER-GALATI, S, *Eastern Europe in the 1980s* (Croom Helm, London, 1981), £13.95.

GATZKE, H W, *Germany and the United States: A 'Special Relationship'?* (Harvard University Press, Cambridge, Mass, 1980), £10.50.

GROSSER, A, *The Western Alliance: European-American Relations since 1945* (Macmillan, London, 1980), £10.00.

HACKEL, E, KAISER, K and LELLOUCHE, P, *Nuclear Policy in Europe: France, Germany and the International Debate* (Europa Union Verlag, Bonn, 1980).

KRIPPENDORFF, E and RITTBERGER, V, *The Foreign Policy of West Germany: Formation and Contents* (Sage Publications, Beverly Hills, Ca, 1980), £6.00.

MARQUINA, A, *Defence and Security in the Programs of Spanish Political Parties* (Instituto de Cuestiones Internacionales, Madrid, 1980), $1.75.

MCCAULEY, M, *East Germany: The Dilemmas of Decision* (Institute for the Study of Conflict, London, 1980).

MYERS, K A, *NATO: The Next Thirty Years. The Changing Political, Economic and Military Setting* (Croom Helm, London, 1980), £14.95.

NELKIN, D and POLLACK, M, *The Atom Besieged: Nuclear Dissent in France and Germany* (MIT Press, Cambridge, Mass, 1981), £10.85.

ROBINSON, W F. (Ed), *August 1980: The Strikes in Poland* (Radio Free Europe Research, Munich, 1980).

SEZER, D B, *Turkey's Security Policies* (International Institute for Strategic Studies, London, Adelphi Paper No 164, 1981), £2.00.

SMYSER, W R, *German—American Relations* (Sage Publications, Beverly Hills, Ca, 1980), $3.50.

INSURGENCY AND TERRORISM

BUCKLEY, A D and OLSON, D D, *International Terrorism: Current Research and Future Directions* (Avery Publishing Group Inc., Wayne, NJ, 1980), $7.95.

JANKE, P, *World Directory of Guerilla and 'Terrorist' Organizations* (Harvester Press, Brighton, 1981), £30.00.

NORTON, A R and GREENBERG, M H, *International Terrorism: An Annotated Bibliography and Research Guide* (Westview Press, Boulder, Colorado, 1980), $20.00.

PURCELL, H, *Revolutionary War: Guerilla Warfare and Terrorism in Our Time* (Hamish Hamilton, London, 1980), £4.95.

SCHAMIS, G J, *War and Terrorism in International Affairs* (Transaction Books, London, 1980).

MIDDLE EAST

ADAN, A, *On the Banks of the Suez* (Arms & Armour Press, London, 1980).

AMIRSADEGHI, H, *The Security of the Gulf* (Croom Helm, London, 1981), £13.95.

BAKHASH, S, *Khomeini's Revolution* (Sidgwick & Jackson, London, 1981), £7.95.

BRECHER, M, *Decisions in Crisis: Israel, 1967 and 1973* (University of California Press Berkeley, Ca, 1980), £15.00.

BROWN, R L, *Anwar Al-Sadat and the October War: Factors Contributing to the Egyptian Decision to Go to War. October 1970 to October 1973* (California Seminar on Arms Control and Foreign Policy, Santa Monica, Ca, 1980), $2.25.

CHUBIN, S, *Soviet Policy Towards Iran and the Gulf* (International Institute for Strategic Studies, London, Adelphi Paper No 157, 1980), £2.00.

DEEB, M, *The Lebanese Civil War* (Praeger, New York, 1980), $24.95.

FUKUYAMA, F, *New Directions for Soviet Middle East Policy in the 1980s: Implications for the Atlantic Alliance* (RAND Corporation, Santa Monica, Ca, 1980).

GURKAN, I, *NATO, Turkey and the Southern Flank: A Mideastern Perspective* (National Strategy Information Center, Washington, DC, 1980).

KELLY, J B, *Arabia, the Gulf and the West* (Weidenfeld & Nicolson, London, 1980), £15.00.

KHALIDI, W, *Conflict and Violence in Lebanon: Confrontations in the Middle East* (Center for International Affairs, Harvard University, Cambridge, Mass, 1980).

LONG, D E and REICH, B, *The Government and Politics of the Middle East and North Africa* (Westview Press, Boulder, Colorado, 1980).

MOHAMMED, K S, *The United States and the Palestinians* (Croom Helm, London, 1981), £12.95.

MROZ, J E, *Beyond Security: Private Perceptions among Arabs and Israelis* (Pergamon Press, Elmsford, NY, 1980, $8.95.

PLASCOV, A, *A Palestinian State? Examining the Alternatives* (International Institute for Strategic Studies, London, Adelphi Paper No 163, 1981), £2.00.

ROSEN, S J, *Soviet Strengths and Vulnerabilities in the Middle East* (RAND Corporation, Santa Monica, Ca, 1980), Papers Series.

SELLA, A, *Soviet Political and Military Conduct in the Middle East* (Macmillan, London, 1981), £15.00.

SHAKED, H and RABINOVICH, H (Eds), *The Middle East and the United States: Perceptions and Policies* (Transaction Books, New Brunswick, 1980), £14.50.

TIBI, B, *Arab Nationalism: A Critical Enquiry* (Macmillan, London, 1981), £20.00.

TREVERTON, G (Ed), *Crisis Management and the Superpowers in the Middle East* (Gower Publishing Co, Farnborough, Hants, Adelphi Library, vol 5, 1981), £9.00.

YODFAT, A and ARNON-OHANNA, Y, *The PLO: Strategy and Tactics* (Croom Helm, London, 1981), £10.95.

SEAPOWER

ALFORD, J, *Sea Power and Influence: Old Issues and New Challenges* (Gower, Farnborough, Hants, Adelphi Library, vol 2, 1980), £8.50.

BRITTIN, B H, *International Law for Seagoing Officers* (Naval Institute Press, US Naval Institute, Annapolis, Md, 1981), $25.95.

GRIFFITHS, M, *The Hidden Menace: Underwater Mines 1776— 1972* (Conway Maritime Press, Greenwich, 1981), £5.50.

HANKS, R J, *The Unnoticed Challenge: Soviet Maritime Strategy and the Global Choke Points* (Institute for Foreign Policy Analysis, Cambridge, Mass, 1980), $6.50.

HANKS, R J, *The Cape Route: Imperiled American Lifeline* (Institute for Foreign Policy Analysis, Cambridge, Mass, 1980), $6.50.

JANE'S, *Jane's Fighting Ships 1980—81* (Jane's, London, 1980), £40.00.

MOORE, CAPTAIN J, RN, *Warships of the Soviet Navy* (Jane's, London, 1981), £8.95.

VELDMAN, J H and OLIVIER, F, *West European Navies and the Future* (Royal Netherlands Naval College, Den Helder, Holland, 1980).

SOVIET MILITARY STUDIES

BAYLIS, J and SEGAL, G, *Soviet Strategy* (Croom Helm, London, 1981), £5.95 pbk, £10.95 hard.

BERTRAM, C, *Prospects for Soviet Power in the 1980s* (Macmillan, London, 1980), £12.00.

CHUYEV, Yu V and MIKHAYLEV, Yu V, *Forecasting in Military Affairs: A Soviet View* (US Government Printing Office, Washington, DC, 1980).

COLTON, T J, *Commissars, Commanders and Civilian Authority: The Structure of Soviet Military Politics* (Harvard University Press Cambridge, Mass, 1979), £16.25.

DEANE, M J, *Strategic Defense in Soviet Strategy* (Advanced International Studies Institute, Washington, DC, 1980).

DONALDSON, R H (Ed), *The Soviet Union in the Third World: Successes and Failures* (Westview Press, Boulder, Colorado, 1981), $12.00.

DUNCAN, W (Ed), *Soviet Policy in the Third World* (Pergamon Press, Elmsford, NY, 1980), $35.00.

DOUGLASS, J D, *Soviet Military Strategy in Europe* (Pergamon Press, Elmsford, NY, 1980), $30.00.

FINLAY, D D, *Some Aspects of Conventional Military Capability in Soviet Foreign Relations* (Center for International and Strategic Affairs, University of California, Los Angeles, 1980).

ISBY, D, *Weapons and Tactics of the Soviet Army* (Jane's, London, 1981), £15.00.

JACOBSEN, C J, *Soviet Strategic Initiatives* (Praeger, London, 1980), £13.00.

KELLEY, D R, *Soviet Politics in the Brezhnev Era* (Praeger, New York, 1980), £6.50 pbk, £14.25 hard.

KLINGHOFFER, A J, *The Angolan War: A Study of Soviet Policy in the Third World* (Westview Press, Boulder, Colorado, 1980), $22.50.

LIDER, J, *Military Force: An Analysis of Marxist—Leninist Concepts* (Gower Press, Farnborough, Hants, 1981), £12.50.

LONDON, K (Ed), *The Soviet Union in World Politics* (Westview Press, Boulder, Colorado, 1980), $27.50.

MENAUL, S, *Russian Military Power* (St Martin's Press, New York, 1980), $25.00.

SALLAGER, F M, *An Overview of the Soviet Threat* (RAND Corporation, Santa Monica, Ca, 1980).

SCOTT, H F and SCOTT, W F, *The Armed Forces of the USSR* (Westview Press, Boulder, Colorado, 1980) £16.25.

WICH, R, *Sino—Soviet Crisis Politics: A Study of Political Change and Communication* (Harvard University Press, Cambridge, Mass, 1980), £9.00.

STRATEGY

CALDWELL, L T, *Soviet-American Relations in the 1980s: Super-power Politics and East—West Trade* (McGraw-Hill, New York, 1981), £6.55.

BENNETT, B W, *How to Assess the Survivability of US ICBMs* (RAND Corporation, Santa Monica, Ca, 1980), Reports Series R-2577-FF and R-2578-FF.

BERTRAM, C, *Strategic Deterrence in a Changing Environment* (Gower Publishing Co, Farnborough, Hants, Adelphi Library, vol 6, 1981), £9.50.

CHESTER, E W, *The United States and Six Atlantic Outposts: The Military and Economic Considerations* (Kennikat Press, London, 1980), £14.95.

CLINE, R S, *World Power Trends and Foreign Policy for the 1980s* (Westview Press, Boulder, Colorado, 1980), $20.00.

COLLINS, J M, *US—Soviet Military Balance: Concepts and Capabilities, 1960-1980* (McGraw-Hill, New York, 1980), £21.95.

GARN, J, COFFEY, J I, LORD CHALFONT, and BLOCK, E B, *The Future of US Land-based Strategic Forces* (Institute for Foreign Policy Analysis, Cambridge, Mass, 1980).

GIRLING, J L S, *America and the Third World: Revolution and Intervention* (Routledge and Kegan Paul, London, 1980).

KRAPELS, E K, *Oil Crisis Management: Strategic Stockpiling for International Security* (Johns Hopkins, Baltimore, Md, 1980), $15.00.

LUTTWAK, E, *Strategy and Politics: Collected Essays* (Transaction Books, London, 1980), £10.00.

McGOWAN, P and KEGLEY, C W, Jr, *Threats, Weapons, and Foreign Policy* (Sage Publications, Beverly Hills, Ca, 1980), $20.00.

MENAUL, S, *NATO in the Eighties: A War Winning Strategy* (Institute for the Study of Conflict, London, 1980), £2.00.

RECORD, J, *The Rapid Deployment Force and US Military Intervention in the Persian Gulf* (Institute for Foreign Policy Analysis, Cambridge, Mass, 1981), $7.50.

RONFELDT, D, NEHRING, R and GÁNDARA, A, *Mexico's Petroleum and US Policy: Implications for the 1980s* (RAND Corporation, Santa Monica, Ca, 1980).

ROYAL INSTITUTE OF INTERNATIONAL AFFAIRS, *President Reagan and American Foreign Policy* (Royal Institute of International Affairs, London, 1981), £3.50.

SARKESIAN, S C, *Non-Nuclear Conflicts in the Nuclear Age,* (Praeger, New York, 1980).

GODSON, R, *Intelligence Requirements for the 1980s: Analysis and Estimates* (National Strategy Information Center, Washington, DC, 1980).

GOLDMANN, M I, *The Enigma of Soviet Petroleum* (George Allen & Unwin, London, 1980).

GRAY, C S, *Strategic Studies: A Critical Assessment* (Hudson Institute, Croton-on-Hudson, NY, 1980).

GRAY, C S, *Strategy and the MX* (The Heritage Foundation, Washington, DC, 1980).

HANDEL, M, *Weak States and the International System* (Frank Cass, London, 1981), £15.00.

HOEBER, A M, *The Chemistry of Defeat: Asymmetries in US and Soviet Chemical Warfare Postures* (Institute for Foreign Policy Analysis, Cambridge, Mass, 1981), $6.50.

INTERNATIONAL INSTITUTE FOR STRATEGIC STUDIES, *Strategic Survey 1980* (International Institute for Strategic Studies, London, 1980).

SCHNEIDER, W, Jr, *US Strategic Nuclear Policy and Ballistic Missile Defence: The 1980s and Beyond* (Institute for Foreign Policy Analysis, Cambridge, Mass, 1980), $6.50.

SEATON, M B, GARDNER, P D, and PORTER, R E, *On Deterrence* (RAND Corporation, Santa Monica, Ca, 1980), Papers Series P-6468.

SINGER, J D and WALLACE, M D, *To Augur Well: Early Warning Indicators in World Politics* (Sage Publications, Beverly Hills, Ca, 1980), £11.25.

STEIN, A A, *On Misperception* (Center for International and Strategic Affairs, University of California, Los Angeles, 1980).

TREVERTON, G, *Energy and Security* (Gower Publishing Co., Farnborough, Hants, Adelphi Library, vol 1, 1980), £8.50.

USSR ACADEMY OF SCIENCES, *USA: Military-Strategic Conceptions* (Hayka, Moscow, 1980).

WAR AND SOCIETY

ALBERT, S and LUCK, E C, *On the Ending of Wars* (National University Publications, Kennikat, London, 1980), £14.85.

BERES, L R, *Apocalypse: Nuclear Catastrophe in World Politics* (University of Chicago Press, Chicago, 1980), £12.00.

BEST, G, *Humanity in Warfare* (Weidenfeld & Nicolson, London, 1980).

KALDOR, M, *Democratic Socialism and the Cost of Defence* (Croom Helm, London, 1980), £17.96.

MANDELBAUM, M, *The Nuclear Revolution* (Cambridge University Press, New York, 1981), £8.95.

RAMBERG, B, *Destruction of Nuclear Energy Facilities in War: The Problem and the Implications* (D C Heath, Lexington Books, Lexington, Mass, 1980), £12.50.

RAYMOND, G A, *Conflict Resolution and the Structure of the State System: An Analysis of Arbitrative Settlements* (Allanheld Osmun, Montclair, NJ, 1980), $22.50.

THOMPSON, E P and PALMER, E, *Protest and Survive,* (Campaign for Nuclear Disarmament and Bertrand Russell Peace Foundation, London, 1980).

UNITED STATES CONGRESS, OFFICE OF TECHNOLOGY ASSESSMENT, *The Effects of Nuclear War* (Croom Helm, London, 1980), £7.95.

WEAPONS SYSTEMS

ALFORD, J (Ed), *The Impact of New Military Technology* (Gower Publishing Co, Farnborough, Hants, Adelphi Library, vol 4, 1981), £10.50.

BIDWELL, R S (Ed), *Brassey's Artillery of the World* (rev. ed. Brassey's Publishers Ltd, Oxford, 1981) £??.00

DUPUY, T N, HAYES, G P, and ANDREWS, J, *The Almanac of World Military Power* (Jane's, London, 1980), £25.00.

INTERNATIONAL INSTITUTE FOR STRATEGIC STUDIES, *The Military Balance, 1980—81* (International Institute for Strategic Studies, London, 1980), £6.95.

JANE'S, *Military Communications, 1980—81* (Jane's, London, 1980), £42.50.

JANE'S, *Infantry Weapons, 1980—81* (Jane's, London, 1980), £40.00.

JANE'S, *Military Vehicles and Ground Support Equipment, 1981* (Jane's, London, 1980), £40.00.

JANE'S, *Armour and Artillery* (Jane's, London, 1980).

JANE'S, *Weapons Systems, 1980—81* (Jane's, London, 1980), £40.00.

LAIBLE, R C, *Ballistic Materials and Penetration Mechanics* (Elsevier Scientific, Oxford, 1980), £29.25.

Chronology of Main Events of Defence Interest, April 1980— March 1981

JOANNA CHAPMAN

2 April: *Uganda:* Lieutenant General Abdallah Twalipo, Commander of the Tanzanian People's Defence Forces, confirmed that half the 20,000 Tanzanian troops would withdraw by 6 April, a year after entering Uganda and overthrowing President Amin's régime, having successfully trained the Ugandan troops to replace them.

4 April: *Afghanistan:* Tass reported that agreement between Afghan Foreign Minister, Mr Shah Mohammad Dost, and Mr Andrei Gromyko, his Soviet counterpart, had been ratified by the Presidium of the Supreme Soviet. The agreement concerned the terms of the temporary stay in Afghanistan of a limited contingent of Soviet troops, after Soviet intervention in December 1979.

5 April: *India:* Assam was declared a disturbed area after repeated outbreaks of rioting, in protest against the inclusion of immigrants in electoral registers, had led to over 80 deaths.

6 April: *Turkey.* Mr Ihsan Sabri Caglayangil (Justice Party), President of the Senate (Upper House), took over as acting President of the Republic following Mr Korutürk's retirement from office and failure to elect a new President.

7 April: *Iran:* Following a meeting of the Revolutionary Council, Ayatollah Khomeini stated that control of US hostages, held since November 1979, would not be transferred to the Government of Iran. President Carter announced further measures against Iran.

10 April: *Gibraltar:* A joint communique issued by UK Foreign and Commonwealth Secretary Lord Carrington and Spanish Foreign Minister Sr Marcelino Orega Aguirre, announced agreement in principle to reopen the land frontier between Gibraltar and the Spanish mainland and to suspend other restrictions imposed when General Franco closed the border in 1969.

12 April: *Liberia:* President Tolbert was killed and his Government overthrown in a military coup by a People's Redemption Council of junior military personnel under the leadership of Master Sergeant Samuel Kanyon Doe. The suspension of the Constitution, imposition of martial law and suspension of habeas corpus were announced on 25 April.

17 April: *Afghanistan:* The Afghan Government formally proposed talks with the Iranian and Pakistan governments to discuss questions pertaining to the normalisation of relations and to the situation in the region as a whole.

18 April: *Zimbabwe:* Full independent status was formally conferred on the Republic of Zimbabwe after a transitional period of 4 months during which the country had been administered as the British dependent territory of (Southern) Rhodesia under the governorship of Lord Soames. Zimbabwe became simultaneously the 43rd member of the Commonwealth. Diplomatic relations were formally established between Zimbabwe and a number of Western countries including France, the Federal Republic of Germany, Italy, the United Kingdom and the United States.

20 April: *Honduras:* In the first national elections since 1971 the Liberal Party won 35 out of 71 seats in a new Constituent Assembly with the task of choosing a provisional president, drafting a new constitution and establishing procedures for the election of a civilian president.

22 April: *Luxembourg:* A special European political cooperation meeting of the European

Economic Community (EEC) foreign ministers adopted a two-stage plan to take action against Iran, including diplomatic sanctions and limited economic measures, to be taken immediately, with further measures if necessary.

22 April: *Iran:* It was reported that 100 people were killed in several days of fighting between the Iranian Army and Kurdish guerrillas after Kurds allegedly besieged army garrisons around Sanandaj and Saqqez and as units of the Iranian Army were transferred to the Iraqi border because of tension there.

24 April: *Afghanistan:* The Press Trust of India News Agency announced that Herat was under direct Soviet control and that the Governor had been arrested. Fighting was also reported in Uruzgan province in central Afghanistan.

24 April: *Iran:* The United States launched an airborne commando operation to rescue the 52 Americans held in Tehran. The operation was abandoned in its early stages at a desert area in eastern Iran following the failure of 3 of the 8 Sikorsky RH-530 helicopters involved. As the force prepared to evacuate in darkness a helicopter collided with a Hercules C-130 transport aircraft, killing 8 men. The rescue operation was fiercely denounced in Iran.

27 April: *Colombia:* A siege of the Dominican Republic Embassy in Bogota which began on 27 February with the seizure of 57 hostages in the embassy by 16 members of the Colombian left-wing guerrilla organisation M-19, ended when the guerrillas were flown to Cuba together with 12 diplomatic hostages.

28 April: *Falkland Islands:* Talks on the Falkland Islands resumed in New York between representatives of the United Kingdom and Argentina with a representative of the Islands' legislative council taking part for the first time.

30 April: *United Kingdom:* A group of armed Iranians (calling themselves the Group of the Martyr) seized the Iranian Embassy in London taking 26 hostages, among them 4 Britons, and

demanded the release of 91 fellow Arabs imprisoned in Khurzestan. After protracted negotiations and the deaths of 2 of the hostages, members of a British Special Air Service (SAS) team penetrated the embassy on 5 May, killing 5 of the 6 gunmen and brought out the 19 remaining hostages.

2 May: *Pakistan:* President Zia-ul-Haq of Pakistan left for a 6-day visit to China at the invitation of Chairman Hua Guofeng.

4 May: *Yugoslavia:* Marshal Josip Broz Tito, President of Yugoslavia, died aged 87 after a protracted illness. Political functions previously held by him were subsequently reallocated in a major reorganisation of the League of Communists of Yugoslavia (LCY) and state structures in accordance with proposals made by the President some 10 years previously.

10 May: *Cuba:* It was reported that several Cuban MiG fighter aircraft attacked and sank a Bahamian Defence Force patrol boat in Bahamian waters 20 miles north of eastern Cuba, after the boat had taken in tow two Cuban fishing boats on charges of poaching in Bahamian waters.

13 May: *Brussels:* A 2-day ministerial meeting of the NATO Defence Planning Committee (DPC) called for the total and immediate withdrawal of Soviet troops from Afghanistan.

13 May: *Uganda:* It was announced in Kampala that President Binaisa had been relieved of his authority by the Military Commission of the Uganda National Liberation Front (UNLF). An interim government was established under Mr Paulo Muwanga, Chairman of the Military Commission.

14 May: *Poland:* A 2-day meeting of the Political Consultative Committee of the Warsaw Treaty Organisation (Warsaw Pact) nations issued a statement calling for a world conference on international problems and proposing a European conference on disarmament and *détente* (which Poland offered to host).

16 May: *Vienna:* Talks were held between Mr Edmund Muskie, US Secretary of State, and Mr Andrei Gromyko in a meeting which constituted the first high level US—Soviet contact since Soviet intervention in Afghanistan.

17 May: *Pakistan:* The 11th session of the Islamic Conference of Foreign Ministers opened. Afghanistan's membership was suspended at an extraordinary session in January, but 8 Afghan rebel leaders attended as part of the Iranian delegation. Syria, Libya, South Yemen and the Palestine Liberation Organisation (PLO) objected to a resolution calling for the establishment of a standing 3-member (Iran/Pakistan/Islamic Conference) Committee on Afghanistan.

17 May: *South Korea:* Martial law was extended throughout South Korea, all political activities were banned and many political figures arrested, including the prominent opposition leader Mr Kim Dae Jung. The move followed a wave of strikes and widespread demonstrations in support of demands for wage increases in line with the recent 12 per cent rise in the cost of living.

18 May: *Soviet Union:* President Giscard d'Estaing of France met for talks with President Brezhnev on European security and international issues. The decision to hold the meeting was taken without consultation with Western Allies and received with reserve by the latter although the initiative was welcomed by the German FR Government.

18 May: *Peru:* Fernando Elaunde Terry (Popular Action Party) was elected President, winning 45.4 per cent of votes cast, in the first general elections to be held since 1963, bringing to an end 12 years of military rule.

21 May: *Republic of Ireland:* Mrs Margaret Thatcher, UK Prime Minister, and Mr Charles Haughey, Irish Prime Minister, at a meeting in London, agreed to hold regular meetings on a continuing basis in order to develop new and closer

political cooperation between their two governments.

23 May: *Mozambique:* President Machel of Mozambique and Mr Robert Mugabe, Prime Minister of Zimbabwe, at a meeting in Beira reached agreement on joint operations between the two countries to halt rebel activity.

27 May: *South Korea:* Tanks and infantry moved into Kwangju, capital of South Cholla Province, and reoccupied the city following demonstrations which began on 18 May in protest against the extension of martial law and the arrest of Mr Kim. It was estimated that numbers of those involved had risen from 5000 to 20,000 on 19 May after parachute troops had been flown in to suppress the initial demonstration. Estimates of casualties varied between 170 and 475.

28 May: *Turkey:* A curfew was imposed in Corum following a riot in which 22 persons were believed killed. The riot, quelled by the intervention of the Army, was thought to have started after rumours among the Sunni (orthodox) Moslem majority that Alevis had set fire to a mosque.

29 May: *United Kingdom:* The Foreign and Commonwealth Office stated that 6 or 7 US cargo ships would be sent to Diego Garcia (part of British Indian Ocean Territory) beginning in July. Lord Carrington, Foreign and Commonwealth Secretary, said the move was part of a long-term US programme for strengthening its military capability in the Indian Ocean area.

31 May: *Mauritania:* At the request of the Mauritanian Government, France completed withdrawal of a paratroop unit and about 100 military instructors, stationed in Mauritania since late 1979 after Morocco's occupation of the former Mauritanian sector of the Western Sahara.

1 June: *Cuba/German Democratic Republic:* Cuba and the GDR signed a 25-year treaty of friendship and cooperation.

1 June:	*South Africa:* Damage was estimated at R5,800,000 after attacks on the SASOL I synthetic fuel plant complex at Sasolburg (50 miles south of Johannesburg). Mr Oliver Tambo, President of the banned African National Congress (ANC), claimed that ANC guerrilla units were responsible for the sabotage attacks and for other unsuccessful sabotage attacks at SASOL II.
2 June:	*Iran:* On the initiative of President Bani-Sadr, an international conference to examine 'US crimes in Iran' since 1953 (the time of the temporary flight and return of the Shah) was held in Tehran, attended by 300 delegates from 54 countries including the United States.
4 June:	*Oman:* Diplomatic notes were exchanged in Muscat, the capital, providing for cooperation between Oman and the United States in economic development, trade and security. The US State Department stressed that permission to station military units in Oman would not be sought.
13 June:	*Cyprus:* The UN Security Council approved a resolution extending the mandate of the UN Peace-Keeping Force (UNFICYP) for a further 6 months until 15 December 1980.
17 June:	*United Kingdom:* Mr Francis Pym, Secretary of State for Defence, announced that 160 Ground-launched Cruise Missiles (GLCM) to be deployed in Britain under the Long-range Theatre Nuclear Force (LRTN) modernisation programme would be stationed at RAF Greenham Common, Berkshire, and RAF Molesworth, Cambridgeshire.
22 June:	*Turkey:* Mr Bulent Demir, the Republic People's Party (RPP) Deputy Mayor of Istanbul, was shot dead. Two other members of the RPP, Mr Zeki Tekinel and Mr Suat Karatasli, had been killed on 17 and 18 June respectively.
25 June:	*Turkey:* The 2-day spring ministerial meeting of the North Atlantic Council opened in Ankara. Among the subjects discussed were Afghanistan, *détente,* arms control and disar-

mament, SALT II and the forthcoming Conference on Security and Cooperation in Europe.

26 June: *United States/Kenya:* An agreement was initialled between Kenya and the United States on the use of base facilities. The agreement, which did not involve the permanent stationing of US forces, was made within the framework of the US policy of building up military facilities in the areas bordering the Indian Ocean.

27 June: *Angola:* The Angolan Defence Ministry claimed that a South African force of about 2000, supported by 3 Mirage squadrons, had carried out a number of actions in Cunene Province between 7 and 23 June and that on 24 June another South African infantry brigade, supported by a tank regiment and 2 long-range artillery units, had entered Angola spreading the invasion eastwards to the province of Cuando-Cubango. It was estimated that 300 civilians and 7 Angolan soldiers had been killed. The UN Security Council passed a resolution with three abstentions (UK, France and the USA), condemning South Africa's invasion of Angola and demanding immediate withdrawal of all its forces.

29 June: *Ethiopia:* The Western Somalia Liberation Front (SWLF) claimed that its forces had killed over 8000 Ethiopian and Cuban troops in the Ogaden area in April and May. It referred also to an increase in the number of Ethiopian government troops deployed against it and to an Ethiopian 'scorched earth policy' involving the poisoning of wells and waterholes intended to drive out Somali inhabitants of the region.

30 June: *Soviet Union:* The German FR Chancellor, Herr Helmut Schmidt, paid a 2-day official visit to Moscow for talks with President Brezhnev and other Soviet leaders. A major subject was the December 1979 NATO decision to deploy new theatre weapons in Western Europe and NATO proposals for new

East—West disarmament negotiations. A statement subsequently issued by Herr Schmidt said the Soviet Union was conditionally ready to enter into bilateral negotiations with the United States on the limitation of theatre nuclear weapons in Europe without setting as a precondition the abandonment of the December 1979 NATO decision. Any resulting agreement could only come into effect after ratification of SALT II. This was confirmed on 4 July in a resolution adopted by the Politburo of the Central Committee of the Soviet Communist Party.

1 July: *Poland:* Industrial action at the Ursus factory near Warsaw, in protest against management refusals to increase wages, followed a government announcement that meat prices would rise by up to 60 per cent. Further strikes included those at factories in Tczew and Wdoclawek.

1 July: *Sierra Leone:* The 17th Annual Assembly of Heads of State and Government of the Organisation of African Unity (OAU) was held. Resolutions passed on 4 July included a call for the demilitarisation of the island of Diego Garcia and for its unconditional return to Mauritius.

6 July: *Thailand:* It was reported that Thailand had closed its border with Laos amid an alleged build-up of Vietnamese troops along the Mekong river. Thai officials claimed a link between the attack on a Thai patrol boat by Laotian troops on 15 June and Vietnam's incursion from Kampuchea on 23 June. The United States had announced on 1 July that it would speed delivery of $3 million (£1.3 million) of weapons and ammunition ordered by the Thai Government.

9 July: *Japan:* Talks between representatives of various countries took place during visits to Japan for the memorial service for Mr Ohira, the Prime Minister who died on 12 June; most notably between President Carter and Mr Hua

Guofeng, Chinese leader; between President Carter and Mr Suzuki (elected Prime Minister of Japan on 12 July) and Mr Ito (Foreign Affairs); and between Mr Guofeng and Mr Prem Tinsulanond, Prime Minister of Thailand.

10 July: *Mozambique:* The Government claimed that Mozambique forces had killed 272 rebels and captured over 300 in an attack on the main camp of the Mozambique National Resistance Movement (MNRM) in West Manica province.

10 July: *Austria:* At the 243rd plenary session of the Mutual Balanced Force Reduction talks, the Soviet Union proposed to withdraw a further 20,000 troops from central Europe if the United States agreed to withdraw 13,000.

14 July: *Cuba:* The Cuban Consul in Las Palmas accused Moroccan fighter aircraft of attacking the Cuban Atlantic fishing fleet off the west coast of Africa on 12 July. A Moroccan Government spokesman denied any knowledge of the attack in which one person was allegedly killed and two others wounded.

15 July: *United Kingdom:* The Secretary of State for Defence, Mr Francis Pym, announced the decision to buy the Trident-1 missile system from the United States to replace Polaris as Britain's strategic deterrent in the mid-1990s at a cost of £5000 million over 15 years.

15 July: *Chile:* The head of the army intelligence school was killed in Santiago. The Government attributed responsibility to the Movement of the Revolutionary Left (MIR) and arrested several hundred people. A subsequent series of attacks and kidnappings was made by right-wing groups.

16 July: *Iran:* Following an alleged attempted coup, unofficially reported on 11 July, the ruling Revolutionary Council banned all arrivals and departures by land, sea and air for 48 hours. By 31 July more than 300 people, mostly military personnel, were reported to have been arrested and a total of 36 executed in connec-

tion with the alleged conspiracy to restore Dr Shapour Bakhtiar, former Prime Minister, to power.

16 July: *United Kingdom:* Britain's first Nimrod Airborne Early Warning Aircraft (AWAC) made its maiden flight and the electronics with which it was to be equipped were tested.

17 July: *Ethiopia:* Ethiopia claimed that an attack launched by 14,000 Somali troops on 27 May, penetrating 120 miles into Ethiopia, had been driven back after five major military engagements in which 1300 Somali troops were killed.

17 July: *Bolivia:* It was reported that troops, backed by tanks and artillery, had seized control of the capital La Paz, capturing the presidential palace a few hours after the outbreak of a nationwide military rebellion backed by the right wing. On 18 July General Luis Garcia Meza, commander of the Bolivian Army, was sworn in as President; and the United States suspended military assistance and recalled the American Ambassador.

19 July: *Soviet Union:* The XXIInd Olympiad opened in Moscow. The United States call for a boycott of the Moscow Games as a sign of international disapproval of the Soviet invasion of Afghanistan had led to intense political controversy in the months preceding the games. Sixty-two countries and territories stayed away and 81 countries, including all European Community members except the Federal Republic of Germany, took part.

20 July: *Lebanon:* Mr Takieddine Solh was appointed Prime Minister with the task of forming a government of national unity with paramilitary chiefs and leaders of political parties after 5 years of civil war.

21 July: *Poland:* The largest strike in demand of wage rises, of over 30 factories affected since 1 July, occurred at Stalowa Wola steelworks where 30,000 were involved. On 18 July Polish leaders

had promised to set up a commission to review the demands.

21 July: *United Kingdom:* Meeting in London the Council of the Western European Union (WEU) comprising Belgium, France, the Federal Republic of Germany, Italy, Luxembourg, the Netherlands and the United Kingdom unanimously agreed to abolish with immediate effect the WEU protocol restrictions on the permitted size of FRG warships. The decision was strongly attacked on 24 July by *Pravda.*

22 July: *United Kingdom:* The UK embargo on arms sales to Chile imposed in 1974 was lifted on the grounds that the human rights situation in Chile had improved. The move followed the resumption of full diplomatic relations between the United Kingdom and Chile in early 1980.

22 July: *Honduras:* Power from the ruling Military junta was formally transferred to the Constituent Assembly, dominated by the Liberal Party, which was elected on 20 April. General Policarpo Paz Garcia was subsequently elected as interim President on 25 July.

23 July: *Zimbabwe:* Both Black and White Zimbabwean Members of Parliament approved a further 6 months' extension of the state of emergency imposed on the eve of UDI in 1965.

23 July: *Northern Ireland:* Tension in west Belfast, heightened by the shooting of Michael McCartan, aged 16, by a police patrol, continued with outbreaks of violence on 24 and 25 July.

27 July: *Iran:* The former Shah of Iran died in Cairo aged 60. Iranian officials stressed that his death would make no difference either to the fate of the hostages or to demands for the return of the Shah's wealth.

28 July: *Afghanistan:* Diplomatic sources reported heavy Soviet helicopter activity from Kabul in the direction of Ghazni. It was believed that Russian forces were being sent to crush an

alleged rebellion led by an Afghan armoured division. Further units were reported rebelling in Wardak Province on 1 August.

29 July: *The United States:* The UN General Assembly called on Israel to begin withdrawing by November from all Arab territories occupied since the 1967 war. The United States voted against the resolution and most other Western members abstained.

29 July: *United Kingdom:* Lord Carrington, the Foreign Secretary, left for a 10-day tour of Brazil, Barbados, Venezuela and Mexico, the first by a British Foreign Secretary to the three larger countries of Latin America.

30 July: *New Hebrides:* The Anglo-French condominium of the New Hebrides was proclaimed the Independent Vanuatu Republic. Negotiations between the British and French mission and the leader of the 2-month secessionist rebellion on Espiritu Santo, led by Mr Jimmy Stevens, head of the Vemarana Provisional Government, had been unsuccessful. Father Walter Lini, the Vanuatu Prime Minister, therefore requested the joint British and French military force (200 Royal Marines and French paratroopers) to maintain their military presence on Espiritu Santo.

30 July: *Israel:* A new bill, making united Jerusalem the capital of Israel, was passed by the Knesset.

30 July: *South Africa:* The South African Press Association reported that 27 Angolan soldiers and guerrillas of the South-West Africa People's Organisation (SWAPO) were killed in a South African raid into Angola. The Angolan News Agency reported that from January to June 1980 South Africa had carried out 529 violations of Angolan territory. Unofficial estimates said that during this period 432 guerrillas and 59 South Africans had been killed.

31 July: *Zimbabwe:* The UN Security Council unanimously recommended that Zimbabwe become the newest UN member, the 154th country in the organisation.

31 July:

United States: The US State Department announced that it had approved the sale of engines for 4 Iraqi warships. Congress and Israel objected to the sale. Iraq is listed by the United States as a country supporting international terrorism.

2 August:

Italy: 84 people were killed and 203 were injured in a bomb explosion attributed to the extreme right at Bologna's central railway station.

5 August:

Japan: The 1980 White Paper on Japan's defences was approved by the Cabinet. It said that Japan should build its defence capability in concert with its Western Allies to maintain a military balance of power with the Soviet Union.

7 August:

United States: It was reported that President Carter had signed a document, Directive 59, requiring the US Strategic Command to give priority to destruction of Soviet military and governmental targets instead of previous reliance on the theory of Mutual Assured Destruction (MAD) threatening cities and civilian population.

8 August:

United Kingdom: Cash limits to the Ministry of Defence were increased by £203 million to £10,942 million for the current financial year and the institution of a moratorium on new defence contracts, initially for a period of 3 months, was announced.

11 August:

Zambia: It was reported that border posts had been set up by Zaire some 30 km inside Zambian territory in the extreme north of the country in the disputed border area of Kaputa.

11 August:

Geneva: The Review Conference of the 1968 Treaty on the Non-Proliferation of Nuclear Weapons opened 10 years after its entry into force on 5 March 1970. Delegates from the non-nuclear weapons states accused the United States, the Soviet Union and the United Kingdom of failure to fulfil their treaty obligations. As a result of these and other divisions the conference refused to endorse new proposals designed to halt nuclear proliferation and failed to issue a final conference document.

12 August: *Iran (Kurdistan):* It was reported that Kurdish Partisans were involved in a series of clashes with the Iranian Army and Revolutionary Guards. It was estimated that a total of 40,000 armed men and women had been organised into regular units by political parties opposed to the Khomeini Government.

14 August: *United Kingdom:* The Ministry of Defence announced agreement between the United Kingdom, the German FR and the United States to share development of new medium- and short-range air-to-air missiles, to replace the UK's Sidewinder and Skyflash missiles in the 1990s.

14 August: *German Democratic Republic/Ethiopia:* The signature of a 20-year treaty of friendship and cooperation between the two countries, announced on 15 November 1979, was ratified.

15 August: *Surinam:* The Netherlands reported that Dr Johan Ferrier, President of the Republic since Surinam's independence in 1975, had been dismissed by the National Military Council. He was succeeded by Dr Chin-a-Sen, a state of emergency was declared and the Constitution suspended.

15 August: *Lebanon:* An Israeli communiqué said that an Israeli raid on the coastline in Southern Lebanon was part of a new strategy of periodic preemptive strikes designed to unnerve Arab terrorists rather than reprisals for specific incidents. Israeli attacks continued for several days.

17 August: *United States:* The Federal Aviation Administration announced that armed marshals would travel on flights leaving Florida airports and those in other selected cities to prevent further hijacking of US aircraft to Cuba, 6 of which had been reported in the previous week.

18 August: *Turkey:* The National Assembly voted unanimously to extend martial law, in operation in 20 of the country's 67 provinces, for a further 2 months.

19 August: *Vietnam:* The Vietnam news agency reported that Laos had reported a series of provocations by Thailand including intrusions into Laos airspace involving F105 fighter bombers on 7, 9, 14 and 30 July.

20 August: *Sierra Leone:* An Organisation of African Unity (OAU) committee recognised the Ogaden region as an integral part of Ethiopia. Foreign ministers at the meeting made six recommendations on conditions for the settlement of the Somali-Ethiopian dispute.

20 August: *United States:* The UN Security Council voted 14-1 with the United States abstaining to censure Israel for the recent Jerusalem bill and to call on all states with embassies in Jerusalem to withdraw them. The Israeli Government later criticised the resolution as unjust.

21 August: *United States:* It was reported that the US Defense Department had developed and flown an experimental aircraft, code named Stealth, constructed with radar-resistant material. Some officials expressed scepticism over the potential of the aircraft, developed by Lockheed Aircraft Corporation, claiming that all three test aircraft had crashed due to their peculiar shape.

22 August: *United States:* US State Department announced agreement on the provision of US military assistance to Somalia in return for access to military base facilities at Mogadishu and Berbera. The Ethiopian Government later protested against the agreement, describing it as an act of provocation against Ethiopia.

22 August: *Northern Ireland:* Three soldiers and 5 civilians were injured on the outskirts of Armagh when a car bomb exploded. The explosion followed a bomb attack on 20 August on the Belfast headquarters of the Provisional Sinn Fein, the political wing of the IRA.

23 August: *El Salvador:* 500 government troops backed by two helicopter gunships killed an estimated 17

guerrillas in an 11-hour battle in the south-eastern part of the country. Deaths in military operations in San Vincente and south El Salvador brought to 40 the number of people killed in political violence on 20 and 21 August. A national emergency was declared on 25 August.

23 August: *Syria:* Following a 4-day meeting, the Central Committee of the ruling Ba'ath Socialist Party endorsed statements by Syrian leaders urging closer links with Russia. Western diplomatic sources said that Syria had received T-72 tanks, MiG-25 and MiG-27 jets from the Soviet Union. It was estimated that there were more than 2000 Soviet technicians and military advisers in Syria.

24 August: *Lebanon:* Israeli war planes shot down a Syrian MiG-21 in the first aerial clash since September 1979 over southern Lebanon.

24 August: *United States:* The *Virginia-Pilot* reported that Government and industry officials believed the main computer network to signal a nuclear attack on the United States to be seriously flawed. The system failed twice in June 1979 and put the country's defence forces on full alert for 3 minutes.

27 August: *Somalia:* Mogadishu Radio broadcast reports that Ethiopian troops, backed by fighter-bombers, had invaded north-west Somalia. Somalia forces had stopped the advance though fighting continued. Ethiopia denied the claim, the first Somali accusation of an Ethiopian invasion in the dispute.

28 August: *Malta:* A Libyan military advisory team was expelled from Malta following a dispute which began when a Libyan submarine threatened to fire on a Maltese-licensed oil-rig drilling in an area claimed by Libya as part of its 200-mile territorial limit. The Maltese Government accused Libya of breaking written commitments to have the sea-bed dispute adjudicated at the International Court of Justice.

28 August: *Afghanistan:* Western diplomatic sources reported heavy fighting 150 miles from Kandahar on 25 August. It was also reported that Soviet reinforcements airlifted into Jalalabad earlier in the week had broken a siege of the city by Moslem rebels and that Afghanistan and Moscow had agreed to extend the main runway at Kabul airport and install new navigational aids.

29 August: *Geneva:* The 9th session of the third UN Law of the Sea Conference, which opened on 28 July, ended after tentative agreement on nearly all substantive issues. Many delegates from landlocked countries were less optimistic.

31 August: *Vanuatu:* Mr Jimmy Stevens, the leader of the 12-week secessionist rebellion on Espiritu Santo, surrendered to the authorities.

31 August: *United Kingdom:* An order worth £40 million for 24 Westland Lynx helicopters for the Ministry of Defence, 10 for the Royal Navy and 14 for the Army, was placed with British Aerospace industry at the opening of the Farnborough Air Show.

1 September: *South Korea:* Following elections in which he was the only candidate, General Chun Doo Hwan was formally sworn in as President. A new Constitution came into force on 27 October.

3 September: *Zimbabwe:* The Zimbabwe diplomatic mission in Pretoria (South Africa) and the Consulate in Cape Town were closed. Zimbabwe asked South Africa to close its diplomatic mission in Salisbury.

4 September: *China:* Three British warships, commanded by Rear Admiral Conrad Jenkin, arrived in Shanghai port in the first visit to China for 30 years by a Royal Navy fleet.

5 September: *Republic of Ireland:* The Irish Cabinet approved a £100 million programme of security measures to include an airborne reconnaissance force, deployment of armed officers throughout the State, establishment of preventive patrols and

improved techniques of investigation and intelligence gathering.

7 September: *Iran:* Iran reported that Iranian Phantom fighters and Cobra helicopters had been used in battles along the border with Iraq in retaliation for an attack by Iraqi planes on the towns of Nasrabad and Qasr-e Shirin.

8 September: *Federal Republic of Germany:* The annual 'Autumn Forge' series of NATO exercises was launched. The series included 'Crusader 80', the first comprehensive examination of the system required by NATO to accelerate mobilisation and reinforcement, and involved between 250,000 and 300,000 troops in 25 related manoeuvres from northern Norway to Turkey. The exercises coincided with similar manoeuvres in the German Democratic Republic by Warsaw Pact countries.

9 September: *Iran:* The British mission in Tehran was closed. The Foreign Office said the move was not a break in diplomatic relations.

10 September: *Syria/Libya:* President Assad of Syria and the Libyan leader, Colonel Moamer al Gaddafi, on the latter's initiative, issued a declaration providing for the merger of their two countries into a unified state to be known as 'Arab Masses State'.

11 September: *Turkey:* Turkish armed forces took control of the country through a 5-member National Security Council led by General Kenan Evren, Chief of General Staff, following the third military takeover in 20 years. Martial law was extended to all Turkey's 67 provinces, major political leaders were taken into custody and a round-up of suspected right- and left-wing militants took place. The period leading to the takeover had been marked by economic difficulties, deteriorating internal security and difficulties in electing a successor to President Korutürk.

13 September: *Zimbabwe:* At least 27 people were injured when fighting broke out in Chitungwiza near Salisbury, apparently between supporters of

the Patriotic Front and Zanu (PF). The incident followed reports that about 17,000 guerrillas would be moved from camps around the country to Chitungwiza.

14 September: *Iran:* Tehran radio reported that a helicopter carrying President Bani-Sadr of Iran and Mr Muhammad Rajai, the Prime Minister, was fired on by an Iraqi Air Force jet fighter during an inspection of the border area. Conflicting reports from Iran and Iraq of increased fighting on the border, in the Iraqi port of Basra, and in the Iranian oil town of Abadan, continued to be received.

17 September: *Iraq:* President Saddam Husain of Iraq announced his country's unilateral abrogation of the 1975 border agreement with Iran. The agreement resolved the two countries' dispute over navigation rights in the Shatt-al-Arab waterway separating the two states, and called for the return of the border province of Daih — not subsequently implemented. Iraqi diplomatic efforts early in 1979 for voluntary amendment of the agreement by Iran and the return to Arab sovereignty of two islands occupied by the Shah in 1971 had failed.

18 September: *Soviet Union:* Lieutenant Colonel Arnaldo Tamayo Mandex (a Cuban cosmonaut) and a Soviet mission commander were launched into space on board the Soviet Spaceship Soyuz 38.

19 September: *United States:* Fuel leaking from a nuclear missile exploded at a Titan missile silo in Arkansas injuring 22 maintenance workers, one seriously. Nearly 1000 people living within 5 miles of the site were evacuated.

21 September: *Iraq:* Mr Tariq Aziz, the Iraqi Deputy Prime Minister, left on an unscheduled visit to Moscow for talks with Soviet leaders. The two countries have a 15-year treaty of friendship and cooperation.

25 September: *Singapore:* A meeting of Asian and Pacific Commonwealth heads of Government, attended by Australia, Singapore, Malaysia, New Zealand and the United Kingdom, reached

agreement on the revival of the 5-power defence pact.

26 September: *Pakistan:* President Zia ul-Haq of Pakistan claimed that 2 Pakistani soldiers were killed and 1 wounded in an attack by 6 Soviet-built helicopter gunships with Afghan Air Force markings on a Pakistani frontier post 60 miles north of the Khyber Pass. A similar attack was subsequently reported on 28 September.

26 September: *Federal Republic of Germany:* An estimated 13 people were killed and 200 injured in a bomb explosion at the annual Munich October Festival. Responsibility was attributed to the extreme right-wing 'Hoffman military sport group'.

28 September: *Iran/Iraq:* As Iraqi and Iranian forces continued to fight pitched air, land and sea battles for the control of the Shatt-al-Arab waterway and Iran's oil provinces, the UN Security Council unanimously agreed on a resolution, supported by the Soviet Union, calling for an end to the fighting. It was reported that the Iraqi Army had surrounded Khorramshahr and Abadan, but had met with strong resistance from Iranian defenders.

29 September: *Thailand:* Thai armed forces received American military supplies, including tanks, rifles and ammunition, as Thai intelligence analysts continued to report the arrival of Soviet equipment in Vietnam and Kampuchea and movements towards the Thai border of Vietnamese forces based in Kampuchea.

29 September: *Sweden:* The Swedish Minister of Defence issued an open warning to an unknown foreign power in connection with the presence of an unidentified foreign submarine located in the high security area of the Stockholm archipelago on 18 September.

3 October: *United Kingdom:* Mr Francis Pym, Secretary of State for Defence, announced that talks at military and technical levels on chemical warfare had begun with the United States.

3 October: *United States:* During talks in New York between the Vietnamese Foreign Minister and the Thai Minister of Foreign Affairs, Vietnam proposed an agreement with Thailand to respect each other's territorial integrity within the present borders. The Kampuchean Government had, on 1 October, accused Thailand of providing air and artillery support for Khmer Rouge infiltrations across the border on 11 occasions between 6 and 25 September. Thailand denied the accusation.

5 October: *China:* China protested to the Soviet Union against the entry into China's Inner Mongolian Autonomous Region of Soviet soldiers who left after a clash with Chinese Frontier Guards. Tass News Agency said on 9 October that the incident was an ambush planned by Chinese authorities.

5 October: *Iran/Iraq:* Iraq called a unilateral cease fire for 3 days. Shortly afterwards, Colonel Ramzi of the Iraqi Army claimed that his troops had taken control of the Iranian port of Khorramshahr. Iran denied the claim.

7 October: *Iraq:* A Kuwaiti newspaper reported that 40,000 Jordanian troops, armour and missiles had been deployed on the Iraqi border with Iran. The US State Department issued a strong warning against outside interference in the war.

8 October: *Soviet Union:* President Assad of Syria signed a treaty of friendship with the Soviet Union formally binding his country to closer military, political and economic cooperation.

9 October: *Geneva:* A 70-nation UN conference on conventional arms approved the prohibition of the use of incendiary weapons against civilians, the ban to come into effect 6 months after ratification by a minimum of 20 countries.

9 October: *Iran/Iraq:* Israeli radio monitors said that Libya was airlifting military equipment to Iran in Iranian aircraft via Greek, Bulgarian and Soviet airspace. The monitors said Syria was

also supplying Iran with equipment by air, including SAM-7, RPG-7 and Sagger missiles.

9 October: *Chad:* An unidentified jet aircraft bombed positions held by Mr Hissen Habre, rebel Defence Minister, in the capital Ndjamena, as fighting between Mr Habre's forces and President Goukouni Oueddei's People's Armed Forces intensified.

10 October: *Uganda:* 2000 – 3000 soldiers, believed by Ugandan leaders to be supporters of former President Amin, moved into large areas of north-west Uganda from neighbouring Zaire and Sudan and captured several towns including Arua. Uganda Government forces, supported by tanks and artillery from Tanzanian Army units, regained control of the area on 15 October.

14 October: *United Kingdom:* A 2-day exercise, Priory 2-80, was held to test the readiness of RAF defence squadrons and involved over 200 aircraft from the RAF and from 6 other allied nations.

14 October: *United States:* Negotiations between Israel, Egypt and the United States on autonomy for the Palestinians resumed in Washington. In a concession to Egypt, Israel admitted that proposed autonomous Palestinian authority should have control over land use.

16 October: *Japan:* A Japanese television station claimed photographic evidence that the Soviet Union had established a naval base at the Vietnamese port of Camn Ranh Bay.

16 October: *Iran/Iraq:* The UK Frigate *Alacrity*, armed with missiles, a helicopter and two 200-mm guns was detached from the naval task force in the Far East to join the Royal Navy destroyer *Coventry* stationed in the Gulf of Oman.

16 October: *Afghanistan:* A statement issued after a visit to Moscow by President Babrak Karmal said that the Soviet Union had undertaken to maintain military presence in Afghanistan until government opposition was removed.

18 October: *Ethiopia:* Radio Ethiopia reported that a two-pronged offensive by Somali forces into 190 miles of Ethiopia's south-eastern Bale province between 18 September and 9 October had been driven back leaving over 1000 Somalis dead or wounded.

20 October: *Greece:* NATO approved the reintegration of Greece into the military wing of the Atlantic Alliance, thus ending 6 years of estrangement caused by Turkey's invasion of Cyprus.

21 October: *Angola:* A South-west African Territorial Force spokesman reported that 28 SWAPO guerrillas and regular Angolan soldiers had been killed by South African Defence Forces supported by indigenous Namibian units during a raid into south Angola.

21 October: *Geneva:* The first full-scale preliminary talks on limiting long-range theatre nuclear systems began between US and Soviet delegations.

22 October: *United States:* The UN General Assembly called (97 votes to 23, 22 abstentions) for the immediate withdrawal of all foreign troops from Kampuchea and for all parties to join in a peace conference in 1981. Vietnam, the Soviet Union and Laos rejected the call.

23 October: *Zambia:* The Government imposed an indefinite curfew on main cities. President Kaunda later said that Zambian security forces had thwarted a coup due to have been launched on 16 October. Allegations that South Africa was involved were strongly denied by Mr R F Botha, the South African Foreign Minister. The curfew was lifted on 8 December.

27 October: *Iran:* Iran reported that contact with its troops in the port of Khorramshahr had been lost and that the bridge between Abadan and the port was impassible.

28 October: *United States:* US Naval sources alleged that a Soviet naval base had been established in the Dahlak islands in the Red Sea, 30 miles off Massawa, Ethiopia.

2 November: *Lebanon:* It was reported that Israel was using miniature robot aircraft, about 10 ft long,

driven by a single propeller and equipped with cameras, to photograph PLO bases in southern Lebanon.

4 November: *Chad:* An Israeli radio monitor reported that heavily armed Libyan troops had moved into northern Chad and taken control of an area of up to 125 miles inside the border. Ghana, Gambia and Senegal subsequently broke off diplomatic relations with Libya.

4 November: *United States:* Mr Ronald Reagan, Republican candidate, won the Presidential election with 51 per cent of the popular vote. He was inaugurated as President on 20 January 1981.

7 November: *Lebanon:* In spite of repeated international condemnation, Israeli jets launched a series of air raids on Palestinian guerrilla bases in southern Lebanon. The attacks were seen as retaliation for a Palestinian attack on a town in northern Galilee in which 5 Israelis were wounded.

8 November: *Jamaica:* After a year of political violence, in which 5000 were killed, Mr Seaga, leader of the Jamaican Labour Party, was elected Prime Minister, gaining 85 per cent of the seats.

10 November: *Poland:* The Supreme Court upheld an appeal by the independent trade union Solidarity against an amended charter which included a clause recognising that the Communist Party had a leading role in the State. The ruling enabled Solidarity to call off the strike it had arranged for 12 November.

10 November: *Zimbabwe:* Fighting continued in Bulawayo for the third day between ZANLA guerrillas loyal to Mr Robert Mugabe, the Prime Minister, and ZIPRA guerrillas supporting Mr Joshua Nkomo, Minister of Home Affairs and leader of the Patriotic Front Party. Fifty-eight people were killed and 506 injured and fighting raised fears of the disintegration of the coalition government.

10 November: *India:* The Indian Army took control of oilfields, refineries and the strategic pipelines in Assam after sabotage attempts.

11 November: *Belize:* The UN General Assembly voted in favour of independence for Belize by the end of 1981.

12 November: *Spain:* The Review Conference for Security and Cooperation in Europe opened in Madrid 5 years after the signing of the Helsinki Agreement, despite serious disagreements between the Soviet Union and the West on the timetable and agenda. The conference was due to last until the end of March 1981.

12 November: *China:* The New China News Agency reported fighting on the China/Vietnam border near Friendship Pass. The Agency blamed Vietnamese provocation.

13 November: *Warsaw Pact:* New proposals on Mutual Balanced Force Reductions (MBFR) were published by the Warsaw Pact. They called for a 'collective freeze' for 3 years, during which other powers would undertake not to strengthen their own forces to bridge the gap left by any agreed reduction of Russian and American forces. The proposals were studied by NATO.

16 November: *Guinea Bissau:* It was reported that President Cabral from Cape Verde was removed from power in a coup by Guinean Nationalist officers and replaced by Mr Vierira heading a Council of the Revolution of Guinean Blacks.

25 November: *Jordan:* The Arab League Summit meeting was opened in Amman: boycotted by Syria, South Yemen, Lebanon, Algeria, Libya and the PLO. Syria accused Jordan of supporting members of the Moslem Brotherhood, believed to be responsible for the violence and unrest in the country for 2 years.

25 November: *Upper Volta:* A military coup led by Colonel Syae Zerbo, a former Foreign Minister, overthrew the democratically elected civilian government. The Constitution was suspended and the National Assembly dissolved.

27 November: *Spain:* Gunmen believed to be Basque separatist guerrillas killed Senor Miquel Garciarena Baraibar, the local police chief.

The attack took to 100 the number of people killed in political violence in the Basque country in 1980.

27 November: *El Salvador:* As political violence continued in El Salvador over 70 people were killed in politically related incidents. El Salvador Human Rights Commission estimated 8350 civilians killed since January 1980.

30 November: *Republic of Ireland:* A large cache of arms, including rocket launchers, bomb-making equipment and rifles, was found by police and troops near the border with Northern Ireland.

30 November: *Syria/Jordan:* It was reported that Syria and Jordan had deployed large numbers of troops and tank forces to their common border, increasing tension between the two countries. Prince Abdullah bin Abdul Aziz, Deputy Prime Minister of Saudi Arabia visited Syria and Jordan in mediation efforts to avert fighting.

2 December: *United Kingdom:* A Territorial Army hall in London was damaged by a bomb explosion. Responsibility was later claimed by the Provisional IRA and police feared a new Christmas bombing campaign.

3 December: *Afghanistan:* Western diplomatic sources reported fighting in at least 12 of the country's 28 provinces between Soviet forces and insurgents. It was estimated that the Afghan Army numbered 30,000 compared with 80,000 in 1978.

4 December: *France:* The thermonuclear M4 missile, due to be in service with the French nuclear submarine fleet in 1985, was successfully tested. The missile, a three-stage rocket, has 6 warheads and a range of 2500 miles.

4 December: *Antigua:* Talks opened in London under British chairmanship on the future of Antigua.

7 December: *China/Vietnam:* Vietnam alleged that Chinese forces had seized a string of strategic heights up to 9 miles inside Vietnamese territory.

8 December: *Brussels:* It was confirmed that NATO's Standing Naval Force in the North Atlantic

(STANAVFORLANT) would remain in European waters instead of dispersing over Christmas. Officials would not confirm speculation that the decision was due to uncertainty over the situation in Poland.

11 December: *Brussels:* A 2-day meeting of NATO foreign ministers was held. Amid reports of a military build-up of Warsaw Pact forces along the German Democratic Republic border with Poland it was agreed that a detailed contingency plan would be drawn up with a wide range of political, economic and diplomatic sanctions in the event of any Soviet intervention in Poland.

13 December: *El Salvador:* Senor Napolean Duarte, Christian Democrat, was sworn in as President.

14 December: *Eritrea:* The Eritrean People's Liberation Front (EPLF), the main guerrilla force fighting Ethiopian forces in Eritrea, claimed to have broken an offensive launched on 4 December by an estimated 20,000 Soviet-backed Ethiopian Government troops trying to break through the guerrilla mountain stronghold in northern Eritrea.

15 December: *Uganda:* Dr Milton Obote, former Ugandan President and leader of the Uganda People's Congress Party, was formally installed as President after elections on 10 December.

16 December: *United Kingdom:* Switzerland signed an order worth nearly £250 million for British Aerospace Rapier anti-aircraft missiles.

16 December: *Chad:* Mr Hissene Habre signed a ceasefire in Yaounde, Cameroon, but emphasised his rejection of Libyan participation in the 9-month armed struggle and his view of the Chad government as illegal and illegitimate.

18 December: *Guyana:* Mr Forbes Burnham was formally declared Guyana's first elected President. British observers subsequently detailed irregularities of polling arrangements and registration of voters.

19 December: *Guatemala:* Twelve soldiers were killed and several others wounded in an ambush by left-wing guerrillas, 120 miles west of the capital,

Guatemala City. Three hundred troops, including specialists in guerrilla warfare, launched a search-and-destroy mission with helicopters and land vehicles.

19 December: *Anguilla:* The Caribbean island of Anguilla, which rebelled against rule from St Kitts in 1967, became a separate dependent territory.

22 December: *Iran/Iraq:* Iran reported that over 300 Iranians had been killed in a series of Iraqi attacks along the 300-mile frontier and in Khurzestan. Iran reported that Iranian troops with air and artillery support had attacked Iraqi positions around Dezful.

23 December: *Nigeria:* At the Organisation of African Unity (AOU) *ad hoc* committee emergency summit on Chad, a four-point plan to resolve the crisis was proposed and a draft resolution calling for the withdrawal of Libyan forces from Chad and an end to Libyan interference in the internal affairs of West African countries was tabled. Both Chad and Libya had earlier rejected the meeting.

23 December: *Lebanon:* A UN building in west Beirut was stormed by villagers from southern Lebanon protesting against the failure of UN Interim Force in Lebanon (UNIFIL) to protect them against recent attacks by Israel and its Lebanese right-wing militia allies. UNIFIL was also criticised by Lebanese officials and by the UN spokesman in Lebanon.

27 December: *Nigeria:* A Nigerian infantry brigade, supported by machine guns, armoured cars, mortars and shells, moved into the northern town of Kano in an attempt to end riots which broke out on 18 December. The death toll of the riots was estimated at 1000.

28 December: *El Salvador:* Army sources announced that government reinforcements had checked an offensive launched the previous day by a 1500 strong guerrilla force which had advanced 18 miles from mountain refuges on the Honduras border in northern El Salvador. Unofficial

reports said the area had been declared a zone of military emergency.

29 December: *Morocco:* Polisario guerrillas reported that 300 Moroccan troops were killed, 300 wounded and a large quantity of Moroccan military equipment destroyed in a 3-day battle on the border of the Western Sahara.

1 January 1981: *United Kingdom:* It was announced that a fighting brigade, abolished in the mid-1970s, was to be reintroduced to the British Army of the Rhine (BAOR).

2 January: *China:* After repeated denials by the Chinese Foreign Ministry that Chairman Hua Guofeng, leader of the Communist Party appointed by former Chairman Mao Tse Tung, had resigned, his absence from the official New Year celebrations was seen as confirmation of his resignation.

5 January: *Nigeria:* The Nigerian Government expelled all Libyan diplomats in Lagos.

8 January: *Geneva:* Talks on the implementation of a UN settlement plan for the disputed territory of Namibia (South-West Africa) opened. Delegates failed to reach an all-party (Democratic Turnhalle Alliance (DTA)/ South-West Africa People's Organisation (SWAPO)) agreement on the implementation date for the settlement plan and the conference closed on 14 January. SWAPO continued to support the UN plan but called for intensification of guerrilla action and full economic sanctions against South Africa.

8 January: *Libya:* Colonel Gaddafi announced that Chad and Libya were working towards a merger of their two countries. The Organisation of African Unity and France condemned the planned merger which was invalid under the Lagos agreement of 1979. France announced the reinforcement of its forces in Central Africa, the Ivory Coast, Gabon and Senegal.

13 January: *Poland:* Polish leaders Stanislaw Kania and Jozef Pinkowski received Marshal of the Soviet Union Viktor Kulikov, C-in-C of the Joint

Armed Forces of the Warsaw Treaty member states, in Warsaw. The meeting was attended by the Polish Minister of Defence, Army General Wojciech Jaruzelski.

15 January: *El Salvador:* The United States announced the resumption of arms sales to the ruling junta after confirmation from the US Ambassador that Nicaragua was giving support to the rebels. It was reported that the Reagan Administration had halted all economic aid to Nicaragua while evidence that Nicaragua was a client state of Russia was reviewed.

17 January: *Northern Ireland:* Mrs McAliskey (formerly Bernadette Devlin, MP) and her husband were shot in County Tyrone. A Loyalist organisation was suspected.

19 January: *Israel:* Mr Menachem Begin, Prime Minister, lost his majority in the Knesset and called for an election in July 1981.

20 January: *Iran:* The 52 American hostages, held by the Iranians for 14 months, were freed and flown to Algiers. Agreement was reached in mediation by the Algerian Government on the frozen Iranian assets and deposits made by the former Shah.

20 January: *Ethiopia:* It was reported that an estimated 100,000 Ethiopian troops were deployed on the border with Somalia.

21 January: *China:* It was reported that China had imposed economic sanctions against Holland to protest against the proposed delivery of 2 submarines to Taiwan.

22 January: *United States:* Mr Alexander Haig was nominated by President Reagan as Secretary of State. The nomination was confirmed by the Senate.

23 January: *Northern Ireland:* The former Speaker of the Northern Ireland Parliament, Sir Norman Stronge, and his son were shot dead and their house set on fire. The Provisional IRA claimed responsibility.

23 January: *Soviet Union: Red Star* carried a report on a joint exercise involving the Northern Group of

Forces and Polish Army units. The Southern Group of Forces held a joint exercise with Hungarian troops.

25 January: *Saudi Arabia:* The Islamic Summit Conference opened. It was agreed on 29 January to ask the United Nations to appoint a special representative to mediate between Afghanistan and its neighbours. Also agreed was a call for a world embargo by all Moslem countries against Israel.

26 January: *China:* The 'Gang of Four' — Mr Zhang Chunqiao, Mr Wang Hongwen, Miss Jiang Qing (Madame Mao) and Mr Yao Wenyuan — and associates of the former Defence Minister Lin Biao received sentences at the trial, which began on 17 September 1980, ranging from life imprisonment to 18 years in jail. Madame Mao received the death sentence, suspended for 2 years.

27 January: *Northern Ireland:* Six different towns in Ulster were bombed in what was seen as a synchronised campaign by the IRA.

29 January: *United States:* Mr Haig, the US Defence Secretary of State, ruled out any shipment of arms to Iran, including those paid for before the hostages were seized in November 1979. (These were not a part of the hostage negotiations.)

29 January: *Poland:* Industrial action continued throughout January. A statement issued by the Government implied that it was considering the use of force to ensure order. Solidarity had been fiercely attacked in the Soviet media.

2 February: *Iraq:* The French Foreign Ministry confirmed delivery of the initial batch of Mirage F1 fighters to Iraq. The total order for 60 aircraft was estimated to require 5 years for completion.

3 February: *Iraq:* Reports from London and Washington said Iraq had received about 100 T55 tanks, either from the German Democratic Republic or Polish stocks. The delivery route was allegedly via Saudi Arabia.

3 February: *United States:* President Reagan announced that no more US forces would be withdrawn from Korea.

7 February: *Soviet Union:* The German Federal Republic Defence Ministry said there were estimated to be 180 SS-20 mobile IRBMs deployed, including a small number on the Sino-Soviet border. It was thought that the SS-20 deployment was nearing completion.

9 February: *Saudi Arabia:* Unconfirmed reports from Bonn and London claimed that Saudis and West Germans were informally discussing the possibility of a Saudi purchase of up to 100 Tornado jets to be built in the United Kingdom. The Saudis were also reported to be seeking major purchase of Leopard tanks from the Federal Republic of Germany.

10 February: *Zimbabwe:* Fighting between rival guerrilla factions broke out in Bulawayo, lasting for several days. Fighting also occurred within units thought to have been successfully integrated into the army. Prime Minister Mr Mugabe used regular forces from the former Rhodesian Army to stop the fighting. Guerrillas from the ZIPRA movement loyal to Joshua Nkomo surrendered after being threatened with air strikes. On 18 February the Government decided to disarm the remaining 22,000 guerrillas from ZIPRA and ZANLA and to separate the factions in distant camps. The fighting in Bulawayo resulted in 80 known deaths; unofficial estimates put the actual death toll at nearer 300.

10 February: *Poland:* Prime Minister Pinkowski resigned and was succeeded by Defence Minister General Jaruzelski.

12 February: *German Democratic Republic:* Units of the German Democratic Republic National People's Army and Soviet troops of the Group of Soviet Forces in Germany (GSFG) held an exercise in the southern part of the country.

13 February: *Poland:* Prime Minister Jaruzelski appealed for calm and a 3-month moratorium on strikes;

Solidarity agreed on condition that Government fulfilled its promises, and that new talks brought results on trade unions for farmers (self-management labour law), relaxed censorship and media access for unions.

14 February: *Israel/Lebanon:* Israeli and Syrian air forces were reportedly involved in a series of clashes over Lebanon raising fears of increased fighting. US sources later reported that an Israeli F15 fighter had shot down a Syrian MiG-25 Foxbat, the first such air battle between the world's most advanced fighters.

14 February: *India:* The Non-Aligned Conference of foreign ministers ended with agreement on a new peace initiative to end the Iran/Iraq War: formation of a 4-nation mission to supervise evacuation of occupied territory and peaceful settlement of disputed claims. Similar initiatives were urged for Afghanistan and Kampuchea. Members also called for a more neutral definition of non-alignment.

16 February: *Nigeria:* It was reported that tension was increasing in the northern border region following the build-up of troops, believed Libyan, on the Chad border, and unrest in Kano State.

16 February: *Uganda:* Amidst growing unrest, President Milton Obote asked the United Kingdom to train and organise the Ugandan Army and police force.

18 February: *Spain:* The deadlock on disarmament conference proposals was broken when the United States gave support to the four principles included in the French RM-7 proposal, the most important of which was for obligatory and verifiable reporting of all significant military moves in Europe, extending eastward as far as the Urals.

20 February: *Mozambique:* Reuter reported that Russian naval units had taken position outside Mozambique's two main ports (Maputo and Beira) following a South African raid in January on the African National Congress.

21 February: *Spain:* Basque guerrillas kidnapped the Austrian, El Salvadorean and Uruguayan consuls, demanding the release of 300 political prisoners. On 28 February the four were released unharmed following a newspaper publication of an ETA statement on alleged police torture.

21 February: *Zimbabwe:* Diplomatic relations with the Soviet Union were established subject to the prohibition of Russian links with Mr Nkomo's Patriotic Front Party.

24 February: *Soviet Union:* The XXVIth Party Congress opened in Moscow. President Brezhnev called for renewed *détente;* declared full support for Poland; renewed his offer to withdraw Soviet troops from Afghanistan following signature of non-intervention treaties by neighbouring states; proposed that new arms-limitation talks should include a ban on neutron weapons and limitation on the deployment of US *Ohio* and Soviet *Typhoon* class missile submarines; proposed talks on both the Persian Gulf region and Afghanistan and suggested that new measures of trust could be applied in the Far East. He implicitly accepted the French RM-7 proposal made at the Madrid CSCE conference that confidence-building measures should include all major troop movements. He also proposed a freeze on present Theatre Nuclear Force levels.

24 February: *Greece:* The Greek Government announced the end of an agreement to repair Soviet warships at Syros.

24 February: *Spain:* Pro-Franco rebels attempted a *coup d'état,* seizing the parliamentary building during voting on a new premier. Following an appeal by King Juan Carlos, military chiefs failed to back the rebels and the attempt failed. Sr Sotelo was elected Prime Minister and the alleged leaders of the plot were arrested.

28 February: *Northern Ireland:* The Reverend Ian Paisley invited reporters to see a midnight parade of 500 men, all allegedly holders of firearms certificates, who, he said, were pledged to use

force if necessary 'to defend the freedom of Ulster'.

3 March: *Lebanon:* Israeli air force jets attacked Palestinian bases in southern Lebanon following a Palestinian guerrilla attack in northern Israel. An attempt by guerrillas to cross into Israel by hang glider was foiled when the fliers were arrested after landing.

3 March: *United States:* South Africa was barred from taking part in the UN General Assembly's debate on Namibia.

5 March: *Spain:* The CSCE Conference failed to meet its planned closure date and efforts to find a final draft text acceptable to all 35 delegations failed. The meeting was due to continue until Easter.

7 March: *China:* Vice Premier Geng Biao was named as the new Chinese Minister of National Defence in a Government reorganisation. The new minister had both military and overseas experience.

7 March: *United States:* The US State Department announced that Saudi Arabia would receive AWACS Airborne Warning and Control capability to counter Soviet penetration in the region. It was also announced that Saudi Air Force F15 fighters would receive long-range fuel tanks. Israeli fears of Saudi supremacy were offset by an offer of credit to purchase more aircraft.

11 March: *Belize:* Following ministerial talks between the United Kingdom and Guatemala in London, a full settlement was reached on independence for Belize in 1981 which granted Guatemala access to the sea. No decision was reached over the presence of British troops.

12 March: *United States:* Congress was asked to repeal the ban on military aid to UNITA insurgents in Angola (forbidden under the Clark Amendment of 1976). US military budget proposals before Congress were seen as the reinstatement of military aid and arms sales as tools of foreign policy. Proposed credits were made for Egypt,

Israel, Oman, Kenya, Sudan, Turkey, Jordan, El Salvador and Thailand.

15 March: *Pakistan:* A 13-day hijack of an internal flight in Pakistan by pro-Bhutto gunmen to Damascus via Kabul ended with the exchange of 54 prisoners for 100 hostages. The United States and Pakistan claimed that the hijackers, who remained in Syria, were aided in Kabul.

17 March: *Warsaw Pact:* A 3-week joint Warsaw Pact Command and Staff exercises, 'Soyuz-81' began. Soviet Polish, GDR and Czechoslovak armies and fleets participated in the operations to test the coordination of the action of units and the cooperation between superior HQ staffs, which was directed by Marshal Kulikov, C-in-C of the Warsaw Pact Armed Forces.

17 March: *United Kingdom:* Nigerian President Shehu Shagari paid a 3-day state visit to Britain. It was hoped his talks would lead to completion of arms contracts for aircraft, missiles and warships worth £600 million.

19 March: *South Africa:* South African troops attacked Angolan SWAPO bases from Namibia; South African soldier killed by a Mozambique border ambush aroused threats of retaliation by South Africa.

21 March: *NATO:* At the conclusion of NATO's crisis management exercise Wintex/Cimex 81 a number of weaknesses were indicated which included civil defence, lines of communication, air and chemical warfare defence and reserves and stock.

22 March: *Soviet Union:* Soyuz-39, the USSR spacecraft, was launched and successfully docked with Salyut-6/Soyuz T-4 orbital complex.

23 March: *Central African Republic:* After violent demonstrations against newly elected President Dacko, France reinforced the military garrison in the capital Bangui.

25 March: *Morocco:* Polisario Front guerrillas, estimated at 3000, were reported to have attacked a Moroccan garrison at Guelta Zenmoir in the

	Western Sahara 20 miles from the Mauritanian frontier.
27 March:	*Poland:* A 4-hour strike was followed by talks which led to agreement on a number of points, thus enabling a threatened general strike to be called off.
30 March:	*Thailand/Indonesia:* The hijack of an Indonesian Airways internal flight in Sumatra on 28 March, which was flown to Bangkok, ended when about 20 troops, believed to be mixed Thai and Indonesian, stormed the plane. It was later suggested that the Thai troops had received training from the British Special Air Service (SAS).
31 March:	*United States:* President Reagan was shot in the shoulder by a young man who seriously wounded two other men as the President was leaving a hotel in Washington.
31 March:	*NATO:* Allied discussion began on NATO policy regarding Theatre Nuclear Force talks with the USSR. It was reported that the United States was seeking rejection of President Brezhnev's proposed freeze on TNF deployment.

The Chesney Gold Medal

THE CHESNEY Gold Medal is awarded by the RUSI for any specially eminent work in the field of military science or national security.

CHESNEY GOLD MEDALLISTS

1900 Rear Admiral Alfred Thayer Mahan, USN
1907 Major General Sir Frederick Maurice
1909 The Hon J W Fortescue
1910 Sir John Knox Laughton
1911 Professor C W C Oman
1913 Colonel Sir Lonsdale Augustus Hale
1914 Sir Julian Corbett
1919 Major General E D Swinton
1921 Major General Sir Charles Callwell
1924 Professor G A R Callender
1925 Captain Sir George Arthur
1926 Vice Admiral Sir Herbert Richmond
1927 Brigadier General Sir James E Edmonds
1928 L G Carr-Laughton, Esq
1929 Colonel H C Wylly
1930 Dr C E W Bean
1931 Commander C N Robinson, RN
1932 Colonel C de W Crookshank, MP
1936 Professor Spenser Wilkinson
1950 The Rt Hon Winston S Churchill, MP
1955 Sir Arthur Bryant
1963 Major General J F C Fuller. Captain Sir Basil Liddell Hart
1965 Marshal of the Royal Air Force Sir John Slessor
1968 Professor Arthur J Marder
1973 Professor Michael Howard
1975 Captain Stephen W Roskill, RN

Index to Advertisers

Arab Defence Journal	xix
Army Quarterly	216
Barr & Stroud Limited	194
Brassey's Publishers Limited	296
British Aerospace Dynamics Group	xxii
British Limbless Ex-Servicemen's Association	xvii
British Shipbuilders Limited	xxi
Canadian Defence Quarterly	138
Défense Nationale	232
Eurometaal nv	230
Ferranti Computer Services Limited	xxiv
Flight International	283
Foreign Affairs Publishing Company Limited	295
Frank Cass & Company Limited	122
Geerings of Ashford Limited	123
Graseby Dynamics Limited	150
Ian Allan Limited	215
Institute of Strategic Studies, Pakistan	283
International Institute for Strategic Studies	26
Islamic World Defense	282
Kingswood Publications Limited	xviii
Lasergage Limited	213
Mullard Limited	149
National Defense Magazine	137
Pergamon Press Limited	xxiii
Rolls-Royce Motors Limited	231
Royal Institute of International Affairs	123
Royal Star & Garter Home	xvi
Royal United Services Institute	xx
SAPEF Limited	232
Soldat und Technik	27
Systems Designers Limited	214
Tijl Periodieken bv	26
United Service Institution of India	296
Vickers Shipbuilding Group Limited	195

For information regarding availability and cost of Advertisement Space in this and other Brassey's publications please contact:

Brassey's Advertisement Department
Pergamon Press Limited
Headington Hill Hall
Oxford OX3 0BW
Tel: (0865) 64881
Telex: 83177